SEX, SPROUTS & SPIDERS

Jill Madge

I dedicate this book to the memory of my/our very lovely Dad (Fatherchops). We could not have wished for better. (And who I forgive for giving me his chunky hairy legs).

Also to my very lovely and long suffering Mum whose entire house I have managed to clutter with all my treasures (junk and building materials) and without whose care, support and rescue from spiders, I would never have got this far.

ACKNOWLEDGEMENTS

I would like to say a very big thanks to all who have inspired me to write this book: in particular life's constants throughout; all the animals of course - closely followed by Francisco, Beata, Jamie and Becky and of course the real Daniel – the true versions of which made working life in a pub so much fun for so many years.

PS I miss you all loads so if you ever fancy coming building houses with me let me know – even if it is just to make the tea!

A big thank you to all whom I have forced to read this and who have helped me to get it to here.

Special thanks must go to Phil the computer whizz at Microchipz for rescuing my book from disaster on numerous occasions (and at such short notice) and for being so patient and helpful to some one who computers hate.

Thank you all.

CHAPTER ONE
THE OLDE FLAGON INN

As she bent down to take a half pint glass from the bottom shelf and heard, and more worryingly, felt a dull snapping, Melissa knew that today was finally the day. The day her well over-laden bra finally gave up the ghost and the day before the serious diet had to start – again! Carefully Melissa straightened up to continue serving the drink, all the while hoping that the man in front of her was indeed just a lecher and was not looking at her chest because one boob was two inches higher than the other or because there was a weird wire creating a protrusion not dissimilar to a Madonna costume! After a subtle feel, she was relieved to find he was just a lecher as accused. Great – the start of a shift with a wonky boob and a high puncture risk from any sudden movement!

"Hello Dennis!" Melissa said brightly to the new arrival at the bar. "And how are you?" she asked as he scrutinised her in one slow, easy and very creepy gesture which she guessed he assumed was subtle, having practised for his eighty-six years since leaving the womb and spotting his first pair of boobs. "A half of the black stuff – in a handle." He instructed loudly, which he knew she already knew and which she was well aware that the only reason he had a handle was that they were stored on a shelf above the bar and he (not very) secretly got his kicks from watching the women who served him thrusting their chests nearer to him watching them straining at their fastenings. Then followed the creepiest part - the payment. Several slimy tricks here; 1) to dig his hands searchingly into both trouser pockets for an overly long time and then to remove them both collecting the change up into one hand and then telling you to help yourself thus necessitating the need for you to touch him. 2) To pass you the money and always give you too much – even when he has the right amount because then he can run his fingers along the underside of your palm – Mmmmm very erotic thanks – NOT! Or 3) by trying to grab your fingers if you try and avoid his touch by trying to plonk the money quickly into his waiting hand. That whole palaver over with, there is then the pleasure of awaiting his less than tactful comments about your appearance, the other customers or staff, said in a very loud voice due to his deafness, and of course to complain about the prices at the pub even though he comes in every day. The most worrying thing was that the longer Melissa worked there the more she got to thinking that her and Dennis were more alike than she would care to think about and indeed by the time she reached his age she too would have picked up any of the additional aggravating habits she had not already acquired. The groping and lechering would be good to work on sooner rather than later, she thought to herself whilst adjusting her left boob.

The Olde Flagon Inn where Melissa worked was the most unimaginable of places. A true example of life being stranger than fiction with a whole host of priceless characters and additional extras from a £45.000.00 Steinway grand piano in the skittle alley, down to a larger than life (suspected steroid abusing) goat called Dennis (not named after the octogenarian of the same name, although the personalities bore remarkable similarities). The Olde Flagon was an eighteenth century coaching inn situated on top of a hill high up on a tiny cross roads complete with old village demarkation stone nestling in one of it's grassy verges, in the middle of deepest darkest Somerset.

The pub oozed beautiful old features from its mullioned windows and slate tiled roof to the stable door and large carriage

house at the end of the building. Old metal rings thick with decades of black paint were dotted about the length of the building
as tethering places for animals. Colourful, overflowing window
boxes nestled beneath lattice, leaded windows which were still
the originals evident by the tiny bubbles trapped in the yellow
tinted glass and by it's imperfect clarity making you feel you may
have had one too many before you had touched a drop. To the
side of the building was an enormous and wonderfully planted
high walled garden complete with pond and behind that a paddock with two geese and loads of happy rare breed chickens running around, rooting and scratching about in the steaming piles
of horse manure, watched over by Dennis, the obscenely large
and appropriately menacing goat, and of course, the three horses whose actual poo it was. Inside was a fabulous old inglenook
fireplace made from the local creamy coloured stone blackened
over the years with a sooty residue. Large dark grey flagstones
covered the whole of the floor, angular steps turned into amazing undulations worn shiny in places by the passage of more
than two hundred years of weary travellers and revellers alike.
Large oak beams also darkened with soot and smoke protrud-
ed across the ceilings decorated with the old horse brasses and
thick, slightly faded curtains with bright hunting scenes hung at
the windows. Old earthenware bottles that once contained ale
and ginger beer cluttered dark shelves along with unusual orna-
ments interspersed by beautiful copper pots and pans glistening
in the dull light of the old-fashioned wall lights and lanterns.

Melissa had been working at the pub for just over four and a
half years and loved it. It was her life. A series of very bad career
decisions mixed with a fiery temper and an inability to keep her
thoughts to herself – oh and huge credit card debts - led her to
The Olde Flagon. Originally Melissa started when her monthly
outgoings exceeded her monthly incomings whilst working as a
builder in partnership with her Dad and her brother Tony. Their
company was set up when their Dad having retired at forty nine
began to tire of so much spare time on his hands and it was also
a way of giving his children an extra helping hand, mainly in an

3

attempt to get a rather lazy son who was of the opinion that the world owed him a living, to get off his rather large behind and make something of himself. They bought two crumbling old houses and a building plot in the nearby town of Slapperton to convert into flats to rent out. Melissa was not afraid to have a go at anything and with her slightly arrogant attitude of 'if they can do it so can I' she was fortunately, albeit annoyingly to others maybe, good at most things and building turned out to be no exception. Melissa revelled in the joy of a new ability learned and from wood-work to wall building, laying and levelling concrete floors; she en-thusiastically toiled and indeed conquered. Obviously there were times when rescue from the eight legged residents of Slapperton was required with Melissa's utter fear of spiders, and her painting talents meant a gallon more paint being required than if anyone else had done the job – not to mention a restyled floor and set of clothing – but on the whole a valuable member of the business, not afraid to work but unfortunately also not afraid to spend. Me-lissa's 'live for today because tomorrow you could be hit by a bus and then where would not buying that lovely pair of boots have got you!' attitude only applied to money but meant that a second job was required whilst the building business was in its early stages of only absorbing money and not actually producing any, and so when that week's June Slapperton Journal (the towns font of all knowledge – albeit generally ill informed, inaccurately reported and miss-spelt) was advertising for bar staff Melissa was there like a shot. What started as just three shifts a week soon turned into six shifts and so well did she get on with the proprietors that they wasted very little time before offering the job of actually managing the bar on a full time basis.

The pub was leased by Bruno and Michael, a slightly eccentric gay couple. Michael was forty and Czechoslovakian from poor almost peasant-like beginnings and Bruno was sixty and from Colombia, nephew of a previous president of Colombia and de-scendant of the Italian royal family, very well educated, highly intelligent with an amazing memory, fluent in five languages and a wonderful pianist. The two-some made an interesting if highly volatile pair. Michael cooking and rearing rare breed chickens and Bruno running the business and playing 'mein host' when he could fit it in between his horsey duties (being a very keen huntsman and owning three ridiculously expensive horses). Eventually however, ambitions and needs adjusted sufficiently to cause them to separate and so sadly after eighteen years and much glass throwing, Michael left the pub for a new place and even older but more solvent man and that left Melissa, Bruno and Charlie alone to cope at The Olde Flagon.

Charlie like Melissa had started in the June just one week apart but Charlie had started at only thirteen as a washer-upper and kitchen help on a Sunday lunch. A bright girl, pretty and natural with no pretensions, hit it off immediately well with all she encountered and especially well with Michael. He was completely charmed by her and how keen she was to help and learn. This of course was perfect because as time went on so he became more disillusioned with the whole cooking thing and took advantage of Charlie's good nature and natural cooking ability meaning that by the time she was fifteen he would leave her in the kitchen to cook and he would sneak upstairs to watch the football. Thrown in at the deep end Charlie thrived and automatically took over when Michael left all together. Bruno was forced to make more effort and take fewer days off and threw himself into cooking interesting dishes for Charlie to complete. It was his coping mechanism, cooking late into the night most evenings and then of course waking up to burning smells and a smoke filled kitchen, generally due to having had a glass of wine permanently attached to one hand throughout the entire cooking process like a weird extension of his arm causing him to nod off at the table whilst waiting for his latest gastronomic concoction to finish simmering or whatever.

The Olde Flagon had a very broad range of patronage from all walks of life. Due to the high-brow nature of Bruno with his classical music concerts held in the pub and performed at by world renowned musicians and his international business connections from when he had proper high ranking employment with the large multinationals, a certain type of customer was guaranteed to come. In addition to the horsey 'air-hell-ows' (as Melissa liked to call them) with their huge attention seeking guffaws, to go with their huge (everything except beer) beer bellies and huge noses and huge egos, with their equine faced wives with their huge diamonds and haughty manners, were the ordinary 'business lunchers' from neighbouring firms and quarries to the rustling old 'polyester wrinklies' with their sparking static clothing in bold and generally wildly clashing colours and truly mesmerising hats and accessories. In addition to them was the passing trade – poor innocents expecting pie and chips for under a fiver, generally tourists obvious from the second they walk in the pub that it was not their kind of place on principal because of the prices, not because they would not be made welcome – money is money after all! Then of course there were the sneaky rendezvous people – all obvious in that they barely kept their hands off each other and if they ordered food it was always something to share. It never ceased to amaze Melissa that regular patrons whom she was very familiar with would bring their mistress and their wife to the same place and even sit on the same favourite table. Once she was even about to compliment one of these women as to their new hairstyle and how much it suited her when she suddenly realised that it actually was in fact a new mistress and not his wife – a remarkable clone-like version may be who nagged less was all Melissa could assume after she remembered to close her aghast mouth. Finally of course there were 'the regulars'. These came in two basic categories 'regular regulars' and 'irregular regulars' (truth be known all the customers would fit into the irregular category as there was not one normal person amongst them – as if some weird force was bringing all of societies oddities together in one place). The 'irregular regulars' were the once or twice monthly diners or concert goers and the 'regular regulars' once or more a week people – amazing characters all! And then there of course was Melissa's man. Well, all right, not her man at all, but if it was a fair and just world and chemistry rated over luck at being in the right place at the convenient time, then he was as close to being her man as you were likely to get! The atmospheric chemistry upon the two seeing each other was very intense. His dark (stereotypically but so apt) smouldering eyes were harsh and stern looking and searched out only hers until of course the gaze was returned and then neither could sustain it, both looked sharply, simultaneously away as though bitten or stung. It was the weirdest non-relationship Melissa had ever had with anyone. Playing her role in the pub Melissa's bar was an equivalent of a stage – a place to become a different person - the braver version of herself. The bar forcing the shy person to speak up, be heard – even sometimes overcompensating for the shy interior. Eye contact had always been a favourite sport of Melissa's at school, with almost daily staring contests in dull lessons which she always won, and yet here with him a quick stolen glance and away. More puzzling to her than that was his inability to hold eye contact too. Here was this man Daniel Palmer, a self-made millionaire, a confident businessman and fifteen years Melissa's senior, sitting at the bar – just the two of them in the pub, but with him sitting sideways on at the bar thus staring along the bar and not over it at Melissa; not being rude and ignorant, far from it, always very attentive in their conversations – but again, always stolen glances not intimate eye contact. This man's presence in the pub was both thrilling and awful. Always arriving early – generally before the pub was truly open - and Melissa's heart raced from the moment she saw his headlights appear. However composed she tried to be pre-empting his arrival she always managed to be in the wrong place at the wrong time; switching lamps on, drawing curtains or stoking the fire, all keeping her away from the safe protection that the bar ensured. If she happened to walk near him as he entered the pub they were like two magnets repelled from each other in a ridiculous attempt to keep out of each other's body space. Psychologists would have had a field day with their behaviour – and that is before we even get to the small matter of how clumsy Melissa became, flustered and generally developing whole sentence 'spoken dyslexia'. Daniel had been visiting the pub for the whole time of Melissa working there. Initially very private, keeping himself to himself, buying his pint of Murphys and taking it to sit at a large oval and always kept reserved table (on account of the fact that it had the capability to seat six and because it was the nicest table should nice regulars arrive) to smoke an occasional cigar and stare into the fire, alone with his thoughts. For Melissa it was complete lust at first sight. So much so she could not really talk to him, "Hello" and the price of his pint was all she achieved for probably two whole years. One day when he and a friend were sat recuperating after a game of squash she was brave enough to ask them if they knew what the opposite of a meniscus was - because it is something we obviously all need to know – and conversation grew from there. Both of them being brave with a third person to smooth the way and chatting almost like ordinary people – but never for too long – Melissa could not trust herself not to show herself up for too many sentences – family 'verbal diarrhoea' carrying her away to places best not considered.

The real icebreaker for the three-some was the day of the prawn cracker. Tony an authentic Chinese chef who was so tiny he could barely reach the kitchen unit and who in his baseball cap could pass as a fifteen year old was actually thirty-six. Remarkably if you managed to persuade him to remove the cap he looked a good ten years older due to his rapidly balding head – probably not actually helped by the hat. He had a passion for dressing up and after a trip to Scotland he returned with the full kilt ensemble, including those peculiar shoes which tie up after criss-crossing laces up over knee high white socks, and of course a sporran. Once Melissa took him and a friend of Bruno's, who was on holiday in England, to Longleat Safari Park Tony shocked them all by wearing what can only be described as a Red Indian outfit – fortunately without the headdress. Melissa was not sure who had more photographs of them taken that day – the lions or Tony. So anyway, Tony turned up to work one day with some prawn crackers for them all to nibble on. Well as much as Melissa had frequently seen cooked prawn crackers, she had never before seen raw ones, nor had she ever considered what form their rawness might take – until that day. So fascinated was she by them that Melissa took one out to the two men (Daniel and his friend Nigel – the only customers in the pub) and asked them to identify the mystery object. The small silicon-like translucent, almost transparent flat disc was more like plastic than food and they could not decide what it was and moreover food did not even enter into their list of guesses. Melissa did not tell them what it was; instead she left them to ponder and brought out a bowl of cooked ones to give them. So that was it, prawn cracker mystery solved and friends for life. The next time they came in Nigel suggested that they remain at the bar instead of moving away and so that was what they did, and continued to do. That of course then set a precedent for non squash playing night visits so that when Daniel came in on his own Melissa assumed that he probably felt obliged to remain and talk rather than sit and stare into the fire and so it was over the years of two pint visits Melissa slowly found out all about 'her man'.

Daniel was a quiet and unassuming man who on occasions Melissa did begrudgingly have to share him with other customers coming into the pub, as he always seemed to know everyone. As time went on she found out all about his various business interests, one of which being a large local building firm, and he seemed to find it quite refreshing to have found someone to have to tell about himself who did not already know who he was and therefore had no preconceived ideas as is often the consequence of living in a rural community where everyone knows everyone else's business – or at least thinks that they do however distorted the information has become through the village jungle drums. The more that Melissa discovered the more surprised she was at the modest manner he had in explaining his quite phenomenal achievements including the fund raising and building of the new Community Centre in near by Slapperton, and the restoration of the town's historic old clock and tower. If only Melissa could find out a truly vile habit or irritating flaw, life would be a whole lot easier, she thought to herself.

CHAPTER TWO
IT HAD BEEN A BAD WEEK FOR SPIDERS

It had been a bad week for spiders. Spider incident number one happened late after work one night. Melissa entered her bed-room and waited for the energy efficient bulb to flash and 'tink' on (a thing which annoyed her intensely on the occasions where instant light was called for – which was whenever you entered such a minefield of a bedroom). Hanging her jacket on the handle of the ski-machine, Melissa made to go back out of the room to the bathroom, when something caught her eye and stopped her dead in her tracks. Dumb-struck and with the familiar uneasy goose pimples prickling their way up all over her body, Melissa looked properly up at what had distracted her, only to see 'Horris', the huuuuuugest great heart shaped bodied spider with enormous legs, hairier even than her own, laughing evilly down at her from the ceiling above the entrance and more importantly exit to the room. Major dilemma time; as all spider phobics are aware, these massive spiders are bound to jump on you as you go underneath them in order to make your escape – and anyway, who in their right mind leaves the room whilst letting Horris out of your sight and thus to potentially vanish and then appear again later, always when you are asleep, merrily wending his way through the Artex to-wards you whilst you innocently sleep with your mouth wide open, snoring or indeed dribbling, only to have Horris whose eight little feet cannot possibly hold the weight of his shoe box sized body on the ceiling and consequently he will fall down directly on to you and run around your bed, onto your body and in and out of your mouth! So not wanting to risk this unthinkable incident, Melissa backed a safe distance away from Horris, not taking her eyes off him, whilst desperately trying to figure out what to do. Ages, possibly weeks later, armed with a coat hanger in one hand and a shiny metal waste bin in the other, Melissa was poised ready to deal with Horris. She was not happy with the decided method of rescuing herself due to the fact that a) Horris could easily be poked by the coat hanger but not drop into the bin and of course land, with a thud, onto her, running frenziedly all over her. Or b) could run down the hanger's length onto Melissa and run frenziedly all over her. Or the worst thing that could happen and therefore the most likely c) because Horris was *so* big, he could grab the coat hanger and bin out of Melissa's hands and use them as weapons against her! Luckily at that very moment of indecision, Melissa's parents arrived back from a late session in the village pub (a complete opposite of The Olde Flagon which was three miles away from their home). 'So maybe there is a God!' Melissa thought to herself as she heard her parents noisily entering the hallway downstairs in a drunken effort to come in quietly. Melissa's Mum could always be relied upon to rescue her from her hairy-legged friends. As she came up the stairs she found Melissa still in situ with her impromptu weaponry and fear-struck expression. Grabbing a long handled feather duster propped up in the corner of the bedroom (never of course used, but the good intention was there) Melissa's Mum unceremoniously poked at Horris who obediently hopped straight onto the duster after which she plopped him even less unceremoniously out of the landing window. Grateful, but knowing how cunning Horris and his kind could be, Melissa insisted that her Mum thoroughly check the duster over *and* put it back downstairs in it's cupboard so that Horris could not easily climb back up to taunt her – in case he had been sneaky enough to hang onto the duster as she suspected.

That night as Melissa lay on her bed, trying, but failing to get to sleep, she looked thoughtfully around her. Thirty years old, still living with her parents, no life to speak of except that of her work for Bruno as the manager of the pub, and to top it all a body becoming more and more reminiscent of the Michelin blimp with each passing moment. Only last week Lucy, her best friend from school, when discussing how cold she had got on her motorbike said "Well it's like…you know where you have cellulite on your bum and so even though you are warm your bum is still cold to the touch?…Well my whole body felt like that after being out for twenty minutes on my bike!" 'What does she mean?' Melissa thought, "You know on your bum" 'My whole body is like that! Oh except of course for my hands and feet, which due to the bad circulation most likely caused by excessive chocolate or cake binges coating all my arteries, means they are always stone cold even without cellulite!' Still without the faintest notions of sleeping, Melissa looked around the dark shadows that made up her bedroom. It was every mother's nightmare (well except Melissa's who with four untidy children had resigned herself to the mess many years before).

There was no more than a pathway of visible carpet from the bed to the door and what there was of that Sydney (named after the country for some bizarre reason) one of the family's two dogs lay in, stretched out as long as he could possibly make himself. Syd, as he was more commonly known, a liver and white Springer Spaniel was Melissa's very best and most reliable friend in the world. He was old, smelly, going deaf, blind in one eye and completely without the other (but it was sewn shut so that he always looked as though he was mischievously winking) and even though he could fart for England, and frequently made efforts that you would not forget it, Melissa loved him to bits. As he snored noisily she continued to survey her belongings jammed in around him. To his left a cross-country ski machine and to the left of that a treadmill. Behind that a weird stomach crunching device and on the windowsill a set of pastel coloured girleee weights. All of these things were used sporadically in a 'get skinny and gorgeous' attempt from time to time, along with the other equipment which had long since overflowed into her youngest brother's old bedroom, including a rowing machine, full multigym, step machine, rebounder mini trampoline, an exercise bike and an old hula hoop (free with a bus load of empty Hula Hoop crisp packets – great diet plan that was!) In total hundreds of pounds worth of equipment – none of which Melissa actually remembered it saying that you actually had to *use* to get the body of a gladiator – surely just buying it should have been enough! To the right of Syd, to the rear and ahead were clothes and shoes. Every where you looked were clothes hanging off the ski machine and treadmill (an extra use they neglect to feature in their adverts!) hung off the doors of the wardrobe and the bedroom door, hidden in the two drawers beneath the bed and jammed on the double hanging rail as well as being stuffed to bursting in the huge wardrobe; in fact so stuffed was the said wardrobe that the hanging rails had bent and then sheared into two due to the excess of weight – consequently the whole thing had needed a complete internal rebuild with metal rails and a middle strengthening support and an extra rail halfway down for shirts and tops which practically doubled it's capacity and then was immediately taken advantage of. For all these clothes however very few actually fitted at this current moment in time. The sizes varied from a gorgeous schoolgirl size twelve to a fat bloater size twenty. The saddest part of which was that more than half of the clothes had never been worn, or indeed had ever had their labels removed. Melissa, ever the optimistic pessimist, thought that she could incentive diet; buy something gorgeous with a view to slimming into it. WRONG! Even after the first ten failures in incentive purchases she still could not take the hint and ran up staggering credit card bills in an attempt to regain her figure and burst her wardrobes. When her clothing situation depressed her too much Melissa started on shoes. Known as Emelda Marcos to her family, Melissa's feet became her focus as they were not fat and even though they were large, they never made her bum look big or created unsightly belly rolls!

Still as sleep evaded her, Melissa watched the shadows cast by the bright moonlight shinning through the curtains, that were never drawn unless the sun created a reflection on the screen of the full size television at the foot of her bed. Shelves on the wall were loaded to buckling point with videos and trashy top-ten best-seller novels. A great collection but it always reminded her of the dull life she led which allowed so much time for such vegetablised leisure activities. Then, of course, there was the additional clutter, boxes of junk stuffed into one wardrobe and on top of another, important 'might be useful one day' sort of stuff like flippers and a car boot sale collection couple of boxes, just waiting for a cold winters day to wrestle with the most common and ignorant members of the general populous offering a pittance to the level of wanting to destroy the item in front of them rather than take their insulting amount. Additionally, a fairly large collection of cuddly toys, a lot of them too big to be anything but in the way, but one the perfect size to be sat up on top of the wardrobe wedged between two midi system stereo speakers with a straw hat for holiday use resting at a jaunty angle on it's head. Finally there was the weird stationery and packaging fetish. For Melissa's room contained more items of stationery than most busy working offices, including all sorts of weird shoe boxes and smaller packaging containers and rolls of gift wrap plus emergency birthday cards. For such a chaotic room it was terribly well organised and functional (in an extremely messy and unappreciable to the ignorant on-looker sort of a way).

Spider incident number two happened the following evening. Whilst innocently watching a film on the telly alone, or so she thought, out of the corner of her eye, and not even realising that her peripheral vision could even reach that far, Melissa suddenly saw Horris the spider's big brother 'Borris', run across the arm of the sofa next to the armchair she was sitting on, and up and over Melissa's seat where the two arms were touching. Melissa leapt up and watched in horror as Borris ran down the back of her seat. Desperately looking back and forth in the chair, she waited for Borris's next move. Suddenly she saw it; one of Borris's boots was carelessly dangling out of his hiding place! Melissa quickly grabbed the TV guide and slid the corner of it along in-between the cushions of the seat, thus scooping Borris out. He hastily legged it up the back of the seat and just as Melissa thought he was getting away, he tripped, presumably over one of his carelessly tied boot laces, and Melissa ruthlessly squashed him until he fell crunched up on the floor, at which point she dropped the Argos catalogue on him and then stamped up and down on it for good measure. Heart still pounding, breathless and sweating from fear, Melissa gingerly sat back down to watch her film, ruined now by the constant need to keep watching out for any of Horris and Borris's family to take revenge on her and sure in the knowledge that she must now know what a heart attack must feel like!

Spider incident number three happened the following morning. The day before spider incident number two Melissa's parents had gone on holiday and left Melissa alone in the house dog sitting. Normally Melissa got up late in the mornings due to the late nights she kept from working in the pub and her Mum always got up at the crack of dawn to let the dogs out for a wee. Monday morning Melissa was rudely woken by the younger of their two dogs barking to go out downstairs at the back door, located directly below her bedroom. He barked two or three times before it registered that only she was at home and therefore had to get up. Fumbling her way over Sydney, the older dog, still snoring loudly by the side of her bed, and through the obstacles that made up her room, Melissa got downstairs only to find that Jasper had in fact already shat on the carpet, and quite some time ago by the look of it! After reprimanding the dog, mainly along the lines of "Why the hell did you wake me up if you were going to crap anyway?!!!" Melissa cleared up the aforementioned turd and went to thoroughly wash her hands and put the kettle on. After filling the kettle she noticed that the dog's water bowl needed filling up and so whilst absentmindedly talking to the dog, she picked up the beige Tupperware jug (which every house she had ever been in seemed to have) and turned the tap on to full pelt in order to fill the large container quickly. Then she looked from Jasper back to the job in hand only to see the most massive spider she had ever seen in her life running rapidly up the side of the jug towards her hand. Horror-struck, Melissa slung the jug into the sink at which point the high-pressure water hit the side of the up-turned jug and splashed violently, deflecting back out of the sink in all directions, but mainly at Melissa. As fast as she could she shoved the spout of the mixer taps across so that the water gushed directly into the second sink. As her goose pimples appeared and she got that nasty cringy feeling spiders always had on her, Melissa evilly switched on the hot tap in order to give the 'Conan' of the spider world a painful and hideous death. All this and it was not even **7am**, she hadn't even had a cup of tea **and** it was only the third morning of the two week holiday her parents had gone on!

CHAPTER THREE
THE SUPERMARKET

It was Saturday lunchtime and Melissa met Sally, her best friend, for their weekly shop and cup of tea. Melissa had been relaying some funny occurrence that had happened in the pub, whilst idly squeezing some Galia melons testing them for ripeness on the fruit stand, and it was during an enormous guffaw, which Sally was renowned for, that she looked up and saw him. Panic struck, her heart thumped uncontrollably – after it remembered to work at all, her stomach lurched and her knees, so reliable until that point, seemed to have forgotten their role in life. Sally stopped mid sentence "What's a matter with you – you've gone really pale?"

"DO NOT look round – but he's here!" Naturally she swung her head straight round to look. "I said DON'T!" 'What is it with people that when they are told that, that they straight away feel compelled to anyway' part of Melissa wondered whilst the other part concentrated on her face overcompensating for its previous lack of colour and turned beetroot or possibly even aubergine!

"Well go and say hello then."

"I can't do that!"

"Did he see you?"

"I don't think so but he must have heard us – you honking like a goose!" Melissa looked around at him again and he was flicking through a car magazine.

"STOP IT! HE'LL SEE US!" Melissa urgently hissed.

"Well that's the idea isn't it? Anyway, he has." Melissa sneaked a look over at him and sure enough Daniel's cheeks had coloured up a very flushed shade of red and he quickly made his purchases and stalked off very self-consciously out of the store, his eyes fixed purposefully ahead, so much so that he stumbled as a small child waddled into his path.

"Oh God! How embarrassing was that?! He's gone and we never said hello. He'll think we were laughing at him. That's probably why he went so red!" Melissa said, pacing about around the now discarded melons.

"He definitely saw us – so why didn't he say something, or at least smile up at us, or wave? Very odd. Quite excellent in fact!" Sally said grinning.

"What do you mean 'quite excellent?' It's not bloody excellent – we have just blatantly ignored each other! A prime out of the pub opportunity ruined! He won't even wanna come into the pub again if he thinks we were laughing at him not at…" Sally butted in "It's excellent because you both reacted the exact same way. You are both like a couple of beetroots. You have both regressed to pre-pubescent teenager status! Now we both knew you were crap around him…but now you know that you have just as bad an effect as he does on you. Excellent!"

CHAPTER FOUR
SUNDAY AT THE PUB

Sunday at eleven o'clock Melissa arrived at work and without so much as taking her coat off, she walked purposefully through the kitchen, did the usual morning pleasantries with the staff and looked meaningfully at Charlie who immediately put down the vegetables she had been peeling and followed Melissa, who was armed with a yellow carrier bag, into the cellar. Once in the cellar Melissa pulled out a large tube of paper and theatrically unrolled it for Charlie's approval.

"Daaa da!" Melissa musically fan-fared and began fastening the five feet long diet chart to the back of the cellar door. Charlie laughed "You daft cow! That's great!" and they stood back, both admiring the huge chart. Melissa had spent some time carefully marking off a poundage countdown on either side of the chart and at the one stone mark had drawn a large red band across the whole width boldly printed with 'ALMOST SKINNY!' and at the two stone mark 'SKINNY!' Both girls had far more than that to loose but Melissa had decided a little encouragement would not go astray. Melissa unpacked the scales from the yellow bag. "Sorry about the dust and fluff – I didn't have time to clean them properly – it'll only be out of belly buttons, I expect!" she laughed trying to brush the worst of it away. The scales were truly quite gross looking. They had been very expensive when

Melissa had bought them years before but with age and steam from the bathroom they lived in, the top covering had begun to curl unpleasantly at the edges leaving still sticky glue exposed to the bathroom fluff and hair to adhere to.

"Right then, you can go first." Melissa told Charlie.

"No-oh. You!"

"But you have much less to loose than me!"

"They're your scales!"

"I made the chart! Take off your shoes!"

"Bitch!" Charlie said, complying with mock annoyance.

"Right then…switch that button there." Melissa pointed to a small button on the front edge of the scales. "Then wait for zero to appear."

"Then what?"

"Get on!" Charlie assumed the position, head bobbing up and down, desperate to see what the nasty number would be. "Stand still. You're like bloody Noddy! Look ahead. The scales will wait until you keep still and then they will flash up your wait three times." Charlie stopped swaying long enough to for the scales to register.

"OH MY GOD! SHIT! I never knew I weighed that much!" Charlie said and leapt off the scales as though they had burnt her. Melissa got on, but having weighed herself more recently than Charlie was less shocked, although equally appalled by her weight.

"Pick a colour – but you can't have the purple one!" Melissa fanned out a selection of brightly coloured felt tipped pens. Charlie selected neon blue and Melissa carefully wrote their weight in large shameful figures at the top of each person's side of the chart in each person's chosen felt tip pen.

"I still can't believe it! I am never going to eat again!" Charlie exclaimed whilst fiddling awkwardly with her huge clumpy platform soled shoe that did not seem to want to go back on. "I have put on nearly two stones since the last time I weighed. SHIT! FAT BITCH! We aren't telling anyone our actual weights are we?"

"Well, I won't tell anyone yours if you want. It will be between us and the beer delivery guys!"

"Huh?" Charlie's brow furrowed in confusion.

"Well, they will see the chart when they bring in the barrels won't they!" Melissa laughed. As realisation dawned, Charlie laughed too and they made their way back into the pub.

Sunday lunchtime at The Olde Flagon was always busy and the bright late autumn sun had brought all the walkers with dogs and the cyclists out to come and sit in the pub's beautiful, prize-winning beer garden. The regular Sunday crowd were at the bar; lecherous old Dennis sat in a low chair just to one side with his regular phlegmy throat clearing cough, next to him George – even older than Dennis, retired farmer and really grumpy old bastard material when he felt inclined and would argue black was white for the sake of it, particularly in discussion with Dennis. Next to them Nancy and Henry or rather Nancy and 'Sniffer' as the two 'Old Gits' (as staff referred to Dennis and George) referred to him. Henry was a heavy snuff user and one of his trade-marks in addition to his 'crunchy with grease' beige corduroy flat cap – which he was forever leaving the pub without – necessitat-ing a member of staff, generally Melissa, to have to touch said object in order to 'put it safe' for him until his next visit (Melissa did have her doubts as to anyone wanting to even touch it with-out protection; let alone steal it!) was the 'snuff handkerchief'. The true colour of the garment people preferred to imagine was red with white polka dots – rather like one you would tie to a stick if you were leaving home, containing all your obviously 'tiny' belongings in the days of Peter Rabbit; actual colour of hanky unfortunately however, was *brown,* red and white polka dots – predominantly brown in fact and worse than that, the build up of the brown was witnessed by all unfortunate enough to watch him blow his nose and the recycled snuff come back out. Peculiarly the regulars never ate crudities and bar nibbles after Henry's arrival. But for all this, a nicer couple you couldn't hope to meet. Both in their late sixties and fit as fiddles, straight up, good humoured and lovely company and when conversations were dwindling, you could generally rely on them to snipe a bitchy comment or six along the bar at each other, which was always good sport to be a spectator of. Nancy was attractive, tall and slim and had a mop of wild grey hair that Melissa loved because she knew that it was exactly as hers would be given a few years. She had a wickedly mischievous personality and people lit up when she spoke with them. She was a fabulous cook and loved picking Bruno's brain for new and unusual ideas and so they could be often seen swapping recipes in a huddle away from the others. Next to them at the bar were Eric and Mary. Again real old characters, the same age group as Nancy and Henry. Mary was really sweet and 'momsie', softly spoken and had slightly frizzy, over-permed hair. Eric was…well, just Eric – a law unto himself. Always dressed in tweed suits with a huge expanse of waistcoat showing, not quite, but nearly, straining at the fastenings and always decorated with a long length of fancy chain, presumably attached at one end to a pocket watch (but in all the years she had worked there she had never seen him look at it, and being the slight eccentric that he was, she would not have been at all surprised if there was no watch at all, or even something bizarre like a piece of cheese attached to it). Eric was a musical sort, for example; he would not stop whistling, and how Mary had put up with him for so long was a complete mystery that only being stone deaf could excuse – which she unfortunately, or fortunately, wasn't. Eric would even ask questions and half way through the answer would strike up with a few bars of some hymn or other – something that regulars at the bar never failed to find humour in, particularly upon him joining in discussion with a stranger at the bar.

So, whilst the normal antics were going on, Melissa continued serving the steady flow of customers, catching snippets of all their conversations, and it was whilst finishing serving a shockingly brightly-dressed fifty something lady (who looked like her hair was acting two-fold as a head covering and a bird's dwelling – about whom George would refer to as 'a Mutton' as this was how he referred to any women who were dressed in anything remotely eye-catching) that she spotted him. Standing away from the bar with his hand protectively on his nephew's shoulder whilst the nephew fiddled with the chinstrap on his cycle helmet.

"Hello." Melissa smiled a welcome, feeling her colour rise and her stomach churn. He smiled back and watched as Melissa caught the bottom of the pint glass she was lifting over the beer pumps against the top of one of the said obstacles and splashed the top quarter inch just about everywhere. It had always been one of life's great mysteries to Melissa as to how the tiniest amount spilled from a mug or glass actually covers the most enormous space once released from its confines. Reddening still further, she proceeded to make yet more mess cleaning up the spillage as obviously having topped back up the remaining beer she caught the glass again on a different pump. Daniel looked on in quiet amusement and Melissa wondered if he was cringing on her behalf.

"Right then, what can I spill on...I mean get for you?" Melissa quipped. "The usual?"

"Aaa, yes please – I'll stand well back!" he grinned wickedly at her, impressed at her ability to so easily laugh at herself.

Melissa had been planning their next meeting all of the previous night. She had not reckoned on it being quite so soon however.

"You had a lucky escape yesterday." Melissa started.

"Yesterday?"

"Yes, at the supermarket." Daniel coloured slightly.

"I didn't see you." He looked puzzled. 'Playing it like that are we' Melissa thought to herself – good, much less embarrassing than having thought to have been ignored.

"Well, my friend Sally and I were there together and we had decided that I had to proposition the next bloke I saw – only there weren't any and we only spotted you as you were leaving!"

"Sounds like you had a lucky escape mate!" Henry said, winking at Melissa.

"Oh, I don't know. I'm not so sure!" Daniel said back to Henry as he and his nephew took their drinks out into the garden with that quick backwards smile and glance when he reached the door.

CHAPTER FIVE
A FOOT ON EACH CHEEK OUGHT TO DO IT

Monday. Day two of diet. It had been going well so far, Melissa having only been awake for fifteen minutes and as yet had only had a pint mug of tea. She lay propped up against a mountain of pillows, with the duvet pulled up snugly around her, with just a quiff of wayward hair visible to the outside world – if the outside world had been able to see in that is. Sydney Spaniel maintained his normal position stretched out along the length of the drawers in the bottom of Melissa's bed, where the warm central heating pipes ran underneath the floorboards beneath him, loudly snoring and twitching his feet gently as he chased rabbits, or more likely chocolate cake, in his dreams. Melissa heard a loud bang and a succession of bumps emanating from downstairs. Knowing that she was alone in the house, with the exception of the dogs, she would normally have been frightened at such a noise but as it was *their house*, after the initial fright she smiled down at Syd who had popped his head up at her for reassur-ance, no doubt from feeling the vibrations through the floor, and laughed as she listened out to make sure she heard the completion of this clatter, namely that of a scrabbling of claws on plastic; in order that she knew Jasper, the cause of the noise, was OK having just fallen off and overturned the two seat sofa near the front lounge window in an effort to climb up into the windowsill to watch the world go by. It was a bad habit that Jasper had acquired when everyone went out. It caused much amusement to any passers-by who saw him with his huge fluffy body and nose awkwardly squashed up against the window, precariously balanced on a windowsill half the width of his wide body. Jasper was an over-sized Welsh Border Collie with long mane-like hair. He had the most marvellous gentle temperament for a Collie and he was low level sound hearing impaired or "Bloody belligerent!" Melissa's Dad always accused. He also had the most beautiful haunting colour scheme; his face was completely split in two, one half black and one white including white eyelashes on the white side and black eyelashes on the black side – actually very spooky to look at until you got used to him. The scrabble, scrabble and thud could be heard from downstairs, then a thundering of heavy, clumsy dog charging up the stairs and Melissa looked across to see a worried looking Jasper appear in her door way obviously having frightened himself half to death.

"Hello dopey dog!" Melissa laughed "you all right then?" Jasper's ears, which had been frightened back behind his head, perked straight back up to their normal happy looking position as he almost seemed to grin at the relief in seeing a reassuring face. Before Melissa could stop him, he had taken a couple steps into the room and then leapt from the doorway several feet, up over Syd who growled (like an old man grumbling) annoyed at him for the disruption of the nice dream Melissa supposed, and landed heavily on the bed, but more specifically, heavily onto Melissa.

"OW! GERROFF YOU BIG DOPE!" Melissa playfully pushed at the big over-grown puppy whilst Syd winked on from below through his one eye, grumpily growling at Jasper who completely ignored him. Jasper tried licking Melissa's face as he got more excited at this game until she buried her head underneath the covers and confused him not knowing where she had gone. Jasper tilted his head first one way and then the other, completely flummoxed at Melissa's apparent disappearance, and then in exasperation started batting and pawing at the lump in the bed until Melissa with tears pouring down her face, stuck her head back out at him laughing uncontrollably as he pounced at her, so happy to have found her again. The mail arriving noisily through the letterbox was the only thing that saved her, as on hearing a possible attack Jasper jumped from the bed and exited the room as loudly as he had arrived, barking bravely as he tumbled down the stairs. Melissa reached a hand out to affectionately ruffle Syd's head who raised his eyebrows disapprovingly as if to say 'bloody idiot!' and spuddled (a technical term that the family had for his circling round several times prior to lying down) around and around until he found a comfortable position in which to resume his cake hunt.

Melissa scowling, swung her legs resentfully out from under the duvet and slowly forced herself out of bed. The sloth with which she moved was due to her lack of enthusiasm for the task that awaited her; namely the gym. Although truly crap at dieting for any length of time Melissa was always good, for a while at least, once she actually committed herself to it, obsessively attending between four and five times a week and sometimes even getting up before eight to get there! But as with the best-laid plans and all that, it was just not to be. Whilst precariously balanced on the loo, mid-wee, artfully putting on socks without causing to either break flow, or pee anywhere other than down the loo, and then putting feet into the leg holes of jog pants – no, not those vile stretchy things which the hugely obese (and of course Slapperton men) wear out with shoes and tank tops, with sagging asses or even worse; pulled up to above waist height and worn with at least one hand kept firmly in the pocket, the other hand, when free, just blatantly scratching, poking, prodding and generally fondling genitalia – unaware or just uncaring of who is watching them do it. So 'NO', not like that, but not a shell suit either, nearly but definitely actually not! Not shiny and did not sound like a cheap carrier bag when it moved either! Anyway, we digress; it was the bra that caused the problem. Normally a fairly simple procedure (well, for women at least!) having had more than eighteen years of bra wearing exper-ience, but today,

'GYM DAY', disaster struck. With both hands on fasteners either side of her body, arms stuck out like wings, before arriving in to clasp together, Melissa's face took on the frozen expression reminiscent of the Edvard Munch painting "The Scream" (but obviously Melissa was having a much worse hair day!) as a shooting pain shot up and down her back, so intense was the agony that it even managed to stop her wee in it's tracks! Some how the 'would-be gym skiving' nerve jammed itself in-between…well hey, who knows …but all Melissa knew was that it bloody hurt and with every little movement made the likelihood of a very red loo seat shaped ring around her cellulite covered rear, a very real possibility on account of the fact that the pain was making a certain part of her body not actually want to go anywhere. Hideous images flashed into Melissa's mind of four, no better still six, gorgeous firemen breaking down the bathroom door and extracting her from her undignified position (complete with trousers and her most ugly knickers around ankles) one on each thigh and one on each wing where her arms were still sticking out like an oven-ready chicken, still holding onto the unfastened bra, whilst the other two firemen had a boot on the top of each bum cheek trying to ease her numbing body from it's porcelain prison. Luckily, or not, she could not quite decide, Melissa eventually fought through the pain and completed her dressing and the wee had gone back to where ever wees go when frightened away. The pain however became an inter-mittent type fault and remained for the rest of that week. 'Diet ruined then, no gym, so out with the fish fingers!' Melissa thought.

CHAPTER SIX
I WANT A FABULOUS BODY

A week later, Melissa looked up from her favourite, or prob-ably more accu-rately; least hated treadmill, to the clock on the wall, it was 7.47 am. *Seven bloody forty-seven AM!* I must be mad!' she thought to herself, raising her eyebrows at herself reflected in the mirror to emphasise the point. "Let the ritual punishment begin!" she muttered under her breath, dumping her towel and water bottle down on the floor. The reason for it being her least hated treadmill was on account of the fact that it had a large fan in-between it and the next one. Provided Melissa got to the machine before a neighbour arrived, she could set the fan to point directly at her and to remain in the same position, not revolving left and right, and on full power. It was only hav-ing done this that she would then step up and programme the machine to 30 minutes at fast pace, slight incline, walking. It wasn't that Melissa disliked exercise; it was just that she found it boring. The music was never turned up loud enough to hear properly over the noise of her heart thumping, the loud pant-ing breath and thudding of her feet, but the worse aspect to the whole ordeal was the mirrors; the whole bloody place was full of them and the whole treadmill wall was one huge mirror! 'What sane person would want to see them-self running? Even the skinny people surely could not enjoy watching all their bits jiggling about – even if they were skinny bits – and the poor 'cuddly' ones, well there's a whole different story!' Melissa thought every time she set foot in the place. 'You just manage to entice the lardy ones into the gym and the first thing they do is shove you in front of a mirror and make you watch the body that you already knew was vile, do things you had only before ever had to imagine. Who knew that belly-rolls could move in such a gravity defying, wave-like undulations?' Melissa caught her puzzled expression in the mirror and looked at her reflected body under a baggy t-shirt, with a badly fitting bra and trousers with a waistband that had become slightly too tight even though it was elasticated, and was reminded of a ferret caught in a sack *and* on speed! 'Is it any wonder there are so many people out there who open up gym membership only to stop in the first week?' Melissa wondered and saw her frowning face looking back at her again.

To entertain herself whilst walking, Melissa watched all the other reflected gym users in the mirror, and even though she knew she looked rough, growing redder and redder with each passing step, so it was quite heartening every time she spotted someone in a worse state of sweat and blubber than herself; always quick to share a smile or a mutual roll of their eyes at their joint exertions. The skinny people were always too focused on the job in hand, even before they got to the torture method of choice, to spare a grin at the sweat drenched fatties.

"Hello." An 'in-betweeny' (neither fat nor skinny) got onto the treadmill next to Melissa, "I thought it would be busier."

"Yes, but that's because the sensible people are still in bed or tucking into their breakfasts!"

"Here bloody here!" she called back over the noise of the fan and exercise machines, as she slowly set one of the prefixed programmes going.

"I think this is about the norm' for this time of day, but I can't be sure as I've only just started back after several months of not coming and regaining all my weight so hard lost before!" Melissa said rolling her eyes at herself in frustration.

"Yes, me too – so easy to get out of the habit of coming!" Melissa glanced at her and thought that she would not even be at the gym with a body that size, at all!

"Well I'm awful in the mornings and stopped coming early at weekends because all you got was second-hand garlic and curry fumes. It stunk in here!" Melissa said wrinkling her nose in disgust at the memory.

"Ohh!" the 'in-betweeny' coloured up "I had a curry last night. I don't smell do I?" she started subtly sniffing about herself in panic.

"Oh, God no! You don't smell!" Melissa's exertion flush covered for her embarrassed face, "It was all the men. You're fine. Honestly!" The 'in-betweeny' half smiled a thank you but was obviously not convinced. They did not speak again after that. Melissa shot the 'in-betweeny' a reassuring glance but all that was reflected back was the fear like a rabbit caught in the car headlights, and in true rabbit style, the little nose twitches, as she continued trying to check herself for fumes.

When the last ten minutes flashed up on the screen of the treadmill, slightly bored with people-watching, Melissa began her 'mantra'; once when reading a health magazine she had come across an article promoting positive thinking and that chanting your mantra twenty times each day should be channelling positive energy into helping achieve those goals that you wanted to achieve. Quite depressed about the general state of her life – or lack of it, Melissa had thought up her mantra whilst dog-walking to help pass the time when not text messaging Sally. The article had said it was best chanted 'out loud' and at least twenty times, so Melissa figured that ten minutes on a treadmill pacing her mantra out in her mind would surely be much better, and at worst, what harm could it do? Walking the dogs she had done it out loud, but that was in the middle of a country lane with only the dogs and an occasional cow to hear her rantings; in the gym Melissa thought it was best kept internalised, or else she wouldn't be getting strange looks just because of her beetroot coloured head! After many practise versions with the dogs,

Melissa's final mantra was 'I want Daniel Palmer, a fabulous body and to be happy....I want Daniel Palmer, a fabulous body and to be happy...' which she said to herself over and over in perfect rhythm with her steps. On the treadmill just mentioning his name made the previously flagging steps more determined and enthusiastic, suddenly more worthwhile. Sometimes the mantra was just 'I want Daniel Palmer', because she knew that getting him would give her a fabulous body because the weight would just drop off from being in 'lust' and because of the inevitable quantity of sex they would be having – both things of course would result in the 'happy', the other request from the mantra. So, in this happy and deluded vein, she walked and chanted, only stopping when the heaven sent digital beep sounded and the treadmill decelerated itself for the disembarking procedure.

CHAPTER SEVEN
THE BET

At the pub the shift had ended for Charlie and Kathy, the pretty and bubbly waitress. All the early arriving polyester clad 'wrinkly army' had eaten and gone, so the two giggling girls came out of the kitchen and joined Melissa at the bar, as was the daily ritual. No sooner seated than armed, cigarettes in hands; the long deep drag, the instant rush, then the ease of intenseness in their facial features as they both got their longed for fix.

"So what are we going to do with you then? We have to get Mel a bloke some-how!" Kathy started off their contemplations looking first at Melissa and then at Charlie. "It's no good you waiting for them to ask you, you're just going to have to proposition someone!" Kathy continued.

"God no! I couldn't do that. How awful would that be?" Melissa demanded "And besides, no one nice ever comes in here!"

"Look, they're not going to ask you because you are too confident and intim-idating!" Kathy told her, flicking the ash from her cigarette expertly into the clean ashtray.

"Me, confident?!" Melissa interrupted "You are joking!" she didn't query the 'intimidating' part of the accusation because she was well aware that her all but complete lack of attention in the last four years had made her build up a kind of armour, feeling that for what ever reason men didn't like her, rather than let them think they had succeeded in getting to her and hurting her by this snub, she was ready to 'repel borders' even before the thought had crossed their minds; and unfortunately her rapier wit and even sharper tongue, on occasions, did frighten off meeker, duller witted men.

"Well even if you don't feel it, you certainly come across that way! Accept it. You are going to have to do the pulling, isn't she Charlie!" It wasn't a question, it was a command. Kathy was a 'don't mess with me' kind of a girl.

"I'm sorry Mel, but I think she is probably right."

"What do you mean 'probably' – DEFINITELY!" and Kathy viscously stubbed out her cigarette, as if to emphasise the point.

"Anyway – I thought you were supposed to be giving up those cigarettes!" Melissa retaliated.

"The doctor said an occasional one wouldn't do any harm to the baby – in fact – it's good for me." She stated and Melissa and Charlie exchanged glances (eyebrows shooting off the tops of foreheads type of thing).

"He did!" Kathy exclaimed, catching their expressions. "And anyway, I have cut down – I'm only on about ten a day now; I only smoke in the evenings."

"Yeah, so we see." Melissa said, nodding at the used ashtray.

"Stop changing the subject anyway!" Kathy regained her original train of thought as she lit up again.

"Yeah, I reckon we should have a challenge. A bet to make you ask someone out." Charlie said, her eyes sparkling mischievously looking first at Kathy and then Melissa.

"No way! I can't do it!" Melissa said as Charlie grabbed an order pad from off the bar and began to write out the terms of their 'contract'.

"Let's see…*I Mel, promise that I will proposition or kiss – with tongues* (so you don't wriggle out of it by kissing Henry)"

"Uggghh!" both Kathy and Melissa chorused in unison.

"As, I was saying… *'that I will proposition or kiss (with tongues), someone by….*"

"The end of the month!" Shot in Kathy.

"Oh come on, no!" At least give me until New Years Day, cuz at least then I get helped by the mistletoe thing!" Melissa pleaded. Charlie and Kathy looked at one another.

"Yeah, all right then." In begrudging stereo – i.e., one in each of Melissa's ears.

"Anyway, what is your punishment for not doing it going to be?" Charlie asked, "Oh, I know." Kathy said slowly, grinning broadly. "She can baby-sit for my kids two nights a week for two months!"

"Good one!" Charlie said and started writing, wearing a huge smile on her face.

"No! Now I know you are joking. That's just too cruel! Anyway, who in their right mind would trust me with their kids? You know I'm phobic!"

"I'd trust you, and it will be all the more incentive for you to proposition a fella then!"

"So…*I Mel, promise that I will proposition or kiss (with tongues) someone by mid-night on New Years Day.…*"

"2005! You know what she's like; this could go on for decades!" Kathy interrupted, pointing her finger at the pad and tapping where she wanted it inserted.

"Good point. *2005. I understand that failure to do said task will mean baby-sitting two nights a week for two months for Kathy's 'Children of Satan' (and no fobbing them off with my Mum!).* Right, now sign it!" Charlie finished off by under-lining it with a flourish.

"No. I refuse." Melissa laughed.

"Sign it!" they demanded in unison, and then laughed when they realised.

"OK, sign it or I will tell Silver Van Man everything that you've ever said about him!" Kathy threatened, referring to their nickname for Daniel Palmer.

"It might help my cause if you did!" Melissa quipped back.

"Not the way I'd tell it!"

"It will never stand up in court you know – making me sign under duress."

"Just shut up and squiggle. We're helping you!" Charlie said thrusting the contract at her. And so it was; a hideous challenge, hanging in mid air. It was impossible Melissa thought; a) because she was not brave enough to proposition anyone, b) except Silver Van Man, the men that came in the pub were either married (oh, including Silver Van Man) or ugly, or gay or 'the other' and worse in Melissa's mind than the aforementioned categories: posh! She knew that there was just no way she could ever go out with a posh bloke. She imagined the sniggers of taking an 'air-hell-oh' home to meet the family, and knew that they would never let her live it down – her brothers still ribbed her about a boyfriend she'd had when she was seven (nearly the most recent boyfriend!) of whom they swore he was so ugly that he had a bolt through his neck! (As far as all the girls were concerned at the time, and ever since, quite the contrary was true of his physical appearance, but brains-wise though she was inclined to agree!). Luckily Melissa could not imagine a 'hooray' wanting her with her broad Somerset accent and laugh like a drain either, so problem solved. Then on top of all that of course was the other problem; children! They could not have – and indeed they knew it – picked a worse punishment as far as Melissa was concerned. Even as a child the signs were there; a more stylish and grand dolls pram Melissa's parents could not have bought (Melissa's Mum wanting her not to miss out like she had) and after the very first day, she emptied out the dolls and fancy bedding on the floor and carried bricks around the garden in it!

CHAPTER EIGHT
MARLENA

D ue to the staffing problems at the pub due to its out-of-the-way location, the usual estimated seven-mile catchment area of advertising for staff had to be expanded slightly, more specifically in fact, to Poland. The Olde Flagon was a really nice place to work, Melissa and Charlie both proving this claim by both having stayed for so long. Unfortunately though, the pub was out in the wilds (part of it's attraction for some) and so transportation was essential and basically English people would rather claim 'dole' money off the Government than wait at tables or clean, and so finally through a friend of a friend of a friend who had also been forced to resort to abroad for staff to find good care for her invalided mother, so too did Bruno for kitchen help, day-time waiting staff and cleaner. Unfortunately for Bruno, this necessitated offering accommodation due to the slightly excessive commuting from Poland without; and so it was that Marlena arrived at The Olde Flagon.

Melissa and Charlie, and indeed everyone they discussed it with, had always been told how poor Poland was and that food, clothing and the like were in short supply and of poor quality when it came, so when the moment arrived for Marlena to finally make her entrance Melissa and Charlie were some what taken a back. Marta, Marlena's aunt who already lived locally having married an English pillock too gullible to see Marta for what she really was about, had picked Marlena up from the station (only later did Melissa discover that she had made her wait for four hours before she actually got her, even though the station was only half an hours drive away). The two women together made quite a scene; Marta barely five feet tall, had a shock of peroxide blonde hair which appeared to have been styled into a pixie type cut until she swung her head around and revealed the most awful and obviously fake long and curly hair piece. She was actually dressed quite stylishly, but unfortunately from the same age group as her niece, twenty years her junior, which was quite well betrayed by the tell-tale lines already quite well established on her unfriendly and stern face. In complete contrast, Marlena was five feet ten, jet black (from a bottle) long hair, very heavily made-up eyes with thick black eye-liner over her top lids in a kind of Egypt meets the Sixties way. Dressed completely in black from her excessively high, laced up, Doctor Martin style boots (known in Poland as 'underground' boots) to her three-quarter length obviously 'good quality' leather jacket. So much for no money and poor quality clothes, Melissa thought! Lack of taste yes, but lacking in money, certainly not apparent!

"Is Bruno here?" Evil-looking mutton-dressed-as-lamb dwarf demanded, ignoring the polite 'hello' and welcoming (or at least she had intended it to be, smile; perhaps it had been mistaken for wind?

"Ahhh, yes. You must be our Polish lady!" Melissa ignored evil dwarf and smiled at the eclectic mix of fashion before her, with the most penetrating and 'staring' blue eyes. "I'm Melissa; I'll just get him for you."

Introductions were made and Marlena settled into the room which was to become her home for the next few months, then without a backwards glance or a 'goodbye', evil dwarf bitch left the building.

Marlena, it turned out, was quite a character. She had excellent English and a good sense of humour. She was quite quiet initially, as one might expect after a twenty-four hour bus trip in addition to being made to wait for that extra four hours. There was one major fault however, instantly apparent....bad dress sense aside...she was much too attractive and slim for Melissa's liking – particularly in the already scarce male situation she found herself in.

BUM!

CHAPTER NINE
MARLENA'S "CARE IN THE COMMUNITY"

Within a week of arriving, Rob, the local lothario, had made it his business to be the first to bed the 'new blood'. It seemed an appalling trait of all the youngsters in the surrounding villages to the pub, and indeed the village in which she grew up, that everyone must sleep with everyone. In the small group of farming contractors that Melissa, in the summer, opened the pub early for and shut it late (because of their beseeching telephone calls to her telling her at 11.45pm that their convoy of tractors and farming gadgetry were only a couple of miles away, and so please don't shut the pub yet) there was only one girl that regularly came in with them, as opposed to five lads, and she was a lovely bubbly 'girl-next-door pretty girl, only everyone had carnal knowledge of her and worse still, she seemed proud of it. Melissa even heard one of the lads saying one day that he thought that Debbie was a really nice girl, but there was no way that he would be going down the aisle with someone that half the church had slept with. In the village that Melissa had lived in since she was six, the same thing was true; herself excluded and her next-door neighbours, also outsiders, everyone only dated within the village, after the novelty of one relationship wore off, they moved on to the next, leaving them in their thirties pretty well back to the people they started with, and generally their

43

second cousins. It seemed to Melissa that if they left the village boundary that the sky might fall in or something, because to Melissa's mind the pickings were not rich enough (in the non-monetary sense) to bother with, let alone try them all out. So... Marlena's arrival in the pub meant a metaphorical new skirt to chase, and foreign at that, it would always be a conversation piece and so Rob spent a lot more time in the pub trying to impress her sufficiently to persuade her to come home with him. What Rob was unaware of however, was that Marlena's city that she lived in, was from her description at least, the sex capital of Poland; there were more sex clubs than any other form of business and everyone seemed to be involved, and consequently their attitude towards sex was much less inhibited and 'no holds barred!' Even less was Rob aware that what he had actually met in Marlena was the female equivalent of himself. Marlena's attitude towards sex was very practical; if she wanted sex she would let you know in no uncertain terms, and when she had satisfied her needs it was over, irrelevant of what position that left her victim in. It caused no end of laughter to Melissa and Charlie as she relayed the shocked expression on Rob's face the morning after the night that Marlena decided to go home with him (a night she had chosen purely because it had been the first day she could be bothered to shave her legs) when he had dropped her back at the pub and leant across to kiss her goodbye she was already out of the car and shutting the door. He gave her the filthiest of looks and then drove off spinning his wheels in some loose gravel on the junction at the edge of the car park. Charlie and Melissa thought it was excellent that he should feel used in the same way he had treated most of the women in his life. Rob avoided the pub for several weeks after that, but once he eventually came back in again, he and Marlena became 'sex buddies' – when ever Marlena chose, of course. Melissa watched the situation play itself out and could see that what Rob was actually up to was trying to make her want him and chase after him in the same way all the other misguided girls did, until he tired of them and moved on; albeit whilst he was seeing at least one other girl too. Melissa could see that it was really denting his ego to be treated so indifferently, particularly as she had said no to sex with him more often than she said yes, not a situation that he had ever been faced with before. It entertained Melissa no end, to see Marlena toying so heartlessly with him, particularly after the appalling way he had treated so many really nice girls that he had brought into the pub, let alone the ones she had never met. Marlena reminded Melissa of one of those nasty wildlife documentaries where the hideous creepy crawlies are shown having rampant sex, only then for the camera to pan around and come back a while later to see the female mercilessly munching on the male's body.

It never ceased to amaze Melissa just how much Marlena was sexually lead; even down to the typical male sex fiend's habit of indiscriminate shagging, i.e. without actually caring about whether or not they fancied them; indeed, ability to breathe seemed to be the only necessary criteria for those men and her. In the first few months of Marlena being at The Olde Flagon, Melissa wickedly used this to her advantage directing any unwanted male attention she was getting at Marlena, who bizarrely did 'the deed' with two of Melissa's least favourite pursuers. One was a quite attractive man who had taken a fancy to her whilst she was out with Sally one night; attractive though he was when the brains were being handed out unfortunately he must have held the door open for everyone else, because two minutes in conversation with him were like two hours; the most mind numbingly boring two hours ever! A bit harsh possibly because Melissa did find out how to change the drive shaft on a tractor with your teeth (well, at least that is what she thought he said) and unfortunately he knew where she worked so after having successfully putting him off when he asked her out that night, he then repeatedly turned up at the pub and pitifully attempted to chat her up all night – much to the amusement of customers present, watching Melissa uncomfortably squirm at his unwanted attentions. Not having built a sufficient bond to have considered herself a proper friend with Marlena at this

45

point and still a bit wary of her since she expressed an interest in women as well as men, and that included her if she was interested, the second Marlena came and sat herself down at the bar when she finished her shift that night, Melissa made a point of introducing him to her and let nature take its course.

The second pursuer was Roger Bevan. Roger was a character who if you made him up would never be believed, a real case of fact being stranger than fiction. Melissa guessed he was in his late forties, because he would never let on. He was only about 5'8" but really big built and sporting an enormous beer belly. He was a builder by trade and whatever the weather was doing he was always wearing shorts and on the rare occasion one would see him without his standard baggy jumper with a large hole on the belly (fraying badly at the edges leaving peculiar undulating squiggles of wool waiting to catch in something and unravel some more) he had arms like Popeye the Sailor and rough, calloused hands the size of shovels. His arms were the size of most people's thighs. He had wild curly hair that was thinning slightly so that you could see his bare skin catch the light in-between the curls, and he was always trying to convince Melissa that everyone thought he looked like Tom Selleck when he was younger and with his hair cut shorter, but Melissa could not see it herself. What Melissa could see in Roger was Romany Gypsy with his brown weathered skin, wild hair and vivid blue eyes which were sparkly bright and with the light in the right position when he stared at you made him look quite mad; quite the opposite to the 'sexy' which Melissa was sure he thought he was achieving. Roger had a very well known reputation as a serial womaniser and was particularly fond of married ones – until they got too attached that is. Giving Roger his due, as much as she wasn't won over by his charms, she had seen him in action and witnessed lots of women that fell for his corny chat-up lines. Melissa's favourites were when he honed in on a particularly plain looking woman, which would do in the absence of an attractive victim, and then flirt outrageously with her and tell her what beautiful eyes she had or a gorgeous smile. He was clever, Melissa acknowledged, because he knew that the plain women would be well aware of their beauty or lack of it, and would not take too kindly to out right lies, well not in most cases at least, and so he cleverly commentated on specific attributes that were nice, she had even heard him use eyebrows, which nearly caused her to spit out her tea she had found it so funny.

Melissa had met Roger the second night that she had worked at the pub. He and a group of his building team did a regular pub-crawl on a Friday night and had a pint in each venue, or two if there were attractive women around. The first time Melissa set eyes on him had been quite unnerving because he just stood in front of her staring, never losing eye contact with her where ever she moved around the bar, other than to lasciviously run his eyes long and lingeringly up and then down her body, remaining slightly longer in the breast area, and then back to her face causing Melissa to flush with embarrassment. The group asked her a few questions about where she came from and Roger complimented Bruno on such a good find for the pub, and then they went on their way. As soon as they had gone Bruno warned Melissa what a womaniser he was, and that he advised that she have nothing to do with him, other than to serve him beer of course. The following night at a similar time, the group, joined by two girls this time, arrived again and Roger did the same unnerving staring thing up until Melissa had enough, and to the amusement of his friends asked him if he had something in his eye due to the fact that he was making a funny face at her. He had flushed momentarily and retaliated by telling her that he had been struck by her beauty. Melissa laughed out-loud at him and told him that surely he could do better than that, and all his mates laughed and assured her that he couldn't. Roger had relentlessly perused Melissa, not exclusively of course, for all the time she had known him. Their banter in the pub kept the regulars in the pub entertained, particularly when Roger secretly bet Dennis one night when Melissa had out-scored him magnificently in the 'put-down' stakes which Roger had resorted to when flattery had been exhausted; that he could have

47

bedded her by Christmas. Dennis laughed and took the £10 bet and then, of course, to ensure he won, told Melissa all about the conversation and offered to give her half provided that she didn't. Melissa told him that the money wouldn't be necessary even if she hadn't have known about the bet there was absolutely no chance of it happening. Roger was always telling Melissa that she would end up a miserable, lonely old woman and she told him that if he really was the only alternative then the miserable and lonely really would be preferable and that she would start buying cats now. So Marlena's arrival really was a Godsend as far as Melissa was concerned, and he immediately turned all his charms on to her and that entertained her no end and made Marlena feel flattered at all the attention.

CHAPTER TEN
IT'S NOW OR NEVER

Thursday night, not Melissa's night for working really, but lately she was doing more of them than not. Thursdays were also 'lads night out' for Daniel so sometimes he came in but very rarely, so when at quarter to six Melissa walked through from the kitchen with her pint mug of tea, dunking the teabag unceremoniously about with her finger-tips, it was no wonder she dropped it from inches above the mug with a huuuge splosh and of course a tidal wave of hot tea that counteracted this, upon spotting him there waiting uncertainly just inside the door.

"Hell-low!.....Ow!....Shit!....Bugger! You're keen!" Melissa said rescuing the teabag and throwing it into the bar bin, splatting as it hit the swing top and sending rivulets of brown tea all down the length of the plastic (clean it up later Mel thought... now calm down...breathe!)

"Uhh yeah, ummm, I hope it was OK, but you did say to me and Nigel that if ever your car was outside that we could come on in."

"God, yeah – of course its OK, you just startled me a little." His face relaxed a little as he sunk down onto his favourite bar stool.

"So what d'you know then?" Daniel asked as she concentrated on pouring his Murphys without spilling it or breaking anything. It had become their usual patter – one or other always asked it. Melissa sneaked a direct eye contact look at him but on reaching target both looked away, him slightly before her she noticed.

"I know that door handles for Suzuki jeeps cost twenty eight bloody quid! It's doubled the whole car's value! What about you?"

"Caaw, that's a bit steep, you ought to have thrown it away and bought a new one!" Melissa had bought the jeep to drive in bad weather rather than risk her beloved MR2 in the snow. It had become something of a joke between them that she was obviously filthy rich - even though they both knew she was not (especially Melissa!) "Me...?" he paused looking along the bar and away from Melissa's stare, "I know that Binkleys are robbing bastards...they have just charged me ten quid for a twenty-two mil' swept tee and I don't even reckon that it's swept!...Hang on, I'll show you!" Daniel left the pub and came back a couple minutes later with the plumbing fitting.

"Naaaah. No way is that swept." Melissa examined it, "That's just a slightly off centre 'equal tee', probably a rejected equal tee in fact! You've been conned. Take it back!" Melissa instructed bolshily.

"Well I argued and argued with them and they would not have it, but I'm still not convinced, so I need to get another somewhere else so I can take it, show them what a proper one looks like and tell them to shove it!" Conversations like this were fine, not your ordinary type of thing but then there were not too many barmaids that would know one piece of bent copper from another; but it was the time during which they both relaxed, a fraction, neutral ground. It was non-threatening, non-sexual and yet the underlying buzz of his closeness, heightened by his slightly uncomfortable, not quite nervous, behaviour, made Melissa's insides lurch uncontrollably. 'What was it about him that did this to her?' Melissa often wondered. She watched him 'not' looking at her. 'Now be analytical and unbiased for a moment' she told herself. 'Right.' She assessed, 'he was OK looking but not drop dead gorgeous. With every haircut his almost black hair was becoming more and more grey, and it was coarse looking, almost wiry hair (not the stereotypical 'cawwhr', imagine running your hands through that girls!) and yet for all it's lack of resemblance to Richard Gere's lovely grey hair, it was still definitely an urge that had very vividly stuck in her mind as something she would kill to be able to do. And then there were those eyes…harsh, sometimes cold eyes; deep, dark, almost evil looking sometimes, penetrating and smouldering, secretive eyes which gave nothing away. It was so unfair to fall for someone with such unreadable eyes as normally her finely tuned people watching skills would have had his eyes betray him by now – but hell! What chance did she have, they couldn't even prolong eye contact for more than the briefest of moments anyway! He was nearly fifteen years older than her but as much as she preferred older men it was not an essential requirement, it just meant that there was just slightly more chance of them having grown up a little; having decided what they wanted out of life. Then there was his status of millionaire and something of a local 'somebody'. Money of course was always nice, but ultimately, mad though she knew she was, if Melissa got money she wanted to have either earned it, inherited it or won it herself. The being a big fish in a small pond just meant that even more people had an opinion on you; and where money was involved so inevitably is the green eyed monster, and Melissa knew without doubt that if he was a penniless window cleaner she would still want him. So it was none of these things individually, and yet when he walked through the pub doorway that first day, you could have knocked her down with the proverbial feather; or set fire to her hair, and she would not have had the slightest notion of anything except him – oh, and maybe the smell of burning hair at some point and only then because that is really bad! It has to be beyond us, chemical or electromagnetic-al or some other such something as yet unexplained or defined.'

'Oh God, what have I been saying? Have I been staring? Have I been dribbling? What's he been saying? I haven't been picking my nose without realising have I?' Melissa's thoughts brought her back to reality with a bump! The outside door creaked and banged and Melissa and Daniel both looked around; it was Charlie arriving for work. It always disappointed Melissa to have to share his company, but sometimes the distraction of a new conversation helped them along the way.

"Hi Charlie Poohbag – you OK then?" Melissa asked. Daniel and Charlie both smirked.

"Yeah, fine thanks – Hello." And proceeded to strike a match from the brick on the bar and then breathe in deeply on her cigarette. After that none of them knew what happened, most especially Melissa whose mouth seemed to take over whilst her brain switched to autopilot and Charlie and Daniel looked on first in surprise and then shock.

"Ummmm errrr, ummmm I'm really sorry about this but I need to embarrass both of us for a moment." Melissa began saying to Daniel. At this she had his full attention and he looked at her with a bemused and puzzled smile on his face all expectantly. At this extra attention and already knowing what she was about to say, Melissa's face flamed red but she had committed herself now and was determined not to be beaten. "Uuuhhhmmm, Oh God!…Ummmm..Oh yeah, whatever you do, you are not allowed to answer OK?" she implored of him, eye contact for once never faltering.

"I'm not allowed to answer?" he asked slightly confused but grinning and rubbing his chin in mock consideration.

"No, definitely not!" Melissa replied sternly, as Charlie puffed on, watching this unexpected turn of events, not knowing what Melissa would say next but very keen to hear.

"OK, ummmm, well you know I told you that the girls made me this bet?" she looked up for acknowledgement, having been intently staring at the lemonade and cola dispensing machine whilst she composed her words into some semblance of order.

"Yee-eh-ss." He said considering it slowly.

"Well I've had a good think about it and I'm afraid you're it! So ummm, sorry about this but would you like to come for a quickie in the cellar with me please?" Daniel's eyes nearly popped out of his head as his eyebrows momentarily left his face. Melissa held his gaze then looked bashfully away and then quickly over at Charlie who was gesturing thumbs up signals wildly just out of Daniel's field of vision. When he looked to follow Melissa's gaze to Charlie she turned her face away but the raised edge of her cheeks clearly betrayed her facial expression.

"And I'm not allowed to answer you say?" He returned his attention back to the still embarrassed Melissa, having regained his serious composure.

"No you are not! I am sorry for doing that to you but now I have won. No baby-sitting! Oh, and the cellar is that way, down the corridor – if you needed to know." She bravely shot at him, try-ing to keep the humour but belie the intent too as she pretended to busy herself doing the evening's candles. Charlie meanwhile was snorting out the water she had just been drinking.

"Oh my God Mel!" She spluttered, "I can't believe you just said that!" from her new position behind the bar as she dragged a beer cloth over the spat out water with her foot. "Bet definitely bloody won! Well done you! Oh my God!" she repeated at a loss for words, "I'm so shocked!" Charlie kept looking from Daniel to Melissa to try and gauge his response. Daniel's gaze kept return-ing to his pint and to Melissa – widely smiling. Finally he spoke again, "Wouldn't it be a bit cold in there?"

"That just adds to the thrill, and anyway, right now the heat from my face would keep us warm." Melissa could feel her cheeks were still smouldering. It was partially from embarrass-ment and partially from delightedly observing the expressions flitting across his face; the impenetrable mask permeated for just a moment. 'God, what a buzz!' Melissa thought.

They tried to resume a normal conversation, the three of them, but so many looks were being shot about that it was impos-sible. Luckily pint number two was coming to an end and all Melissa found she could do was concentrate on the relief she felt at successfully winning her bet and more importantly not having offended Daniel in the process.

"And I'm definitely not allowed to answer?" He raised his eyebrows provocatively at her and stared long and hard with a mischievous sparkle in those wicked eyes. Melissa stared him out for a while before saying very quietly again, "No." He smiled broadly and finished the last of his beer keeping eye contact with her the whole time. As he put down his glass he said, "Guess I'd best go then."

"Yeah, byeee. Cheerio!"

"Byeee." Charlie laughed, making the e in her goodbye waver uncontrollably along with the cigarette still wedged in her mouth.

After the door had safely closed behind him, but not before he had paused momentarily to smile at the two girls once more, they both watched in silence for his car lights to go on then Charlie squealed out "Oh my God! You did it! You bloody did it! I just could not believe my ears!"

"I know...I really thought I was going to blow it and it was going to all come out wrong or that he'd go mad or something!"

"You aarre joking! What man would go mad at being asked for sex by someone?!"

"Oh, I know, but he's married and he might have thought I was taking the piss or something."

"Naah, you've got no worries there. He seemed quite flat-tered. Good job he wasn't drinking when you asked him, I reckon he might have choked!"

"What, like you did?!" Melissa smiled and fidgeted nervously. "But what if he goes away and thinks about it and can't face coming back in here again?"

"He'll be back. But what I don't get is why wouldn't you let him answer?"

"Oh, well that's easy: a) cuz I would not have wanted to hear him actually say no and dash all my dreams and hopes of the last four and a half years, b) cuz he's married and may not have felt comfy saying yes even if he had wanted to say yes in front of a witness, and c) he might have said yes!"

IT'S NOW OR NEVER

"What the hell's wrong with him saying yes? It's what you've wanted all along!"

"I know but what could I say to that? If the shock didn't kill me, I couldn't go off into the cellar and do it over a barrel (well, not the first time at any rate!) Besides, whatever I would have said in response would have come out badly – you know what I'm like! It would be like Paul Shepherd at school all over again."

"What are you on about? Who the hell is Paul Shepherd?"

"At school Paul Shepherd, who was in the fifth year when I was in the third year, found out that I fancied him and one day he came up to me and said "I hear that you fancy me?" and so embarrassed was I that my fantasy was standing in the flesh next to me that I said "Oh yeah, but I was only messing about." And he said, "Well I bloody well hate being messed about!" and skulked off and I stood by and let him go! I blew it big time! And this would be no different – I'd followed him round school for years! Now with Daniel if he had have said yes then I would probably have said "Err, umm thanks, but I was only joking – I'm afraid of spiders, couldn't go in there!" when in fact it is my all time favourite fantasy with him!"

"So say, "great, come on then!" and drag him off kicking and screaming into the cellar!"

"Oh God! I just couldn't. I'm too bloody shy and inexperienced! And if I turned down an opportunity like that I'd have to kill myself…painfully and very slowly!"

55

CHAPTER ELEVEN
FANCY A QUICKIEEE?

Melissa spent the whole of the following day distractedly thinking about the night before. Every time she thought about it brought a smile to her face and a glow to her cheeks. 'What if he doesn't come in? What if he does but it's not the same? Oh God! What have I done?' Melissa asked herself, worrying about the consequences of the previous night's events.

At 5.30pm Melissa was already at the pub busying herself with the night's preparations, so at 6.15pm when the door creaked it's opening warning and Melissa had already greeted all of that evening's expected staff, her heart raced and pounded loudly and her stomach churned as she waited to see who came through the internal door. Through the large stained glass panel that made up the top half of the door, she could make out the out-line of two men, greatly differing in heights, and that was it; the sick feeling of panic and fear and they were in through the door.

"Hello!" and "Hi-ya Mel!"

"Cawwr – you're early!" She exclaimed, looking up at the clock behind her, "Oh, and Hello – of course!" Barely daring to look at them.

"Ah, yeah, well we came straight here from squash tonight cuz I'm going out this evening so we only have time for one pub and so obviously it was straight up to see Mel – no contest!" Nigel said, smiling broadly.

"Your usuals?" Melissa enquired, "or may be you'd like something from the cellar?" She bravely flashed a bright mischievous smile at Daniel. Nigel missed the comment, but a smile flickered across Daniel's face and he looked back at her, but by then she had removed her attentions to the pint she was pouring – amazed with herself that she had been brazen enough to say that, let alone look at him for any length of time.

"So who won then?" Again a stock conversation, but anything would do whilst she tried to regain her composure from such a brave attack. The visit passed raucously, with the usual 'Oh she's so good – just watch her do that – no time wasted – three things on the go at once – and all the time smiling – oh that smile' and on it went; all of this from Nigel, who was a lovely man, short and cute and cuddly with not a bad word to say about anyone (which ordinarily would have annoyed Melissa as she did not consider it honest that one person could truly tolerate everyone they met, but with Nigel it was OK, he was such a likeable character that he might just prove to be the exception to the rule for Melissa). He was nine years older than Daniel, but although his dumpy exterior would mislead you, he was actually a very fit bloke, terrible hair though. Nigel's hair was very thick, very dark grey and brushed completely across from one side of his head to the other, as though trying to cover a bald spot or a receding hairline – but the odd thing was he had neither; just a weird, wig-like hairstyle that Melissa was always telling him he needed cutting. He was also very easily impressed, especially when he had the beer in him, or just plain infatuated, or drunk; and she knew it was not drunk, although that said after three pints he was definitely anybody's!

At the end of pint number two, Nigel asked Daniel "Have we time for another one do you reckon?"

"Ahh, yes, just a quick pint." He said glancing up at the clock above the till. "Mellll!" He called to her as she made her way across the pub, "Can I have a quickieee please?" And there it was. 'Oh my God! He's reciprocated. He wants me!' Melissa thought not daring to look at him right away. When she did she could see that he had been watching her every move, waiting to see her reaction. His face was challenging, questioning, but moreover smiling. Melissa's too was smiling; all pursed lips and cheekbones (well, where they would have been if she had visible ones!) 'Very clever!' she silently congratulated him, but as she put the head on his pint a moment later he looked at her straight and said, "You didn't answer." Melissa grinned and blushed; or maybe even blushed then grinned, but Nigel saved her "Oh no, that's extra!"

"Oh, not necessarily!" Melissa shot back and then began serving another customer who had appeared leaving Melissa not able to fully appreciate the result. The pub became really busy after that and Melissa was unable to chat with them any more, other that to shout and wave goodbye when they said they were leaving. Again through the throng though Melissa was able to see that customary pause and double take in the doorway, and he smiled as he caught her straining her neck to see him. 'He does want me..doesn't he?..or may be he is just trying to figure out how my mind is working – well good flippin' luck!' she thought.

CHAPTER TWELVE
SKINNY DIPPING

It was Saturday night and it had not been looked forward to with too much enthusiasm by Melissa since Daniel had already said that Nigel could not make Squash that week and therefore visitation possibilities were low. The pub had one couple arrive for dinner at six and no sooner had they sat down at their table that the sound of the door went again. It was with only idol curiosity and the fact that the job required a welcome from her that she looked up and her face immediately broke into a smile as she beckoned Buddy, the scruffy pub Collie dog, away from tripping 'her man' over, parked as she was across the entrance. Buddy glared at her and then looked up sharply at him, and begrudgingly followed her directions to move – no doubt cursing them under her breath as she went, if her facial expression was anything to go by.

"You've got cold hands! So what have you been up to then?" Melissa asked as their fingers accidentally brushed as they exchanged money.

"Ha, just a bit of plumbing – put a new shower in. The plumber couldn't come for a month and I couldn't be bothered to wait any longer and so I did it myself."

"I see. A man of many talents." Melissa mocked him gently. He smiled and the usual small talk and pleasantries were exchanged. After a while Melissa said, "Funny question for you...well I suppose most of mine are!" He laughed and waited expectantly. "Have you ever been skinny dipping?" He looked across at her where she was now sitting copying the blackboard menu onto a note pad not far from his seat. He was smiling, as if to say 'where does she come up with this stuff from – and where is it going?'

"Ummm, no. I can't say that I actually have."

"You are joking!" You must have! I thought, well...oh, well that's not at all embarrassing!" Melissa covered her face behind her hands momentarily and felt the heat come to her cheeks as they started colouring up. He was still looking at her inquisitively.

"It's just that one of the waiting staff's Dad came in the other day and told me he had just been talking to someone who'd been skinny dipping with me, and well Charlie and him were both really shocked. Well, I thought I'd ask you, cuz I was sure you would have done it too, as I thought just about everyone else would have, and well I guess I thought wrong!" She could not look at him glowing as she was.

"It does sound like a good idea, now that you mention it." He flashed a smouldering look at her, eyes sparkling mischievously again.

Melissa's stomach lurched at the unexpected flirtation and her colour deepened some more. "Oh, yes, you must. I can highly recommend it, but wait for the summer or else go abroad – Greece is good!"

"What, to rub in to protect you from the cold?"

"Yeah, now there's an idea!" they locked stares, grinning. Melissa did her best after that to concentrate on the copying up of the menu, but it was futile, reading the same lines over and over again, and ended up distractedly doodling in the margin instead.

"So what's Nigel's excuse for not squashing tonight?"

"Ah well, he's got some Nigerian Gospel singer visiting this evening – a bit heavily into the old religion is old Nigel. He's one of those people who say 'bless you' when you sneeze. I mean, what is that all about? I wanna say 'thanks' and take a bow – but what for?"

"All I ever do is ask if I've got snot in my hair!" Melissa said as he smirked. 'Oh God! Is it any wonder I can't get a bloke!' Melissa thought. "Ah well perhaps sneezing is some religious experience we're having – yeah, don't Jews say gazuntite or gazuntag or something too? See, definitely religious!" They both laughed as they contemplated this. A while later Daniel got up to leave. Melissa still no further ahead on the menu, having written the same thing at least twice, looked up.

"Right, I'm off on me way. A hot bath is beckoning – there see, I shall be skinny dipping!"

"Good for you! Ba-byeeee!" she laughed as he left smiling a wicked smile. 'Oh if only to be sharing that bath!' Melissa thought. But major progression, major eye contact today and he was really animated and chatty, more like he is when Nigel is around. 'I must remember to think up other flirty things to ask him about...but what?.....Bloody customers, anyone can see I'm busy!' Melissa thought smiling through gritted teeth at the couple who had just come in.

CHAPTER THIRTEEN
A MAGICAL GALAXY

Friday night. The wind had been gusting very powerfully and Melissa went through the usual evening preparations, nervously glancing up every time the wind spitefully, Melissa thought, made the door creak. Dead on six o'clock it finally opened but instead of 'her man', her smile dropped slightly as Charlie walked in.

"Hi!"

"Hello." Charlie responded quietly, lacking the normal bright smile and enthusiasm. She thumped her bag down heavily on the small table next to the bar, lit up a cigarette and slumped down in a chair by the fire. Slightly concerned by her uncharacteristic demeanour, Melissa grabbed her huge mug of tea from the bar and went around and joined her, enjoying the distraction of an impending visit.

"How come you are here so early then?"

"Yeah, sorry about that." Charlie replied, still in the same lack-lustre way.

"No, I don't mean cuz of that, what's up?" Charlie's eye didn't have their normal sparkle and her smile didn't quite make it to them, or even to its normal happy shape.

"Oh, it's just me and Pete; we've had a bit of a row." And with that she stubbed out her half smoked cigarette and produced a huge bar of Galaxy chocolate – almost magically Melissa thought, wondering why she had not acquired this trick herself – from under the table. Charlie unwrapped it and shoved a large chunk in her mouth with it barely touching the sides before purposefully breaking off another similar sized piece and ramming that in too.

"Chaaaarrrrlieee! What are you doing! What about the diet?" Melissa looked on in shock as the large bar was fast disappearing, and it did not even look as though she was even going to get offered any.

"I don't bloody care! Bloody men!" And in went another piece of chocolate as if to emphasise the point before the preceding bit had even had a chance to leave on its way downwards. "I deserve it! I need it! I've had a shitty bloody day and right now I don't care!" At this point the door went again and they both looked up expectantly; Charlie nearly as excited by Melissa's hype about 'the visits' as she was, but it was only Rick, the only male member of staff currently employed.

"Hi!" He said lumbering in and flopping down at their table. He was a tall, well built seventeen year old with a lovely nature, which made him very popular with the customers, but with an annoying habit of not knowing when to shut up and an even more annoying haircut. He was quite an attractive lad, but unfortunately chose to slick down his dark hair with some sort of wet-look mousse, which reminded Melissa of her Grandad's Brylcreamed hairstyle, not too dissimilar other than the fact that Rick's style seemed to come from an age preceding his, where a centre parting was the thing – Melissa preferred her Grandad's look.

"You're bloody early too! What is it with everyone today? I know; I was bored!" Melissa whined a poor attempt to mimic a teenager. "You're bloody mad you are! Help Charlie eat her chocolate and save her a few calories."

"NO! You bugger off!" She yelled through a mouthful of chocolate, holding what remained of her Galaxy bar protectively towards her chest. "They are my calories and I intend having every one of them!" At this point the door creaked again and in blew Daniel. Caught slightly off guard, Melissa carefully, so as not to trip up embarrassingly in front of him or spill tea down herself, tried to coolly make her way back around the comfortable side of the bar, after having exchanged meaningful looks with Charlie.

"Hello, what's all this then?" Daniel asked grinning as he spotted the chocolate wrapper in Charlie's hands.

"Don't ask!" Melissa said, trying to hide the fact that she had just clouted her head on the archway leading into the bar by being brave and not crying or rubbing it, as she picked up a pint glass from the shelf.

"Ahh, like that is it Charlie. Diet's going well then?"

"Well enough that at least I won't have to go to the bloody gym tomorrow if she finishes that ALONE!" At this they all looked at Charlie, who coloured slightly from the excessive attention.

"Anyway, thinking of food, I've got something for you to try out." Melissa retrieved a large bright pink carrier bag from the other side of the large square shaped bar. "We've been given a load of sample crisps to try so you can help with the testing."

"Oh, OK then." Daniel agreed, putting his glass back down on the bar. Melissa picked it up and topped up the missing inch or so, of Murphys back up, as was customary for him (other customers would have had it poured properly in the first place, letting it settle before adding the head).

"Right, first one....the lovely pink wrapper must be prawn cocktail." She pulled a face whilst saying this, not for her dislike of prawn cocktail but because since she was a baby, probably in an effort to impress her three brothers (and be one of the boys, she thought with the benefit of hind sighted contemplation) that she had always hated anything pink. She pulled open the bag and popped a crisp in her mouth before offering them across to Daniel who was licking the newly created stout froth moustache from off of his top lip. Her expression, in the middle of doing this, instantly changed as the burning sensation hit the back of her throat and the coughing began. Grabbing for the nearest drink she gulped a mouthful of the still hot tea adding to her discomfort. Daniel, Charlie and Rick, the latter two who had joined Melissa behind the bar upon hearing the rustle of crisp wrappers, watched on in delighted amusement.

"Not prawn cocktail then?" Daniel asked grinning.

"Ahhh, I think I can safely say no to that!" She spluttered attractively as she turned the packet over. "Jalapeno Peppers! Hmmm, probably quite nice if you were expecting it!" They all worked their way through the seven different weird and wonderful flavours; all of them downing copious amounts of fluid after the Jalapeno Pepper flavoured ones Melissa was gratified to notice. At 6.30pm there were sounds of movement on the stairs above and Charlie and Rick left the stools they had been sitting on for the crisp testing and headed for the kitchen; that being the early warning system that the boss was approaching.

"Well, I can't decide whether I should stay for a quickiee cuz I have to get back and cook tea tonight." He kept his eyes fixed on his nearly empty pint glass. Melissa nearly choked on the tea she was drinking. 'Did he just say quickiee? Shit! He did! Did he mean anything by it? Oh God! Shit! Well I'm game if you are springs to mind – nope, bugger, just can't say it. WHY IN GOD'S NAME NOT? I'M SO CRAP!' she debated with and scolded herself madly.

"Yes, well there's a decision." Was all Melissa could manage. 'But there it was, an intentional use of the word on his part, that would do nicely for now! Not as good as leaping over the bar and dragging him to the cellar but my response was as close as my cowardliness would allow.' Melissa thought.

"Yes, I think I will." He said and looked probably meaningfully up at Melissa; but again those unreadable eyes and guarded expression. Melissa smiled and poured another pint, glad that she was keeping him that little bit longer.

"So it's Saturday you're not here then did you say?"

"No the one after." Melissa replied whilst thinking 'the same weekend you are going to be away or else do you seriously think I would be going anywhere? How sad is that, that you only arrange time away so as not to be here when he's not. Christ, he probably only comes here for the well-kept beer, not the clumsy, Rubenesque bar maid!' Melissa scraped at the melted wax and the stumps of candles in the candlesticks lined up on the bar adjacent to Daniel's seat in quiet and nervous contemplation of 'the quickieee'. 'Perhaps it just slipped out. May be it was Freudian? But what if it was intentional...may be the treadmill mantra was doing the trick!

CHAPTER FOURTEEN
LUCY

Melissa's old best friend from school, Lucy, had moved away with her boyfriend when she finished university to be near his place of work. Lucy and Melissa had the same silly sense of humour and had lived in each other's pockets throughout the whole of those all important secondary school years. They had met at a three-day activity course run in the school holidays after finishing primary school and immediately hit it off. Much to their mutual delight they found themselves assigned the same form tutor on the first day of secondary school and remained inseparable from there on in. Lucy's boyfriend Tom, was a drop-dead gorgeous, lovable rogue and always up to mischief, but he worshipped the ground Lucy walked on, and was always showering her with expensive gifts. In short, on paper at least, he was the ideal man, so it was no surprise that when his work took him to Winchester that she went there too. Melissa and Lucy naturally kept in touch but in the form of long and silly letters sent in envelopes filled with sweeties or funniosities that had tickled one of their fancies sufficiently enough to warrant posting it to the other. It was rare that they got together because Lucy was normally doing 'country' type things with Tom on their time off, and also letters were more fun and entertaining and did not interrupt what you were doing and also could be stopped and started at will dependent upon some exciting gossip occurring – or not.

Lucy was always inviting Melissa to come and stay, so finally when Melissa found out that 'her man' was away for the weekend, she decided that rather than mooning around the pub miserable because he was not coming in, it was best not to be there at all. And so it was arranged. Melissa studied her road atlas, not having the slightest idea in which direction Winchester would be found, and then all fuelled up, oil checked and ready to go, off she ventured into the most vile and miserable weather imaginable.

When Melissa eventually pulled up outside what she hoped was Lucy's house she was a nervous wreck. She had driven around every round about within a ten-mile radius of Lucy's house at least twice, in an effort to make sense of Lucy's rather dodgy directions in the unrelenting rain. The directions were in fact very accurate, but relied upon you noticing silly small and irrelevant road markers, as opposed to the may be slightly more helpful, whopping great church, multi-storey car park or Petrol Station that was next to the actual road junction you were to take and were much easier to look out for than a small sign covered by an over-grown hedge – or even a combination of the two would have been helpful.

"Hey you!" The petite blonde, bubbly and massive 'chested' Lucy rushed out the front door and hugged Melissa. "You found us OK then!"

"Yes, just about, but don't give up your day job!"

"Cheeky cow! Come on in. I have cake!"

"So I should bloody well think!" Melissa said before putting her nose in the air and in her best BBC newsreader voice saying, "I am a guest and I expect to be waited on hand and foot – now get that bloody kettle on!" Melissa instructed bossily but with a huge smile on her face as she struggled through the front door and down the cluttered hallway with her belongings.

Melissa unceremoniously dumped her bag down and flung her coat on top and then went and sat at the lovely old-fashioned country pine table that they had rescued from a skip many years before on a drunken night back from the pub. The table held fond memories for both girls as the Police had come past when they were having a rest from carrying its awkward mass the mile or so home, wearing four-inch stilettos. The natural resting position was to lean on it or sit on it, as indeed Lucy did; however, it was at this point that they discovered why such a lovely old thing was being discarded. In one fluid action Lucy jumped enthusiastically up onto the table as its legs at the far end creaked and toppled in on themselves. Lucy slithered backwards to the ground along the table's length as though it was a child's slide, and Melissa nearly wet herself laughing. Eventually, when they managed to contain themselves long enough to turn the table up the other way, in order that they might carry it with its loose legs contained inside its interior, Melissa reached across to pull out a leg whilst at the same time getting one of her heels caught in the grass verge at the side of the pavement, causing her to topple into the up-turned table. In true Melissa style, no sooner was she down she quickly spun herself around and with the offending loose legs in each hand, she steadied herself in her would-be boat and began a fairly impressively coordinated rowing action. Lucy had tears pouring down her cheeks at both the fall and then the boating image that Melissa had managed to create.

"Come in number 9, your time is up!" Melissa shouted.

"But Sir, we don't have a number 9!" Lucy responded.

"Number 6 are you all right?" Both girls yelled in unison. Such a nice time they were both having that they did not see the two Policemen appear around the corner on the other side of the road, until it was too late that is.

"Lucy!" The harbour Police are here!" Melissa smirked, trying but failing miserably to regain her composure as Lucy was pulling Melissa's shoe from the verge whilst revealing her red knickers, thankfully in the days before thongs were very popular, as she bent over without bending her knees in her very short skirt.

"Evening ladies." The Policemen said in unison as they surveyed the scene. "Ahoy there me hearties!" Melissa raucously replied, still rowing her table. "Now what on earth are you doing – out rowing the seas – at this time of night?" The older of the two men asked good-naturedly.

"Melissa clambered unceremoniously out of her boat, supporting herself on her makeshift oars.

"Well Officer, we were on our way home with our new table and stopped for a rest when it capsized." Melissa explained seriously. Lucy meanwhile, could contain her amusement no longer and snorted terribly as her laughter escaped, after which both girls screeched with laughter at the fact that she had snorted.

"Where are you headed?" The younger Police officer asked smiling.

"Only over to Cherry Tree Lane." Lucy replied.

"Yes." Melissa added, "It has a bench opposite the turning and in case you don't spot that there is a bloody great big petrol station too!" The girls giggled again as Lucy passed Melissa back her shoe.

"Do you have a license for that boat?" The older officer addressed Melissa seriously.

"Oh God Mellieee, they're going to arrest you." Lucy laughed.

"Drunk in charge of a vehicle is a very serious offence ladies, so you will have to escort us over to the Police car and we are going to have to bring your 'boat' as evidence." The older officer said in a matter-of-fact tone.

"But it's a table!" Melissa said bewildered as they were ushered over to and helped into the back of the Police car. Lucy was still giggling, thinking how exciting the evening was becoming. After driving for a few minutes, to Lucy's obvious disappointment they passed the petrol station, and the bench, and turned into Cherry Tree Lane.

"Which house ladies?" The driver glanced at his rear-view mirror at them.

"Twenty-three. Does this mean you aren't going to arrest her?" Lucy asked, genuinely dismayed.

"Not this time. Next time we catch you out rowing this late though with no lights on your boat you'll get the book thrown at you." The older officer said grinning as both men got out of the vehicle outside of Lucy's house and opened the back doors to let, and help, the two girls out. As the girls went around the end of the vehicle they saw the end of the table-come-boat protruding from the boot before the men easily removed it and put it and its legs, or oars, on the lawn outside the front door.

"Oh, thank you ever so much, you've been great!" Melissa said, relieved at not having to walk any further in her high heels.

"Yes thanks. I still think you should have arrested her though." Lucy pouted, "Would you like a cup of tea?" Lucy asked as she concentrated hard on lining up the key with the lock, which apparently she did by sticking out her tongue and screwing up her face, and after three attempts pushed open the front door.

"No thanks, we have to get going – more pirates to catch!" The young officer laughed through the open window of the patrol car as they waved and drove off.

"What are we going to do with it now?" Melissa asked as she lent on one of the good legs of the table as she bent down to take her shoes off.

"Aaaahh – leave it there. We'll sort it out in the morning."

"I said would you like a sandwich!.....Earth to Melissa!.... Earth calling Melissa!"

"Oh, what, sorry?"

"Where have you been space cadet?"

"Oh, I was back in Cherry Tree lane having just brought this table back. Happy days." Melissa sighed dreamily.

"Soppy cow! Sandwich?" Lucy demanded, laughing as she too reminisced.

"Not if we are having chips later."

"You mean you had to ask? Of course. Tom has become a chip Nazi, he says I am getting too cuddly and has banned me." Lucy pouted for effect.

"Bloody good job he's had to stay away then, else I would have had to seriously hurt him." Melissa said as she automatically shot her eyes up at the ceiling upon hearing a loud thump. "I thought you said Tom was away?" Melissa asked with a concerned edge to her voice.

"I did. He is. That is Kick."

"It sounded far too loud for him." Melissa said, still looking at the ceiling as she listened.

"Naahhh, hang on a mo." Lucy said as she held up her palm as if stopping traffic. With that Melissa concentrated on the heavy thudding moving away from overhead and moved her head in the direction the thudding was travelling. The thudding moved from the room above the kitchen, and went quiet for a short while before resuming louder than ever down the wooden staircase. As Melissa swivelled around in her seat to face the corridor that lead away from the stairs, she burst out laughing as Kick, a very slightly built, but beautiful black cat, nonchalantly made his way into the room and wound himself first around the table leg and then hopped up onto Melissa's lap.

"KICK!....How the devil are you, my handsome old boy? You frightened me to death! What have you been eating? LEAD!"

"I know, isn't it amazing. We get the smallest, runty looking cat ever, who stamps!"

"That's incredible! I honestly thought it was a person stomping about up there." Melissa grinned in disbelief. "Now where's that cake?"

Later that evening, after fetching two massive portions of fish and chips, Melissa and Lucy talked and talked and ate more cake and drank copious quantities of tea and wine late into the night. Kick, the cat, entertaining them periodically by showing off his party trick of fetching plastic bottle tops that you throw for him just like a dog. Eventually, they made their way up to bed. Melissa had the misfortune of sleeping in the spare bedroom, where the other semi Lucy's house was attached to was only a wall away. Only unfortunate because the sadistic sods next door had a wind chime stuck up outside their bedroom window next to Melissa's window and it was blowing a gale outside.

"Bloody marvellous! Wind chimes and a cat with anti-gravity boots stomping about. Just what you need for a peaceful nights sleep." Melissa muttered to Kick as he pushed his way into the room.

The following morning, after Melissa had made herself several large mugs of tea whilst she nosed through Lucy's pile of glossy magazines, Lucy finally came downstairs with her blonde fringe stuck out at a gravity defying 90 degrees from her head.

"What have you done? Been asleep on your face?" Melissa exclaimed upon seeing the state of Lucy's wild hair.

"Certainly feels like it!" Lucy replied as she reached her hand about tentatively until she found her wayward fringe and tried squashing it flat to her head again with the palm of her hand. It did work until she removed her hand, at which point it boinged straight back into its previous sticky-outy position. As Melissa got up to put the kettle back on again, Lucy went over to the back door to let Kick out. Kick was just as happy to stay inside but with a gently nudge up his backside with the massive pink fluffy slippers with rabbits faces on and big stuck up ears, he begrudgingly stamped outside. Lucy was just closing the door behind him when she glanced around the garden and realised that the bird table was lying down on its side.

"Crikey, it must have been really windy last night, look, the bird table has blown over!" Lucy said as she stepped outside and made her way down the stepping stones dotted across the lawn towards the up turned table. Melissa watched in quiet amusement as she could see the giant bunny ears attached to Lucy's feet bobbing about as she stepped from stone to stone whilst holding her dressing gown firmly closed around her. Melissa was just plopping the tea-saturated teabags into the pedal bin one by one when suddenly Lucy yelled out. Startled at the sudden outburst, Melissa jumped and flung soggy teabag number two half way across the kitchen, where it landed with a rather loud splat. Ignoring the mess she had made Melissa ran out the back door, ooh-aahhing at every step as her bare feet made contact with the cold stone path and wet grass.

"WHAT IS IT? WHAT'S HAPPENED?"

"There's a dead bird!"

"Oh God! Is that all?"

"Yes, but it's under there!" Lucy said, pointing miserably at the bird table.

"What are you on about?"

"Well I bent down to lift the bird table back up and as I moved it so I spotted it underneath."

"So what have you done with it?"

"Dropped the table and yelled out." Lucy said quietly, embarrassed at her pathetic reaction.

"Oh, right, so if it wasn't dead it certainly will be now." Melissa laughed at the absurdity of the situation.

"Oh God! Don't say that! You mean you think I may have killed it?" Lucy panicked, "Quick, help me lift it up!" Melissa bent down and pulled up the end of the bird table without waiting for Lucy to retie her dressing gown closed. Sure enough, when the table was properly righted, there was on the floor a beautiful little brown speckled bird.

"Ohhh, that is so sad." Lucy said, as tears started to form in her eyes.

"Wow! What are the chances of that happening? You are wandering about, minding your own business, when all of a sudden SPLAT!" Melissa smacked her hands together to emphasise her point. "A bird table, of all things, falls on you and kills you!"

"Oh don't!" You're sick!"

"No, really!…what are the odds of that bird pecking about in the exact spot that the table edge was going to land?" Melissa asked as they both stared intently at the poor inert little body.

"More weird though surely, is why isn't he squished flat? You know, pizza pavement?" Melissa looked at Lucy, seriously waiting for an opinion.

"You really are gross! But now that you mention it you are right. That is an awful lot of weight that has hit it, and at speed. What shall we do with it now?" Lucy looked about the garden for something to scoop it up in.

"Ummmm, you don't need to worry on that front…Kick has just run off with it!"

"Oh God no! Kick! Put that down immediately!" Lucy shouted as she ran towards Kick who was quickly leaving the scene of the crime down the side of the house with the dead bird hanging out his mouth. Lucy continued the chase with her fluffy bunny slipper ears wiggling comically as she hurried along, making a tragic but hilarious mockery of the whole sorry event.

CHAPTER FIFTEEN
HYPNO BOYD

Exactly five minutes to six o'clock and Melissa whizzed around the pub doing her last minute jobs of slicing lemons, restocking the white wine fridge and fetching ice from the cellar. 'THE CELLAR', every time she entered it shivers shot up and down her spine, and it was not because of the regulated twelve degrees temperature or because of the suspected ghost either! Leaving the cellar and passing by the window opposite the door to the ladies loo, Melissa peered expectantly out through the wobbly glass at the car park beyond. (The view was completely obscured by the 'wobbles' but Melissa new from experience that it could not disguise the outline of a large silver van within its undulations, and indeed dust, as she inquisitively rubbed a finger over the indentations and then wiped the pale grey dust off into the leg of her trousers – classy chick!) Slightly disappointed Melissa went back into the bar, it was still early, all was not lost! Suddenly the front door was rattled as someone attempted to open it, and then the doorbell shrilled out. Still clutching the ice-bucket in her hands, Melissa's heart lurched and beat frantically in anticipation, but as she reached up to undo the top bolt of the front door her pulse almost stopped as she realised that it was not Daniel, but instead was Bill or rather 'Mobile Phone Bill' or 'Phone-Bill' for short, as he was referred to being as there were more than two Bills that frequented the pub. Melissa slowly drew back the bolt, knowing that even if 'her man' arrived straight afterwards that the evening would be ruined, because three is always a crowd and never more so than when that third is 'Mobile Phone Bill – or the other two that said!

"Hi ya Mel How are you?" Bill said enthusiastically as he barged on through as soon as the door was undone.

"Hello! Yeah, fine thanks, and you?"

"Pint a Carlsberg please – yeah, can't complain I suppose. Working too hard and underpaid, you know how it is!" Melissa passed the pint across the bar and placed it down next to Bill's bulging black leather wallet, large set of keys and two very different but state of the art, mobile telephones. "Packet of plain crisps too please Mel." He said as though the thought had just occurred to him, even though he had the same thing every time.

"So you got any holidays booked then?" Bill asked, running both his hands through his very sparse, curly and wet-look gelled hair on either side of his head. Melissa often thought Bill had missed his true vocation in life as a hairdresser, as every conversation she had with him, even on a twice or more weekly basis, could have been scripted by the 'nice but dim' girl who washed your hair prior to having it cut, and then swept up the debris later, in between whiles she scalded your head, then allowed freezing water to run down your neck and of course finding out where you last went on holiday, where you were going next on holiday, and of course where you would like to go. Naturally of course, this girl was always exceptionally pretty, had a mini-skirt which barely covered her thong and had multicoloured stripes running in uneven chunks through her spiky hair, oh, and standard regulation of at least two piercings, in either her navel, eyebrow and nose as well as the five in each ear (and of course, that is just the visible ones!) Bill however, did not measure up in any of these categories Melissa was relieved to think as she thought of his rather rotund body over-loading a thong, due to the belly overhang NOT in the over filled department, well she assumed, certainly not something she knew personally nor was it a thought on which she wished to dwell! Luckily to draw her attention away from these unnerving images, the door opened and in walked Daniel. As is human nature, upon hearing the door open, Bill strained his body around on his stool to see who was coming in, and said an enthusiastic hello when he recognised who it was. Daniel's face seemed slightly unfriendly as he returned the welcome but in a more polite and restrained way which only emphasised the pleasure exuded when he returned Melissa's welcoming hello and hugest of smiles. Bill was sitting in Daniel's usual seat and so he took his Murphys to the other end of the bar away from Bill's belongings (what would be handbag contents, if he were slightly more effeminate). Daniel hunched slightly over his pint and looked very tired and stressed.

"So, any gossip and scandal for me?" Melissa asked removing his pint that he had drunk an inch or so from and topping it back up. He looked up at her with his hands still in the position they had been in before she removed the glass from them.

"I'm bloody knackered is all I know!" Daniel said, at first serious and then grinning as he watched Melissa spill the overly full glass sending streams of creamy froth down the sides of the glass and onto the bar.

"Oh look, I spilt it – just for a change! She said catching Daniel's eye before reaching for a clean beer cloth from the shelf and wiping up the puddle.

"Any of the lads been in?" Bill asked (as per usual) referring to the farming contractor lads who contributed a large percentage of their earnings to the up-keep of the pub.

"Nope, not since before your holiday." Melissa answered, annoyed to be disturbed from any contact with Daniel.

"And where is Bruno tonight – out on the pull?" Bill continued with his regular line of questioning, and cackled loudly as if he had said something particularly clever.

"Nope, he's at the theatre tonight, and with a woman, before you ask." Melissa replied matter-of-factly.

"No! Really?" Bill bellowed excitedly.

"Yes. Really."

"Oh my God! Has he turned?"

"Bill, you are a very sad man." Melissa answered, "And a nosey old git!"

"Hey! Less of the old – I'm only six months older than you!" Daniel's eyebrows nearly shot off his head at this remark. Melissa did not look young for her age she knew, but Bill just seemed so much older in his mannerisms and appearance (not in maturity – for he certainly was far from that!) and the look on Daniel's face clearly reflected the fact that he did not think they were the same age either. Daniel purposefully picked up his glass and glugged a large way through its contents.

"Wow! You got a thirst on then?" Melissa asked surprised at the speed with which he downed his normally savoured drink.

"Yes and no. I only really stopped for a quickieee!" He replied, standing up and throwing back the rest of his stout in a couple of gulps. Looking at the surprised and obviously disappointed Melissa with a strange and meaningful glance (if only she knew what the hell it meant!) he placed his empty glass down on the bar, said goodbye and then moved to leave. He turned at the door, as was customary, and gave her that same strange look, put a hand up to wave, bid regards to Phone-Bill and left. Melissa sadly watched him drive away, and then with both hands picked up his glass with the froth still clinging to the inside, and took it over to the glass-washing machine, holding onto it as if by doing so she would somehow feel closer to him; then realising how ridiculous and pointless this was, up-turned the glass into the empty basket on the draining board.

"You'll never guess what I did at the weekend Mel!" Bill said, bursting rudely into Melissa's thoughts.

"No, what's that then?" Melissa unenthusiastically replied as she made her way back over to face him at the bar.

"I got hypnotised!"

"Really?" Melissa asked with genuine interest, surprised by the unusual and very unexpected subject matter raised.

"Yeah, to give up smoking."

"Soooohh, does it work?"

84

"Well, I can honestly say I have not touched a fag since I left the hypnotist at lunch-time on Saturday, and I had a packet in my pocket on the way home and in the car there were some too."

"Wow! That's really great! Where did you go? What did they do to you? Did you know you were hypnotised?" Melissa bombarded him with questions, fascinated for probably the first time ever by all he had to say when it dawned on her that from amongst his normal handbag type contents on the bar his cigarettes, of which he was a chain smoker, were indeed absent. Bill went on to relay his whole hypnotic experience and before he left for the evening, Melissa took down the hypnotists telephone number, even though she was not really sure that she would pursue the issue herself but did think 'Hey – one never knows – does one!' and screwed up her forehead immediately wondering what had brought on the posh impersonation all of a sudden, 'we're not all locked up see!' she continued to think.

Thoughts about the hypnotist played on Melissa's mind until eventually she could stand it no more, and dialled the number.

"Hello – I'm sorry I am unable to take your call right now, but if you leave a message I will return your call as soon as possible." A friendly American accent softly relayed. Melissa pressed the 'end call' key on her mobile telephone and tapped it thoughtfully against her chin. She had not considered that he would not be there, and having plucked up the courage to call was now feeling incredibly disappointed to be delayed in this way. Again Melissa tapped in the number (still not having figured out how to use 're-dial' – even though she had had the phone for more than two years!) The American voice message answered again and after the beep Melissa nervously gabbled, "Hi, my name is Mel, I'm a friend of Bill's who you stopped smoking last Saturday. I am calling to find out if you can help me with weight loss, so please call me back." And Melissa continued to leave details of how she could be contacted. Having hung-up (as much as you can actually 'hang-up' a mobile) Melissa smiled to herself, pleased that she had set the ball rolling in her pursuit of a gorgeous body. She knew that she could not be cured 'per se' or else everyone would have already done it and sold their stories to 'Flab Obsessive Monthly' and the like (which Melissa liked to read for inspiration with her carrier-bag full of calories from the supermarket) but what Melissa actually hoped for was a will-power boost and a craving for vegetables and not the cream covered carbohydrates which were one of her closest friends.

Just as Melissa pulled up outside the pub that night, her mobile phone started 'diddly-dee-ing' its appalling attempt at a piece of classical music. After a mad panic to fumble the phone from the deepest darkest corner of her bag before it got swallowed up into the black abyss forever, or stopped ringing, Melissa grabbed it just in time and said hello.

"Hi, is that Melissa?" An American voice drawled softly from the earpiece.

"Oh, ummmm yes?" She said uncertainly.

"Hi, thanks for calling me earlier, its William Boyd here. Sorry I was with a client when you called, but in answer to your question, yes, I have had great success with weight loss candidates and I am positive I can help you."

Desperately needing to hear these words Melissa eagerly tried to arrange a time to see him but as he was based in Nottingham and spent every other two weeks here, Melissa had to be content to wait until the following Monday for her first session. As Melissa made her way around the side of the pub to meet the awaiting Bessie, the pub's Rotweiller, who was by now frantically wagging her stump of a tail causing most of her rear end to waggle endearingly too, in her desperate effort to say hello, and get a biscuit of course, having been made all the more frustrated by knowing that Melissa had arrived a good few minutes before Bessie actually got to see her. It was with a glad heart that Melissa started work, knowing that she only had a week to go before her whole life could change, and finally for the better! Not to mention that it also left a whole week in which to over-indulge in all her favourite foods knowing that after Monday she would no longer fancy any of them!

Monday finally arrived and Melissa was so relieved, if for no other reason her over-indulging was beginning to wear her out with so many trips to the supermarket to buy all her favourite multi-billion calorie most favourite craved for foods. It is hard work feeling stuffed all the time too, especially without the necessary time in which to sleep off the bingeing due to not actually stopping eating! 'Hypno Boyd', as Melissa had programmed him into her phone, had rung her that morning to confirm the appointment and to check she was happy about the directions she had been given to find him – but really to also remind her that he only accepted cash. Melissa busied herself with the normal crappy morning television and a long leisurely breakfast awaiting her Mum's return from the supermarket with various surprise goodies and at the very least fresh, still warm bread.

Melissa had to get herself organised as she needed to go and get some cash for the hypnotist and get showered and changed as she was going straight from Hypno Boyd to the cinema with Marlena and Jo, a friend of theirs who used to work at the pub as a waitress when Melissa first started, and there would be no time to change in between.

During the week of awaiting the appointment Melissa had kept making notes of all the things she felt were relevant to the hypnotist to know about her food habits. She added to them as and when something of interest occurred to her. She was really looking forward to being hypnotised. It had always been a subject that had fascinated her ever since a friend had been hypnotised at a stage show in Tenerife. The best thing about that evening she remembered was watching him watching himself on a video camera play back that a neighbouring table of shell-suited holiday makers had been kind enough to show him when he did not believe that he had been hypnotised. At one point the hypnotist had told him that he (the hypnotist) was invisible and then he proceeded to run about the room carrying a space alien type puppet with long dangly legs – which of course for the slightly inebriated 'Chuggy' as they knew him, was convinced that this thing was alive and whizzing around the room under its own power. Chuggy looked frightened to death – it was priceless!

Having picked up Marlena there then ensued a ridiculously long, stop start journey stuck in a five mile traffic queue caused by the left over dregs leaving from the Pilton Pop Festival, known to the rest of the world as Glastonbury Festival, even though Glastonbury was another seven or so miles on from Pilton where the festival was held. Obviously Glastonbury and the legendary ancient Isle of Avalon etcetera etcetera, blaaaah blaaaah blaaaaah was bound to score more Brownie points with the weirdy hippies, low lifes, travellers and druggies which seemed to make up a large percentage of the one hundred thousand plus crowd which attended although all the customers in the pub would have you believe a lot of 'normal' people went too, but Melissa personally had her doubts. They arrived in their droves in all manner of conventional and unconventional transportation including the largest number of VW camper vans of varying ages and states of disrepair together at any time in the world. The temperature gauge in Melissa's tatty old jeep she had decided to give a run crept higher and higher as they inched slowly along amongst hundreds of vehicles all trying to cut into the traffic queue as they exited from the festival site. There were also the army of backpack clad festival goers of all ages in a dress uniform of ridiculously expensive logo emblazoned t-shirt, baggy trousers with the last nine inches from what should be the bottom missing, trendy sandals or trainers and numerous plaited friendship bracelets and a floppy fishing style hat that you used to have to be bribed to wear to keep the sun off as a kid. Oh, and of course, not forgetting the 'not less than £100 or not worth bothering with' designer sunglasses. Then there was the all important 'keep it till it drops off so that you can tell your mates where you've been' hospital style fluorescent festival entry band. Add this to the minimum of four days without washing even though you have had copious amounts of sex, all with different partners, drunk too much, been sick – part of which splashed back onto your shirt too – and spilt four days worth of food and drink down the same shirt as it would have been 'uncool' to bring a change of clothes 'maaaaan'! Following slowly behind the hoards at a walking pace you could almost see the odour seeping out of them, enhanced now by the sun on their rain dampened shirts. Ironic really that the environmentally obsessed should be creating their very own hole in the ozone layer. As by now may be already quite obvious, Melissa was not a big fan of the festival and all it entailed. Never having actually been herself all her stories came direct from the lads in the pub who emptied the septic tanks on site for the duration and towed out the stuck vehicles filled with the lighting equipment and flashy electrical musical instruments and sound systems. The most entertaining stories were of course the poo related ones. In particular of the year before last when the septic tanks were being emptied by the huge dance tent and someone accidentally set the pump to blow not suck and filled the tent and lots of dancers with thousands of gallons of human excrement. Melissa's bias was not fully without justification as for a week either side of the festival, shops for miles around sold out of everything including basic essentials and the dirty hippies that the festival attracted camped in verges all around the surrounding lanes to the neighbouring villages leaving a whole load of rubbish and mess behind them and generally having also liberated the contents of several sheds and garages and even the occasional petrol tank – if not the whole car. Whilst Melissa acknowledged that of the travelling fraternity they were not all bad people the ones that were bad however, ruined the reputation of them all. Melissa knew that relatively 'normal' people frequented the festival too because the pub got filled with mouthy young Londoners whose mobile phones rang persistently and whose voices could be heard a hundred yards away so keen were they to let everyone around them know that they were there and going to the legendary 'Glastonbury'. So there Melissa was, dawdling along in a rapidly overheating car, using up valuable shopping time for Marlena who was going to look around Glastonbury whilst Melissa was being hypnotised so that someone knew exactly where she was.

"Don't let them out you tosser!" Melissa yelled to the car in front as yet another VW camper van tried to edge its way out into the traffic queue, much to the amusement of Marlena at her sudden outburst.

"Just you try and push in front of me and I'll have you with my bull bars!" Melissa yelled again. Marlena watched on in curious bewilderment and amusement as Melissa continued her abuse at the drivers and walkers alike, all oblivious to her anger. Melissa caught sight of Marlena's face. "I know its pointless shouting at them but it makes me feel better! Dirty bloody hippies making me late and ruining your valuable shopping time don't forget!"

"Oh yeah – dirty bloody hippies!" Marlena shouted out too – rather too loudly out of their widely open windows whilst travelling at the same walking pace as the accused.

"Yes, very good Marlena, but don't forget we cannot lock ourselves in and we are stuck in a traffic jam and every year people get stabbed at this do."

"Oh, do they?" Her eyes widened in disbelief. "In that case 'out the way you dirty bloody hippies'!" She whispered quietly. They laughed and the jeep engine protested noisily before stalling.

"Oh God! Now we've had it!" Melissa said as she tried to restart the engine whose temperature gauge was now just a millimetre away from the 'explosion imminent' position. The engine faltered and on the second try started up – fortunately at the same time as the traffic made a huge five or six hundred metre surge forwards. They were off again, the dirty and ripped white hood that acted as a roof flapping noisily behind them; it was some come down from the MR2 and that's for sure Melissa considered it appreciatively.

Finally they arrived in Glastonbury and managed to find a car parking space in the high street. The pavements were busy with an array of weird and wonderful people all dressed in brightly clashing colours and all shod with the same Glastonbury footwear of sandals, painted patterned desert boots or nothing on their feet at all. There was also a large amount of hair. Hair everywhere you looked, sprouting from every orifice, sticking out in wildly matted clumps from every head, armpit and even sprouting in abundance from the bottoms of the dungaree clad women's trouser legs. Skinny scruffy dogs followed their owners on lengths of old twine, often wearing a neckerchief for a collar; animals more smartly dressed and much less smelly than their owners. Strange sounds of a whole host of musical instruments from guitars to penny whistles all jostled for their place amongst the varying beats of tom-tom drums and singing. Everything a different rhythm and type of music – all attempting to cadge some money rather than do something so alien as work for a living. And then there were the smells; every person you passed had their own petchuli oil or marihuana cloud encircling their whole body and trailing wafts of noxious sent behind them. Even the shops had their own powerful odours; joss sticks burning in every available space in between the healing stones with their 'magical Glastonbury' powers.

Marlena – a Glastonbury virgin, looked around her in wonder trying to absorb the complete sensory over load that is Glastonbury. She did not say anything just silently took it all in with a quizzical look on her face.

"Something else isn't it?" Melissa asked screwing up her face in distaste at a particularly smelly vagrant passing by them.

"Yes. Does anyone here brush their hair?" She asked in her clipped Polish accent as a prime example of the Glastonbury 'White Rasta' went past (no beads or stripy hat though, just matted hair).

Melissa uncurled the piece of paper retrieved from the depths of her hand bag and smoothed it out enough to read her hand scrawled instructions from between the crumples of its surface.

"OK, so we need to find the Tourist Information Office." Melissa looked down the High Street for a familiar sign. "And there it is." She said nodding in the direction of it. "And it is supposed to be on the opposite side of the road to that. Come on, let's get skinny!"

The two girls headed off down the street, Marlena tottering in her five inch platform heeled shoes which she wore everywhere outside of the pub. Opposite the Tourist Information Office; that reminded Melissa of a pretty Dickensian cottage complete with wobbly glass and slightly bowed windows. The girls looked across the road and saw a large sign swinging in the breeze with 'East meets West' and a sunset emblazoned upon it. Butterflies donned their boots and began to tap dance in Melissa's stomach as they wandered beneath the sign and into a tiny cobbled alleyway. They stopped outside a large blue door where the sunset logo was repeated above a door bell and antiquated old intercom. Melissa got out her mobile phone and called Hypno Boyd, as she had abbreviated him to, to let him know that she was outside. (Why couldn't we just ring the bell like normal people? She thought as she nervously awaited his reply).

"Hello….the bloody answer machine is switched on! Now what?"

"Leave a message; perhaps he is screening his calls."

Melissa dialled again and just as she had finished telling the answer machine that she was outside his door, there was a shuffling of latches and a creaking of old hinges as the old door swung open and a man popped his head out.

"You must be Mel." He said extending a well tanned hand. "Hi I'm William Boyd. Come on up!" Melissa and Marlena arranged to meet in the pub across the road and then with a worried expression Melissa turned and followed Hypno Boyd up the flight of stairs a head of them, and then up another and another. Melissa's face reddened from the exertion and she began to breathe heavily. 'Perhaps this was how he planned to make her skinny!' Melissa thought to herself embarrassed to hear herself huffing and a puffing.

Melissa followed Hypno Boyd through a series of doors dotted along the winding corridors and eventually led her through to his room. It was small and square with two school-type plastic moulded chairs in the centre, a pile of rugs on the floor to the side of a massage style table and a tiny white porcelain sink with a large rectangular mirror above it.

"Come and look at this view!" He beckoned enthusiastically as he walked over to the window and extended his arms out wide (Melissa thought he was going to say 'taaa daaa!' so proud he was of it). Melissa cautiously moved over and looked out. Through the high position of the window you could see the ruins of Glastonbury Abbey as clearly as if they were in your own back garden.

"Isn't it great?" Hypno Boyd enthused.

"Aaa yeah, lovely." Melissa hesitantly replied.

Hypno Boyd continued staring out of the window for quite some time and then as if suddenly remembering why he was actually there, he turned his head sharply back to reality – staring at Melissa as if un-unnervingly absorbing her thoughts for a moment, and then gestured for her to sit down.

Melissa was not sure what she had been expecting. An American and a hypnotist and working out of Glastonbury was bound to have been a bizarre combination and sure enough; it was. Hypno Boyd was in his late forties with very darkly tanned skin and jet black, slightly greying shoulder length (at the back only) hair. His thick hair had a definite wave to it so that where it brushed along his shoulders it curled upwards and outwards; in a way that old ladies on the street would have stopped on the street to compliment him on his lovely curls as was the law apparently with slightly insane old ladies – if trips out with her curly haired brother were anything to go by. He had a thick, more obviously greying beard and jet black furry-caterpillar style eyebrows. His eyes were very dark brown, almost black, surrounded by lots of 'laughter lines' Melissa generously assumed given his age. He was a trim build and Melissa guessed only about five feet seven inches tall if his big hair was flattened against his head when he was measured. On his feet Melissa was relieved to see that he was wearing fairly ordinary black leather shoes, black socks (always a good taste indicator she was of the opinion) but above the socks were some black leather trousers which creaked every time he moved. To make matters worse, on top of this was the loudest shirt outside of Hawaii. (Obviously the black sock theory had been shot to pieces!)

Hypno Boyd crouched down to open a brown soft sided file case and fiddled about removing a large A4 notepad and a tiny white box which rattled as he opened it and removed two pills from its multicoloured contents. Throwing his head back he quickly swallowed the pills followed by several noisy gulps from a plastic disposable cup which had been by the side of one of the school chairs.

"Vitamins." (Pronounced vight-a-mins) he said rattling the box at Melissa. "Do you take them?"

"I buy them but generally forget to take them after the third or fourth day."

"You really ought to get into them – they are really just so good for you if taken in the right quantity and combination. Right then, lets begin." He said plonking himself lightly down in the plastic chair opposite Melissa and crossing his right leg over his left so that his ankle rested on his knee enabling him to comfortably lean his clipboard on it for support. "OK, I just want to go through what hypnosis is all about and so that you know what to expect and what you can realistic hope to get out of it then we will get right into it.

"Uh yeah, OK, but before we start I have been making a list over the last week of things that I consider will be important to you in understanding my eating habits and patterns and the sort of self-destruct things that I do to ruin diets. Also, I think that it is important that you understand that I am not looking for a lazy way out of dieting; every year for several years now I have lost three stones which I have done through five times a week sessions at the gym and severely restricting my food intake. I do understand what it takes to diet and I am prepared to do it, the reason I am here is because I want you to take away my food cravings – or at least trade them in for cravings of a healthy variety like fruit or celery and not sweets and carbohydrates."

"OK, that is great, and it will speed up things immensely you having pin-pointed your specific problem areas." Hypno Boyd scribbled frantic notes with his fountain pen making loud scratching noises as he swirled it flamboyantly over the page. Melissa watched him curious to know what he could possibly be writing so early into the session and how he could go out in public wearing that shirt. Perhaps it was part of the hypnosis technique; 'watch my shirt, watch my shirt, you are feeling sleepy...' Melissa thought to herself.

They talked for three-quarters of an hour. Predominantly about him Melissa later reflected. He was actually a very interesting person to talk or rather to listen to, and clearly was well into sport and health and fitness – even if he was a bit of a Sixties type throw-back underneath those creaking leather trousers.

"OK then, I think we're ready!" He said flicking the back of his hair up with both of his hands simultaneously in a remarkably effeminate manner. "OK, if you'd lie down on the couch and make yourself comfortable then we'll begin."

Melissa lay down nervously on the phlegm green massage table and watched him as he crouched again at his briefcase and removed another set of pills. He swallowed two of apparently the same type as before again washing them noisily on their way with several loud gulps of water. He dragged his chair over to the side of the couch by Melissa's head and then touched his temples with both hands and closed his eyes as if in a trance momentarily. He took several extremely deep breaths exhaling loudly in a long and very controlled manner and then he opened his eyes, did the now incredibly annoying hair flicky thing and then he reached down and switched on a small CD player which was under the couch and weird haunting; what Melissa considered to be birthing music filled the room.

"Are you feeling relaxed?" He asked producing two tiny brown bottles.

"No, not at all." Melissa replied laughing nervously.

"OK, hold out your index finger."

Melissa cautiously held out her index finger and Hypno Boyd dripped a single drop from one of the bottles with a teat pipette and then two drops from the other.

"Wipe that under your nose." He instructed as he did the same thing to himself.

"Why? What is it?"

"Hypno Boyd smiled at her caution and showed her the labels on the bottles. "They are essential oils; the first was incense and the second one lavender. Smell them."

Melissa slowly lifted her finger towards her nose and wafted her other hand over it; a technique they had to use in chemistry lessons to prevent oneself from deeply inhaling vile substances, and being as Melissa could not even bare to walk into a Body Shop without retching because of the overpowering mixture of scents mixed with the high heat in the shop, then she knew that this was likely to be something she would not be wanting to take a big sniff of.

"Ugggghh!" Melissa responded turning her nose up in disgust.

"You don't like it?" Hypno Boyd asked astounded.

"NO! It's vile!" She replied still with her faced screwed up as she could still smell it.

"What does it remind you of?" He asked watching for a response.

Immediately without having to think Melissa said "Glaston-bury."

"Yeah right, with all its mystical powers and legends." He said empathising.

"NO!" Melissa said appalled at the thought, "Because of all the dirty hippies and travellers! It reminds me of that other rancid perfume they wear Petunia or Petulis Oil or whatever it is called; ugggghh, gross!" Hypno Boyd laughed at her candour.

"Well it is a shame that you feel like that but it is an important stage in the hypnosis because it will help you to relax and as you will be having several sessions it will help your brain to associate the smell with being relaxed and hypnotised and it will take you into even deeper levels of hypnosis."

"Well OK then." Melissa said begrudgingly wiping it under her nose.

"OK, lie back and start to breath deeply." Melissa watched him from the corner of her eye as he sat with his eyes closed next to her inhaling and exhaling deeply.

"Breathe in…….breathe out……breathe in…….breathe out…..let the air slowly fill your lungs and then slowly release it through your mouth. Good." He told her as Melissa did her best to mimic his movements. "Now breathe even deeper. Take that air right down in, deep, deeper than before, right down into your diaphragm then fill your lungs right up to capacity…….. then breathe it all back out as slowly as you took it in."

This continued for what seemed an age but amazingly Melissa found that she did feel much calmer; even though she couldn't stand that God awful smell up her nose.

"You are very relaxed and calm. You will continue to breathe deeply knowing that with every breath you breathe in you are taking yourself towards the new you. You are walking through a large field." Hypno Boyd continued speaking very slowly and calmly with very little change in the level at which he was talking and it was quiet too; a mere background suggestion amongst the weirdy birthing music that Melissa felt surrounded her.

"At the far end of the field is a door. You make your way over to the door and as you draw near a large key magically appears in your right hand. This is the key to your mind. You use the key because you are all powerful and unlock the door to your mind. You walk through the door feeling happy that it is a good thing that you are about to do and once you are through the door you lock it back up knowing that you are safe and that you are all powerful and that nothing can happen that you do not want to. The key magically appears back in your hand where it stays always and you find yourself in another field. As you walk along through the field you see a cave ahead of you with a very large entrance, it is dark but very welcoming and you are drawn towards it because of the love and warmth you can feel exuded. You enter the cave and see a pathway downwards made up of seven steps. You climb down the steps and with each step, seven, six, five, you find yourself becoming deeper and deeper into hypnotic trance, four, three, two..." Hypno Boyd reached forward and with his thumb applied pressure to the middle of Melissa's forehead, "....deep hypnotic trance, deep hypnotic trance, deeper and deeper...one. You reach the bottom of the steps." He released the pressure and Melissa surprisingly felt her body relax further into the couch even though she would have said if asked at that particular moment in time that she was already fully relaxed. "You have reached the healing beach. You walk out into the glorious sunshine and feel the warm sun on your back and the warm sand between your toes. You feel great and happy and secure and warm. At the far end of the beach you see two palm trees, hung up between the two palm trees is a huge white hammock which you know is your hammock. You make your way over to the hammock and get in. You lie there relaxing, swinging gently knowing that everything is right and this is where you want to be. As you lie there peaceful....."

'Hang on a minute' Melissa thought to herself, I'm still trying to get in the bloody hammock!' As soon as he had mentioned the word hammock Melissa had been having a comedy moment trying unsuccessfully to get into it. 'Concentrate' Melissa told herself; surely this should not be happening? I can't be hypnotised' she thought despondently.

"You have a beautiful mind. You have a beautiful body. To make your body more beautiful and to turn it into the best version of yourself that you can you need to start from within. You need to love yourself and because you love yourself you will treat your body like a temple. Your body is a temple and you will respect and love your temple by only putting the best things into it." Hypno Boyd rambled on in the same vain until he took Melissa back to reality and led her back along the beach after crash-landing out of her hammock – well that is how it happened in Melissa's mind at least. Back up the seven steps blaaah blaaah blaaah until she locked the door to her mind and the key magically disappeared into the palm of her hand.

"Eyes wide open, wide awake!" He instructed and Melissa's eyes almost involuntarily flew open. "How do you feel?"

Melissa thought about it for a while as she sat up, other than feeling a bit weird from having been lying completely flat, she didn't feel any different from normal.

"OK" she replied rather disappointed. "So how do you know that you actually did hypnotise me then?" Melissa asked con-frontationally.

"Rapid eye movement indicates dream sleep." He said mat-ter-of-factly.

"Oh right, but surely if I was just awake and imagining myself walking through fields and down steps and falling out of the hammock my eyes would have been moving anyway?"

"Yes they would have, but not in the same way."

"But surely if I was hypnotised I would not have imagined this whole comedy sketch of me falling in and out of the hammock and also whilst you were on about me loving my body as a temple I was thinking to myself 'hippie shit, hippie shit, hippie shit'; surely that's not right?"

"Hypnosis is a very misunderstood thing. You should be com-pletely aware at all times of what is going on around you. You were hypnotised." He tried to assure her. Melissa hopped off the couch and picked up her handbag and paid him.

"Right, same time tomorrow then. Oh, you're not driving are you?"

"Yes I am!" Melissa exclaimed panicked at the way he had asked.

"It's OK but some people take longer to come out of really deep hypnotic trances and so when you get to your car and stand beside it, stamp your feet and imagine you are a tree and your feet are your roots burrowing down into the ground to get the firmest footing they can."

"Oh, right, marvellous!" Melissa said, her sarcasm lost on him.

As she left the building after trudging down the three flights of stairs, wondering all the while if she had or had not been hypnotised, Melissa switched her telephone back on and it instantly beeped. Text message from Marlena to say that she had got bored and so had gone back to the car. Melissa stood outside of the jeep and opened the door to fling her bag unceremoniously onto the back seat.

"How did it go?" Marlena asked excitedly.

"Hang on I have to be a tree a minute."

"What?" Marlena demanded, her face a puzzle trying to decide if her English had failed her.

"I said I have to be a tree a minute, hang on." Melissa shut the door again, stamped her feet several times, said aloud "I'm a tree, I'm a tree!" whilst waving her arms up above her head (even though he had not instructed her to do that bit) and then looked around to see if anyone had been watching and got into the jeep.

"What was all that about?" Marlena asked astonished at what she had just seen Melissa do.

"Don't worry, we're in Glastonbury, everyone is strange here! Hell, they were already staring at us because our clothes are colour co-ordinated! We're strange here just because we aren't strange enough!" Melissa laughed and explained in precise detail what she had just done and why.

"So now we can go and test it out, and if there was ever a good place to test out your will power then the cinema has to be it!"

Melissa felt an overwhelming feeling of happiness entering the doorway of the cinema. Having met up with their friend Jo outside in the car park, the three girls headed over to the calories and Melissa continued her normal cinema visiting rituals of filling a bag with wicked sweeties, buying a bottle of still water to wash it down with and then going over to the popcorn department to buy an ice-cream and an all important cup of tea. Melissa was somewhat surprised that a huge voice from deep inside her had not at some point shouted at her for being a pig and was slightly disappointed that no one had announced over the tanoy system 'would Melissa step away from the sweets; put the bag down and step away!' But no, not even a squeak. Melissa voiced these concerns to the others and they all decided that if it was going to work at all then perhaps it would kick in a little way through the ton of confectionery. Allow her a few and then make her stop, allowing her to take the nearly full bag home like normal people instead of feeling compelled to force every last calorie down before the advertisements were through and even though she felt quite sick half a bag ago, and worse still that of the entire bag she really only enjoyed the last two which she always savoured because they were the last and had to last as long as possible. Melissa really did think she needed help!

The following day Melissa set off on her own to see Hypno Boyd, happier that this time he was not some weirdy pervert. Weirdy yes, pervert less likely. Melissa's on-going worry was merely that he would get her to cluck like a chicken every time the doorbell went or some such thing which she was fairly sure that she would do to amuse herself with the more irritating clients were their situations reversed. When she arrived outside of the large blue door which led up to Hypno Boyd's room it was already open and so knowing already that there were some chairs in the waiting room before his room Melissa made her way up the hundreds of stairs so that she might have chance to catch her breath before the session today. Eventually Melissa heard the sound of someone on the stairs way below effortlessly running up them rhythmically tapping their way all the way up to where Melissa was waiting. Having assumed that Hypno Boyd was on the other side of the closed door she was waiting outside of, she was quite surprised to see his face appear around the top of the stairs as was he to see her.

"The door was open so I came on up – I hope that was OK?" Melissa explained doubting by his expression now that she had done the right thing.

"Sure. Fine. No problem. Come on in." He smiled warmly and Melissa enviously noted that he was not even a little short of breath after his energetic climb as she got up and followed him into his room, screwing up her eyes as his even wilder patterned shirt than yesterday's seemed to be moving before her eyes making her feel momentarily giddy. He invited her to take a seat again as he fished about and retrieved his 'vight-a-mins' and took several different coloured ones all with a disturbing flick of his head chased down by a plastic cup full of water that he had filled from the tap in the sink.

"Would you like some?" He asked waving the empty cup at Melissa.

"No, I'm fine thank you."

"You know you really must drink a lot of water it's good for the soul." He said as he sat down on the chair opposite resuming his cross-legged position of the previous day to rest his file on his leather trousers that he had on again; creaking strangely with every movement. He flicked his hair out from where it was partially caught up in his collar and then he straightened his back, closed his eyes and breathed in and exhaled deeply a few times whilst Melissa watched on.

"So!" He said unexpectedly opening his eyes and addressing Melissa, "How is it going? Noticed any changes yet?"

"What you mean that something SHOULD have happened? I knew it! I knew I hadn't been hypnotised! I knew it the second I couldn't get in that bloody hammock!" Hypno Boyd watched her as she flared up with his head on one side and then scratched away with his pen as he made some notes.

"It is perfectly normal for you not to notice anything happening yet." (Yes, would say the con-artist Melissa thought) "We have yet to re-programme you. It has taken years for you to learn your bad habits they will not go straight away." He said calmly.

"Bill stopped smoking immediately and he's been smoking for the same amount of time that I have been fat!" Melissa accused.

"People are all different." Hypno Boyd calmly explained, used to encountering sceptics to his chosen field of expertise. "Some people are much easier to programme than others. People who question everything, shall we say those of us who are more intelligent are less easily manipulated generally and therefore take some time to allow their inner-selves to open up and accept what I am telling them."

Melissa narrowed her eyes as she stared at him trying to decide if he believed all this crap that he was spouting or if he was just some badly dressed confidence trickster as she suspected he was who could just as easily use the exact same excuses just trying to flatter her ego to make her continue coming.

"Well may be you are right. But why don't you stop with all the 'my body is a temple' crap and just tell me from now on that I hate the smell, sight and taste of chips and cakes or make me crave lettuce?"

"I do not agree with putting any negative thoughts into your head. We must do everything for a good reason not for a bad one. This will work as it has with Bill's smoking, but you have to give in to it fully and listen to what your body tells you."

"I listened to it last night and it sent me straight to the ice-cream and popcorn just like normal and it thought that stuffing the lot down in record breaking time was lovely. I listened to what it said and there was not a mention of lettuce leaves or stopping what I was doing!"

"You are just going to have to trust me. Four more sessions and you will be cured. But it is up to you." Hypno Boyd stared at her meaningfully. Melissa thought it was just because he was in pursuit of her money however; but what if he was right? What if he was genuine and did have the gift and she was about to walk away from being cured forever? As much as Melissa thought it was all a big con deep down she just knew that as did he, that she couldn't take the risk and so she agreed to the rest of the sessions. Positive mental attitude after all! If she believed that it was going to work then maybe it would.

Melissa was hypnotised another four times. The second, third and fourth times were all much like the first; wrestling on the hammock each time and not feeling any different. Going home after each session was no different either, and just to be on the safe side, she stopped outside of her car each time and pretended to be a tree just in case she had been hypnotised and was not actually aware. Perhaps that was where he was getting his sport Melissa wondered; knowing that all of his clients were out there stamping about and pretending to be trees before they got into their cars to go home. The fifth and final session was different however. As Melissa was lying on the couch trying very hard to wipe all thoughts from her mind and concentrate on relaxing, she suddenly felt her whole body sink further into the mattress. It was a very strange and involuntary movement and again, had she been asked she would have said that she was relaxed and so revelled in the new found sensation, so much deeper into the couch that she had sunk than ever before and it made her bones feel somehow disconnected momentarily to allow all the tension to completely drain from her body. Today she managed to get into the hammock on the second attempt and found herself swinging happily in it feeling the sun warming her body as instructed. At the end of the session as he brought her back round and made her wake up, her eyes shot open and she felt almost giddy as she sat herself upright. Assuming that it was just the head rush from having been lying dead flat and from looking at his madly patterned shirt again she thought nothing of it. Melissa paid Hypno Boyd and shook his hand as he wished her good luck and told her to keep thinking positive and happy thoughts. Melissa found herself five minutes later standing in a long queue in the Post Office some way up the road from where she had been with Hypno Boyd, with absolutely no memory of how she had got there, not even recalling going down the horrible flights of stairs from his room. As Melissa stood in line she felt very odd and it reminded her of dreaming about herself but being aware of the fact that she was on the edge of the dream scene looking in, as well as doing the actual dreaming. The more she thought about it the more she became aware that she was not actually hearing the normal hustle and bustle sounds around her and that they were somehow muffled. Suddenly it dawned on her that she was probably still hypnotised. "Oh my God! He actually did it!" Melissa mumbled out loud, unaware of the strange glances that she was receiving. Melissa was thrilled that it had finally worked out and now had faith that she was cured of eating naughty food. Happily, but not liking the odd and cloudy headed state she was in, she decided to do the tree thing there and then in the Post Office. And on having completed the stamping and grounding of herself she opened her eyes and the proper noise of the busy Post Office filled her ears; including a grumpy old man shouting at her to move up the queue so that he could get in the door.

Melissa wandered happily back to her car and thought to herself that perhaps she had misjudged Hypno Boyd after all. Right up until she drove past a fish and chip shop and the marvellous smell caught in her nostrils. Surely that should not be happening. She did not stop however but that was because of God's nasty intervention and not because of Hypno Boyd because there was no where to park. Or was it her hypnosis kicking in, she could have parked further away or gone around the block until a free space appeared? Erring on the positive Melissa decided it was the hypnosis and so was rather dismayed to find out that when she got home and saw a big cream cake waiting for her in the fridge that even though she momentarily thought about it as she gobbled it down, nothing different to the normal guilty thoughts kicked in. Conned as she suspected or maybe she should have a few more goes now that she had finally felt hypnotised?

CHAPTER SIXTEEN
MAD DOG LADY

Bruno was away on holiday and it had been a fairly busy Sunday lunch time; and it was only half way through. Melissa returned from delivering a bottle of wine to some customers at a table, having to ask two people to move first themselves and then their Highland Terriers from being in the gang-way to the bar. The two offending ladies shot her looks of disdain, particularly when she asked them to move the dogs as well as themselves, but Melissa was in a good mood and so raised her eyebrows and rolled her eyes internally only and continued to serve the man waiting at the bar who preceded the ladies in the queue. Melissa smiled and apologised for keeping him waiting and he accepted it good naturedly and then because it was so busy and for no other reason Melissa was convinced; he ordered a round of cocktails. Happy thoughts! Melissa cheerfully began mixing up a couple of Bloody Marys 'with the works'.

"EXCUSE ME!" Her happy thoughts were rudely interrupted by one of the dog women yelling (ladies had obviously been an inaccurate presumption).

"WHO DO WE SEE FOR A TABLE FOR LUNCH?" She continued yelling, her grey sort of 'bobbed' haircut stuck out wildly as if blown by the wind, even though it was a sunny and windless day.

"That would be me." Melissa said sweetly – very put on and very sarcastically – if they had known her.

"WELL?"

"Well…" Melissa quietly replied as she continued making cocktails "When I have finished serving this gentleman…." She nodded at and smiled at the man in question, who returned the smile and then rolled his eyes conspiratorially at her, "I will be right with you – won't keep you a mo!" She smiled, one love to me, Melissa thought. The dog woman glared at her and then muttered something to her equally unkempt looking friend, but ultimately had no option than to either wait or leave.

"Sorry to keep you." Melissa approached them after finishing serving her nice customer. "There is a table there." Melissa said pointing to a small table for two behind the two women in the corner with tables either side of it already occupied by jovial diners. "Or, if you'd rather, there is a larger table through there." She said and gestured through to the woman's left towards the restaurant.

"IT'S RESERVED!" Mad Dog Lady said harshly, scowling at her.

"No, I'm sure it's not." Melissa replied calmly, smiling sweetly at her although now it was beginning to become an effort to stay nice.

"YES IT IS!" The nutty dog lady yelled again, starting to attract attention from the other customers around her.

"No, I am sure you are mistaken, I'll go and check." Much to Mad Dog Lady's disgust Melissa slipped out of the bar, put her head around the corner of the room in question to look at the table; even though she already knew it was empty and not reserved, and came back. "Yes, it is definitely available."

"IT'S NOT VERY NICE! CAN'T WE SIT SOMEWHERE ELSE?" Mad Dog Lady demanded rejecting one of the most popular tables in the restaurant.

"Where else would you suggest?" Melissa asked as the pub was full but for the two tables offered.

"THAT ROOM THERE!" She pointed regally across the open plan bar to an apparently empty room. Melissa looked at her watch; it was nearly 1.30pm it was unlikely that they would get many more diners now.

"Um, yes." She said "If you want to sit at a table for 'twelve' people." She emphasised the ridiculousness of this request "Then I suppose it is OK." Mad Dog Lady glared at her again and without so much as a thank you, her and the other clearly nutty dog woman and the two Scotties on hugely long retractable leads which had not been retracted, but which it was clear to everyone but them that they should have been, wandered off around the far side of the pub.

Much later there were only three tables left with diners and Melissa was chatting to Eddie at the square bar on the side farthest away from the dog women. Eddie was a good friend of Bruno's who was riding the horses for him whilst he was away and baby-sitting the other animals and chickens and Marlena. He was an unusual looking man, not unattractive but very tall and gangly looking as though he had been stretched on the rack (but stopped prior to huge organ damage and death obviously) and had as yet not adjusted to the size of his new body. He had the strangest tightly curled, gingery-grey, fuzzy, matted looking hair and wore it in a style not too dis-similar to Daniel's friend Nigel, perhaps they shared an optically challenged barber Melissa thought, only Eddie's hair really looked as though he had a false hair piece plonked in the middle of it; accentuated by the fact that when he touched his hair he seemed to hold it at the edges as though straightening that section up. His glasses were terrible too and he obviously chose them without the benefit of his wife's help. They had large metal frames but they looked to have been bent around the shape of his head as opposed to resting on his nose like normal; they fitted the contours of his face like trendy wrap-around sunglasses but lacking any of the style and making themselves a very distracting feature to puzzle at whilst talking to him. He wore the most awful brown and grey patched jodhpurs (designed that way, not repaired) which did nothing for his lanky body and indeed made Melissa keep expecting him to turn around and for there to be a huge square flap held closed by two enormous buttons like a cartoon depiction of long-johns. As Melissa and Eddie chatted, so there was an occasional yelp of a Scottie dog, high pitched and desperate as it whined in an attempt to get some of Mad Dog Lady's meal. As they talked so the dog noises became more frequent, more high pitched, more intrusive and more annoying and Eddie and Melissa raised eyebrows at each other awaiting the reprimand of the dog; however it was not forthcoming. For a couple of minutes more they talked; now about the fact that they could not believe that the woman was not telling the dog to shut up, when with one piercing squawk as if to emphasise this point Melissa had had enough. She walked over to the far side of the bar next to where the dog women were sitting and very politely said "I am sorry, but will you keep your dogs quiet please as we do still have other people in the pub dining."

Mad Dog Lady spun around and slammed down her cutlery against the side of her plate, oblivious to the gravy she was splattering her companion with. Melissa flinched at the evil flashes Mad Dog Lady's eyes blazed at her as she shouted back "NO! I WILL NOT!" Melissa's jaw dropped: not the anticipated type of response.

"You will not." Melissa said calmly but glared back at her.

"NO! AND I CANNOT BELIEVE YOU HAVE BEEN SO RUDE!"

Puhhh, *me* rude? Melissa thought to herself. "I am sorry but your dog is making an awful noise and it is not fair on the rest of the people in the pub. She answered, still politely even though it was not deserved.

"IT HAS NOT! IT HAS NOT BARKED ONCE! I SHALL BE COMPLAINING TO YOUR BOSS ABOUT YOU! HE IS FRENCH AND HE LOVES DOGS! HE WOULD BE APPALLED TO HEAR THAT YOU HAVE SPOKEN TO ME LIKE THIS! YOU ARE NOTHING!"

That was it. She had stepped over the line. Now Melissa was very angry and her hands started shaking as if to emphasise the point. "No, your dog has not barked once it has been

SCREECHING and WHINING. My boss is not French he is Colombian and when you complain to him here is his card." Melissa said putting the small business card she took from the top of the till onto the bar. "I AM MELISSA AND ACTUALLY I AM THE CO-LICENSEE HERE AND WHAT BRUNO WOULD BE APPALLED AT IS THAT I LET YOUR DOGS BOTHER OTHER CUSTOMERS IN THE PUB AND AS THE CO-LICENSEE I AM TELLING YOU THAT WHEN YOU COMPLAIN MAKE SURE YOU DO IT OVER THE PHONE BECAUSE YOU ARE NOT WELCOME BACK!" Melissa turned and walked back to Eddie, where Charlie was also now standing. Melissa was still shaking with fury but was able instantly to resume a normal conversation when Charlie asked her if she wanted her to buy any more cotton wool for the first aid box as well as blue plasters. "What is that to shove in the customer's ears?" She quipped at which Eddie and Charlie laughed, much to the annoyance of Madder Than Ever Dog Lady who glared at the three of them probably assuming that they were laughing at her.

"I WANT OUR BILL!" The up until then quiet one of the twosome demanded.

"Certainly." Melissa tapped the figures straight into the till "That's £35.30 please." Melissa said overly pleasantly. The woman thrust a wad of crumpled notes at Melissa which she intentionally laboriously uncrumpled and smoothed out slowly in front of her.

"I CANNOT BELIEVE THAT YOU HAVE SPOKEN TO US IN THIS WAY!" She shot at Melissa whilst hastily fleeing from the bar as if in fear.

"AND I CANNOT BELIEVE that you would bring your dogs into a pub and let them behave like that and go mad when politely asked to keep them quiet. Oh yes, and you still owe me thirty pence!" Both women glared at her for the reprimand and scrabbled about in their purses for the outstanding coins.

"WHO COMPLAINED?" Maddest of dog women demanded.

"No one. Just me. Your dogs were making a dreadful row!"

"THEY WERE NOT! WHO WAS IT? IT WAS THEM WASN'T IT? BLOODY FROGS!" And glared at a table with four Belgium people who fascinated by the disturbance had all turned around to watch.

"No it wasn't, I told you it was me. Now out you go!" And Melissa motioned towards the door with her hands making wide sweeping movements.

"WELL I WON'T BE COMING BACK!" Quieter dog lady stated at the door in a futile attempt to save face.

"Good, because YOU ARE NOT WELCOME!" And as the scruffy foursome left the Belgium table cheered loudly.

Melissa apologised to them for the disturbance and told them that she hoped it had not ruined their lunch. "No, it was brilliant! You were great! Is she mad?"

CHAPTER SEVENTEEN
BLONDE STOMPING IN A DOG POO

It was Tuesday night. Charlie was having the night off to go and celebrate her 18th birthday the following day by staying away for the night with friends in a seedy hotel in Weston-Super-Mare. Quite a strange choice Melissa thought but more frightening than Charlie's bad taste in birthday destinations however had to be the fact that Melissa was now left behind the bar when Bruno was left in charge of the cooking when potentially it could get busy. As per normal Melissa arrived at about 5.40pm and went through her regular opening up rituals. At 6.05pm the door creaked open and in walked two women. Melissa's instant thought was 'lesbians' because two weirder women together she had only ever seen before had been lesbians and whilst Melissa acknowledged that all lesbians were not ugly, butch, tough, menacing and in need of a shave; it was the first feeling that came to mind whenever she saw two dodgy looking women together, particularly on the wrinkly side of forty. Outrageous though she knew this was, particularly as the two bi-sexual girls she knew were very attractive; although one of them did meet the 'in need of a shave' requirements but then she was foreign! So any way, the two odd women walked in on this dull and gloomy Tuesday night and thankfully booked a table for later that evening and left; without so much as an orange juice. This left Melissa alone once more with just Buddy the dog, a huge mug of tea and The Fosseway magazine for company. Knowing that Bruno would not start in the kitchen until 7pm Melissa picked the comfiest seat in the bar, and coincidentally the one 'her man' always sat on, and idly flicked her way through that weeks highlighted events. At 6.30pm she was joined by Marlena for her pre-work couple of cigarettes as she was not allowed to smoke upstairs in the pub, but no other customers appeared until the lesbians returned at 7.15pm. It was a strange sort of a night; the pub was at it's tidiest on account of lunchtime having been unusually quiet and because of that all the bottling-up was done and the place all clean and sparkling. Until 8.30pm there was not a single other customer nor bizarrely any telephone calls. Four more weird ladies trooped in; strangely attired apparently poor relations to the already present women and Melissa waited patiently behind the bar with her best fake smile plastered onto her face sure that an order for one drink and four straws was about to be placed. Surprisingly though they did in fact have a drink each and not one was devoid of alcohol or had 'juice' as part of its name. They even ordered food, which easing Melissa's previously overly judgemental conscience slightly for her unkind assumption earlier was for one bowl of chips and four forks. Having smugly come back to the bar from delivering Bruno his latest food challenge for the evening, the four women were sitting on the only reserved table in the whole, almost empty pub – a pet hate of Melissa's. One of the women felt the evil glare directed at them on the back of her head and said "We sat on the reserved table, is that all right?"

"Oh, it doesn't matter.." Another one of them said matter-of-factly, I put the sign over there."

"Actually yes it does matter. That table is specifically reserved for later on this evening hence the reserve sign so please move somewhere else, I am sure you can find another table." Melissa directed this final part of the sentence to the woman who had moved the sign as she gesticulated at the array of empty tables all around them. Begrudgingly the women got up and moved to another table and Melissa pointedly replaced the reserved sign and cleaned the wet rings that the condensation from the cold glasses had left on the wooden grain of the table top. Melissa returned the evil stare that the arrogant sign moving lady gave her as she relocated and soon desisted when she realised that she was seriously outclassed in the biggest bitch stakes. When she returned to the bar Marlena who had appeared and watched the exchange with interest asked her who had booked 2A, the reserved table, as she had not heard the phone go. Melissa whispered to her that no one had and Marlena chuckled at Melissa's nastiness but Melissa defending her actions by explaining that it was the principal of the thing and had they asked she would have let them but as they didn't and moved the sign humiliation was required. Turning away from Marlena Melissa's attention had been caught by a noise behind her and she turned around to be brought up short when she realised that 'her man' was standing patiently waiting at the bar. Instantly her stomach lurched and then having realised that he had probably caught her at her worst, her cheeks flared red and glowed with embarrassment.

Daniel was smiling at her just taking it all in "Hello!" he grinned. "Hi Marlena!" He waved as she retreated back to the kitchen amused at Melissa's discomfort and utter lack of composure.

"Hi, how are you?" Melissa responded desperately trying to compose herself whilst at the same time kicking herself for driving to work with the window open and not attending to her 'big hair' in between whiles; safe in the knowledge that it was Tuesday and that he would not be in, or so she thought.

"Nigel was away at the weekend and so I thought that I had better come in and see you."

"That was dashed decent of you, thank you." She put her best posh voice on and smiled directly into his dark seemingly unblinking eyes.

"So what have you been up to then?" He asked.

"Not a lot."

"The gym?"

"Well sort of, I went three times and then…" Daniel raised his eyebrows in anticipation of the excuse. "Now don't look at me like that, this is a bonafide 100% genuine reason. I came home from the gym the last time and had a shower but when I got out I realised that I had left the towels in my room…so I whizzed across the landing to get them, dripping wet, and my bloody ski-machine jumped out and I kicked it! So now I am broken."

"Broken?" He smirked.

"Yes broken! You may well laugh but I have hardly been able to walk for days and the nail on my little toe is all loose. I've had a horrible week, the only nice thing that happened was on Monday and that is only because I am a nasty bitch."

"This I've got to hear." Daniel said giving her his full attention.

"Well there was this really vile woman here, all snooty and arrogant (oh and very petite, attractive and blonde)."

"Obviously a bitch!" He interrupted.

"Yes, exactly!" Melissa smiled. "Well she left here and I could see her wandering around outside admiring the flowers and then the cheeky bitch picked a load of them! Well I was all set to go out there and give her a piece of my mind when all of a sudden she was flapping her arms wildly and hopping about and so I thought wickedly to myself 'good she's been stung', but it was even better than that because then she started scuffing her feet repeatedly along the grass and then examining the soles of her shoes. It was great, she had stood in a bloody great pile of dog poo and even better than that…" Melissa paused for effect. "She was wearing white canvas shoes! They would have been straight in the bin! Brilliant! But better than that canvas is quite absorbent so it may even have soaked in!" Daniel's face lit up at Melissa's unconcealed amusement at the poor woman's misfortune, his eyes sparkling wickedly as they crinkled at the edges into attractive laughter lines.

"…And it doesn't stop there because Bruno arrived back whilst she was trying to scrape the poo off of her shoes and so he caught her with his bunch of begonias in her hands and he went ballistic! Even with the door shut we could hear him shouting abuse at her; he was going wild waving his hands about and practically chased her off of the premises. In the end she flung the flowers at him and made a run for her car, so there is probably poo in there now too! So that is why instead of the normal lilies today we have begonias." Melissa said pointing to the vase containing five large round headed beautiful red velvety looking flowers.

"She was going to take all of those?" Daniel asked incredulously.

"Yeah I know, cheeky bitch. There actually were two more but their heads snapped off when she flung them at Bruno."

Daniel finished his pint and as Melissa was pouring him another he said "Oh, I have a joke for you."

"Oh right then, go on." Melissa said passing the pint over and spilling a little as she put it down which ran in a long creamy line down the length of the glass and soaked into the red bar cloth beneath. "Whoops!" She said topping back up and then spilling it some more as she replaced it. Daniel watched with amusement as the beer cloth changed from bright red to burgundy as it became more and more beer soaked and Melissa became more and more flustered.

"Shut up laughing at me and tell me your joke."

"Right, well this man walks into a bar with a cat and an ostrich and buys them both a drink. They stay there for a few rounds and only the man and the ostrich buy the drinks the cat never once puts his hand in his pocket. The next day all three return and the same thing happens and this goes on every day for a week. Finally the bar man says to the man "What's the deal with the cat and the ostrich mate?" And the miserable looking man explained.. "Well I found this magic lamp and I rubbed it and sure enough out popped a Genie and he said he would grant me a wish..."

"I thought Genies give out three wishes." Melissa interrupted.

"Yeah, cut backs I assume." Daniel ad-libbed and Melissa smiled. "Anyway, as I was saying before I was so rudely interrupted… "So I thought long and hard and eventually I asked for a long legged bird with a tight pussy…"

Melissa burst out laughing, "That's awful!"

"It made you laugh!"

"Yes, but its still awful!"

"OK, you do better then."

"Oh, that's not fair; I'm no good at jokes."

"Go on, spending half your life in here you must have heard hundreds."

"Well just cuz I hear them doesn't mean I'm any good at telling them."

"Go on, tell me just one." Daniel insisted locking eyes with her until she flushed and looked away.

"Oh, all right then. There is this frog…and somehow or other he hops and struggles his way to the top of an enormous tree… hops along the highest branch and all of a sudden flings himself off! SPLAT! He lands on the ground and off to froggy hospital he goes and then later on he comes back with one leg in a plaster and covered in cuts and bruises and struggles and hops all the way back up to the top of the tree again. He hops along with his broken leg to the end of the highest branch and hurls himself off SPLAT! He lands on the ground and off he goes to froggy hospital and this time he comes back with a broken arm as well as a broken leg and lots of cuts and bruises. He makes his way back up to the top of the tree and staggers along the highest branch and flings himself off once more. SPLAT! He hits the ground and is taken off to froggy hospital. Meanwhile from a nearby branch two crows have been sat watching all this going on and one crow says to the other "Don't you think it's time we told our Kevin he's adopted?" Melissa burst out laughing and laughed and laughed and laughed until the tears poured down her face. "I love that joke!" She managed to splutter out in between laughs, it did not matter how many times she heard it she still laughed until she cried and then laughed some more when she watched the puzzled people's expressions on the people that she told as she went into hysterics and Daniel was no exception.

"It's funny, but it's not *that* funny." He told her his face crinkling up into an attractive smiled nonetheless bemused by how much it had clearly tickled Melissa.

Melissa eventually managed to calm herself and wiped the tears from her cheeks with the back of her hand.

"You've got some mascara down your face." Daniel smiled pointing to her cheek.

"Melissa flushed with embarrassment and then to Daniel's surprise ducked down behind the bar in front of him.

"What are you doing?" He leant forwards and peered over the bar to where Melissa was crouching down on her haunches wiping the mascara away after wetting the end of her finger on the end of her tongue.

"What, have you got a mirror down there?" Daniel asked incredulously, again confusion furrowing his brow.

"Naah. It is just the back of the beer pump." Melissa explained standing back up straight. It's not as clear as a mirror but you can see the general image. She pointed to the brass surrounding the lager advertising fascias along the bar.

"Most ingenious!" He commented "Anyway after all that excitement I have to go I'm afraid."

"Cooh, it doesn't take much to excite you does it!" Melissa flirted.

"Much less than you could possibly imagine!" he smiled wickedly at her and then he suddenly remembered, "So how's your toe now?"

"Painful and the nail still feels wobbly. I must have looked a right sight though if anyone had seen me naked and dripping, water everywhere, holding one foot in the air and hopping up and down, swearing like a trooper hoping that the pain would go away."

"Hmmm, yes, I'll just hold onto that thought for a moment." He closed his eyes and grinned as if imagining the scene.

Melissa blushed furiously and looked up at him through embarrassed lashes as she imagined her flabby, dimply naked body and assumed that he'd be imagining the same thing. From

SEX, SPROUTS AND SPIDERS

the expression on his face however he clearly couldn't be, but then he did not know what atrocities her clever black clothes covered especially as his wife no doubt was beautiful and skinny and gorgeous.

"Has it gone black under the nail?" He asked all serious again.

"Well half of it is I suppose, the bit nearest the bottom."

"Aahh, well then you'll need to pierce that to release the pressure, it will hurt a lot less then."

"Really? I don't like the sound of that!"

"No, seriously. I hurt my foot at a friend's house and one of the dinner guests there was a doctor and he said he'd sort it out for me. He took me into the kitchen, heated up a needle and pushed it through the nail."

"Ugggh!" Melissa exclaimed having a very vivid picture in her mind.

"Yeah, well it is ugggh, because a whole load of blood jetted out and where he had been treating me up at the breakfast bar sitting across two stools, the blood spurted up and fell straight into the chilli-con-carne that was on the counter beside us."

"Oh God! That's gross!"

"I know. Me and him didn't eat any of that, funnily enough!"

"That's terrible! But it helped you did it?" Melissa asked still frowning as she imagined all his friends tucking into their meal.

"Oh yeah, you ought to do yours."

"Naaah, knowing my luck the nail will fall off and not grow back again, then I'll have deformed feet."

"How many people actually get to see your feet?" He asked mischievously.

"That's' not the point. They're gross enough already."

"Surely nothing a good shave wouldn't put right?"

"Out! You're barred!" Melissa laughed pointing at the door.

Daniel smiled and waving his hand at her he grinned and left the pub, looking back just as the door closed behind him.

CHAPTER EIGHTEEN
DENNIS THE GOAT

About eight years ago Michael bought Bruno a young kid (baby goat not a child) as a retaliatory gift for what had been considered as a useless gift of a spider tie pin that in actual fact had been bought after much consideration and indeed expense, and yes, the whole story told it was a lovely and thoughtful gift unless you know, as Bruno did, that Michael was in fact spider a spider phobic too. So as a form of retaliation Michael knew that Bruno would also find the goat a distasteful gift and so it began: Dennis the Satan goat.

Melissa was assured from all of the regulars around at the time that Dennis was a lovely and cute little chap for quite some time. However, as with an increasing number of modern families these days, Dennis grew and grew and grew into a rebellious adolescent and soon became a fondly infamous character at the pub because of his overly playful nature in the butting department. He even got a personal mention in 'The Good Food Guide' and not for his suitability for eating either!

Dennis made for particularly good sport when some one went out to feed the chickens and horses at the pub because he was the stereotypical walking dustbin and was well aware of the treasures contained within the bright yellow buckets carried by the poor, some times innocent whose turn it was to feed the

animals.   The best sport was always to be observed when a
stranger ventured out into the paddock; Dennis was a master
at his craft with his dopey looking 'love me' face and droopy
ears he looked all fluffy and cuddly, very very big but definitely
huggable and indeed he would, but for a short time only, even
allow you to lovingly pet him whilst he 'affectionately' nuzzled
at your hand before trying to chew your sleeve.   The fun only
truly began if there was no gate between you and him, a fact
that Melissa never really believed for more than four and a half
years of referring to him with affection, for with no gate after
a while if there was no food boredom would quickly set in and
so it would begin.   (At this point it is very relevant to know that
Dennis was either crossed with a donkey or that he was a serious
steroid abuser for he was massive; standing way above the average person's waist height)   Dennis would start gently nudging
the side of his head into your thigh or stomach – OK- belly, and
you would think awwww how lovely and affectionate he is and so
smooth the tufty fur on his head in between his horns.   At this he
would start to push more forcefully against you and you would
begin to feel slightly uneasy, only now looking properly as those
huge gnarled horns and wondering what he could possibly need
those for.   As you think so your smoothing falters and you begin
to panic and so gently you push him away by his obvious horn
handles…but then BINGO!   He's got you – you have provoked
him fair and square.   You have initiated an offensive move so let
the games begin!   Who can get across the paddock quickest and
if it is you, will you manage to get the fiddly catch on the gate
open before his huge powerful head makes contact with your
rear?

Respect and trust for your owner – or at least the person who
feeds you, one would assume; one would be forgiven for thinking – but no, this is Satan goat, and although he might let you off
one day he'll certainly get you back twice the next day to make
up for it.   Many is the time people have gone running past the
pub rear windows which look out onto the paddock, flinging a
yellow bucket away from them as Dennis, head down is in hot

pursuit. Many times afterwards the best bruise competition has been held in the pub for the most successful Dennis hit.

Mel had always been very fond of Dennis; fooled like all the others who had not personally encountered him by his lovable looks. She defended him constantly to all who would speak badly against him. She even made a model of his head and mounted it on a plaque as if to appear as a hunting trophy for Bruno's 60th birthday. One day though that all changed. Some months after Michael had left the pub and his beloved animals he had made a visit and was slightly worried about Dennis's health. Knowing how fond Melissa was of Dennis he asked her to keep a special eye on him because he had always suffered with bad hooves from being trodden on as a baby by one of Bruno's horses. So, in order to put Michael's mind to rest and especially because Dennis had been moved to a new field down the road from the pub to keep Bruno's other horse company, and of course hopefully keep the weeds down. Melissa had persuaded Bruno to buy Dennis his own house to protect him from the weather; no easy feat when you are dealing with a man who thinks that animals are just that – animals and don't need waterproof housing because that it what their thick coat is for.

So one morning, armed with a bag of carrots and a Polaroid camera, Melissa keenly set off to visit Dennis to record him and his lovely new house for Michael. Upon arriving at the field's gate neither horse nor Dennis were anywhere to be seen. Melissa waited and waited and called and banged the gate but with no response. Slightly worried, Melissa thought that Dennis might have been unwell in his house, and of course the more she imagined him lying crippled with pain, unable to move to show her how bad he was, the more she worried. With some reluctance, but knowing that she'd never forgive herself if anything happened to him and she had ignored the opportunity to check – and happy in the knowledge that she had protection bribery in the form of food: carrots and lots of them, she entered the field. It was as she was only metres away from his house that Dennis popped his head up from amongst a huge gorse bush.

Upon seeing his new victim he came charging over but in a non-aggressive, 'happy to see you' sort of a way. She of course should have run then whilst she had the chance, but so chuffed was she to see him after so long of him being away from the pub's paddock that she chatted to him happily as he approached. He was also very happy to accept the offered carrots whilst he gave her the once over. He was very taken with the Polaroid and did snuffle it once or twice with a stomach orientated interest. After a while of munching, his boredom level was exceeded and the camera became the sole object of his attention. As Melissa kept moving it away and trying to distract him with carrots the more he wanted to get it and before she knew it he had tossed his head at her arm and sent the camera flying clean out of her hand where it travelled quite some height before thudding dully down into a large clod of sodden earth. Melissa was more than a little bit panicked by this and started backing slowly away from Dennis who by now had lowered his head fractionally and was barging gently against her with his side just behind his shoulder. Warning bells started going off in Melissa's head and sure enough, just as she quickly turned to assess the distance between them and the gate - her only escape – so he started butting into her, head down and powering forwards.

"NO DENNIS! NO!" she yelled pointlessly as though he was a dog and she simultaneously grabbed his horns in order to stop the ramming. Game on of course as far as Dennis was concerned and with all his force, she hoped, he butted against the strength of her arms with her quite substantial body weight behind it. She successfully held him off for what felt like days, whilst deliberating on what her best course of action might be. If she ran to the gate could she open it in time or would he impale her with his horns up against it, affectively helping him in his quest for victory, she wondered. Meanwhile Dennis appeared to have stopped pushing so she warily let go of his horns to see. Seizing the opportunity he reared violently up onto his back legs and flailed his front ones around in the air frighteningly close to Melissa's face before thudding back to the ground. Melissa's heart was thumping out of her chest; never before had she been so terrified. He was massive up close and clearly, to Melissa's mind at least, he wanted to kill her! (Obviously camera shy!) Not knowing what to do she grabbed at his horns again just to force him to stay on the ground.

"Why are you doing this to me Dennis? I'm your friend!" Melissa told him pitifully willing him to stop. Again, after some time had passed he eased up on the pressure he was exerting and finally she decided there was nothing else for it; she shoved Dennis away from her as hard as she could and then 'legged' it across the fifty yards to the gate. Dennis instantly regained his footing and reached the gate only mere nanoseconds behind Melissa getting through the gate and banging it shut behind her. She leant against it close to hyperventilating where she had been so frightened and had run faster than she had thought it possible for such an un-streamlined and lumpy body. Dennis stood there looking evilly at her, no doubt chuckling to himself Melissa thought. Then, before she had had the chance to properly compose herself Melissa then heard a thundering noise and it was getting closer. Looking up into the apparent direction of the noise Melissa saw Seiggy (short for Siegfried) Bruno's three years old un-broken colt galloping down the steep incline towards them. It was an amazing sight; mane billowing out dramatically as he stormed at them – well specifically it appeared, at Dennis. One look from Dennis at what was coming was all it took and he was away like a shot, running along the length of fence furthest away from Seiggy, almost as frightened of his approach as Melissa has been of Dennis.

"And why couldn't you have come ten minutes earlier, huh?" Melissa asked him exasperated. "Aren't you the gorgeous boy then – look at you!" What Melissa knew about horses you could write on the back of a postage stamp, she preferred a different kind of horse power; however she was very much in awe of the magnificent beasts and looked on in wonder at the beautiful horse standing arrogantly in front of her. Melissa tentatively stuck out a hand to smooth Seiggy's head as he tried to ascertain if she was friend or foe and more importantly; if she had food. Judgement made Seiggy spun around violently and kicked out his back legs high up into the air, looked back as though to emphasise his disgust and he galloped away as dramatically as he had arrived.

Melissa drove back to the pub in a state of utter shock and gave a very energetic and flamboyant version of events to which Charlie, Marlena and Bruno hooted with laughter, particularly Bruno who loved Melissa's rendition laughing until the tears poured down his face.

"Ha! So finally you believe me! Your lovely cuddly Dennis is only good enough for dog food!" he laughed holding his stomach where it was aching from laughing so much. "I would have paid good money to have seen this. Will you come back down with me so I can watch?" He asked as Charlie and Marlena continued to snigger.

"Piss off the lot of you! I could have been killed!" This caused a further eruption of guffaws. "Anyway you need to go and rescue the camera please and more importantly the carrier bag in case one of your beasts eats it's and dies." Melissa said dramatically. "I'm going home to get some sympathy!" Melissa tossed her head in the air and left to another eruption of laughter.

CHAPTER NINETEEN
GOOSEY, LUCIFER & CHOCOLATE GATEAU

For such an awful week Wednesday actually started well. Melissa woke up in a positive frame of mind, or more precisely knew that she had to get out of bed and have a shower as her hair was in such a God-awful state that not even putting it up could disguise it; it was either wash it or wear a bag over her head! Being as for the first time 'ever' Melissa had more than three spots at one time the bag was quite an inviting rescue aid, but nonetheless twenty minutes later she was sitting with her wet hair dripping over her breakfast of soup and fruit – day one of the soup diet - AGAIN!

It was busy in the pub that lunchtime and Melissa was kept well entertained by that day's customers and even had the good fortune of finding her mobile 'phone after an hour of searching for it. She was positive that it was either lost or stolen and with no way of checking about the 'lost' theory having turned it to silent vibrate mode whilst at work so that calling it would not have helped unless the 'losing' it had involved it dropping inside the metal dog biscuit tin behind the bar in order that it's vibrating could be made audible by the echo from the tin.

At home later Melissa ate her lunch, which consisted of vegetable lasagne and half of a truly awful cheap excuse for a chocolate gateau, buy one get one free (so bad they had to give them away Melissa thought later having completely ruined her diet in style) all picked up from the local 'eight-till late' whilst buying the essential lottery tickets. After her lunch feeling more than a little bit sick, Melissa continued typing up her 'novel' instead of having her customary afternoon siesta until 5.20pm then rushing to leave the house by 5.30pm. The book really seemed to be taking shape and the enthusiasm with which the girls at work had received her first chapter had really spurred her into action. She had begun the book several years previous as it had started in the form of letters to a friend. When Bridget Jones' Diary came out; before even leaving the cinema the friend had called her and told her what a great film she had just seen and that it was as though she had been sat watching letters that Melissa had sent her coming to life. Melissa was truly touched by this compliment to her letter writing skills but later kicked herself that she had not had the where-with-all to do something about a book before, as that same friend had been telling her the same thing right back during their school days. Clumsily tapping her way around the keyboard Melissa's fingers slowly began to remember the letter's various locations in order to regain her once speedy touch typing skills. So engrossed was she that it was 5 o'clock before she knew it and more surprisingly she had managed to go for a whole hour without a single cup of tea; quite an achievement!

Exactly half an hour later Melissa pulled up outside of the pub. Only the Land Rover was there meaning that Bruno was still making the most of his day off; Melissa hoped so at least because he had been looking a bit weary lately and deserved to let his hair down – what little there was of it. As she closed the door and fiddled with the keys to her 'beloved', never stopped talking about it MR2 Melissa heard the distant click-clacking of Bessie's overly long nails excitedly tapping on the concrete path to the side of the pub where she lived. "Where's my best girlieee then?" Melissa yelled out taking one last admiring backwards glance at her car before catching sight of the beautiful huge Rotweiller who was excitedly spinning around behind the large wrought iron gate panting a smile of massive 'don't mess with me' teeth at her. "There she is!" Melissa called out excitedly rounding the corner leading to the garden gate. Bessie threw herself at the gate in a desperate bid to get closer to her quicker. "Where have you been then?....where have you been?....hello!...yeah yeah I know." Melissa stuck her hand through the bars and got slobbered over between whines for her trouble. "Let me in then...go on...get out of the way of the gate." Melissa soppily chatted with her, the dog jumping about like a puppy nudging boisterously at her left hand coat pocket waiting for her daily treat. "Yeah, I know, hang on then....get off my bloody feet you clumsy cow! Go on, you are ruining my suede!" Bessie bounced on regardless all hyperactive at the prospect of whatever biscuits she knew Melissa had in her possession. "Sit down then; you know the drill!" Bessie immediately sat, shuffling excitedly about on her bum. As Melissa fumbled with the zip on her coat pocket so Bessie became more and more impatient almost hopping from one back leg the other in her attempts to remain seated but also cope with the excitement which was making her whole body shake and her lips quiver. Finally Melissa managed to release the spiteful zip and Bessie's gingery eyebrows by now were nearly touching each other where her face was so keen to know what the hold up on the biscuit front was. Once Bessie was suitably bribed and petted and Melissa's black suede boots were both clearly marked with large brown foot prints, Melissa went through to the kitchen from the back door of the pub and began her daily ritual of hanging up her coat and bag and getting the bar set up; but not before switching on the kettle of course! As Daniel had not visited on Tuesday night Melissa's hopes were high that he would appear tonight instead and so it was with a cheerful anticipatory buzz that she went about her bar chores. Would he come or wouldn't he – she dare not hope too much because fate, God or whoever would no doubt piss on her fireworks if she got too cocky about his what should be destined arrival. So instead she went about her work trying to pretend that he would not be coming and therefore to act like she didn't care what he found her doing when he arrived (so long as she wasn't picking her nose or pulling the knickers from out of the crack of her ass of course!) even though normally of course she would plan it in such a way as to have to put the candles in the holders for when he was sat at the bar so that she had an excuse to stay near him and chat whilst serving the dual purpose of finding something constructive to do with those clumsy 'tell all' hands.

Time was ticking on. OK, so he really wasn't going to come after all – BASTARD! Melissa thought to herself as she tapped playfully on the window pane at Gigi, or Goosey as Melissa called him – a rescue goose who lived in the paddock at the rear of The Olde Flagon and tapped the glass for attention in the hope of extra food. He got really aggravated if you stopped talking to him, to the point of honking and screeching like he was being beaten to death in order to regain your attention, and of course at times the entire pub's. "Bastard hey Goosey!" she stopped tapping and stared at his pretty and inquisitive face. All that was missing were eyebrows to complete his expression and he'd be perfect, she thought chuckling out loud as she imagined him with Bessie's for a moment and smiled at the weird picture she had conjured up. Melissa did always think too that it actually looked as though his beak had at some point fallen off and been clumsily stuck back on due to there being the apparent signs of a badly glued join where it met his face in between his eyes.

Melissa sat there for quite some time whilst hugging the huge mug of tea she was occasionally sipping from, watching Goosey's antics when out of the blue – completely unprovoked, Lucy, the other goose, advanced on him hissing loudly and with her long white neck out-stretched and lowered for attack. Lucy was a beautiful, large, completely white goose with bright blue eyes in contrast to Goosey's muted brown colours and was brought to the pub when it was decided that the reason Goosey was so noisy and tapping the windows all the time was because he was lonely. They had suspected this for some while but it was finally proven beyond any shadow of a doubt when the old kitchen dishwasher was put in the paddock awaiting collection by a scrap merchant and Goosey was always to be found gazing longingly at his reflection in the shiny stainless steel sides and especially in the glass panel at the front. So enamoured was he that he would sit there all day and hiss at you if you came anywhere near him and his obviously beautiful new mate. So, back to the point….Goosey was startled by Lucy's unexpected attack but quickly spun round and retaliated. In an instant the two geese were entwined in an elaborate head-lock viciously pecking at each other's necks, shoulders and wings, each the perfect mirror image of the other. Their wings were flapping and widely outstretched as they aggressively laid into each other, their honks becoming unbearable screeches as they released their holds and just chest barged on another. Melissa looked on first in fascination and then in horror as the fight went on and on gaining in ferocity with each passing moment. In a desperate albeit pathetic attempt she opened the window and yelled at them. Banging the window closing arms loudly against the frame in an effort to distract the pair.

"Oyyyy! Hey! Goosey!" bang bang bang and then she started whistling in short loud bursts still desperately trying to get their attention in the hope that they would stop. Unfortunately – for Goosey that is – it worked and he looked around losing concentration for the job in hand, enabling Lucy to grab a better beak hold under the top of his wing where it joined his body and she began ruthlessly and viciously stripping away at the soft downy feathers there. Her new position created equal opportunity for Goosey to reach the same part on her body and he quickly made up for lost time pecking away at a more ferocious rate. Lucy escaped Goosey's grasp and tried to scuttle off gaining a few goose lengths on him, head down, wings outstretched but Goosey was soon in hot pursuit; the pair honking and screeching still. Backwards and forwards across the paddock they chased, it was almost comical, first one in the lead and then the other; all that was missing was the accompanying black and white era chase scene music. Eventually with one final grab and a honk for good measure, Goosey saw Lucy off and made his way back to Melissa who he could see waiting for him at his window. "What the hell was all that about?" she demanded of Goosey still quite shaken at the worrying prospect of them actually having damaged each other. As Goosey waddled the last few steps to the window Melissa could see the evidence of the fracas as Goosey had acquired a white fluffy beard of Lucy's downy feathers the entire way around his beak.

"What do you look like you dozy bugger!" she laughingly exclaimed as he swooped his head endearingly from side to side running the underside of his beak along the windowsill. At that point Melissa heard the creak of the old metal front door closer as it pulled the heavy door shut. Her heart pounded and she felt the blood run from her face.

"Hello!" Bruno called out brightly as he purposefully walked across the pub towards Melissa. Both gutted and relieved at the same instant Melissa replied brightly back "Hi, I can see you have had a good day!" she said smiling at his complete change in demeanour and body language from the last time she had seen him. Instead of the hunched up plodding about he was all up-right and exuding a happy 'vibe' without having to say anything.

"Oh yes. I've had a lovely time." (Got laid Melissa thought wickedly to herself). "Yes..." He reflected his eyes closing momentarily and smiling "...a truly lovely time!" (Yep, definitely got laid then!) he plonked his floppy satchel style bag he always took with him on his days off down at his adopted desk, i.e. the dining room table nearest to the kitchen. (Melissa always wondered if he had some secret butterfly catching fetish or something because with a bag like that all that was missing was a net).

Melissa began to tell him about the Goosey and Lucy incident that she had just witnessed as they both made their way back into the bar and Bruno poured himself a large glass of white wine. So engrossed was she in her tale in fact that she did not even hear the bar door open and wasn't aware of the customer until Daniel was standing right up at the bar.

"Hello! Murphys?" she quickly recovered her surprise and flushing the traditional red.

"Yes please." He said bemused. It always puzzled her that they had to go through this because he always without fail drank the same thing and yet he got quite funny if she was so presumptuous as to start pouring without his acknowledgement – funny bugger!

"So anyway…they were really going for it!" Melissa continued, turning to face Bruno as the Murphys slowly poured.

"Hello Daniel! It sounds more like they were mating to me!" Bruno said matter-of-factly.

"I'm just going off to wash my hands a mo." Daniel said waving his filthy black hands at her comically.

"Do you know anything about geese bonking?" Melissa asked Daniel when he returned directly staring but laughing into his eyes. He held the stare a moment longer than they normally managed before his face furrowed slightly in thought and then looking between them both replied "No sorry, I don't."

"We'll just have to ask Charlie when she gets here, she'll know." Bruno said and wandered back out through the gothic style archway and out through to the kitchen and his private living quarters beyond.

Melissa looked down at Daniel's hands as he was fiddling with a blue paper towel trying to wrap it around the index finger of his left hand. "What yah done there then?"

"Cut it on a bloody rusty old door catch on an old shed and it won't stop bleeding."

"Is it bad?" Melissa stared concerned at his finger. He unwrapped the paper towel and showed it to her.

"Not really look."

"D'you want a plaster?"

"Naaah, its stopping now."

"Course you might die." Melissa smiled mischievously into his eyes.

He awkwardly passed over the money for the pint with his unwrapped injured hand. As Melissa sorted out the money into the till's compartments she exclaimed "Uggggh - this one is covered in blood!" and wiped the offending 20p off in the beer towel on the bar of a similar dark red colour in front of him. "I hope you haven't got AIDS!"

"Oh well, probably."

"Oh well, so long as you had fun getting it I s'pose!" she grinned at him again and he smiled back eyes sparkling.

"So, what do you know then? Any scandal or gossip?" she asked.

"Well…ummm…"

"You are going to say no aren't you?"

"Well there must be something after all this time." He wrinkled his brow and stared at the bar top thinking. It had indeed been five days since his last visit and she was glad that he was as aware of it as she was. "But what about you then – you must have done something?"

"Yeah right!" She answered sarcastically them both knowing that this was unlikely due to the hours she spent at the pub. "Oh yeah, I went to the cinema Monday and saw Ocean's Eleven. It was really good; but anything with the gorgeous Mr Clooney in would be I suppose!"

"Yeah, if you say so!" he humoured her smiling.

"Oh there is something! Melissa remembered.

"Yes?" He made himself more comfortable on his stool and eagerly awaited what she was about to tell him.

"Yes. I had a romantic candlelight dinner!" She scanned his face to observe his reaction.

"Oh yes. Who with?" He asked feigning much less interest than he had previously shown at the first mention of the remembered tit bit.

"Me and Marlena!" She whispered conspiratorially at him leaning further across the bar to him and glancing in the direction of the kitchen in case Marlena had appeared for her regular 6.30pm cigarette.

"You did?" He laughed and quizzically raised his eyebrows.

"It all started perfectly innocently. We were wandering around shopping, pretty well had bought all we wanted and we came across this Italian place and my feet were aching so I suggested we had our pre-cinema dinner there because from the outside it just looked like a quiet little Mediterranean style café. Inside it did too only the downstairs was completely reserved for a party later and so we were ushered upstairs where it looked like someone had forgotten to pay the electricity bill! It was *SO* dark!" Melissa was really into her subject now and barely paused for breath not really noticing as Daniel watched her animated expressions intensely as she told her tale. "It was really dimly lit with those funny little tea light things in large dark blue, barely see-through glasses. Hell, it would have been lovely if I had been there with a bloke!" Melissa said as Daniel butted in smirking mischievously with amusement. "Did she play footsie with you?"

"No, I didn't sit that close to the table, but she did keep trying to look into my eyes, asking what it was that I kept looking at behind her as she moved her head about trying to catch my stare!" Melissa mimicked Marlena's actions and found herself consequently staring deep and meaningfully into the face of the man with whom she would have ideally loved to have been sat in that restaurant with. Her self-consciousness soon took control of her momentary lapse of shyness and she looked down and fiddled nervously with a loose thread on the beer mat lying on the bar in between them.

"So what were you looking at then?" he asked barely able to contain his amusement.

"Well luckily, I could see the busy roundabout outside, so the darker it got the more the headlights came on and the more the flashing distracted me nicely."

"A roundabout, how fortuitous!" At this he heartily laughed out loud, deep and pleasing. Melissa grinned, glad to have amused him as she knew telling him would and revelling in watching him reacting so attractively; her stomach lurched again. "You weren't tempted then?"

"God no! Hell other than not being remotely attracted to women, I know where she's been!" Daniel smiled as Melissa enlightened him "Everywhere!"

"So how is the diet going then?" he asked having partially composed himself.

"Oh God! Don't ask!" Melissa said going over to pick up the now ringing 'phone. I just can't get motivated! Hello, The Olde Flagon….." When Melissa finished detailing the information from the 'phone call she walked back over to begin replacing the candles in their holders. The door creaked open again and in scuffed Charlie; barely picking up her huge platform soled shoes, along with Rick one of the waiting staff. Greetings were exchanged around as Charlie struck a match from the brick on the bar and drew heavily on her cigarette.

"There's a present for you in the kitchen." Melissa said.

"Oh yeah – what job's he left for me to do now? Peel a sack full of onions?" Charlie asked despairingly.

"Oh no. Nothing like that – I bought you this present." Charlie and Rick both turned and exchanged a knowing look and then slung their cigarettes into the nearest ashtrays and then raced each other into the kitchen. As with Bessie they knew what form Melissa's presents usually took. Daniel looked at Melissa bemused as if awaiting an explanation to why they would have run off quite so unexpectedly when suddenly they heard Charlie say "NO – Gerrofff! It's mine!" Shouting whilst returning back out to the bar with Rick following behind in hot pursuit. Rick was armed with and pathetically waving around a hopeful but as yet unused spoon as Charlie stood the other side of the bar tucking her spoon into a whole chocolate gateau; not even having bothered to fully unwrap it, let alone go to the trouble of cutting a portion.

"Charlie!" Melissa and Daniel both exclaimed, equally shocked at her keen-ness to wolf down the gateau. (Melissa's surprised stemmed purely from the fact that she thought only *she* did such terrible things!).

"Oh, go on Charlie, let me have some." Rick whined waving his still unused spoon sadly at her.

"That's a soup spoon Nick." Melissa stated raising her eyebrows at him questioningly.

"Oh, I know, it was the first thing I picked up."

"Mmmmmmm mmmmmm, this is lovely thanks Mel."

"Umm I did kind of buy it for you to share really." Melissa motioned at Charlie to acknowledge Rick's existence.

"It was buy one get one free – I didn't think they were very nice – else you would most likely have never seen it."

Charlie smiled at this in between mouthfuls knowing unlike Daniel, that what she said was absolutely true.

"Oh all right then....come on Rick!" Charlie commanded and led them off into the kitchen.

"Oh, and Rick, now that I have rescued you some cake..." Melissa called after them.

"Yeah yeah, you want a gallon of tea...I'll put the kettle on." He begrudgingly mumbled at her.

"Thanks!" she smiled to his retreating back.

"Is it someone's birthday or something?" Daniel asked, still not quite believing what had just passed before him.

"Oh, that, no – I just saw it so I bought it."

"Oh." He replied not seeming to really understand what would motivate a person to actually do that. It was chocolate gateau, what further explanation is necessary – obviously a girl thing; poor men! Melissa thought.

"Right! Just time for a quickieee!" Daniel said draining the last of his Murphys having previously glanced at his watch.

"Ahhh, well talking of quickieees..." Daniel looked up attentively his interest raised. "I wondered if you would take part in a psychological experiment with me?" Melissa looked up at his expectant face as he butted in with a definite "Yes." Melissa smiled at his enthusiasm particularly as he was yet to find out the nature of the experiment.

"You don't actually have to do anything."

"Why not?" he butted in again sounding disappointed. Melissa acknowledged this with a wicked look from under partially closed, suggestive eyes, but continued on filing his reaction away to moon over fully later.

"All I need for you to do is to agree to consider something."

"Yes, I'll do it!" Melissa laughed at the interruption this time before trying to explain, and he stared back at her long and hard smiling in earnest at her.

"See Charlie and I have been psychoanalysing me and why it is that every year I lose three stone and then instead of losing that extra one stone and really happy with my size that instead I pile it all back on again. From previous dieting we know that money doesn't motivate me enough and so what we decided was it must be sex that was lacking i.e. even after losing all that weight year after year I still don't get rewarded at the end of it with any form of gratification and hence end up thinking what was the point and put it all back on again; comfort eating because no one wants me. Sooooo, where you come in is that I need you to agree to 'CONSIDER' only (because of course I do not want to morally compromise you) that if I lost four stone that I could be your sex slave." Melissa put the completed pint onto the top of the bar, hoping that he didn't notice how badly her hand was trembling.

"Yes, I will DEFINITELY 'CONSIDER' THAT!" He said having not so much as flinched at such a proposition. "It will be good fun yes!"

"I would have asked someone else but unfortunately no one nice comes in here – so you are it – sorry." She cringed lowering her embarrassed face.

"It will be great fun - yes." He repeated as though he had only heard part of the question, and not the 'consider only' part.

"Yes?" Melissa queried. This had not gone at all as she had envisaged – much better – but she would have to think about all that again later, right now she needed to compose herself before her heart pumped itself right out of her chest.

"Right, ummm great. Thanks. Now think of a different subject for us to talk about while I get my normal colour back."

He laughed easily, watching her flap her hands about comically trying to cool herself down and then watched her fumble nervously about with a candle trying to put it in the wrong way up in its holder – and succeeding, and then trying to pull it back out without drawing too much attention.

"How will I know?" He asked wickedly (obviously she hoped that four stones might be self evident). She spun around to face him, locked eye contact and as calmly and seductively as she could replied "Oh, you'll know! If I get anywhere near to losing that much weight you'd better stay well clear of the entrance to the cellar door because you will no longer be safe!"

"Right. OK then!" Satisfactorily appeased he smiled a huge sexy smile that quite took Melissa's breath and ability to speak momentarily away.

"Oh yes, geese!" Melissa remembered and yelled through to Charlie to come out and rescue her only it turned out that a yell was not really required owing to the fact that Charlie had over-heard the beginning of the conversation and knowing in theory what was coming next had tactfully backed away again out of sight for a ringside seat.

"Yes, what about the geese?" She asked innocently grinning at Melissa's flushed face and sparkling eyes already resembling the post sex glow. Melissa explained animatedly again what the geese had been up to and asked if this was some sort of foreplay or courtship.

"Naaah – they don't do that. They just grab round the neck from behind as they mount them – no romance – certainly no 'foreplay'!" She said laughing. Melissa's thoughts had distract-edly been taken over by being grabbed from behind as she was mounted by someone within close enough grabbing distance, luckily her face was already or else it would have possibly betrayed her thoughts.

"In that case..." Melissa dragged herself sadly back to reality "Lucy might be a Howard or Jeremy even, actually scrap that, from the way Lucy was acting he is definitely a Lucifer!" An elec-tronic timer beeped loudly from the kitchen and Charlie scuffed off to attend to it. At the same time Daniel drained his glass and said "I'm off then. And I shall consider that." He grinned as he turned back to face her in the doorway.

"Don't you think too hard mind!" Melissa said and kicked herself for not coming up with something wittier. Although she had rather excelled herself already tonight, she mustn't be too hard on herself, she thought happily.

As soon as the outside door had closed Melissa rushed off to the kitchen.

"YOU BLOODY DID IT! I AM SOOOOO PROUD OF YOU!" Charlie enthusiastically shouted. "I can't believe it! I was shocked that you did it for that bet, but when you said you were going to ask I didn't think you ever actually would! Brilliant! Bloody brilliant!"

"I know! I can't believe I did it! I had the opportunity earlier but right in the middle of him asking about my weight the bloody 'phone rang! I could have ripped it out of the wall and jumped up and down on it! Then before I knew it I was saying it anyway!"

"And did you see him?" He didn't go red or nothing! It was almost as though he has been waiting for you to ask him – he was sooooo calm. Bloody brilliant!"

"How embarrassing though! It will be terrible seeing him the next time he comes in. I won't be able to look at him!"

"You barely do anyway you silly old tart! Get on, you'll be fine!"

"Oh I know but it was such a silly childish thing to say!"

"Who wouldn't be flattered by that sort of proposition? At least you have made it perfectly clear that you are interested in him!"

Melissa heard the bar door open again and bounced excitedly back out to the bar to start what would become a very busy non stop stream of drinkers and diners; and a succession of broken glasses, spilt drinks and ice in drinks which didn't require it and no ice in drinks that did so distracted was she at her newly agreed arrangement.

CHAPTER TWENTY
MUSICAL TESTICLES

The hunt was meeting at the pub Wednesday morning and so Kathy, being the wife of the hunt's terrier man and so a keen supporter, offered to do the lunchtime bar shift in order to see all of her friends whilst getting paid to do so. In addition as far as Melissa saw it, it meant that Melissa didn't have to be at work an hour and a half early in order to accommodate the red and black coated visitors and their many hangers-on which would have of course meant getting up even earlier – heaven forbid – and also meant that Melissa who was really anti everything about hunting and so certainly was relieved to be able not to have any part of seeing them off on their murderous mission.

At two minutes to 9 o'clock Melissa's Dad woke her up by yelling at her from her bedroom doorway. "Melly-belly, wakey wakey!" he called cheerfully, making his way unsteadily through the scattered bedroom debris. "This bloody room gets worse and worse!" He angrily shouted as tea slopped over the edge of the mug that he was carrying and scalded his hand as he tripped over the hairdryer flex lying dangerously and still plugged in across the pathway to the bed. The shouting and thumping as he banged into things brought Melissa rudely to her senses as she gratefully took the mug from him. "Ohhh Syd! Have you farted – or was it Melissa?" he yelled out screwing up his face in utter disgust at the noxious smell permeating his nostrils. Sydney looked up out of his only eye at him and seemed to wink at her Dad as he sighed a deep 'you woke me up to ask me that – of course it was me!' sort of indignant sigh and rolled over on his back with his huge furry feet raised up in the air propped up on one side against the bed.

"Phwaah – he stinks!" Melissa's Dad disgustedly stumbled from the room as Syd did a proud and audible encore, her Dad hanging on the ski-machine for support at the trickiest part of the exit.

Melissa switched off her alarm clock that was not set to go off for another half an hour and propped herself lazily back against the pillow mountain and slowly sipped at her tea, listening to her Dad cursing Jasper downstairs whose wee he had just discovered in one of his shoes by putting his foot in it, and to Syd snoring loudly again whose upturned feet she could just see over the edge of the duvet twitching about as he slept. The next time she looked at the clock it was twenty to ten. She couldn't believe it; she had just daydreamed away forty minutes, mainly thinking about Daniel and the previous night's unprecedented visit at 9.30pm. Melissa thought back again and smiled. Being Tuesday and seeing as how lately he had been coming in on irregular evenings, Melissa hadn't really thought that he would be coming. So much so in fact that when her 5pm 'siesta' alarm call went she snuggled up further into her duvet before deciding he would not come so why prematurely exit such a comfortable cocoon to prepare herself for 'a visit' that probably wasn't going to happen. She reached out an arm to reset her alarm for twenty minutes later and went back to sleep, not even bothering to replace the clock on the bedside unit; just plonking it down by her head. It seemed like only seconds later that the alarm was hammering loudly all through her head as it went off right next to her ear and disturbing her from a surprisingly deep wave of sleep. Heart pounding at the shock Melissa leapt out of bed before she was fully awake, thinking that she had over slept. Just as she was regaining control of her breathing, after realising that she was not in fact late for the school bus which had left about fifteen years ago as she had momentarily convinced herself in her semi-consciousness, she caught sight of her hair in the mirror of the open wardrobe door and that woke her right up. "God must hate me!" She said out loud to her reflection, desperately tugging at her hair in an effort to tame its huge, fluffed up sticky-out-ed-ness. "Need a wee, need a wee, need a wee" she spoke to herself out loud again as she clawed at her frizzed up, truly alien style head covering whilst simultaneously jiggling about crossing and uncrossing her legs in an effort to stem the flow. In the end the wee won and she stumbled off to the bathroom, more than a little concerned that she would get her trousers and knickers down before the pee came out. "Aaaaahh." She sighed in relief as the long warm stream gushed loudly at first and then quietly tinkled into the pan. "Right – back to the problem!" Again she said this out loud as she washed her hands, carefully checking both sides of the bar of soap for stray pubic hairs that always seemed to frequent soap, before using it.

She inspected her big hair in the mirror above the basin. The lighting was much brighter in here which only accentuated the problem. Glancing at her watch she panicked "Shit!" It was twenty-five past and she normally left the house at half past. Rushing back to her bedroom she pulled her hair vigorously into a tight pony tail and began twisting from it's base so that it wrapped in on itself to form a French pleat. Once the twisting was complete holding the pleat firmly in place with one hand and rummaging awkwardly about with the other through the contents of the wardrobe shelf that she used as a dressing table with all her make-up and girlieee paraphernalia on it until she found a clip and firmly pressed the fasteners together over her thick bunch of hair. This was usually a very successful operation and confidently Melissa began to spray copious amounts of hairspray all over her head before looking back in the mirror. BIG MISTAKE. For when she did catch her reflection she was horrified to see that her fringe had frizzed up into sticky-out ringlets. Desperately she brushed at the offending hair that was still wet from the hairspray over-load and tried to gently smooth out the frizz. Melissa's hair was naturally wavy and if left to dry on its own, or in damp weather conditions coiled up into generally pretty ringlets and as a consequence Melissa seldom brushed her hair because it was normally the brushing that blurred the ringlets into fuzz. On this occasion however, she was desperate and so brushing was the last and final resort excluding scissors! So, maybe God didn't hate her so much after all – she thought hopefully as her fringe regained some semblance of normality, but at that exact moment, just to prove her wrong the hair clip holding back the thick pleat of hair to her head, twanged open under the strain and slid down the back of her neck and onto the floor; releasing the heavy hair from it's glamorous twist which slinkily unravelled into a not displeasing wavy style; the hairspray having tamed the frizz. Melissa rummaged in the wardrobe again until she found a small hand mirror and held it up to inspect the back and side views of her head in case she had been lured into a false sense of security by a seemingly all right front. Happy enough with what she saw, and lacking the time to do anything else, she quickly applied some more Max Factor 2000 Calorie mascara (See even my mascara is fat! She told her reflection despairingly) and then hurried into her high heeled suede boots and out of the house.

When Charlie arrived at the pub at 6.15pm that night Melissa smiled disappointedly at her as she came in and lit up her customary cigarette.

"He won't be coming tonight." She inhaled deeply "I've just passed him going the other way and he looked like he was wearing a suit."

"Oh." Melissa said quietly "Which way was he going?"

"I don't know, we saw him on this road, not at the junction – he looked really smart. I waved and he looked at me but I don't think he recognised me in Louise's car." Melissa's face dropped with disappointment at another night of not seeing him and wondering where he was going and who he was seeing; perhaps he already had a mistress or several even? She instantly felt like eating: drowning her sorrows in food. She had been good all day and had even been to the gym, but she just wanted to lash out her disappointment at something and food was going to be it – she grabbed a packet of Mini Cheddars off the shelf and began munching miserably.

It was a quiet night with only three couples dinning and Ted who had been forced into fending for himself whilst Pauline his long suffering wife was away, oh and Ralph, the hippy type long haired musical editor and incredibly gifted musician; whose appearance instantly gave the impression of an obviously gifted interior to excuse the eccentric and hairy exterior. All of these people had left by 9 o'clock just leaving Melissa, Charlie and Marlena alone in the pub at the bar (in the absence of Bruno who had left some time before to go to the cinema having been persuaded by Melissa to see 'my Mr Clooney' as she referred to George Clooney in Ocean's Eleven). After about twenty minutes of silly girlieee chit chat, lights appeared coming across the car park and drove fast towards the windows to the left of the front door as they viewed it.

"It's him!" Melissa said disbelievingly her heart missing a beat. She didn't think that the outline of the vehicle looked quite right though "Naaah, wrong shaped van…looks more like a Discovery." She said on closer inspection and with relief as she thought about her hair.

"It'll be Roger." Charlie groaned, "Just what we need!"

"Oh great." Melissa groaned too as it was the right sort of time for him to come, well prior to Melissa having stopped speaking to him that was for being more than a bit rude to her the last time they met about her ever increasing girth – a fact any gentleman would never dream of being so tactless about, particularly when the person doing the insulting clearly ate even more pies than she did! The door creaked open and having convinced themselves that it was in deed Roger, they continued talking, only Melissa looked up to say a courteous hello and only because good manners would not allow her to ignore him completely.

"Helll-oooohhh!"

145

"Hi." Daniel said quietly as he walked up to the bar looking around at the empty pub. "Busy then?" He smiled. Charlie gave Melissa and Marlena a knowing smile and looked around to greet Daniel who was looking slightly uneasy with his hands in the pockets of his black leather jacket (and not a suit as Melissa was slightly disappointed to see – having quite a thing for men in dark suits – probably a bond fetish!)

They all chatted together making funny observations and witticisms and Daniel having previously sloped off, returned from the loo.

"It's a bit dark out there you know? You economising or something?" He asked.

"Oh, sorry. Has the bulb gone then?" She asked whilst going over to check that the gent's light was in fact switched on.

"It's OK, I managed." He smiled.

"Oh, you found it all right then did you?" He laughed in response, his dark eyes twinkling. Melissa bashfully looked away (not really comfortable talking about his bits with the current thoughts she had about him whizzing about permanently in her mind, but not before scoring a direct hit in the staring department.

As the information slowly sunk in Melissa's heart rate jumped up a notch. Perhaps the light had not gone at all – perhaps now that she had made it clear that she wanted him and the pub was empty of customers he was going to follow her in there (on the pretext of supervising – holding the chair stable or whatever) and was in fact going to push her firmly up against the cool tiled wall (no where near the urinals!) and passionately kiss her to within an inch of her life. She gulped back the thought and felt the flush reach her cheeks as she lingered over the thought and then in true Melissa style…made absolutely no effort to come out from behind the bar and take that risk. (Even though it was all she ever thought about – not in the men's toilets normally though!)

Melissa saw Daniel's quizzical look as he watched the series of reactions reflected in her face, clearly puzzled by what she may or may not have been thinking.

"So where is all this 'we've been busy every night – wall to wall customers' you told me about then?" He asked gesturing around the empty pub with his free pint hand.

"I know – lovely isn't it. I told Bruno that if he expected us to come and actually work that we would want a pay rise! Looks like its back to normal so he needn't worry." Feeling awkward with Marlena and Charlie there without the normal excuse for them to leave them alone due to having to start work – Melissa fiddled with The Fosseway Magazine they had been going through when Daniel had arrived. On the outside of the free newspaper was a glossy A4 sheet of advertising half covering the front and rear of the outside of The Fosseway Magazine and Melissa self con-sciously pulled it free of it's staples and began making a paper aeroplane. She had no idea what possessed her to start doing this and spent some considerable time from that second fold through to two weeks later, wondering what weirdness had moti-vated her to do such a thing when the man of her dreams was watching just three 'reach out and grab-able' feet away. She even went so far as to fly the plane out through the bar and into the kitchen doorway – at least it was a 'good' aeroplane, as aero-planes go – she cringed, it was no real consolation! Some how or other they got around to talking about middle names. One of Melissa's turned out to also be Daniel's wife's which Melissa was not best pleased about and then Daniel asked them to guess his – telling them that it began with a 'G' and was 'a good old fashioned Somerset name'. Straight away Charlie guessed George and was right.

"That's a shame – cus I was going to say 'Guuuh'." Melissa said and Daniel looked at her bemused. "On account of the fact that the old country bumpkins couldn't have spelt anything longer!" They all laughed, including Daniel – fortunately, and especially Melissa – her laughter was out of disbelief at what she kept coming out with this evening. Please God kill me now! She thought to herself raising her eyes heavenwards.

"I best get going then." Daniel sighed unenthusiastically before swallowing the remainder of his stout and wiping the small creamy moustache away from his top lip with the back of his hand. Melissa felt her knees buckling as she took the movement in. His hands fascinated her, she was completely hypnotised by them and knew every hair and crease in them, longing for them to touch her. He placed his glass down purposefully on the beer mat and left his hand on it slightly longer than was necessary as if contemplating saying something and then turned and walked to the door, turning completely around and gazing blatantly at Melissa, this time a smouldering look, which Melissa returned smiling seductively (she hoped) and a smile took over his face. He lowered his head down again, just standing there as if poised to speak but then thought better of it, he looked up at her again and turned around and left.

So, that was Tuesday, but now back to reality, and the whole of Wednesday lay out before her and she had lots to do. Tying an old well worn, much loved and overly large man's stripy dressing gown loosely around her middle, she plodded slowly off on painful 'standing too many hours in badly fitting, high heeled boots with twice the body weight they should be carrying' feet to the bathroom. Syd still had not stirred from his deep sleep but she didn't like to go downstairs and leave him to wake up and think that she was still there, so she stamped her foot several times, but because it was already hurting she wasn't making a heavy enough thump and consequently not enough noise or vibration for Syd to hear or to feel. Spotting a clothing catalogue out of the corner of her eye, she picked it up and dropped it from a couple feet above the ground so that it thudded loudly into the thick grey carpet. Success. Syd abruptly lifted his head up at his rude awakening and his eyebrows comically met in the sleep induced confusion his face reflected. Spotting Melissa he relaxed a little (not realising that it was her that caused the nasty thud that woke him).

"Hello. It's OK. I'm going downstairs now." Melissa said from the bedroom doorway whilst gesturing with her hands too in case he hadn't lip read well enough. "I'm going downstairs now." Melissa repeated, wildly exaggerating the pointing down gesture. Anyone watching her would have been forgiven for thinking that she was doing a mad rendition of a Sixties dance. "You know you are welcome to stay there – and if you are going to I'm sorry I woke you unnecessarily - but I didn't want you to be on your own." Did she think that he was going to answer her back or even understand a word? – Well frankly – yes. He stared at her for a while tilting his head slightly as if deciding which he would prefer, and then he flopped his head back down and shuffled his 'chin' gently from side to side getting comfortable again, he sighed deeply and then he shut down his eyelid. Melissa smiled lovingly as she watched all this. He was the most unbelievable dog; every health obstacle he uncomplainingly overcame or dealt with and the whole family made right idiots of themselves over him. It amazed Melissa that when he had to be castrated due to prostrate problems, two years before, that when the vet had offered them testicular implants for the dog that her Dad had not agreed to them. "They would make the testicle more aesthetically pleasing and the weight of them would make Sydney unlikely to know the difference" the vet had told her Dad. Melissa had laughed until she cried when her Dad had told her and then so did he when she wickedly suggested that they ought to have bells implanted instead. So, opting for the warm floor, Melissa left Syd where he was – waving at him as she left the door way seeing him looking up at her and he wagged his stumpy docked tail in response and again closed his eye.

Once downstairs Melissa made another cup of tea for her and took one through for her Dad in his office (otherwise known as the 'glory hole' where all the junk got kept or hidden when there were visitors).

Melissa opened up a can of grapefruit in its own juice, slopped it into a pudding bowl and slowly plodded off into the lounge, grabbing a spoon from the drawer as she went and putting it into her dressing gown pocket before picking up her mug of tea. After balancing her dish carefully on the precariously positioned magazines and clutter on the coffee table she flopped down heavily into the sofa and reached for the TV remote. Selecting

Channel 5, up came Jerry Springer as a guest on 'The Wright Stuff' and she watched them debating the day's topics, not fully concentrating – distractedly looking through her grapefruit for foreign bodies and pips. (It had always puzzled her how it was that they got the skin off the grapefruit so perfectly without leaving any cut marks along the sides of the segments. Did they have a special weirdy machine or chemical that could dissolve it? Or more worryingly were there thousands of people on a production line abroad somewhere with stacks of grapefruits piled up all around them, painstakingly removing every bit of pith, peel and skin off with their nimble fingers darting between rubbing the sweat from their brows, scratching itches, picking their noses and all after visiting the loo and not washing their hands). Not fully concentrating that is until she heard Matthew Wright say "And now over to the 'phone lines – who've we got?"

"Hi Matthew! It's Kathy from Somerset." Beth the pretty blonde in the booth cheerfully informed him.

'BITCH!' Melissa thought looking up enviously at the pretty and bubbly young woman behind the glass screen who introduced the telephone guests.

"Hello Kathy from Somerset – so what do you think about raising taxes by a tenner a week to improve the National Health Service?" Matthew drawled amiably.

"Hi Matthew! Well I reckon they shouldn't have wasted our bloody money....." A familiar loud and broad Somerset accent filled the room. Melissa's ears pricked up to concentrate and she stopped eating to see if it was indeed *their* Kathy "....on that bloody Millennium Dome, then they would have had the millions they need – bloody stupid it tis!" (Yep, Melissa thought, definitely our Kathy – just wait till I see her – dopey cow! Who'd have thought real 'normal' people actually call the show, Melissa chuckled to herself). The rest of Kathy's comments got interrupted by one of the panellists going off at a tangent about the Millennium Dome – lucky, else Kathy would have been late for work Melissa thought and then finished her grapefruit and tea and switched off the TV on the remote control. It flashed off and then straight back on again. Melissa snatched the control back up and pressed the button more firmly and this time as she waved it agitatedly at the screen it flashed on and off twice and then stayed on. "That's your bloody fault that is." She chided Jasper gently, who had charged in to investigate. He looked slightly guilty for a moment until she patted him on his head and gently tugged at his silky soft ears. "Yes, you may well look guilty...chewed it didn't you?" She said waving the remote control questioningly at him. His happy up-right pointy ears dropped a fraction and his tail's frantic wagging slowed down to an uncertain slow pace as Melissa inspected the remote – with its top right hand corner bitten off as though it had been a bar of chocolate. "You're all right dopey!" She said patting her chest and indicating for him to jump up. He leapt up, throwing his whole body at her enthusiastically so that she had to catch him and bundle him up like a baby. This used to be fine – because the last time they had done this he was considerably lighter, but now she struggled to hold him and he slithered heavily from her grasp landing clumsily on his back feet before bounding away to take a run up in order for her to do it again – and properly this time! She managed to stop him in his tracks and distracted him by rolling him over and tickling his fluffy white belly. "Right – enough – things to do Jasper Dog!" He looked up at her disappointed that she had stopped and then leapt to his feet as if to begin the next game. He followed her along as she made her way out to the kitchen with the breakfast dishes and grabbed playfully at the waist tie flapping about at his nose level. Once she had unburdened herself of the crockery and the dog, by removing the slimy drool soaked tie from his grasp and replacing it with an old discarded bone to chew on, she went into the office/glory hole which her Dad had since vacated and switched on the ancient computer. It whirled and groaned as it booted itself up and she flopped down into the operators chair and began the instructions to get into the word processing section in order to access her disk.

For some years now – well probably forever – well at least since Lucy called her from after watching Bridget Jones' Diary

– it had been Melissa's intention to write a book. Initially it had been 'just because it was there' as the great explorer who's name Melissa could never remember) said regarding climbing Everest, but as the years went on and Melissa read more and more of the supermarket top ten best sellers trashy holiday type novels – she became more and more disappointed with their general ability to keep her attention and more importantly to entertain her, with very few of them being good enough to want to recommend to a friend. With the end of each (promising to begin with) book, she became more and more disheartened and consequently more and more determined that she could write one herself - because judging by the book that she was reading last night – she frankly could not do a lot worse. And so it had been that when a humorous idea or observation had come to her she had written it down – generally in the form of a letter to Lucy, (The one with the motorbike and cellulitey ass from earlier) and being as her writing was so truly awful, she had always copied up a second slightly more tidy and legible version on to Lucy, keeping the first scrawl for herself, if it warranted keeping for future reference.

CHAPTER TWENTY-ONE
GLOVE PUPPET

Every lunch-time for as long as Melissa could remember at around 2.30pm Jack, John and Tim turned up at the pub. Jack was quite a handsome man in his early fifties with silver hair but thick black eyebrows. He was always dressed very smartly, head to toe in designer labels, often in pinks and pale pastels which he got ribbed mercilessly about and accused of being homosexual by the more conservatively and 'normally' attired people. Jack, although married, was a notorious womaniser, having met his evil harridan of a wife however, no one really blamed him. He always had several women on the go at once and owning his own rough and ready working Man's Club in Slapperton, he always seemed to have several of his 'groupies' in attendance for all the world to see and for his harridan wife to glare at over the top of her school mistressy glasses. It was a club where whenever Marlena and Melissa visited they only seemed to have five glasses which Jack rinsed out under the tap under the bar as no where visible, even when Melissa cheekily stood up on the toe rest of her bar stool and leant over could any glasses been seen other than the ones actually in use. John, mid forties owned a big chain of nationwide agricultural machinery and engineering works and was one of a whole family of overly large girthed short people who reminded Melissa of Weebles from her youth; the

153

fat little egg shaped people with a weight in their bottoms and the jingle 'Weebles wobble but they don't fall down!' John was a cheery round faced and spherical bodied man with an outrageously behaved wife who in her past, before landing John and his millions, had been known to get her whole house done up by enticing various workmen into her home when they were working on her council house estate and exchanging sexual favours for kitchen units, a new boiler, a re-tiled bathroom and even a resurfaced driveway. By the time she had moved out of her house it was like a classy show home. These days however she could buy whatever she wanted and so she let her hair down by drinking to excess and dancing on tables everywhere they went giving anyone unfortunate enough to look proof that she was a real red head and landing her the nick-name of 'Table Top Tanya' which was much better than the previous title of 'Take a Number Tanya' from the week she had her kitchen fitted and the plumber, tiler, electrician and their mates were all queuing down the stairs outside of her bedroom door when her then husband of the time had arrived back unexpectedly early and had exclaimed loudly that it wasn't the sodding deli counter at the supermarket whilst their front door was still open and so all the gossiping neighbours chatting out in the road heard it all and saw the husband storm out and drive off in his car and saw the front door close soon after and periodically man after man leave the house giving the impression that her kitchen would get finished after all.

Tim was an architect. He was very tall and painfully thin and in his early forties. He clearly shopped in all the same places as Jack and Melissa often accused him of being Jack's clone, particularly as Tim's hair was greying so rapidly that it would soon be as grey as Jack's. Tim had a girlfriend, a very large chested but very plain and dull sort of girl but according to Jack and John he wasn't really interested in sex; and indeed Jack would know as the girlfriend was one of his groupies according to Melissa's Slapperton spies and so they always wound him up about his doubtful sexuality too. As an architect however he was brilliant and had made quite a name for himself.

"Melissa!" Jack sang out as he led the threesome into the pub.

"Oh God….we're closed!"

"Now don't be like that!" Jack laughed placing his car keys onto the bar and then removing his green fingerless gloves and putting them together over the top of them. John waddled in and plonked his keys down on the bar in front of the beer pumps and then Melissa tried not to laugh as he struggled to climb onto the slippery bar stool which wasn't an awful lot shorter than him. Tim sauntered over and leant over the bar at the opposite end and rested his chin in his hands as he intently watched Melissa.

"Bad hair day today then Mel?" Tim said as he rudely examined her up and down.

"Yes, very funny Tim, every day's a bad hair day…hey, you never told me that you had an identical twin!" Melissa accused staring at him Jack and John both looked at him in surprise.

"You never said." John said.

"That's because I don't." Tim said pushing himself up into an uptight position.

"Well who is that then?" Melissa asked pointing to the large squared off black wooden floor to ceiling pillar which was supporting two heavy black painted beams above. Jack looked behind him at the pillar and then at Tim who was coincidentally and uncharacteristically dressed head to toe in black.

"Oh ha bloody ha!" Tim said instantly catching on.

"Obviously he's a lot more interesting than you and not as skinny but other than that an exact match."

"Yes Timothy, she does have a point." Jack laughed at him as he glared at Melissa and then at Jack and all the while John was chuckling into his Gin and Tonic which the three always drank.

"What's that you say Tim….you're feeling a bit cold?" Jack cocked his head towards the wooden pillar whilst undoing the black scarf from around his neck. All three of them watched in amusement as Jack tied his scarf around the pillar at approximately Tim's neck height.

"Now they are identical!" Jack stood back to admire his handiwork and looked assessingly from Tim to the pillar. All of them laughed and Tim went over and stood next to the pillar just as Marlena walked in from the kitchen with her white shirt and tight black skirt on showing off long slim legs under some wildly patterned tights which were black with white zig zags on them.

"Aaaah, the lovely Marlena!" John exclaimed upon seeing her. "Let me buy you a drink!"

"Hello and thank you, I'll have a pint of lager please." Melissa poured out her drink and meanwhile Jack had come up to her and put his arm around her broad 'Russian shot putter-esque' shoulders and stared deeply into her eyes. Belligerently she stared back at him until he laughed and gave a mischievous wink to Melissa.

"Now, beautiful Marlena, may I introduce you to Tim's' identical twin?"

"He has a twin? How cool!" Marlena looked at him impressed at the novelty.

"No I bloody don't! This is supposed to be my twin!" He said standing next to the pillar with his arms folded crossly. Marlena spotted the scarf knotted around the would-be twin's neck and burst out laughing.

"No Marlena! It isn't funny!" Tim said banging his head against the pillar.

"Say cheese!" Jack yelled ad Tim looked up in surprise as Jack flashed his telephone camera at him and then chuckling passed the 'phone around for all to see the image it had captured. Meanwhile Melissa grabbed one of Jack's fingerless gloves from the bar and deftly hid it under the counter. Marlena saw her do it and Jack caught the puzzled expression cross her face and looked around suspiciously to where Marlena was looking.

"Oh no, you've taken one of my bloody gloves again haven't you?" Jack implored Melissa.

"No, I didn't! Bloody cheek! Why would I want one of your scabby gloves? Any thief worth their salt would take both, what use would one glove be to anyone?" Melissa stood with her arms folded staring challengingly at Jack.

"Because you evil woman, the last time you took them you stitched the fingers up!" Jack said glaring at her menacingly across the bar as she and all the others laughed at him.

"You did what?" Marlena asked, not having heard properly.

"Jack left his gloves behind one day and she sewed up the ends of all the fingers so that he couldn't put them on." John explained laughing at Jack. "And another time she covered them with jelly sweets, that was really funny!"

"Actually it was very funny." Tim agreed.

"Was that Tim's twin I just heard?" Jack sniped bitchily. Tim banged his head against the pillar again and then said accusingly to Melissa "You know that I will never live this down no don't you?"

"Was that him again?" John asked Jack wickedly and Tim wandered off in his normal mock strop like a primadonna actress and surveyed the art up for sale around the pub.

"So Marlena, are you coming out with us for a drink?" Jack asked raising his eyebrows suggestively.

"When?" Marlena asked staring back at him not even remotely intimidated by his lecherous gaze.

"Why now, but of course!"

"Where are you planning on going?" She asked non-committally.

"We still have our usual rounds to make. Oh come on. Do say you'll come." Jack begged.

"OK but I have to be back at work later."

"OK, no problem, I'll drop you back off hear myself." He said grinning happily.

Marlena vanished upstairs and came back down a short while later with her black leather jacket and matching handbag which was accessorised with silver studs and chains looping pocket to pocket and to the hook of the large exposed zip creating a menacing punk look. She picked up her pint from the bar and downed the contents in one swift glug, replacing the empty glass down on top of the bar with a bang.

"Right, come on then! Are we going or not?" Marlena said with hands on hips.

"Oh, right, yes, great. Come on lads!" Jack encouraged and all three knocked back the remains of their gin and tonics and Melissa laughed as John slithered off the red fake leather topped stool.

"Bye then Mel!" They all chorused as they filed out through the stained glass door.

That evening Melissa came in and opened up as normal and just as she appeared through the door leading out of the cellar from having filled up the two ice buckets, Marlena was standing in front of the door about to go through it in the other direction.

"Shit! You frightened me to death!" Melissa said putting the ice buckets down on the table nearest them on order that she might hold her chest.

"Oh sorry! I did not mean to scare you!"

"What are you doing down here already? In fact how come you are back already?"

"Ah yes. I need to talk to you. I think Bruno is very cross with me." Marlena said looking worried.

"I doubt that. What's happened?"

"He walked in and caught me naked."

"What on earth was he doing in your room anyway?"

"No, not in my room." Marlena looked at Melissa's bewildered expression.

"Well where were you? He has his own bathroom." Melissa stated as she tried to assimilate the information.

"No, not in my bathroom. Here. In the pub. He is very cross. I think he will want me to leave." Marlena looked sad.

"What on earth were you doing down here with no clothes on?"

"I was with Jack. Bruno walked in. We never heard him. He was furious. He waved his arms around like the windmills at us." Marlena mimicked his gesticulation.

"Marlena, you mean to say that he caught you having sex with Jack down here in the pub?"

"NO!" Marlena looked appalled at the suggestion. "We had just finished having sex. We were just about to put our clothes back on when he walked in and caught me untying Jack from Tim."

"What? Tim was here too?" Melissa asked flabbergasted.

"Nooo! Tim!" Marlena pointed to their newly christened black wooden pillar.

"Oh, Tim's twin!" Melissa relaxed slightly. "Untying him?" Melissa suddenly realised what she had said. "With what?"

"His scarf. He asked me to tie him to it. I think he is a bit kinky." Marlena whispered quietly.

"So let me get this straight, Bruno walked in and caught you naked and Jack tied to that pillar?"

"Yes."

"Wow! You certainly did not waste anytime did you?" Melissa chuckled imagining the scene.

"Yes, so now I need you to speak to him and beg him not to send me home." Marlena implored her.

"Yeah, yeah OK. I'm sure he'll have calmed down by now. Where is he?"

"He only came back because he forgot his wallet. He has gone back out now."

"You do know how old Jack is do you?"

"Yes, he is twice my age. He is not in bad shape for an old man. He gets very excited. He wanted me to hurt him."

"Hurt him how?" Melissa asked intrigued.

"He wanted me to tie him up until it made him scream out where it was so tight. And he wanted me to squeeze him really hard and pull him about roughly." Marlena nodded at Melissa's groin to indicate where on Jack she meant. "I think he is a very strange man."

"You should have run off and left him tied up for Bruno to deal with, that would have made him scream!" Both girls laughed.

"But you will speak to him please." Marlena implored looking very concerned as Melissa struggled to get the images of Jack tied to the pillar and Bruno finding him waiting like an offering to the Gods.

Melissa picked up the ice buckets again and took them over behind the bar closely followed by Marlena who perched herself on her favourite bar stool and lit up one of her short Polish cigarettes from the packet on the bar next to her stool.

Melissa watched Marlena's subdued body language as she worried at a piece of skin down the side of her nail on her thumb in between puffs on her cigarette.

"You know he's married don't you?" Melissa asked Marlena, concerned that she may be unaware of exactly what she was dealing with.

"So?" Marlena replied "It was just sex."

"Oh right, of course." Melissa said, still being surprised on a daily basis on how cold hearted and calculating Marlena was able to be towards men, but watching her to see if her expression betrayed her words.

"You're a bloke really aren't you?" Melissa laughed, only half joking. "Are all Polish women as heartless as you?"

"Men have treated women terribly for years, lying to them to get them into bed. I am not like that, if I want sex I have it, I do not pretend to like them. Most Polish women are as silly as you English. My Mummy told me that if they have a dick then they are a liar and so do it to them before they do it to you." Marlena said very seriously.

"Your Mummy doesn't think very much of men does she? They are not all bad."

"My Mummy hates men. They are all bastards!" She said harshly. "My Dad was a bastard; he left us when I was four years old!"

"Oh, I am sorry. That must have been terrible for you. I cannot imagine not having my Dad around."

"I did not miss him. We did not need him. He was having sex with my best friend's mother and we were playing there and walked in on them."

"Oh God, how awful for you!" Melissa said feeling a lump appearing in her throat at Marlena's obvious pain badly disguised as anger.

"How awful for my Mum. I did not know what I had seen and so I innocently went home and told Mummy that Daddy was tired and so Marta's Mummy had been kind enough to let him go to bed with her."

Melissa watched as Marlena harshly mashed out the remaining cigarette and immediately lit up another inhaling deeply and billowing out a huge cloud of smoke that swirled around her and wafted towards Melissa which Melissa flapped out of her airspace with her hands.

"Whatever did your Mummy say?" Melissa asked using the term 'Mummy' which sat so uneasily with such an outwardly fierce, strong and independent woman.

"She told me to sit down and eat my tea and then she went and threw 'a sid' in her face."

"What is 'a sid'?" Melissa asked confused "Do you mean *acid? She threw acid in her face?*" Melissa asked appalled.

"Yes, acid. That's it."

"Where on earth did she get that from?"

"I don't know. She had bandages on her face for weeks and then I lost my friend. So as I say, all men are bastards!"

"Didn't she get in trouble?" Melissa asked repulsed at the images it conjured up in her minds eye.

"No. The woman would not dare. She knew she had done wrong."

"Wow! Remind me never to upset you or her! Bloody hell!"

"She's a bitch! She deserved it!"

"Was she scarred for life?" Melissa could still not shake the images of a melting face from her mind and terrible screaming.

"Not too bad. I do not care."

Melissa was almost too shocked for words and as much about how cold Marlena's reaction to the acid attack was. As Melissa pottered around the bar slicing up a lemon and an orange and switching on the glass washer she pondered Marlena's revelation

161

and thought that it explained an awful lot about some of Marlena's extraordinary behaviour. At 6.25pm after having chain smoked seven cigarettes, Marlena hopped off the stool, picked up her mobile 'phone, Zippo lighter and now almost empty cigarette packet and went out to the kitchen to start work. Melissa was just emptying the contents of the ashtray into the bin when the door flew open and in burst Charlie loaded down with several carrier bags which banged noisily against the door frame and the fire extinguisher next to it.

"Hello to you to!" Melissa laughed as Charlie plonked the bags down unceremoniously on the floor just inside the door and rubbed her hands where the handles had cut into them and left red marks from the weight of their contents.

"Hello! Pour me a coke will you…I'm knackered." Charlie said flopping down onto Marlena's recently vacated bar stool. "Ugggh it's warm. Who's been sat here with a hot arse?" Charlie asked wriggling around on the bar stool and screwing up her face in disgust.

"Marlena, she's just gone into the kitchen."

"She's keen!"

"She's worried she's going to be sent back to Poland." Melissa said passing over a full up glass of coke with the bubbles bursting frantically above the surface creating its own fuzzy beigey coloured aura.

"Thanks. Why? What's she done now?" Charlie asked not overly interested.

"I think that may be she should tell you that. But make sure she does, you'll definitely want to hear this!"

"Why, what's happened? Tell me?"

"No! Go and ask her yourself and ask her to make me a cup of tea will you please?" Charlie now intrigued slithered off of the bar stool which she was slightly too short to reach the ground without the use of the foot rest, downed the last of her drink and then burping loudly and excusing herself and giggling, grabbed her bags and rushed off into the kitchen clouting them against one of the stools on one side and against the table as she passed by on the other. Melissa meanwhile rooted about on the shelf in between the optics and fished out a black reel of cotton with a fairly thick needle sticking out of the end of it trailing a few inches of its thread in its wake. She pulled the needle out of the paper covering where it was placed perfectly through the centre of the 'o' on the brand name marked across it and whipped out the thread which was already attached and replaced it with a much longer length which she detached from the rest of the reel with her teeth. Reaching under the bar where the pint glasses were stored she retrieved Jack's green glove from on top of the front row and placed cotton reel, threaded needle and glove in a row on the bar. Melissa checked out through the windows to make sure that no cars had arrived and then darted out to the kitchen and grabbed the large first aid box from off of the wall and pulled out a large blob of cotton wool from a packet. Closing the lid of the box and putting the cotton wool to one side, she then went over to the hand basin and washed the grease from her hands. Marlena watched all of this in silent curiosity. Marlena was naturally not very chatty and Charlie because she was in obvious shock from what Marlena had just told her.

"When you have a mo' will one of you wipe a soapy cloth over this please, it's greasy as hell!"

"What are you doing?" Charlie asked finally curiosity getting the better of her.

"I am being creative. You'll see later. Made that cup of tea yet?"

"We're on to it. Patience is a virtue you know?" Charlie grinned.

"Yeah, so they say." Melissa laughed leaving the kitchen with her cotton wool.

A short while later Charlie came out into the bar closely followed by Marlena. Charlie placed her refilled mug down beside the row of beer pumps where Melissa always kept it and then with a quick glance around to make sure that there weren't any customers still, she and Marlena sat at the bar and lit up a cigarette each.

"Oyyy, you skiving cows, haven't you got any work to do?"

"Of course we have, but I've just had a shock and so need a fag to calm my nerves." Charlie said after watching the flickering flame creep up the match towards her fingers and then finally at the last second she blew it out and put it still smouldering into the ashtray.

"Yes, pretty impressive gossip, hey Charlie?"

"Yes, ha bloody ha!" Marlena replied dead pan. It really was amazing how quick to pick up all the weird and wonderful slang terms and expressions Marlena had been. Melissa's favourite expression that she had started using when Marlena got all excited about something was the very Somerset expression of 'gurt'; when Marlena had come out with "and there was a bloody gurt spider" one day the whole pub had been in stitches, sounding so wrong from so foreign an accent to all their local ears.

"What do you think Bruno will do?" Charlie asked as she fiddled with the matches in the brick in front of her, lining a load of them up so that all their heads were parallel with the edge of the brick.

"He'll calm down. He'll probably laugh about it later. He was probably disappointed that the only person getting any action in his house is Marlena."

"What are you doing?" Marlena asked as she watched Melissa cutting up one of the black Murphy's beer towels into funny shapes and put them onto the bar.

"Customising Jack's glove for him."

"What are you going to do this time?" What's the cotton wool for?" Charlie asked pushing herself up on the bar to get a better look.

"You'll have to wait and see. Now bugger off back to the kitchen, there are some customers look." Melissa said nodding towards the car lights having just pulled up in front of the window causing weird shadows up the wall and the ceiling of the pub opposite it.

In between the odd few customers that entered the pub Melissa continued with her task of sewing various bits and pieces retrieved from around the pub to the green glove. Eventually she was finished and she put the glove over her right hand and then hid that hand behind her back and went into the kitchen.

"Say hello to Jack's new friend!" Melissa called out over the noise of the extractor fan and the noisy electric food processor that Marlena was busy grating cheese with. Both girls looked up and instantly burst out laughing at the glove puppet that Melissa had created.

"That's brilliant!" Charlie stopped what she was doing and came over for a better look.

"He'll go mad!" Marlena said as she finished feeding the processor the last of the chunks of the Cheddar cheese and switched it off.

"How did you make the ears stand up?" Charlie asked as she put the glove onto her own hand and flicked gently at the ears on the rabbit face that Melissa had created.

"I put a piece of cardboard off the back of one of the order pads in it." Melissa said smiling as Charlie made it screw up its face and twitch its whiskers.

"I love the tail, that's the best bit!" Said Marlena prodding at the ball of cotton wool that Melissa had stitched to the cuff.

"No, his eyes are the best, what are they made from?" Charlie asked as Melissa stuck her head around the kitchen door to check that she wasn't ignoring a queue of waiting customers.

"Murphys bar towel, both bits, the white is from the writing on the cloth."

"Oh and you made his little teeth with card inside them too! It's Brilliant! I can't wait to see his face."

"How did you make his whiskers?" Marlena asked flicking at them now as the puppet stayed perched on Charlie's hand.

"They were just a drinking straw that I cut into really fine lengths. That was the fiddly bit as the straws were all stripy so I had to cut the coloured bits off to leave the white bits."

"You fussy cow! As it's for fun did it really matter?" Charlie laughed at her and handed back the glove.

With that Melissa heard the sound of voices and made her way back into the bar.

"Crikey, you're brave!" Melissa exclaimed as Jack leant over the bar and tried to see if Bruno was sitting around the corner at his normal paperwork table in the room that led to the kitchen.

"And you are wearing my glove!" He exclaimed catching sight of the underside of his green glove on her hand.

"I shouldn't think this is your!" Melissa banged her hand down onto the bar in front of him so that the rabbit's funny goofy toothed face was staring up at him.

"Oh my God!" What have you done to my glove?" He laughed tugging it from Melissa's hand and putting it back onto his own and having a good look.

"Bruno not about then?" He asked still uneasily checking around him, particularly as the kitchen door opened and Marlena came out.

Bizarrely Marlena barely reacted to seeing him. "Hello. I did not expect to see you back so soon." Marlena said not even smiling at him.

"Well as I forgot my glove...." He said waving his fist so that the rabbit ears flopped about, "...and it's a bit nippy out there so I can't survive without them. Bruno OK with you?"

"I have not seen him since you left so I do not know." Marlena answered and went over and cleared two empty glasses from a vacated table.

"So are you having a drink?" Melissa asked smirking at him. Jack looked at her as he tried to figure out why she was laughing.

"I will to celebrate the retrieval of my glove." He said waving his rabbit covered hand in mock salute at her.

"I should have thought that wasn't all!" Melissa laughed again as she pushed the glass up under the gin optic and waited for the measure to release its contents out over the ice and lemon that she had already put into it.

"Meaning?" Jack asked squinting his eyes and furrowing his thick black eyebrows suspiciously at her.

"Well, two things immediately come to my mind."

"Two?" Jack looked surprised.

"Yes, one of course being that you managed to pull a girl at least half your age…" He smiled looking very proud of himself, "…and two, that Bruno didn't have a go whilst you were tied up!"

"Uggggh. Don't!" Jack said cringing as he poured half of the tonic over the gin and the ice cubes crackled as it bubbled around them.

"Is he very angry?" Jack asked serious for a moment as he lifted the drink up to his mouth and Melissa burst out laughing again.

"What?"

"It's your rabbit! Aren't you going to take it off now?"

"No, you might steal it again. Anyway, I like it." He said causing its ears to wobble again. As they continued chatting the door opened and Bruno walked in.

"Jack. What are you doing here?" Bruno asked looking imperiously down his nose at him.

"Would you rather I did not come in any more?" Jack asked politely.

Bruno stared at him for an overly long time before answering, "No that will not be necessary but I do not expect to discover a repeat performance in my pub unless *I* am invited!" And he swooped off like a dramatic actor exiting stage left leaving a stunned Jack and a chuckling Melissa staring after him.

CHAPTER TWENTY-TWO
FROG WEDNESDAY

The day started like most others. Tea delivered at five minutes to nine by Melissa's Dad because it was Wednesday and so Melissa's Mum who normally delivered it was working over the local shop for the morning; a shop that makes Arkwrights store off of the old Open All Hours with Ronnie Barker look like a poor portrayal of how truly farcical the real thing actually can be. There was the standard wake-up announcement closely followed by the obligatory whinge about the safety issues of crossing the carpet from doorway to the bedside table, and then to complete the awakening: the Sydney fart.

"Morning to you too!" Came the muffled voice of Melissa from where she had buried her head under the duvet in an attempt to evade the noxious fumes. Head still buried Melissa rolled back over and snuggled down further under the covers and closed her eyes again. Just as sleep was overtaking her once more so Marlena was snapped back to reality by her Dad shouting up the stairs.

"I'm off to see your Gran now. The back door is locked. See you later!" With her eyes tightly shut Melissa yelled her acknowledgement from under the duvet.

"Did you hear me? I said I'm off to your Gran's. Are you awake?" Furiously whipping the duvet from over her head

Melissa yelled back her response. "YES! I HEARD! I'M AWAKE! BYEEEE!"

"OK. See you later. Byeee!" He yelled good-naturedly back up the stairs oblivious to the wrath he had incurred by his sleep seeking daughter. Upon hearing the front door being pulled firmly shut from the outside, and then pushed to check that it was indeed properly shut, Melissa grabbed the duvet back up over her head and muttered to herself "Right then, try again!" letting out a huge involuntary sigh she closed her eyes tightly and let sleep envelope her once more.

What seemed like only a minute later Melissa was brought back to reality by the shrill ringing of her old fashioned wind-up travel size bedside alarm. Still in a daze Melissa sat bolt up right, thrust out her hand and grabbed the offending noise maker and switched it off. Now fully awake her heart began to resume a more normal beat and as she slumped back down into her pillow she reached out to replace the clock on the bedside table. The clock replacement was done every day in this same manner, always by feel and never by sight, only this time she slightly over-shot the mark somewhat and managed to dump the alarm clock right into the tepid mug of tea. Upon feeling the unfamiliar surface beneath the clock Melissa looked across from the large mug and wiped it unceremoniously in the edge of the duvet two things occurred to Melissa: 1) That if she drank normal sized mugs of tea then this would not have been able to happen and 2) That this did not bode well as a good start to the day. With that Syd farted his agreement and Melissa buried her head beneath the quilt once more.

A short while later Melissa made the short journey from the bed to the bathroom, trailing her dressing gown behind her along the floor – another daily ritual to avoid having to put it on only to have to take it off again post wee but prior to weighing.

Melissa stood despondently in front of the sink washing her hands unenthusiastically whilst looking at her reflection between the toothpaste splatters on the large bathroom mirror. The harsh un-shaded bathroom light bulb accentuated the white expanse of her pale chins and her normally wild and wavy hair lay lank and flat against her head doing little along with yester-day's leftover mascara smears to improve her forever reducing self-confidence. And now for the real boost...the scales. Reaching out expertly with her flaking lilac painted big toe Melissa switched the scales on and stepped on. The numbers quickly ascended and then wavered whilst it waited for Melissa to keep still long enough. The screen went momentarily blank and then flashed up its judgement: GUILTY! It accused as Melissa stepped down from her sentencing and slowly picked up her dressing gown from where it had been dumped. Perhaps it would be better to just not weigh – ever. Or failing the will power to even keep off the scales – leave alone the chips – may be destroying them would be the thing to do, Melissa wondered to herself as a sleepy Syd joined her at the top of the stairs and they made their way down to the kitchen.

Having grabbed herself a replacement mug of tea of equally large proportions as the first, minus the added and very unwanted calories of the alarm clock, Melissa closely followed by both dogs, went into the lounge and switched on the TV to her usual mornings entertainment of The Wright Stuff. From here the day continued fairly normally with the rush to get changed and to work all by 11.30am hindered by the fact that Melissa could never quite bring herself to leave Matthew Wright and the panel until the very end of the programme; even when the day's topics were of little or no interest to her. On the way to work there was the usual idiot trying to kill her in a bizarre game of 'Car Chicken' the object of which it seemed to Melissa to be for other road users to wait until they were caught behind a stream of nose to tail cars and then upon seeing Melissa approaching at an obvious rate of knots – just pull out and head towards her with no happy foreseeable outcome. Today was slightly more exciting than normal on account of the fact that it was raining and so Melissa didn't get to see the car fully until the windscreen wipers had cleared the screen at a perfect time to coincide with the oncoming car just realising it had done a bloody ridiculous thing and now they were all very likely to die a hideous, messy and high speed death with Melissa's last thoughts being "Damn – Mum was right! I knew I should have changed my knickers!"

It was nearing the end of the shift and Melissa was just doing a few odd jobs to make the better use of the remaining time of a quiet shift. Making her way into the bottle cellar to switch on the troublesome ice machine that she had left to defrost, Melissa was passing by the beer gas canisters in the main cellar when the gauge of one of the large cylinders caught her attention due to the fact that it was showing empty. Stopping to take a proper look Melissa's brow furrowed as she puzzled at how the gas could have got so low without her having noticed before as it was something that she regularly looked at. Begrudgingly having to admit that she was not as infallible as she liked to think, Melissa grabbed for the spanner and rubber mallet and changed over the cylinder. Checking that the valve was securely fastened by saying out loud to herself "Righty tighty – lefty loosey" in order to remember which way to tighten up rather than undo, Melissa happy that she had fully secured the fitting slowly turned the canister's valve to open and listened to the familiar rush of gas refilling the empty beer lines. Melissa liked the strange noises and smiled to herself at what would normally be the last squeaks and groans of the gas pressure regulating itself. A while longer and still the noises were happening only now they were starting to sound more desperate and un-nerving. It was just as Melissa was beginning to wonder if something might be wrong when the sound of violently escaping gas was all she could hear, getting louder and more furious with every moment. The gauge screwed to the wall attached top the regulator started to shake violently and Melissa could see the gas vapour beginning to shoot out wildly all around it. Ducking down behind the spare canisters Melissa with her head instinctively bent down in an effort to protect herself, reached up to turn off the leaking tap. It seemed to take forever for it to close right down and all the while Melissa awaited some hideous explosion or for the gauges to shoot off the wall at her. With her heart beating wildly at what felt like her second near death incident of the day, Melissa purposefully left on the cellar light and walked in a daze back into the bar.

"What's up with you?" Asked Marlena from her usual position at the bar, cigarette in one hand, pint of lager in the other and with her feet resting up on the next stool to hers.

"You'll never believe what just happened to me! The gas canister has just nearly exploded in my face! I think I am about to have a heart attack. Oh and God hates me!"

"Oh is that all. Shit – quite frightening! Get me another beer will you?"

"You heartless bitch!" Melissa said grinning as she snatched away her glass in mock annoyance. After pouring Marlena's pint Melissa called the emergency cellar service and arranged for the gas problem to be sorted out. Luckily the very mention of the words 'gas' and 'leak' in the same sentence instigates an immediate response unlike any other call you make them and so the gas leak was repaired that afternoon. True to their word for once, the repair man arrived within the hour. Melissa showed the man to the cellar and was just describing what had happened when at the point of her telling him that when the gas was turned on that it nearly shot the pressure gauge off the wall, when Melissa could not believe her eyes as the stupid little man switched it on again! As Melissa had already explained the gas was whooshing out of the regulator at a frightening rate. Seemingly unfazed by this the man switched the gas back off.

"Yes, you have a leak." Melissa's face clearly said what a stupid little man he had just proved himself to be and in a rare moment of self control she managed not to express her thoughts of that moment nor to take the mallet and batter him to death with it for exposing her to the danger of the leaking gas again when she had clearly explained what the problem was.

"You can clearly cope from here on in so I'll let you get on with it." Melissa said as she walked across towards the door whilst the man ignored her anyway. 'No free pint or coffee for you, you ignorant shit!' Melissa thought to herself as she closed the cellar door on him. A short while later the stupid little man appeared at the bar to tell Melissa that he had replaced the regulator and so he was leaving. Melissa courteously thanked him for coming so quickly and smiled her most fake smile as he went out of the door.

"Asshole!" Melissa muttered between clenched teeth to the closed door, much to the amusement of Marlena who sat quietly observing – and smoking and drinking, of course!

That evening as Melissa went out through the first cellar and into the bottle cellar to get the ice she had her first look at the new gas regulator. What she saw stopped her dead in her tracks. Placing the yet to be filled ice buckets down on the barrel next to the gas cylinders Melissa took a closer look. In the place where the old regulator had been was now an ugly large expanse of brilliant white paint getting its first exposure to light in years. Around the brilliant white was an irregular shape of the outline of grubby grey-white from where the regulator had been attached to the wall emphasised by the large black holes throughout its shape where the screws had been removed.

Unimpressed at the eyesore the 'Stupid Little Man' had created with his handiwork Melissa then inspected the new regulator curious as to how it worked. The new fitting attached directly to the canister as opposed to there being a length of pipe as with the old system which went to the regulator with a pressure gauge attached to the top of this. So where was the pressure gauge on this new fitting? Melissa puzzled over this question as she ran her eyes along the length of the pipe just in case the new gauge was somewhere obscure. Then in desperation she crouched down and looked at the underside of the new brass fitting, but as she anticipated the 'Stupid Little Man' had managed to exclude the all important gauge altogether. Idiot!

Melissa returned to the bar after collecting the ice, furious at the incompetence of yet another brewery workman and with herself who should have known better than to have trusted him to have done the job properly in the first place, especially as he had already showed her his inability to listen right from the start. It was as she stomped across the pub with her ice bucket that she saw headlights appear in the car park and at that exact moment it suddenly occurred to her that this was the perfect excuse to get 'her man' into the cellar. She could ask him to check that there was no obvious pressure gauge that she had missed before she let rip down the phone at them for their incompetence only to be told that there was one only she hadn't recognised it. Melissa went all hot and cold as a wave of sick fear and excitement overcame her. The question was though could she actually do it? Could she take him into her cellar with all that it implied? Before she had time to contemplate any further the door rattled open and to her mixed relief and disappointment in walked Anna and Ernie. Melissa's face must have mirrored her emotion as Anna's smile dropped a fraction at the less than enthusiastic welcome.

"Are you OK?" Anna asked obviously concerned at the out of character response as she plonked her enormous black leather bag on top of the bar and pushed the ashtray out of the way tossing her long straightened blonde hair as she made herself comfortable on the most sought after bar stool; because it had a back rest on it. Anna was a very striking lady in her early forties and due to her height and slender body that she always dressed in the latest sexy fashions meant that she got no end of attention from both admiring and envious females and dribbling males. Ernie in comparison was fifteen years older, particularly short, grey and balding, but he had a wicked sparkle about him and a mischievous way that endeared him to all and clearly from the way that they looked at each other was yet to wear off even after their ten years together.

"What...oh...yeah...fine sorry. Hello, how are you? Sorry about that I was just away with the fairies for a moment." Melissa started pouring their drinks. Curiously and because she was so distracted Melissa glanced at her watch. It was ten minutes to six. Melissa did a double take and checked that she was not seeing things.

"You're really early tonight." She tried to say as if a casual observation.

"Well we were on our way home and you did always say if ever we were passing and your car was here that we could come on in."

"Oh, don't get me wrong – I am very pleased to see you, it's just out of character for you that's all." Melissa desperately tried to make them feel more welcome as she was genuinely very pleased to see them, just may be half an hour later would have been preferable tonight. Ernie winked at her as he munched his way through his salted peanuts, not at all put out if she had been slightly less welcoming than usual.

Anna and Melissa soon got into their normal conversational topics i.e. Anything weird and obscure. Ernie told them on several occasions that he was staying well out of their discussions as they managed to turn even the most serious of topics into some bizarre matter of hilarity which had the tears streaming down all their faces and contrary to the best of intentions Ernie always did get dragged in.

It was whilst they were in the middle of wiping away some tears that the outside door was opened causing the internal door to rattle. Melissa felt herself go pale and managed to compose herself instantly as the nerves sobered up the intoxicating high from the laughter. All three of them turned to face the door and welcomed Daniel, as they were a regular foursome in the bar who enjoyed each other's company.

"Here, have your stool." Anna offered standing up and offering Daniel his usual seat.

"No, no. You're fine thanks; I'm not stopping long – just time for a quickieee." He grinned at Melissa as she poured out his Murphys. After Daniel had gulped down the first couple of mouthfuls and Melissa had topped up the head, before she could stop herself it was out, "Would you mind checking out my new gas regulator for me please?"

"Is that a euphemism?" Ernie asked winking at Melissa. Daniel spluttered into his beer as Melissa continued. "Only the old one was replaced today but as far as I can see they haven't given me a pressure gauge but I don't want to go shouting the odds for them to tell me I'm being stupid and that of course there is. So would you mind? I promise I won't ravage you."

"That's a shame isn't Daniel?!" Ernie said nodding mischievously at Daniel who smirked wickedly by way of a reply.

Melissa looked questioningly at Daniel to see if he was OK about her request.

"Course I don't mind coming in your cellar with you." He said looking her straight in the eye as she flushed an even deeper shade of red.

"Great, thanks." Melissa replied and was around the front of the bar in an instant before she could change her mind.

"What, now?" Daniel asked rather taken aback.

"Yes, if you don't mind." Without even bothering to reply Daniel took a large swig of his beer and chased almost excitedly after Melissa towards the door to the Ladies toilets that led down the corridor to the cellar beyond.

"We'll give you half an hour and then come looking for you." Anna yelled after them.

Upon opening the door to the cellar Melissa reached around to the left of the door frame and switched on the strip light. Without stopping to wait for it to come on Melissa walked through into the darkness to the far end of the cellar and felt Daniel following close behind with just the cast light from the corridor to see by. The light was always slow to flicker into life but today it seemed to Melissa to be taking forever. The atmosphere in the cellar was electric as they stood there in the dark together.

"Oh come on lights!" Melissa called out, not daring to look at Daniel, just feeling him in such close proximity was nearly too much for her poor racing heart to bare. 'Could he hear it?' she wondered as Melissa was sure it must be loud enough to hear.

"Ahhhh, and then there was light – finally!" Melissa said in relief, "Right, so it's this one that has been replaced." Melissa touched the new brass regulator. "So what do you reckon? Is there a pressure gauge or some new fangled way of seeing how full the gas bottle is?"

"OK, hang on and let me have a look." Daniel chuckled at her gabbling on nervously. "Right, well none of these do anything, in fact I would expect to see the gauge attached to one of these." Daniel said pointing at the three fittings on the regulator. "So, as its not here where else might they have hidden it?" He pondered aloud to himself as he followed the course of the loop of piping leading from the gas canister. After a few more moments, the whole of which were spent standing only centimetres apart, he gave his final diagnosis.

"You are absolutely right. There is no pressure gauge at all."

"So I was not just being a dopey girlieee and I can happily call them up and give them a rollicking without fear of them telling me I am stupid."

"Phone away! Rollock away in fact!" For the first time they made eye contact, the tension was enormous. Melissa broke his stare and hated herself for her weakness.

"Thanks for that then, I really appreciate it." Melissa said as they both simultaneously moved towards the door.

"So this is the cellar then." Daniel stated, stopping in the middle of the pathway through the barrels and turning round to take it all in. Melissa looked at him trying to gauge what he was thinking, all the while desperate for him to touch her.

"Bit cold in here isn't it?" He looked at her with an unfathomable stare.

"Ahh, well it's OK, the ladies is just through there and there's a radiator and a carpet in there." Melissa grinned wickedly at him pointing towards the ladies loo as they made their way out of the cellar.

"Right, I'll keep that in mind." He held her stare whilst smiling the broadest of smiles. Melissa mirrored his expression whilst she looked at him before her. She had never seen him looking so young and bright and his eyes were sparkling. He looked gorgeous and she had never wanted him more. Melissa closed the door behind them both as they made their way out back into the pub. Daniel led the way out into the bar smiling as he held the door open for her.

"Wow, you're looking pleased with yourself." Ernie said to Daniel.

"Bit quick though weren't you?" Anna said laughing at the pair of them as they both exuded pure lust for each other.

"Well, it wasn't bad but we're going to have another go next week." Melissa laughed.

"Oh, great! I'll be there!" Daniel picked up his pint and took a large gulp. Then returned his gaze to Melissa who looked straight away unable to stop grinning. He looked at his watch and then quickly finished off his drink.

"Sorry, but I have to go. Gotta pick my wife up. See you soon."

Melissa and the others said goodbye and she looked at him as he stopped in the doorway and gave her the hugest smile and waved as he left.

"Well, well....look at you! You can stop grinning now – he's gone." Anna laughed at Melissa all flushed and smiling.

"I can't help it, I'm all of a dooo-dah – I've wanted to get him in my cellar for years!"

"Well you've done it now!" Ernie winked at Melissa.

"Nothing happened! (Unfortunately) I really did need him to check the gas regulator!" Melissa protested.

"Yeah, if you say so!" Ernie laughed at her discomfort. "Well he seemed pretty keen to get out there with you – I don't think I have ever seen anyone move so fast!"

"And did you see his face? He thought all his Christmases had come at once." Anna interjected.

With that the telephone rang and Melissa went to answer it glad of the distraction.

"Good evening, The Olde Flagon." Melissa announced brightly. "Oh, hello, yes, how are you? Yes, fine thanks. Paella for four Friday night, yes, no problem at all. Seven o'clock, yes fine. OK, great see you then." Melissa replaced the telephone handset and scribbled down the booking first in the diary and then on a separate piece of paper for Bruno's attention in order that he would remember to buy all the necessary fish in time to make his house speciality of Paella Valenciana; or as Melissa always thought it tasted like: Batchelor's Savoury Rice with rubber bands in it, not being a fan of squid in any shape or form.

The evening continued as it had begun, on a light-hearted and cheery note. There were very few other customers and so after Anna and Ernie finished their meal they rejoined Melissa and Marlena, who was on a night off and had come down for a pint or six and a packet or two of her Polish cigarettes sent over fortnightly for her by her mother. The drink was flowing well and the jokes were flying fast and furious leaving them all with tear stained faces and holding their sides from so much laughing. The time seemed to zoom by and all too soon it was time for Anna and Ernie to leave, which they did in a very wobbly manner rebounding off of several items of furniture on their way out. Much to the amusement of Melissa and Marlena watching as they stumbled out into the foyer and saw Ernie collapse against the wall and start to slide down it until an equally tiddly Anna managed to prop him up enough to regain his footing through a mass of giggling as the pair precariously exited the building.

A short while later Melissa went out through the front door herself and headed along the side of the pub into the darkness of the beer garden. It always frightened her a little going out into the pitch blackness of the garden as it was not unknown for the rats that frequented the chicken feed stores to run along the path that she was walking. As soon as she was outside, before she could even see her, Melissa started calling out for Bessie, in some way hoping that she would protect her from any eventuality – even though in reality she would actually only be able to watch from behind a huge gate and therefore be helpless to assist.

"Where's my Bessie then? Bessie! Wake up you lazy cow! Bessie pooh bag, come on girlieee!" With a loud thump and rattle as Bessie collided with some obstacle in the dark in her eagerness to get at Melissa, she appeared in the dim light at the edge of the feed room at the side of the garden away from the gate. With a loud clatter of overly long claws on concrete as she tried to run faster than was practical, Bessie did the equivalent of a car wheel spin, finally got sufficient traction and flew towards Melissa.

"Hello gorgeous girl! You all right then?" Melissa smiled with pleasure as the spectacle that was an excited Rotweiller. Bessie slobbered her welcome over Melissa's out-stretched hand as she attempted to smooth Bessie's head through the bars of the gate. Melissa pulled back the stiff, highly sprung bolt that held the gate in place and pushed it open for the awaiting Rotty to barge her way out – too excited to wait for it to be opened fully. She thundered off towards the front door of the pub and upon finding it closed zoomed back again to Melissa to hurry her on.

"All right girl, I'm coming!" Melissa laughed at Bessie as she nudged at her hand in encouragement. On opening the pub door Bessie flew past and waited impatiently again at the internal door groaning a deep throaty whine at the door and Melissa to hurry up.

Melissa opened the door a fraction and Bessie shoved her large snout round it and shoved it aside, seemingly without effort. Upon entry she charged towards Marlena who was in her regular position at the bar with her legs up on an adjacent stool. Marlena smiled at the charging Bessie and reeled off a gabble of Polish at her in welcome. Whatever she had said Bessie was happy to hear and jumped up at Marlena resting her huge front feet on her outstretched legs and showering her hands and exposed toes with large slobbery kisses. After her initial excitement wore off Bessie continued about her normal routine of charging around the tables, scavenging for any dropped food and trying to squeeze in between the legs of the furniture oblivious to the fact that she was at least two times too large for the gap, resulting in the usual chaos of nearly knocked over toppling chairs and tables lifted far enough off out of place to cause the salt and pepper pots to fall over and spill. Buddy, who was already in doors, had vanished off to her regular spot, under the table Bruno used as his desk, to sulk owing to her utter disgust at Bessie 'the outside dog' being allowed in her pub.

Melissa grabbed herself a drink and went around and sat in one of the comfy chairs opposite the bar and she and Marlena chatted about the trivial events of the day whilst Bessie lent up against Melissa as she smoothed her and tugged affectionately at her ears. The girls chatted on for some time when all of a sudden there was a knocking at the front door. Both girls turned to look at the door and then to each other. It was 12.30am, who could possibly be calling at his hour? For one hopeful moment Melissa wondered excitedly if perhaps 'her man' had come back for another go in the cellar. She got up and went to the door. It was an old heavy door that contained the stained glass window and it took some effort to open and used to the weight of it Melissa flung it open firmly. The door reacted as Melissa had anticipated for the first foot of opening but then it juddered quite violently and came to a halt not fully open but plenty far enough for Melissa to be able to see that there was nobody there. And in any case, there was a bell – who would knock? It was then that Melissa was curious to see what it was that had caused the door judder so peculiarly across the carpet. Looking down expecting to see a stone or clump of earth Melissa screamed out in horror at what she actually discovered.

"OH MY GOD! IT'S A FROG! I HAVE RUN OVER A SOD-DING FROG!!!!" Melissa looked down horrified at the very large frog lying on its back with his legs spread-eagled in the most undignified manner.

"What do you mean you've run over a frog? How is this possible?" Marlena asked dumbfounded by Melissa's almost hysterical reaction to what she had done and clearly not believing what she was being told. Marlena rushed over to where Melissa was still propping the heavy door open, unable to let go for fear of it running the frog back over again.

"Oh wow! Isn't it cute – so yellow." Marlena said admiring its protruding belly.

"SO BLOODY DEAD! I AM A FROG MURDERER! UGGGGH-HHH!!!!" Melissa shuddered involuntarily as she relived the moment of the door's impact on the frog and it's reverberations up through the timber and through the large brass handle.

"I MURDERED A FROG! I DON'T FLIPPIN' BELIEVE IT! GOD! HOW VILE!" Marlena took in the scene holding on to the door frame for support in her effort to remain upright as she laughed uncontrollably at Melissa's reaction to what she had done and the general ludicrucy of the whole situation. Whilst they both looked at the poor dead frog immobile before them and Melissa held a struggling Bessie back from it by her collar as she whined to investigate properly.

"Well at least it isn't pizza frog." Marlena said between her unstoppable tears.

"What do you mean 'pizza frog'?"

"You know..."Marlena continued to laugh. "He's not pizza. Not squished and flat!"

"OH GOD! THAT'S GROSS! SHUT UP! Get me the coal shovel" Melissa commanded in an unusual display of a lack of manners.

"What? Shovel? Huh?" Marlena asked confused.

"THE BLOODY COAL SHOVEL YOU DOZEY BLOODY FOREIGN PERSON! OVER THERE BY THE FIRE!" Melissa shouted frustratedly, nodding furiously in the direction of the fireplace. Finally understanding what Melissa had meant Marlena made a puzzled face, "What do you want that for?" She asked confused.

"WELL I'M NOT GOING TO LEAVE THE BLOODY THING THERE AM I! AND I'M BUGGERED IF I'M GOING TO PICK IT UP WITH MY HANDS!" Melissa bellowed, now red in the face.

"Oh, OK. What are you going to do with it?" Marlena asked calmly but still laughing.

"Why? Do you want to keep it as a souvenir?" Melissa asked facetiously.

"A sooo-what?

"Just pass me the shovel." Melissa said grabbing the handle of the shovel impatiently. Sickened at what she was about to do, Melissa shuddered again involuntarily as she slowly began to ease the edge of the shovel under the frog. As she gently pushed so the frog was sickeningly jarred along the carpet as opposed to it going underneath the frog as intended.

"Oh my God! GET ON THE DAMNED SHOVEL!" Melissa didn't take her eyes off the inert little amphibian as she desperately attempted to scoop him up without damaging him any further; which under the circumstances was probably for the best as Marlena close to wetting herself from laughing so hard would have been all the support she would have found. Changing her technique, Melissa tried more force and a scooping action that seemed to be working…right up until the frog completely flipped over in a stiff-legged somersault. Surely rigormortis doesn't set in that quickly, Melissa thought to herself appalled. At this unexpected action Marlena whooped out hysterically, unable to contain her laughter's volume any longer.

"It's not funny! Open the door and make yourself useful!" Melissa instructed having successfully managed to scoop him up. Marlena carefully squeezed by the edge of the shovel, which Melissa had stuck outstretched as far from herself as possible as if it were some how contaminated or contagious and unbolted the front door. Melissa rushed out through the opening and flung the dead creature unceremoniously into the edge of the flowerbed, keen to get rid of the body as soon as possible.

"Ugggghhh! That was vile! I cannot believe I murdered a frog – and with a sodding door! God really must hate me!" Melissa said locking the door and coming back into the bar carrying the shovel limply down by her side. Lifting the shovel up to put it back with the other fire tools Melissa glance inadvertently at the inside of it. "Ugggh! Look! The shovel is all wet where the frog was sitting! He was frog pizza!"

"Ooohh! Let me see!" Marlena leapt off her stool and met Melissa half way across the bar.

"You are sick!" Melissa told her, appalled again.

"You're the frog murderer!"

FROG WEDNESDAY

"Ohhhh, I know. Shut up! How the hell could I have known to look out for frogs in the foyer?" Melissa said pulling her hands roughly through her hair, a sure sign of the guilt that she was feeling as she always did this action in times of stress or nervousness.

"Poor thing only wanted a quick pint!"

"Yeah, and he was polite too, knocking on the door like that. What a way to go though – poor thing. He must have had a hell of a headache before he died, and which bit of him got splatted because he certainly didn't look squished."

Marlena kept on laughing as Melissa lamented about what she had done.

"Right, I'm going home, I've had enough of you, you heartless bitch! Why couldn't you have answered the door – you wouldn't have minded murdering poor Freddie."

"Yes, that's right. But it was you! However will you live with yourself!" Marlena laughed evilly at her.

"Lock me out then Satan Bitch from hell!"

"OK, see you tomorrow FROG MURDERER!" Marlena held the door open for Melissa as she patted Bessie on the head a goodbye and then went out to her car parked right in front of the door.

"Oh God! How cruel is that?" Melissa yelled after deactivating her alarm.

"What?"

"Look at this." Melissa instructed pointing in dismay at the window in her car door.

"Protected by Toad Security!" Marlena read out loud. "I don't understand."

"A toad is the same as a frog only uglier. So if I wasn't feeling bad enough already, now, every time I open my car door I will be reminded of my frog murdering status!"

Marlena laughed her way back to the pub door as Melissa got into her car and started it up. As Melissa drove away the last thing she saw was Marlena hunched over as she had still not stopped laughing.

185

CHAPTER TWENTY-THREE
THE FOSSEWAY MAGAZINE

It was a weekly ritual of Melissa's and Charlie's to scan The Fosseway Magazine. The Fosseway Magazine was a free local newspaper full of articles of local interest, write-ups on village plays and pantos, jumble sale extravaganzas not to be missed, weird artists pictured with their even weirder art, wanted ads, for sale ads, what's on in the forthcoming week and where and of course – most interestingly – the Lonely Hearts page. The man that delivered The Fosseway Magazine was a strange extraordinarily quiet bloke. He slipped in, in what can only be described as 'stealth bomber' mode, unheard and barely seen as he put the stack of papers on the table just inside the front door, with his head kept down concentrating on the job in hand and not existing to the public eye. At least once a month Melissa actually spotted him in time to thank his back as he scurried out of the pub but she had never actually seen his whole face.

As the door hinge creaked as it closed the last couple of inches Melissa and Charlie both looked up from their places either side of the bar. No sign of life but then their mutual gaze fell onto the newly delivered stack of magazines. Cigarette still in hand, Charlie flung herself enthusiastically off her stool to go and grab the first copy.

"Right then!" She wriggled about to get comfortable on the stool whilst deftly flicking through and finding the Lonely Hearts page. "Who do we have for Mel today?" It had been agreed many months ago, that because Daniel was actually married and therefore strictly speaking unavailable, that Melissa needed a backup plan for if she never managed to actually win him over, and especially as no one ever really thought that she would and because Melissa thought deep down that it was morally wrong to be even trying. Charlie proceeded to quickly read through all the relevant men, i.e. All except gay ones, and then to systematically cross them off as Melissa rejected them one after the other on sensible grounds such as 'too short', 'too young', 'too old' 'too intelligent' (due to their preferred literature being mentioned and being far too dull to Melissa to be read unless forced to at school), 'too posh', star signs mentioned or 'into green issues', likes football enough to warn you when you have precious little space to endear yourself to your readers, and most worryingly that they felt obliged to mention it 'has a beard' (although Melissa did not have much of a beard issue normally, this unfortunately conjured up images of a beard so huge and matted in her mind that you might find nesting birds, or even a spare change of clothes in it) Generally it left them with about four men who they would later phone when the customers left, putting the poor guys onto the speaker phone so that whatever staff remained could hear what the men answered to the preset questions. It was quite a cunning plan – or so they thought. They called up and listened and if the staff jury liked what they heard, one of them would then call and leave a message along the lines of that they sounded perfect for their friend who would never go on a blind date but is to be found most days at The Olde Flagon pub, so why not visit for a pint and see how you get on. It was perfect really, completely taking away the embarrassment of a blind date situation as Melissa would be completely unaware that he had come in to check her out as opposed to just being any other customer. He would be aware that she was available if they both liked what they saw she would automatically be nice to him and he would pick up on it and respond accordingly and all in a fairly relaxed chance meeting kind of a way.

After the annoying music and advertising stopped and the well-spoken man completed his speech about 'Any problems with the service then please call'…etc and rambled on about nothing just to lengthen the time and consequently the cost of your call, he finally said "We asked the advertiser to tell us about himself…"

"Errr,ummmm,err….my name is Steve. I'm err, ummm forty-two. I, err ummm, cough, cough, like most things really…" Charlie and Melissa exchanged withering looks, cringing on his behalf at the obvious nervousness that he was suffering. "I'm fairly easy-going and like to have fun."

"Next we asked the advertiser what his favourite television programme was…"

"Well, I don't get to see much telly…" he continued, audibly relaxing. "But I s'pose the news and wildlife documen-taries…"

"Switch him off!" Melissa instructed, "Too dull!" she explained. Charlie groaned, "You're SO picky!"

"NEXT!"

"OK, OK!" Charlie pushed the button to end the call and dialled the next number. The posh news reader type voice came through again…."We asked the advertiser to tell us about him-self…"

"Hello, my name is Brian…"

"Oh my God, it's Mr Bean!" Melissa exclaimed in horror as Charlie and she looked at the speaker phone in amazement.

"Shhh! Listen!..." Charlie scolded her.

…. "Oh and eating and drinking – but not to get drunk you understand. Heeee heeeee he, honk honk, haaaa, haaaaa." He laughed (Melissa assumed) visually conjuring up a terrible image of the actual Mr Bean laughing terribly whilst snorting and spray-ing spittle at anyone nearby. "I'm not an alcoholic or anything like that heeeeee, heeeeee, heeeee, honk chhhhh honk chhhhh ahhhhh!"

"OFF!" Melissa yelled. Appalled at the selection of noises they had just been subjected to and now vividly imagining his Mr Bean like features, nostrils flaring and wet lips quivering, going through a rendition that Melissa imagined would be what a pig sounded like on 'fast forward'.

"Next!" Charlie could barely control her laughter as she tapped in the number of the next victim.

"We asked our advertiser..."

"Hi my name is Penny." A bubbly squeaky voice yelled excitedly through the speaker at them.

"Charlie! It's a bloody woman! I'm not that desperate!"

"Aaaa whoops – wrong number – sorry!" She snorted not able to contain the tears now pouring down her face.

"We asked our advertiser..."

"Hi I'm Andrew. I'm forty-five, six feet two. I'm quite fit and I like most things." The confident and cheerful voice came out through the speaker. Melissa and Charlie both exchanged approving looks.

"What television programmes do I like?" He considered quickly, "Well again, a bit of everything I s'pose, I'm not a big fan of the soaps but hey, if I'm there and they're on I watch them – I'm not ashamed!" He exclaimed with a deep and easy chuckle.

"We asked our advertiser to say how his friends would describe him..." Well spoken man told us as though he had just informed us of a news item of the utmost importance and seriousness.

"Oh, well that's a toughie – I wasn't expecting that. Hmm-mmm, well a good sense of humour, always game for a laugh, friendly, p'raps a bit mad and always near a pint glass." He chuckled the same infectious chuckle.

"We asked our advertiser what he would be looking for in his ideal partner....."

"Right now I am looking for someone to take out places, good company and cheerful. I just want someone to look forward to seeing a couple times a week....and we'll just have to take it from there really."

The news announcer came back on the line, "If you want to leave a message for our advertiser please press one on your telephone keypad. If you want to listen to the message again please press two on your telephone keypad. If you would like to hear from some more advertisers please press three on your telephone keypad."

Charlie grabbed the handset and passed it to Melissa. "You have to get him to come he was lovely!"

"Yeah, OK." Melissa said begrudgingly, still thinking she would rather have 'her man'. Obediently Melissa left the standard 'come and meet my friend Melissa at the pub' thing and replaced the receiver.

"Course, he'll be as ugly as sin!" Melissa said emptying the glass washer and putting the basket full of steaming glasses to drain on the bar.

"Yep! Hugely over-weight too. We'll have to have one of us in here pulling and one outside pushing him in from behind just to get him in here – and he'll need three stools to sit on because he's so wide!" Melissa said, only half joking.

"I still think that we should call them all like you said before." Charlie said laughing at the memory of that conversation.

"What? What were you going to do?" Asked Rachel, a part-time waitress, and Rick together, who had just come through from finishing working in the kitchen, looking between them both for information.

"You tell them." Charlie just managed between laughs.

"Oh, well it was just that I said we should call all the 'advertisers' up" She said mimicking the posh newsreader man, "And get them all to come but instead of carrying the stereotypical red carnation or whatever make them all bring really large objects with them."

"What sort of large objects?" Rachel asked smiling as she bundled her dirty waitress's apron up and plonked it on the bar.

"Oh you know, marrows, beach balls, a left shoe, cuddly toy – anything really that would be too big to hide should they chicken out. We would tell them all that we would be wearing the red carnation (or whatever) but of course we wouldn't be, so that if we liked any of them we could identify ourselves but if not they would just think they had been stood up!"

"That's terrible!" Rick said trying to stand up for his fellow man.

"Don't talk crap, its brilliant! Truly inspired! When are we going to do it?" Rachel asked.

"Yeah, and it will also be great for business – cuz they'll all buy at least one drink!" Melissa agreed.

They all laughed at, joked and sampled several more 'advertiser's offerings leaving two more similar messages for people to come and visit Melissa to see if they got on without the normal embarrassment factor that a blind date would normally entail. Melissa laughed heartily along with the rest of them but suspected nothing good would come of it.

"At least if I don't fancy any of them Marlena will shag them!"

CHAPTER TWENTY-FOUR
WHAT IS IT WITH FEET???

"What is it with feet? Your feet are aching from too long and too heavy in inappropriate shoes – so much so that every footstep is a considered movement, with your toes curled up and splayed out as if waiting for nail varnish to dry on them when BANG! You smack your little toe against something – in this particular instance it was the corner of one of the feet of the bloody ski-machine!" Melissa told Charlie and Marlena as they sat at the bar after work one evening. The two girls laughed as Melissa relayed yet another one of her tales, including doing the flamboyant miming to emphasise her point wherever possible.

"I swear it just jumped out at me as some form of ironic punishment as if to say 'OYYY FATTY! TAKE THAT BITCH! If you had been using me for anything other than a clothes stand you would not be so heavy and your feet would not be hurting!' So hard a thwack it was…." Melissa continued as the girls watched on both chain smoking as they listened, "It felt as if my little toe had been ripped right off! The pain was so bad that I wasn't even able to swear where it took my breath away – all I could do was stand there like an idiot holding onto my foot and squeezing it – as if somehow it might take the pain away. On the bright side though the toe singularly hurt *SOOOO* much that I was partially distracted from my gross legs. I don't know about five o'clock shadow, *ten* would have been more accurate! They are utterly vile!"

"Ugggh GROSS!" Charlie said exhaling a huge cloud of smoke as she and Marlena continued to laugh at her antics.

Another shift for Melissa spent in hopeful anticipation, for the first hour, every time the door opened. Another shift ended, full of bitter disappointment and self-doubt as to his true interest in her.

"Two weeks now. This will have been two whole weeks with only one visit a week!" Melissa said sadly.

"BASTARD! All men are." Marlena commented helpfully.

"I know he has got a lot to do for work but I can't help feeling that it is because he is not really interested and I have imagined the whole thing. What would he be wanting a lardy old troll like me for anyway?"

"Yes, that is a good point you fat cow!" Marlena said helpfully again, the two girls used to hearing all this on many an insecure moment.

"I'm too insecure to even loose weight to get him – in case – ridiculously enough – that I get him! *And* I'm too bloody slovenly to shave my monstrously hairy legs because I hate them so much that I try not to look at them for as long as shaving would take – Christ and those feet! Just shoot me now and put us all out of our misery!"

The two girls still laughing looked at each other despairingly and Charlie raised two fingers in the shape of a gun and made the sound effect of a gun firing two shots.

"Two shots?" Melissa asked with a pained expression.

"Yes, couldn't risk not getting you with the first you miserable bitch!" Charlie answered as she blew the top of the imaginary gun and mimed putting it back into its holster. All three of them laughed heartily and Melissa poured Marlena another pint of lager and made Charlie another Snowball – her drink of choice for more than two months. "Waarnicks sales must have tripled cuz of you, you gross bitch!" She said passing the thick and gloopy yellow drink across the bar adorned with a cherry, a stirrer and a straw. In answer Charlie took a long suck from her straw and poked her tongue out.

"Uggghh, gross! Put it away!" Melissa said appalled at the yellow coating that was left on her tongue.

"I'm really sorry to go on about it...."

"Then don't." Marlena interrupted.

"But I don't know what's wrong with me..." Melissa continued glaring at Marlena who Charlie grinned at over her straw. "I seem to have some sort of self destruct button attached to everything that I do. Right now food holds no interest for me but I am piling it down like some mindless android. I'm just eating because it is there and ironically only because I am so depressed with my vile body. How destructive and twisted is that?"

This time both girls simultaneously raised their imaginary weapons and shot Melissa. They all laughed at their remarkable timing. Then Marlena re-holstered her gun, pulled out a much larger two handed invisible weapon (an Ouzi Melissa assumed) and much to Charlie and Melissa's delight gunned down first Melissa and then the whole bar.

"I have only got fat since I have been here." Marlena stated, "So it must be your fault!" she accused Melissa.

"Yes, it most probably is, along with our friend Mr Cheeeseeeeee chips and his friend Shit-loads of ice cream!"

"Shit-loads?" Marlena asked for a translation as they all giggled.

"There is no translation – it's a Somerset slang term meaning 'an awfully large amount'." Melissa put on her best 'posh' accent.

As they continued to laugh Charlie kicked off her huge platform shoes still splattered in cow muck from the farm yard that was outside of her back door at home where she had to park her car. She picked her legs up with the help of her hands and with some effort plonked them up on the stool next to her mirroring Marlena at the other end of the bar.

"Ohhhh-myyyyy-Godddd! Have you seen her socks?" Marlena laughed as she looked at Charlie's socks in horror.

"No, but I can smell them!" Melissa laughed as she made her way over from the glass washer with three pint glasses and deposited them on the shelf underneath the bar.

"No you can't! Can you?" Charlie asked flushing red in case she was not joking.

"Naaaah, you're OK, but let's take a look at these socks." Melissa said leaning over the bar to see Charlie's feet on the stool below as they were not visible from where she was standing. To help Charlie lifted up one sock clad foot.

"Well that's not so bad. I wouldn't be seen dead in them but they're OK." Melissa said assessing the sock critically: they were stripy pink, purple and a dark turquoise.

"Yeah right. Now show her the other one!" Marlena demanded.

"They're all right, I don't know what is the matter with you!" Charlie laughed notably keeping sock number two firmly in its place on the stool beneath the bar.

"Here!" Marlena said triumphantly, having grabbed Charlie's foot and lifted it up via the toe of the sock so that it was taking the full weight of her suspended leg and thus her foot started to comically slide out of the sock. Melissa laughed as she witnessed the two girls fighting over the second sock and more heartily when Marlena finally let go and then sniffed her hand and Melissa watched the reaction on her face and then wipe her hand distastefully down her leg, then onto Charlie's leg and then still unhappy on a wet bar cloth.

"Charlie that is a truly vile sock!" Melissa accused as she inspected the second sock whilst still laughing at Marlena sniffing her hand and then holding it away from her body in disgust; this sock was lime green with pink fat-faced little angels on it, or possibly fairies and they did seem to be carrying wands.

"Separately that one is nasty but together as 'a pair' with the other should be illegal. Quick, call the fashion Police!" Melissa shouted as Charlie pulled her sock back on properly, red faced from all of the attention and the laughing.

"I think I am broken." Melissa groaned as she looked down at her painful feet, "My feet have been hurting so much that I have bought five different pairs of boots in the last five weeks! I bought different height heels, sole widths, some pointed toes some square and all of them have hurt me after a couple of hours. So…" Melissa continued as Charlie and Marlena looked on in horror at the amount of money that would have added up to. "I conclude therefore that it must be my weight as I have eliminated any specific type of shoe as responsible. At the gym even my trainers are hurting me, and the effort of walking on a treadmill for thirty minutes nearly kills me and it never used to." Marlena and Charlie continued to smoke as they listened, rapidly filling the ashtrays with the stubbed out dog-ends.

"My inside upper arms have become itchy to top it all – so wither I have fleas or my stretch marks are enlarging. Reduced 'visits', can't stop eating, bad feet, expanding stretch marks and hairy ankles – does life get any better than this?" Melissa searched their faces in despair.

"Naaaaa, probably not." Marlena laughed trying to lighten the conversation.

"The saddest thing of all is that I know if 'he' was coming back in more regularly I would not be feeling this way. I would be dieting so that I could be proud of my dieting achievement when he asked. It would motivate me to go to the gym and not eat all that crap – but as it is it feels like his interest is lost and my only reason for getting out of bed has been taken away – which I also hate myself for!"

Charlie and Marlena said nothing in reply to Melissa's sad ramblings; both girls had heard it all before but neither of them liked to see Melissa so low and really hoped that she could sort herself out.

Melissa drove home a short while later. She was feeling strange and melancholy and even the music from her stereo was irritating her so she jabbed harshly at the off button.

"Tomorrow I must be more positive. I must fling myself enthusiastically out of bed. Weigh myself as the start of a new beginning – again! I will tidy up my room – well at least enough to see what colour the carpet is underneath all those clothes and shoes! AND I *WILL* GO TO THE GYM! When I come home and shower I will shave my vile legs and I will use moisturiser too! I will start to take pride in my appearance and not go out in scruffy clothes and frightened 'just got out of bed' hair. Oh, and I will not have conversations with myself OUT LOUD!" Melissa looked at herself in the rear view mirror as she pulled onto her drive and switched off the engine. "Yep! Utterly barking!" She said out loud and then after putting her stereo front into its box and into her overloaded bag she got out of the car and trudged across the lawn to the front door with a heavy but ever hopeful heart.

The following day Melissa did none of her 'to do' list and the fact that she had not lay heavily on her conscience and depressed her even more. At four o'clock it bothered her sufficiently to stop watching the truly awful afternoon television – Ainsley Harriet was very helpful in making this decision and Melissa made a large mug of tea and went upstairs to bed. On her way across her bedroom as she picked her way expertly through the obstacles to her bed, her attention was caught by two containers on the shelf in her wardrobe. Curiously she picked one up and started to read the instructions. Once she had finished reading she twirled the container around slowly in her hand and then in an instant grabbed up her dressing gown from off of the arm of the ski-machine, two towels from where they were hanging off the wardrobe and door and some clean underwear from a pile of laundry on a chair just inside the bedroom door and along with the small container she locked herself in the bathroom. No sooner had she sat down for a wee did she suddenly remember her book and her mug of tea. On completion of her wee she went back to her bedroom and turfed the duvet and pillow upside down hunting for her book. Lying on her belly with her arm shoved awkwardly down the side of the bed and her feet flailing around her in an effort to get at the book which was just fractionally out of her reach. With a final grunt Melissa lunged sufficiently far to be able to get hold of the corner cover of the book and drag it up between the wall and the bed. Red and flustered Melissa struggled upright and then returned, with her tea, to the bathroom. Melissa had never had much luck in the past with hair removing creams. Her most memorable experience resulted in a passport photograph with half an eyebrow missing, and that was from removing the hair on her legs! This time she only hoped it would be more successful. Melissa was a sucker for the glamorous advertisements on the television and this new version had really appealed to her and so she had bought two cans of the new hair removal mousse when she had seen them on special offer. Clearly however, something was bothering her about using it on a subconscious level as it was several months now since she had purchased it without being once tempted to use it instead of her trusty razor. With hindsight Melissa realised later that she should have trusted this internal judgement. All Melissa wanted to do was remove her leg hair so she read the instructions again carefully and then she proceeded to clear the bathroom of all clutter that she might possibly, however unlikely, get cream on. Then she plonked her book face down on top of the toilet cistern shoving hairspray and deodorants out of the way in one fluid motion causing a tidal wave of toppling cans and bottles that Melissa masterfully controlled, or so she thought, until one rogue deodorant bottle with insufficient contents to act as ballast to withstand such a knock, toppled over and in slow motion Melissa watched it bounce its way off the metal flush-handle, onto the loo seat, roll a quarter of the way around the edge only to be deflected into the bowl itself by the bleach block holder and into the hideous depths below. Even though the toilet was to all intensive purposes 'visibly' clean, there is something most distasteful about having to shove your hand down a loo. Melissa toyed momentarily with the idea of leaving it down there for the next occupant to have to fish out but only momentarily because if it was one of her brothers she was not sure that they would not just wee straight over the top of it. Gritting her teeth she pulled her sleeve up as high as it would go, closed her eyes and plunged her hand down in the general direction of her target. Being made of plastic and nearly empty however it bobbed away downwards and then surged back up tormenting her as she let out an 'urrrrrggghhh!' out of disgust as her hand made contact with the cold water followed by the edge of the pan. Reaching desperately again Melissa lunged awkwardly and missed and so hence ended up chasing the blue and white container around its unpleasant confines until she finally had it in her grasp and swiped it up and out of the loo and straight into the stainless steel pedal bin that she had stamped on the pedal of which to perfectly synchronise with the exit from the toilet bowl. Still grimacing with disgust Melissa washed her hands with the soap from the pump action bottle at the side of the basin. After finishing her scrubbing she then squirted more of the blue gel soap onto the taps and her hands to then rub them and the pump part of the soap dispenser. When she was finally satisfied with the coating of foaming antiseptic soap she had distributed everywhere she then splashed it all with water from the running tap and then washed her hands again once more for good measure catching her frowning expression in the large mirror in front of her Melissa wondered despairingly if life really had to be this complicated! Reading the instructions once more she then stripped down to her knickers which she was leaving on to do her bikini line. Taking the can with her she stepped into the shower cubicle and just as she was about to close the door she spotted an old shower cap still in its (more than a little worse for wear and thousands of miles of travel) little card board box advertising the posh tropical hotel that it came from. Melissa removed what was to all intensive purposes was a glorified freezer bag, and bundled up her hair into a scruffy bun and pulled the charming hat down over her thick mop of hair. Moving in front of the mirror Melissa tucked away the few wayward strands up with the others and chanting quietly to herself "I must not touch my eyebrows…" over and over, she clambered back into the shower cubicle and closed the door. Taking the lid from the can and dropping it onto the floor of the shower tray,

Melissa shook the can vigorously and began spraying the contents slowly from her ankles completely coating all over her legs. Standing with her legs splayed as far apart as the cubicle would allow, Melissa double checked that she had not missed anywhere and then bent down to put the can on the floor. "Uggghh!" Melissa yelled out as one of her belly rolls made contact with the upper part of her thighs. Melissa looked down at her foam covered belly and then at the bald patches on her thighs from where the foam had rubbed off of. Melissa wiped the foam off her bulges with the back of her hand and reminded herself not to touch her face. Then she touched up the foam-less patches and this time dropped the can on the floor closing her eyes tightly as it clattered noisily on landing. She looked at her watch and said the time out loud to herself in the hope that she would actually remember it correctly later and then she pushed open the glass door and in true 'John Wayne getting off his horse' fashion Melissa waddled out of the shower cubicle being careful to keep her legs wide enough spread apart to keep her thighs from rubbing together and remove the hair removing cream – no mean feat in such a small bathroom with such fat thighs!

Melissa went over to the sink and washed her hands thoroughly and then washed off the taps and the top of the pump dispenser again and then her hands really thoroughly *again,* no way did she want to relive the missing eyebrow experience again!

Melissa looked at her watch again and then picked up her book from besides the sink and began reading to pass the time. She looked a picture. Naked but for a freezer bag shower cap, her black knickers and her foam trousers – gorgeous! After ten minutes was up Melissa took the sponge from the lid of the can and tested an area at the top of her of her thigh. The hair, although looking a bit frazzled and shrivelled did not come off so she spread the mousse back to cover the area and checked the time again. 'Leave on no longer than twelve minutes' the instructions had read. So in true Melissa style after debating with herself if they meant from finishing the first leg or the second and not really concluding anything and not really sure either when she had finished either of her legs, she decided after another five minutes and waddled carefully back to the shower cubicle and rinsed it all off. Then she rinsed down all the tiles in case any mousse had been squirted on them by accident and then she rinsed off her legs again and again for good measure. Happy finally that she had got rid of any traces of the dreaded eyebrow remover, Melissa rested the shower head on the floor of the shower tray whilst leaving it running and hopped out to remove her now more than a little bit soggy knickers and put them in the sink. Back in the shower Melissa rinsed her hands off in the running water and then replaced the shower head in its holder before continuing her normal washing rituals. Having just finished shampooing her hair Melissa happened to glance down and to her horror saw something large and hairy making its way down her thigh. Melissa froze and her goose-pimple body armour made its appearance, even though she was standing in a cascade of very warm running water. Looking back again to what she was sure was going to be the most massive and soggy of all Horris's eight-legged relations Melissa looked in wonder at the large hairy blob which was now just below her knee. Then further up her leg Melissa saw another blob, and further up again another. And then the penny dropped. What she was actually looking at were clumps of soggy pubic hairs and there was an awfully large amount of them. Melissa grabbed the shower head down from its holder and directed its stream at the source of the emigrating hair – a whole new interpretation to 'down under'. To her horror and it has to be said great amusement, more and more tufts of dark curls fell to the floor and swirled around in the whirlpool of water around the plug hole. When all that was going to come out apparently had, Melissa inspected the leftovers, what little there were. To be fair the hair removing mousse had done an excellent job of her bikini line, but Melissa could not say that she was overly thrilled with the bald patches that were more evident than the hairy patches. With a bemused expression on her face Melissa finished her ablutions and dried herself off knowing from experience of the hair on her head that what looked long wet halved in size dry; and this turned out not to be any exception to the rule. On the bright side however, curly and dry made the bald patches appear smaller. All that Melissa hoped was that she didn't have an accident or even worse, something that she never thought she would hear herself think, however unlikely it may be, that she would not 'pull'! The other thing that occurred to her was what a shame it was that it was not something you could go around showing everyone so that they could share the humour of the experience. Not that she would have been brave enough to anyway!

CHAPTER TWENTY-FIVE
GHOSTS

It was a bitterly cold November evening. When Melissa drove along the road approaching the pub she actually drove by the entrance to the car park and the crossroads it sat upon where the swirling fog was so thick. Realising her mistake as the road beneath her wheels started to descend the steep hill quite some way past the pub, she had no choice but to drive an extra quarter of a mile to the end of the road and turn around on the staggered crossroads at the bottom of the hill rather than risk an accident turning blindly in the engulfing mass of fog that put the visibility of the on-coming headlights down to barely twenty feet before they were level with you. Cursing herself for her lack of due diligence, Melissa carefully turned into the opposite road and checking as best as she was able widely arced the car around and came back up the hill straining her eyes to make out the large pub with no outside illumination to guide her. Eventually her headlights lit up the white dashes signifying the road junction that the pub was on, and not really happy that she wasn't actually about to pull across the path of an oncoming vehicle where it was impossible to see, she floored the accelerator pedal and shot into the large empty car park where she pulled into her regular spot to the left of the door. As she pulled on the handbrake and switched off the ignition the headlights cast bright reflections off the diamond patterned, mullioned windows in front of her and all up the few remaining beautiful red and gold leaves of the creeper which covered most of the outside of the building which refused to give themselves up to the harsh winds and weather the exposed building took a battering from. Before Melissa switched off the headlights she scanned the areas around her trying to check that no strangers were lurking. Reluctantly, being petrified of what or rather who might be waiting in the dark; a fear she was positive that she had from watching too many psychological thrillers when she was younger, she got out of the car and even as she hurriedly went around the front of the car to get through the gates into the pub's garden, she could hear Bessie's excited dancing feet; her nails tip tapping as she bounced around, audible even over the noise of her thumping heart. Melissa called out hello to her which immediately made Bessie whine impatiently as a response in anticipation of the biscuit Melissa would undoubtedly have for her and helped calm Melissa's heart rate knowing that in just a moment she would be safely within the confines of Bessie's compound. Bruno had a terrible habit of going out late in the afternoon on his days off and not thinking to put a light on anywhere in order that Melissa could actually see her way safely into the building. She had at one point brought a torch with her but had given up that as a bad job owing to the fact that she worked herself up into a right state waving the small beam it cast frantically backwards and forwards to try and check she wasn't about to be jumped on. Melissa hated going into the empty pub too, groping her way around between the various light switches, pausing at each one to look out for any signs of intruders and listening intently for any sounds to indicate anyone's presence before moving on to the next switch. It wouldn't be so bad but the light switches were laid out for the person in the building turning the lights off to go upstairs to the living quarters and not for people coming into the building in the dark and so it meant passing through dark rooms hoping that no one had left any shopping lying around unexpectedly in order to get to the switch. These days were better because of Marlena living-in there were generally lights on all over, including her bedroom light rather usefully lighting up the pathway from the car park she had to take, but today Marlena had the day off and had gone off early and clearly from the dark that enveloped the isolated old building and Melissa, she was yet to return.

With the pub all lit up and welcoming and the fire crackling away loudly as the dry kindling and excessive firelighters roared up the chimney in the large inglenook fireplace Melissa was still on edge as she clung to her large mug of steaming tea for comfort and extra heat waiting for the first customer to come in. November was a funny time of year and often they could have as little as five people in all night braving the extremes of weather which the large hill they sat on the top of took the brunt of. No matter what it was like a mile away, you could always times it by at least five to end up with the strength of winds up on the exposed hill or indeed the thickness of the fog. Melissa hated being in the pub alone and was only glad that Bruno had two cars so that it never looked as though she was in the pub on her own in case some weirdo came in. Fortunately she did not have to wait long before headlights appeared across the junction from the pub which caught Melissa's eye and got brighter as the vehicle came straight across the junction emerging like a wild eyed monster from the fog. The large outline of a person appeared through the picture in the stained glass of the door and it creaked open and in waddled Ted along with three of the red and gold leaves dancing around beside him.

"Well hello young Mel and how the devil are you?" He asked 'heee heeeing' after his words as was his custom.

"Hi Ted! Hell of a night out there. Am I glad to see you!"

"You are? Can I write this in the diary as a historical event? Mel glad to see me!" Heeee heeeeee hee heeeee Ted laughed as he pretended to write the words on the wooden bar top with an imaginary pen.

"Ha ha very funny. You know I hate being in this place on my own, it's much too creepy!" Melissa involuntarily shuddered at the thought as she checked subconsciously all around her.

"Lovely old building like this? Get away with you!"

"It is lovely but now you aren't allowed to leave until someone else shows up!" Ted laughed at her as she passed him across a pint of his usual beer in an old fashioned handle glass with large bubbled sides.

"Bruno out tonight then?"

"Yeah, hair cut then the theatre or the cinema. He hadn't decided which the last time I saw him."

"That's nice then. Good that he gets away from this place sometimes."

Melissa had been standing in front of Ted where he sat at the bar when all of a sudden she jumped with fright and swung her head around to the left and then turned 360 degrees looking frantically about her and holding her hands on either side of her waist.

"What on earth is the matter with you?" Ted asked rather startled at her peculiar and abrupt action.

"OH MY GOD!" Melissa yelled out still darting her eyes around all over the place. "SOME ONE JUST GRABBED ME!" Ted laughed heartily and then stopped mid-chortle when he realised that she actually meant it.

"It's only you and me here my love." He said gently.

"I'm not joking! Someone or thing has just come up behind me and grabbed me at either side of my waist (or rather where it would be if I had one) and squeezed me. You know, like when you creep up on someone from behind and make them jump. *I can't believe that there is no one there. It felt so real!*" Melissa said dumbfounded and the colour having drained from her normally rosy cheeks.

"Well I don't know about ghosts and stuff but you certainly jumped as if someone had grabbed you. How odd! A groping ghost, that's a new one!" Heeee hee heee.

Melissa remained unsettled then for the rest of the evening and kept putting her hands to where she was sure she had been touched as though she could still feel the warmth from their hands. Whilst they were idolly passing the time the door creaked and groaned open and in walked 'her man'.

"Well good evening Daniel, how the devil are you?" Heee hee heee.

"Mr Dando, long time no see! You well?"

"Nothing wrong with me that a few of these won't cure!" He said nodding his head in the direction of his pint, "Although I'm not sure the same can be said for our Mel here. She's been seeing ghosts! Reckon maybe you should be taking more water with it young Mel." Heee heee heee.

"Ghosts? Really? In here?"

"Groping ghosts no less! Only Bruno could arrange one of them!"

"What?" Daniel asked barely having kept his first mouthful of stout within his lips. Melissa flushed red from the attention of his concentrated stare and retold what she had experienced. When she had finished explaining his expression, as ever, was unreadable. Mid-way through the explanation Rupert Smythe, the local Conservative Councillor and Parish Council 'hooray' had arrived. He was one of the most arrogant, pompous and peculiar men that Melissa had ever had the misfortune to meet. He was very handsome, in an obnoxious smug git sort of a way (on the rare occasions that his head was actually visible that is from the very high position that he kept it up his own bottom. Melissa and Daniel and indeed Bruno and many others had discussed their dislike of him on many previous occasions and so no one present paid him much attention as he walked up to the bar (beyond a nod) and indeed, Melissa did not even pause telling Daniel about her ghostly experience with the exception of a quick hello nod to acknowledge his existence, which she would never have treated anyone else to such disdain and rudeness. The snub was not gone unnoticed and so Rupert Smythe made a point of butting in at what he did not know was the end of the tale.

"Where's my brown envelope then?" Smythe addressed Daniel grinning slyly.

"I don't deal with brown envelopes. Don't use them and certainly wouldn't give one to you." Daniel answered calmly and in an even tone which actually came across as quite menacing along with his dark eyed stare. Smythe flinched slightly at the harsh response to his would-be humour aimed at Daniel's recently passed planning permission for a large barn conversion locally. All three looked at him with disdain in their expressions to think that he was inferring that he had the power to affect whether or not it was passed. Smythe was well-known locally as a stirrer with the local councillors and in fact would have been a hindrance in getting anything passed due to how many hackles he caused to rise. He sheepishly took several sips from his large glass of wine as if hiding from the hostile glares he was receiving. At that moment Smythe's 'friend' he was meeting arrived. The new arrival into the atmosphere which was almost as thick as the fog outside, greeted Smythe with a hearty handshake and ordered a pint from Melissa that Smythe paid for. Then, in what Melissa assumed was his pathetic attempt at regaining a few points in the put-down stakes, introduced him to Daniel, firstly by pretending to forget his name and then by describing him as being the son of his well-known father as opposed to as the well-known builder that he actually was. He then proceeded to pompously introduce the 'friend' by his connection with a big and internationally well known 'dot com' corporation which Daniel quietly acknowledged with a polite nod and then to Smythe's obvious embarrassment asked what it was that the company actually did, apologetically admitting to 'the friend' that he had never heard of it. It worked as the perfect insult but it was not intended, it was merely that Daniel was not an admirer of the computer age and was still battling hard to avoid accepting it into his world. Smythe seeing he was beaten retreated with his friend to a corner of the pub furthest away from the bar.

"Well Ted!" Daniel drained the rest of his glass, "Nice seeing you but I'm afraid I have to get back."

"Only one pint Daniel, that's just not right me son!" Heeee heeeee heeeee.

""Yes, tell me about it. Dinner will most likely already be in the dog – poor dog." He said glancing up at the clock behind the bar.

"May as well stay and enjoy yourself – better to be hung for a sheep than a lamb!"

"Yes and helpful advice like that is probably why you're getting divorced Ted!" Melissa scowled at him.

"Yes Mel, you're probably right." Heeee heeee heeee.

"Bye then." Daniel waved straight faced from the doorway.

"Byeeee!" Melissa and Ted both chorused in coincidental stereo.

"Nice bloke that Daniel. You'd do well to find yourself a chap like him."

"Yeah I know, but he's already spoken for."

"I didn't actually mean him you mischievous girl. You better stick with your groping ghost – or there's always me!" Heeee heeee heeee heee heeee heee heee.

CHAPTER TWENTY-SIX
SPROUTS

Christmas in the pub was not looked forward to with much enthusiasm. Christmas parties created lots of extra work for everyone and Melissa was not fond of the weird customers that always seemed to appear at this time of year. Loud drunken youngsters brought there against their will with staff works outings that would have all much preferred a night bowling in a loud and brightly lit alley rather than the quiet subdued atmosphere that The Olde Flagon offered with its skittle alley, cosy lighting and completely music free environment (unless there was a concert on), conducive to conversation not raucous parties. People who were appalled not to be able to get Alco pops of any description and even more appalled that they were served their bottled lager in glasses. Bruno and Melissa were both 'Baaahhh Humbugs' about Christmas. Bruno hated all the naff decorations expected in a pub and Melissa hated having to put up all the naff decorations and unpack them from old boxes dusted with cobwebs awaiting spider encounters with every bauble removed. For Melissa however, Christmas was dreaded because it was a time for children and parties – parties involving being part of a couple from which Melissa was always excluded. Every year Melissa hoped it would be the last alone but with each new Christmas nothing ever seemed to have changed – other than maybe an upward dress size or two, and that sort of change she could well do without!

So it was with the normal delay tactics that the Christmas decorating was put off until finally Melissa had to 'bite the bullet' and begin the tedious job of rooting through all the old cobweb covered decorations to find enough to put back up which had not been damaged from being ripped hurriedly down the year before. After a long time spent untwisting what seemed like miles of hideously kinked and entwined bulb covered cables Melissa finally completed her mission and set about putting up lengths of fake pine garland which she attached to the dado rail and then twisted the newly untangled lights back up amongst them. Two and a half hours later Melissa finally finished including upstairs in the alley – where only the tinsel and truly naff decorations were allowed to go. Melissa clumsily made her way back downstairs with the large metal step ladder she had been using, constantly banging it first against one side of the stairwell and then the other taking with it several coats and discarded aprons strewn along the banister. Entering the kitchen at the bottom of the stairs she could hear Marlena clinking glasses about as she cleared up the bar from the remainders of the lunchtime session. Melissa plonked the ladder down on the floor whilst she half-filled the kettle and switched it on. After untangling an apron from one of the legs, Melissa picked up the step ladder back up and made her way back out into the bar jarring the end loudly on the kitchen door frame as she went. At the sound of Melissa clattering about Marlena looked up from checking that night's bookings in the diary and smiled broadly at her.

"Hello you old slapper! I just put the kettle on d'you want one?" Melissa asked as she bounced the ladder off a table edge.

"Aaa, yes please." She continued smiling raising her eyebrows wildly at her. Melissa looked curiously at her for a split second before concentrating on manoeuvring the ladder around the hairpin bend which the furniture obstacles created. As she rounded the corner Melissa stopped dead in her tracks as she became aware of the cause of Marlena's eyebrow imbalance.

"Aaahh, hello!" Melissa looked at Daniel who was sitting at the bar in front of her, "God, what time is it then?" She said quickly swinging around to look at the clock above the till, clattering the noisy ladder's legs against a chair with her wild movement and its emphasised effect through the long see-sawing length.

Daniel looked at Melissa in front of him and smiled an amused hello to her.

"Anyway…." Melissa said coming to her senses only slightly, "it's Monday, what are you doing here?"

"It's Monday what are YOU doing here?" He laughed back at her, apparently revelling in her discomfort.

"I've been decorating. What's your excuse?"

"I came up to see the decorations of course!"

Melissa smiled and made her way on through the pub banging her ladder on just about every item of furniture between Daniel and the cellar door. Daniel looked on, clearly amused at Melissa's ladder driving skills.

"Would you ummmm, like a hand with that?" He chortled as the ladder made impact with the outer cellar door – very loudly.

"Not if you value your limbs at all thanks!" Melissa said as she vanished through the now open door and it banged closed very loudly against the only half way through ladder. Some more bangs, crashes and thuds ensued and both Marlena and Daniel stared at the closed door only imagining the chaos Melissa was creating within the cellar. A short while later Melissa reappeared at the door and tried to re-enter the pub with some semblance of dignity, tugging down the bottom of her fleece jacket which had ridden up revealing her normally well covered behind and running her hands through her hair in a vain attempt to tame its wild mass. Daniel smiled broadly at her as he watched her nervous fidgeting. Growing redder with every step Melissa poked her tongue out at the two of them as a coping mechanism and skulked purposefully off to the kitchen to make her tea. As she passed by the large kitchen window Bessie whined at her and waved a muddy paw pitifully at her as she scraped it down the window which she was looking through balanced on her hind legs.

"Hello girlie! You all right then?" Melissa greeted her enthusiastically glad of the escape from her thoughts for a moment. Fishing about in the scrap bucket that lived on the inside windowsill of Bessie's window, Melissa pulled out a large piece of left over steak probably from off of the plate of a toothless wrinkly that lunchtime she presumed, and flung it out of the small open window to the waiting and very pleased Rotty. As Melissa got back to the job in hand, desperate to get back to 'her man' but also concerned about the problems that it presented ie that of where to sit and what to say when not protected by the safety of the bar, she caught sight of her reflection in Bessie's window and stopped horrified in her tracks.

"Oh my God!" Melissa tipped back her head and looked up in despair, 'you really do hate me don't you?" Melissa tugged at her hair for a few futile moments and then quickly made the drinks, took a huge deep breath as she passed through the doorway and made her way around the front of the bar spilling hot tea behind her as she went.

"Bad hair day then?" Marlena asked laughing and catching Daniel's eye.

"A very good hair day actually, today it is my head that is the problem!" Marlena and Daniel both looked confused. "Here. Coffee. Don't mind the lumps that is just where the arsenic didn't dissolve properly."

"Arsenic?" Marlena questioned, her English letting her down for a very rare moment.

"Yes. Arsenic. Nasty poison. Here, quick, drink it all!" Melissa said gently pushing the mug further towards her.

Daniel chuckled quietly at their banter and observed Melissa's silent mental struggle over which stool she should sit on. It was a huge quandary. Too close and it would look too forward and Melissa knew that they would both feel uncomfortable and he would have been to close to be in focus when she looked at him. Too many stools away would seem stand-off-ish and she really wanted to be as close as she could anyway. Melissa opted for a one stool gap. She sat on the stool one stool away from him and immediately plonked her mud splattered boots (from visiting Bessie earlier) on the foot rest of the stool next to Daniel, leaving her legs in his direction even when looking away from him. Happy momentarily, Melissa picked up her huge mug of tea and took a large slurp and managed to create a tidal wave across its surface as she set it down.

"But it's OK, cuz I'm not clumsy!" Melissa said as she flushed red and wiped up the spilt tea with the beer mat. They were all quiet momentarily as Melissa cursed the awkward situation she found herself in and wished she could think of something witty to say.

"Nice decorations." Daniel said as he looked around taking in all of Melissa's hard work, "But umm no mistletoe I notice." He smiled mischievously holding Melissa's gaze.

"Yeah, I haven't seen any yet. Mind you that is probably a good thing else I have to spend the next few weeks avoiding slobbery kisses off lecherous old gits. Hah! Yes, you've got all that to look forward to!" Melissa told Marlena. "Avoid anyone called John and you have the worst of them avoided."

"Great! Can't wait!"

"Right, I'll have to love you and leave you I'm afraid." Daniel looked at Melissa standing up to take his final gulp of Murphys. He replaced his glass on the bar, "Bye then." He spoke to Marlena across the bar.

"Yeah, bye." She smiled.

"See you then." Melissa looked up at him.

"Bye." Daniel replied staring at her intently. If only she could read those dark meaningful eyes. She knew he was trying to convey something, but hey, knowing her luck it was just trapped wind!

"Bye." Melissa said again smiling bashfully. He moved toward the door and turned back and smiled broadly at her as he quietly pushed the door open and left. Melissa watched the lights of his large van come on and him leave the car park. Only when she could no longer see the red glow of his tail lights did she turn back to face the bar and an awaiting Marlena.

"Look at you. He's gone now, you can't stop smiling." Marlena laughed at her, all flushed and happy.

"Oh, I didn't realise that I was." Melissa said flushing a deeper shade of red and smiling more broadly.

"Looks like you need to get some mistletoe. Oh and a hair-do!"

"Don't I know it!" Melissa said laughing as she put a hand up to her wild hair in despair.

More than a week passed and everywhere Melissa went she looked out for mistletoe. Normally at this time of year it was coming at you out of every shop doorway but this year, the only time that she had ever really wanted some and it was harder to track down than rocking-horse shit. Melissa was getting desperate and desperate times call for desperate measures.

Friday night Melissa nervously paced around the pub trying to complete her evening jobs as she waited for those headlights to appear signifying the arrival of 'her man'. At ten minutes to six he arrived. It felt as though she had been waiting for an eternity and now that the moment had arrived her heart pounded and her breathing became all erratic. "Oh my God, I'm going to have a heart attack! Just when I finally have him in my sights!" Melissa panicked talking to herself as she loitered by the inner door giving him chance to get out of his van. Slowly Melissa opened the door and stood just behind the still bolted outer door until she could make out his outline through the wobbly external door's glass. Just as she undid the bolt and opened the door so a second set of car lights appeared. "No!" Melissa yelled under her breath and determined that her plan was not to be ruined now, worried that her heart would not take that level of stress again Melissa looked out to see the new arrival was only the part-time chef arrived half an hour early – God really did have it in for her!

"Hello, am I too early?" Daniel said standing awkwardly outside realising that Melissa was acting slightly strangely.

"No, perfect timing to check out my new Christmas decorations in fact."

Daniel looked slightly bewildered, "Well come on in then!" Melissa instructed beckoning him in wildly with the hand that wasn't holding onto the door. He walked awkwardly past Melissa, trying to avoid contact as there was not really enough room for them both to pass freely in the small confines of the foyer and looked quizzically at her raising his eyebrows further still as she popped her head out around the door in the direction of the chef's car and then closed the door on him. Daniel stood only a short distance from her and Melissa was glad of the dim lighting which would have hidden her embarrassment a little bit at least. Melissa took a deep breath, "Right, well as you know I have been unable to find any mistletoe so I thought to myself what else is festive and seasonal. So obviously sprouts came to mind." Melissa watched Daniel as he took in all this information, his face was a picture of confusion but he was smiling slightly as he watched Melissa gabbling nervously on in front of him.

"Well come and see then!" Melissa beckoned him the short distance over to her. Daniel stepped forward towards her and as Melissa looked up she realised you could not actually see now that their bodies were blocking out the extra light coming through the stained glass window from the main door. "Oh, well they are up there I promise! Put your hand up there." Melissa told him pointing up above their heads, gutted that he could not see her invention properly. Daniel reached up as he was instructed and tentatively felt about above their heads.

"Uggghh, sprouts!" He said as his fingers made contact with the cold vegetables strung together on a piece of garden wire with a tinsel bow tied at the top of the grape styled bunch.

"Good huh!?" Melissa excitedly questioned.

"Uh, yes. Ummm great." Daniel said unsure of what madness this was and he moved to pull open the interior door clearly expecting her to follow.

"Where are you going?" Melissa panicked as he seemed to be getting away, "Come back you are s'posed to be helping me to test them out!" Daniel still looked confused and stayed holding onto the door handle, probably for security.

"Come on! I want my Christmas kiss!" Melissa demanded frustration making her abnormally brave.

"Oh right!" Daniel smiled broadly as realisation finally struck and he let go of the door and moved towards her. They stood beneath the sprouts and even once their eyes had adjusted to the lack of light from the closed doors there was still not enough light to see so much as an outline of each other's bodies. For all that though they stepped together and Daniel reached out his hands and gently rested them just above where Melissa's waist ought to have been - happily Melissa noticed, just above a belly roll. They both leaned in together and with perfect timing and not so much as a nose clash, which Melissa would be clumsy enough to achieve even if she could see – they kissed. It was long and lingering and it was the most gentle and loving kiss that Melissa had ever received. Not a passionate embrace as she had dreamt of, but better because of the obvious feeling behind it. Melissa's knees went weak as they broke away and laughed gently; Melissa at least because of the relief of it finally happening.

"Well, sprouts certainly work OK for me!" Melissa said embarrassment always making her fill a quiet moment.

"Yes, I would have to agree."

Melissa went around the other side of the bar and pulled his pint, sneaking glances at him, too embarrassed to look at him straight on.

"Phew, I'm all embarrassed now." Melissa said flapping her hand in front of her face in an effort to cool down her burning face. Daniel looked up at her and laughed deeply. "Well that was an interesting start to the evening. I rather like that hallway now." He grinned wickedly at her.

Melissa looked up through her lashes coyly at him. "Well I have to say I have always detested sprouts before now. I think you have just changed my opinion!" Melissa passed across his pint and placed it in front of him watching him sitting there grinning and flushed as he watched the head on his Murphys settle.

Confident and very relieved that she had done a good thing and that it was well received by him, Melissa plucked up the courage to continue with her current train of thought, they both looked up upon hearing the door rattle and creak its opening warning from outside and in walked the chef.

"Hello then!" he called out happily looking at them both and grinning as he passed on through to the kitchen. "Tea I assume Melissa?" He hollered from the kitchen doorway.

"Yes please." Melissa called back smiling inanely still.

"Of course you do realise that I have been here for five years now and six Christmases, so I figure that you owe me at least another eleven kisses." Daniel smiled but looked confused.

"Six Christmases and six birthdays, oh and that does not include New Years Day or Eve, oh, or your birthdays!"

"Well perhaps this is going to be a good Christmas after all." He grinned wickedly at Melissa who flushed an even deeper red thrilled to have achieved such a great response from him.

The following Tuesday Daniel arrived early again. He had been in twice in between whiles but once was with a friend and on the other occasion he arrived later than another couple even though it was still well before six o'clock; Melissa had had a good mind to tell them they were closed. Melissa's heart raced again upon seeing his lights and went through and unbolted the door. Daniel was several yards away from the door when Melissa opened it and he smiled widely upon seeing her.

"Now are you here early cuz you're thirsty or because you wanted to compare sprouts versus mistletoe?"

"Ohhh, well since you ask…" Melissa's heart lurched in her chest hoping with all her heart he would not make some excuse and leave them both too embarrassed to speak ever again. "Both seem like a good idea." Melissa let the door close behind him and he stood underneath the bunch of sprouts waiting expectantly. Melissa flushed and moved in towards him, heart pounding nervously. Again they moved in together in an exact replication of the first kiss. Intense and heady but still slightly restrained. Again they giggled nervously as they pulled apart and Melissa stepped back under the mistletoe just a couple feet away from where the sprouts were hanging. Daniel followed her lead and as he stepped forward into the lighter end of the foyer Melissa could see he was grinning all over his face and his eyes were sparkling and lit up with an intensity that only lust could have caused. They kissed again giggling affectionately.

"Hmmmm, I like them both. It would be a hard decision to choose between them." He chuckled as they both walked through to the bar. Melissa could not stop herself smiling. She could feel her cheeks aflame and felt more alive than ever before.

Two customers chose that moment to walk in leaving the two of them to snatch sneaky glances at one another as Melissa tried to make normal conversation with all three of them. Daniel too mirrored the same expression and colouring. Melissa wondered how something so simple could have such a profound affect on a person and why hadn't she thought of it years ago – and more concerning to her now…where would it all lead?

CHAPTER TWENTY-SEVEN
FREAKY PHONE CALLS

It was Christmas Eve day. There were quite a few groups of office workers who had come out for a boozy lunch together before finishing for the holiday period and so there was quite a happy feel to the pub and lots of high spirited laughter interspersed with the banging of gaudily patterned crackers with naff gifts inside. Marlena had the day off and had gone over to her horrible auntie's (poisoned dwarf) house as they did their celebrating the day before 'normal people' Melissa had teased her. Kathy had become too uncomfortable with her large baby bump hindering her carrying trays of food and as she was beginning to suffer with hideously swollen ankles she had done her final weeks work the previous week which left Charlie cooking with Rick and Bruno flapping about serving the ever increasing numbers of customers which was becoming ever so amusing to watch as with every additional drink the normally straightest of guys thought it only right to flirt mercilessly with Bruno and one even pinched his bottom. Melissa grinned at Bruno as he rushed past her with a steaming bowl of chips and he scowled back at her and told her off for laughing. The ironic thing was that if he had so much as hinted at a flirtation with any of the men concerned they would have hit the roof and been mortally offended but somehow on their terms it was all right. The telephone started to ring after finishing serving a large group of rowdy regulars who were on their annual Christmas Eve pub crawl where they made it their mission to have one pint in every pub within a radius of five miles of The Olde Flagon. Needless to say Melissa did not actually see them again once they had begun, a fact that she was actually quite relieved about.

"Good afternoon The Olde Flagon." Melissa said cheerfully as she watched two of the lads in front of her start waltzing each other around in front of the bar.

"Ummm, yes, hello…is that Melissa?"

"Why, who's that?" Melissa laughed at the strange male voice, as one of the two dancers snatched up one of the long stemmed lilies from the arrangement that Bruno had put together and held it between his teeth as their waltz became a tango.

"Ummm, you don't know me but I advertised in The Fosseway Magazine and they told me to come in and see you but I was phoning to say that I am not able to make it over Christmas because my Mother's had a fall and I have to look after her for a while….Hello, are you still there?" Melissa could feel herself growing red. What a pillock, she thought to herself. Don't men listen ever? She had a good mind to tell him that he was supposed to just visit the pub to see if there was naturally chemistry between them and not phone up! He had completely missed the whole point and misunderstood the message that Charlie had left for him. He also sounded a lot older than forty-five! Melissa instantly took a dislike to him with his painfully slowly spoken and broad Somerset accent.

"Ummm what, yes. I'm still here, but who are you?" Melissa said acting dumb but was getting quite flustered. With that Charlie appeared at the doorway of the bar and spotting Melissa's panic stricken face asked her if everything was all right. Melissa covered the mouth piece of the telephone and whispered to her that it was one of the Fosseway men. Incredulously Charlie stared at her and then grabbed the phone from Melissa's hand positioning it so that they could both hear what was being said.

"….Yeah so I got chickens to feed and the dog to walk, but normally after that I can come out, but not obviously with my

Mam bad like she is. I don't stay out late mind, no later than nine, so when shall we go out?"

"Look, I am really sorry but I don't know who you are but I think someone has been having you on. I have to go its busy here, sorry bye." Melissa said putting the phone hastily back into its charging pod and quickly checking around the bar to make sure that no one was waiting for a drink.

"Forty-five my ass! He sounded more like sixty! He sounded awful. Whatever possessed him to ring? Charlie managed to ask in between giggles.

"Yes very bloody funny! I bet he wears a brown hand knitted cardigan that his mother made and with his dinner spilt down it and that his trousers are held up with bailer twine"

"Oh yes! Those really high waisted trousers like 'The Old Gits' wear that finish just beneath their chests and have a belt around the middle and then the braces clipped to the waist band a foot away from their belt."

"Ugggh yes, you're probably right!" Just then the telephone starting ringing again.

"Melissa is that you?"

"It's him!" Melissa hissed. Charlie burst out laughing.

"Please go out with me Melissa; I know you are single and lonely. Its not nice being lonely, say you'll come."

"I don't know what all this is about but I don't think it is very funny so stop ringing." Melissa said sharply and banged the handset down on the counter.

"Meany!" Charlie laughed at her through the tears streaming down her face.

"Piss off! The guy couldn't take a hint there was no point being nice and he must be odd else someone else would have answered his advert and so he could pester them. We are probably the only ones."

"He'll probably turn up here next and become your stalker!" Charlie said just rubbing the back of her hand across her cheek in time to catch a tear before it ran under her chin.

Melissa laughed and felt guilty about how mean she had been to the poor man on Christmas Eve, he was right; she did know what it felt like to be lonely. "Yeah, you're right, it was mean. I'll ring him back, do that one four seven one thingy for me to get his number a minute." Melissa asked Charlie as she went across to the other bar to serve an approaching customer.

"You're going to go out with him?" Charlie's jaw dropped in disbelief.

"No, ring him and apologise, suggest he rings up one of the women advertising in The Fosseway."

With that Melissa started pouring drinks for her customer and just as Charlie was about to dial the numbers into the telephone it started ringing.

"Right yes, certainly. No worries, see you then, thanks, Merry Christmas!" Charlie said.

"Who was that?"

"Just another two to add to the Perringchief's table tonight." Charlie said amending the booking in the diary. "You realise that means that we can't do one four seven one now though. You have just ruined that poor man's Christmas. You evil girl." Charlie laughed. Melissa felt dreadful.

CHAPTER TWENTY-EIGHT
FRANCE

It had been exactly three weeks since the second sprout kissing incident and Melissa had not seen her man at all in all that time. One or two weeks with not having seen him over the Christmas period would have been disappointing but not altogether unforgivable due to family commitments and the whole general socialising that Christmas necessitated. Three weeks however was an inconceivably hideous length of time to stay away from the pub particularly when one was as insecure as Melissa and indeed after she had kissed him on two separate occasions.

"Oh God!" Melissa yelled heavenwards whilst she tugged her hands roughly through her mass of curls pulling her hair so hard in frustration that she achieved a temporary facelift for the benefit of anybody watching. "I've frightened him away haven't I?"

"Don't be daft. He's a man. He kissed you back. Twice!" Marlena said matter-of-factly as she ferociously mashed her glowing cigarette out into the large grey ashtray on the bar. Immediately she picked up her Polish packet of cigarettes, which were merely in a thick paper package rather than a box, and she deftly squeezed and pushed at the wrapper until a single cigarette popped half way out of the packet. Without even momentarily removing her harsh stare from the job in hand, she snatched the exposed end between her scarlet painted lips and lit it from her

Zippo lighter which was adorned with a Chinese style dragon, a large tattoo of which she also had on her right arm. In one fluid motion she had lit the cigarette and expertly flicked the lid down with a loud metallic clunk as she exhaled a massive smoke cloud. Melissa was leant against the bar in between the beer pumps, with her elbows resting on it and her head resting in her hands. Without having seen any warning car lights or having heard any car doors closing, the outside door was pushed open and the silhouette of someone appeared in the stained glass of the internal door. Melissa stood up from her leaning position in time to see Daniel walk into the pub. Instantly her face glowed red, which for once was rather fortuitous as it made the red palm prints Melissa had achieved resting her head in her hands for so long not quite as obvious.

"Well hello! Long time no see!" Melissa yelled enthusiastically.

"Yes…tell me about it! I had to go unexpectedly to France."

"France?" Was the best reply Melissa could come up with.

"Yes, my wife's father died so we had to go out there and deal with the arrangements."

"Oh that's very sad. Was he there for Christmas then?" Melissa asked relaxing slightly as she at least now had an explanation for his absence which did not involve her.

"No, not on holiday, he lived there. He is, sorry, was French."

"Oh I didn't know. Is your wife French then too?" Melissa asked, her curiosity getting the better of her.

"Yes. She only moved here when she went to university at Oxford. She has been here for more than twenty years but has not lost her French accent at all."

"Is her mother still in France then?" Melissa asked as Marlena quietly sat at the end of the bar watching the two of them.

"Well right now no, she came back with us. Her Mum is understandably in a bit of a state and so when we said we had to go back to England she could not bear to be left and so we brought her with us. They live in a bloody great castle which Max, my father-in-law, had bought as a building project for his retirement so I can see that she would not want to be knocking around there all on her own at a time like this."

"A castle, how fabulous. Has it got turrets and a moat?" Melissa asked having already visualised a romantic French Chateau in the styling of the Walt Disney fairy tale castle.

"What are turrets?" Marlena asked breaking her silent vigil and looking puzzled.

"You know, pointy hat like things on the top of towers." Melissa said whilst looking at her to see if she understood. Seeing that she was looking a bit confused Melissa doodled a rough sketch of one on one of the order pads on the bar.

"Ohhh, thanks. Carry on."

"Turrets yes, a moat no." Daniel laughed at Marlena. "It has certainly had one but currently it is being used as an orchard. There is a bridge to get into the castle main entrance but at the moment it is held up with scaffolding and not at all obvious what you are travelling over. It's nothing that can't be reinstated though. It will be wonderful when it is completed."

"How old was he?" Melissa asked.

"Only 61, its no age." Daniel said sadly.

"How did he die?" Marlena asked billowing out a cloud of smoke.

"Heart attack." Daniel replied turning to face her, "At least it was quick." Daniel said thoughtfully staring into his glass.

"So do you think your mother-in-law will move here permanently?" Melissa asked as she topped up the head on his pint.

"Well actually no. Right now we are just in the process of sorting out our affairs so that we can go back and live out there." Daniel said as he watched Melissa's face take on a sad confused expression.

Attempting to regain her pre-shock composure Melissa, who had significantly paled at this news clumsily knocked the side of her booted foot against the empty bottle bin behind the bar which caused all the bottles to chink and clunk noisily against one another.

"Forever?" Melissa asked appalled.

"Well, the initial plan is for me to take over where Max left off on the building and renovating. I am taking several of my boys to do a load of the work as there is plenty of room for them all to live in."

"But you have your business here; you surely cannot just drop everything and go?" Melissa frantically interrupted.

"Well France is not that far away." Daniel smiled at her reaction. "There are regular flights and I have managers who will run everything in my absence. Plus of course there is always the telephone." Daniel mockingly answered touched by her obvious concern.

"Wow, who'd have thought it?" Melissa said, "Do you speak French?"

"Not much but I can shout loud and wave my hands about." Daniel laughed as he gesticulated wildly to emphasise his point.

"So when are you going?" Melissa asked, too sad to even smile at his attempt to be funny.

"The end of January or first week of February. Can I have another please?" Daniel waved his empty glass from side to side trying to catch Melissa's attention as she was staring miserably into space.

"Oh, yes, sorry. Miles away."

As Melissa was pouring his second pint the door creaked open and in walked a rather red faced man who before Melissa could welcome spotted Daniel and enthusiastically approached him, hand outstretched to greet him.

"Daniel Palmer! How the devil are you? Long time no see! Have you had a good Christmas? Let me buy you a drink!" The red faced man enthused as he energetically pumped his arm up and down not letting it go for a moment.

Melissa watched on with interest as Daniel watched his arm being moved against its will and smiled at the man but without the genuine voltage required to light up his eyes as would normally happen.

Melissa said hello to the strange new-comer as he took off his blue anorak to reveal a terrible 'Christmas Wally Jumper' as they were referred to by Melissa and her brothers, which generally meant that they were a thoughtless gift, bought at the last moment, never large enough so that there was always a three inch gap of exposed flesh between the cuff and the wearer's hand and so tight that every belly roll and sign of 'man breastage' was cleverly accentuated by the explosion of colours which were generally making up a wild pattern that only the blind would truly appreciate. In addition to the Christmas Wally Jumper were the compulsory silly socks with reindeer or Santa or Bart Simpson on them and of course the musical Christmas tie. Red faced man conformed on all counts as he went over to the table in front of the bar and hung his anorak over the back of one of the chairs exposing brightly coloured flashes of his socks as he moved where his trousers were not quite long enough and setting off the monotone diddly diddly diddly electronic sound of 'Santa Claus is Coming to Town' when he stood upright and stepped back to the bar. Melissa. Daniel and Marlena watched him as he chuckled, pulled up his jumper to show the cause of the irritating sound which exposed a large white expanse of shirt covered belly with a black tie with Santa on a sleigh pulled by reindeers fronted by Rudolph whose red nose was flashing on and off completely out of time with the music.

"Good huh? The kids bought it for me." Red faced man waved his belly around to them all holding the bottom of the jumper up to his chest to make sure that none of them had missed out and then when he was satisfied that they had he pulled the jumper back down setting the tie off again with the movement.

Melissa caught both Daniel's and Marlena's eye in turn whose faces at what they were all seeing were a picture.

"A pint of 6X for me love, in a handle if you please, and I'll get Daniel there his one."

"Thanks Derek, that's very good of you. Your family well?" Daniel asked before drinking a very large amount of his pint. Melissa's eyebrows rose as she saw the quantity he had drunk and immediately recognised the signs that Marlena and she were about to be abandoned with a nutter.

"They are all right as nine-pence! And we have another one due in May."

"Another?" Daniel almost spat out his beer. "Have you not figured out what is causing that yet?" Daniel laughed at him good naturedly.

"You would have thought we might have by now. This'll be it though, the last one. Dillis is getting a bit old for it all now – she'll be fifty next year and ten is a nice round number."

"Ten! You have ten children?" Marlena, herself an only-child, asked unable to contain her surprise.

"Yes Lovely. We is very fertile we is. That's an interesting Somerset accent you got there then. Where you from then? Are you one of them illegal immigrants I hear so much about on the telly?"

"If she was Derek she would hardly tell you she was would she?" Daniel pointed out chuckling.

"Naaah, I s'pose not. Beautiful eyes you got there Lovely… and my…aren't you a big lass?" Derek said as he watched Marlena remove herself from her stool and take her ashtray to empty in the bin behind the bar.

Melissa watched Edward watching Marlena in an admiring, albeit unnerving manner and the tip of his tongue shot out and wet his lips in a most repulsive way. Marlena stared at him unsmiling.

"Goodbye Daniel, hopefully see you before you go." Marlena turned her attention towards Daniel who had finished his drink in record breaking time and was just replacing his empty froth coated glass on the bar.

"Yes, I'll be in. Byeee for now. Derek, nice to catch up with you again, can I put one in for you?"

"Oh, you aren't going are you Daniel? Stay and have another won't you?" Derek asked nudging him with his elbow as though that would some how persuade him.

"Sorry Derek, I'd love to but I really must dash. Dinner will be in the dog and all that!"

"Oh yes, fair play. Can't upset the little women-folk now can we!" Call in when you are passing; I have a lovely new machine."

"Yes, thank you. I'll do that. Nice seeing you. Give my regards to the family. Bye Mel. Byeee" Daniel said having edged backwards towards the door desperate to escape.

"Byeeee!" Melissa called out with much more enthusiasm than she was feeling. Not only was her man leaving but she was now left having to put up with this odd man who had rushed him to finish his beer he was so awful. Bloody marvellous!

"So you must be new then?"

"You come here a lot do you?" Melissa asked dumbfounded to being accused of being new having been working there for more than four years.

"Oh yes, Bruno and I are like this." He said crossing his second finger over the first to display their obvious closeness.

"Oh, right. And which one are you? The one on the top or the bottom?" Melissa asked wickedly as she mimicked the crossed fingers that he had just displayed to her and gestured towards them to highlight her point. Marlena, who had come back into the bar at this point to get a pen, chuckled at Melissa and at the confusion showing on Derek's face.

Melissa picked up Daniel's empty glass and placed it upside down in the white glass washer basket that was resting on the draining board behind the bar. As she watched the creamy foam slowly slide down the sides of the glass she sadly wondered how many more times she would get to see him.

"I say! I say!....." Derek's words broke through her thoughts and she swung back around to face him. "Is Michael cooking this evening?"

"Ummmm no. He's in America." Melissa said smugly watching his face for a reaction having already pretended to be a good acquaintance and a regular customer.

"Oh that's nice; he works so hard, the break will do him the power of good!"

"It's not a break, he lives there."

"Why?"

"Why not?" Melissa said evasively, protective of a certain level of privacy that her former and currant bosses were entitled in the gold fish bowl that was owning a pub; observed by all whether invited to or not. And just wishing he would leave her to her misery.

"What about the pub, who's doing the cooking?"

"Bruno and Charlie, the same as they have for the last year or so."

"Well bugger me. I didn't know that. Probably gone off to find himself a good woman. It's about time they both did. Not right two nice men like that having to take care of themselves with no woman to comfort them." Melissa nearly choked on her tea at that little gem; but it never ceased to amaze her how naïve people were about Bruno and Michael.

"You are probably right." Melissa agreed watching Derek as he struggled to put his anorak back on as one of the sleeves had tangled itself in the struggle.

"Would you like a hand with that?" Melissa asked watching him go even redder in the face with his exertions and his repeated setting off of that damned Christmas tie. By the time Melissa had got around the front of the bar Derek had given up struggling and had removed that arm from attempting to get it in the sleeve and untangled it.

"Oh no, that's OK lovely. I've got it sorted now. Give my regards to Bruno. Tell him Derek from the Traction Engine Club. Nice to meet you. Byeeeee."

'Bloody traction engines – I might have known.' Melissa thought to herself. The Traction Engine Club people met in the function room of the pub once a month throughout the winter. Melissa had had the misfortune one evening to do the bar for one of their meetings and had told Bruno that if she ever had to do it again he would die a very hideous and premature death at her hands. The whole evening had been spent watching a slide show of old traction engines, the highlight at the end being a black and white video recording of an old steam train with a special interview with a railway worker discussing the contents of his lunch box – with no *double entendre* intended – more was the pity; he had kippers in it.

"Has the weirdo gone?" Marlena asked sticking her head inquisitively around the corner of the bar to look.

"Yes. Didn't you like his outfit then?"

"Yes, excellent. Especially the musical tie. Did no one tell him that Christmas is over?"

"Clearly not. More importantly he frightened 'my man' away!" Melissa said pouting exaggeratedly at Marlena.

"Your man is going anyway. Looks like you ought to have taken that Fosseway man up on his offer after all. Well assuming that his Mother is better and that he has got time for you after all his animals but before his 9pm bed time!"

"Yes, thanks for that! I'll just slit my wrists now!"

"Someone will turn up."

"Yes but I don't want any one else." Melissa said pathetically. "I don't even remember the last time that a nice looking man came in here even!"

"That's cuz there are none around here as you told me on my first night here."

"You say that and yet you sleep with them all anyway you old Slapper!"

"So anyway…" Marlena ignored the comment, "You will just have to be less fussy or become a Lesbian."

"Pass me the knife will you."

CHAPTER TWENTY-NINE
DASH THE DOG AND BUTT HEAD

Time passed slowly for Melissa through the quiet winter months and April was a welcome change from the dreariness and depression she had suffered at the absence of 'her man'. It was a sunny Thursday morning when Melissa was rudely awakened by the shrill ringing of the home telephone. Upon first being disturbed from her sleep Melissa scowled and pulled the duvet up over her head in an effort to block out the nasty row. Several rings later and there was still no obvious sound of anyone else moving around in the house; Melissa considered not answering the 'phone but then a guilty conscience got the better of her in case it was an emergency, and so with much grumping and groaning with no one to hear but the dogs, Melissa flung the duvet off of her and swung her legs carefully over the oblivious sleeping Sydney lying in his usual position along the length of the bed, and forced herself up and out. Grabbing her dressing gown off the handle of the ski-machine 'en route' out of her bedroom, she had managed to get one arm in as the rest of the dressing gown trailed along the floor behind her at the point of reaching the telephone on the landing when it stopped ringing.

"BLOODY MARVELLOUS! WAKE ME UP AND DON'T EVEN GIVE A PERSON SUFFICIENT TIME TO GET TO THE PHONE! YEAH, THANKS THEN!" Melissa shouted at the 'phone on the wall as she eventually untangled the belt of her dressing gown, which had caught up around the dragging sleeve, and thrust her arm in punctuating her exclamations with the final angry knotting of the belt. Rubbing her bleary eyes Melissa went into the bathroom and without bothering to close the door behind her, plonked herself down on the toilet for a wee. At the exact moment that the trickle turned into the customary gush the telephone started ringing again.

"YES, OF COURSE! WAKE ME UP, HANG UP THE SECOND I GET THERE THEN WAIT TILL I AM MID WEE AND RING AGAIN! DON'T YOU KNOW IT'S MY DAY OFF?" Melissa shouted at the telephone visible from her seat on the loo as she waited for the flow to stop. Naturally it was one of those ridiculously long wees and Melissa rocked her head impatiently from side to side in time with the rhythm of the stream of urine making contact with the toilet bowl as she had her had poised ready with a hurriedly snatched wadge of toilet paper, which of course unravelled from the dispensing holder a good two feet longer than she had actually expected due to the force with which she had bad temperedly wrenched at it. Finally she had finished and quickly splashed water over her hands as a token gesture towards hand washing and then wiping the excess wet off of her hands into the side of her dressing gown she just managed to snatch the telephone from the wall on what must have been its final ring.

"HELLO!" Melissa shouted crossly.

"Mel, is that you?"

"Lucy? Are you all right?" Melissa's voice changed to that of concern.

"Thank God! Where have you been? I have been ringing for ages."

"Yes I know, you woke me up and then when I got there you hung up so I went for a pee and you rang during that too so you had to wait till I'd finished."

"I bet you washed you hands didn't you?" Lucy teased.

"Shut up! What do you want?"

"I'm at Bath hospital. Tom's broken his back."

"Oh God. Lucy I'm so sorry." Melissa felt the blood drain from her face as a thousand thoughts dashed around about Tom who had always been a fan of extreme sports now unable to move. "How did it happen?"

"We were visiting Mum and Dad and he had gone mountain biking with a group of the lads. He hit a tree root and was catapulted over the handlebars and landed right on his back."

"Can he move at all?"

"Well for now he is lying on his back and he must not move anything for six weeks."

"What you mean he can move?" Melissa interrupted.

"Well yes. Unbelievably he has cracked vertebrae but they said if he keeps still for six weeks he might be lucky and be all right. Fortunately his spinal cord has not been affected."

"Oh, thank God for that. How lucky is he?" Melissa breathed a sigh of relief. Melissa took down all the details of the ward name and visiting times, more specifically she wrote on her hand with her Mum's eyeliner pencil she had grabbed from the bathroom, and promised to visit. She replaced the telephone handset onto its wall mounting and then went back into the bathroom and returned the now rather blunt pencil to the glass shelf she had removed it from. She stood in front of the basin and washed her hands more thoroughly (well the palms of them at least so as not to wipe off the message) and whilst doing so rubbed at a few toothpaste marks on the side of the basin with the nail brush. It never ceased to amaze Melissa at how there were always splatters of toothpaste all over the mirror. Some vain person in the household must stand there watching their reflection as they cleaned their teeth in order to spread it so far and wide. Melissa took a sponge from the cupboard under the sink and ran it over the large mirror's surface paying special attention to the tiny splatters. When she had finished her make-shift cleaning effort the mirror was a mass of misty smears and even though she actually thought it was a preferable way to view her reflection at this time of the day she did not think her Mum would be of the same opinion. In the absence of a suitable cloth or cleaning materials (without making the effort of going downstairs – and if she did that she would probably not come back up) Melissa scrunched up the hand towel and made a cleaning pad from that which after much elbow grease gave a surprisingly pleasing result, which was a lot more than could be said for her reflection which she scowled at and rubbed a large black mascara smudge away from under her right eye. Then in order to ease her curiosity Melissa brushed her teeth with her normal amount of enthusiasm and upon returning her purple handled toothbrush to the blue mug with the big fat fish on it with protruding lips on it (which Michael, Bruno's ex had bought for Melissa on one of his day's out because he said the pouty face reminded him of her when she was in a strop) she looked up and checked the mirror. Happily there was not a single splatter. Smiling to herself and bundling up the towel and dropping it into the laundry basket as she passed by, Melissa made her way downstairs closely followed by Sydney who had met her at her bedroom doorway and who she reached out to pat on the head as she went to go down stairs in front of him. Downstairs Melissa stuck her head around the lounge door where Jasper was sound asleep precariously balanced along the length of the windowsill with the tip of his bright pink tongue hanging out of his mouth.

"OYYY DOPEY!" Melissa called out. Jasper visibly jumped at the rude interruption to his sleep and swung his head around to the direction the noise had come from. "Some guard dog you are!" Upon coming to his senses and spotting Melissa he flung himself off the windowsill and leapt towards her happily snapping playfully at her dressing gown belt as Sydney simultaneously barged at him to be first through the door to the kitchen and growled a warning to Jasper to behave himself.

"What have you done with Mummy then?" Melissa asked Jasper as he jumped up and put his paws on Melissa's belly as he surreptitiously used it as a sneaky method to check out the contents of the kitchen units for steal-able food. As soon as Jasper heard the word 'Mummy' he was off headed towards the front door in search of her.

"Stupid dog! I said where is she?" Melissa told Jasper as he rushed back to the kitchen presumably to see if Melissa's Mum had sneaked in past him and on not finding her there he turned tail and zoomed back off to the hallway excitedly barking having convinced himself that Mum was hiding there somewhere. Melissa filled up the shiny chrome jug kettle and spotted a note weighed down under the tea bag's lively looking pot with farm yard animal characters depicted running around on it.

'GONE TO WESTON – BACK IN TIME TO FEED THE DOGS – SEE YOU LATER' was what the paper had written on it with a big smiley face drawn at the bottom with only one tooth. Sydney barked standing at the back door with his hot breath misting up the area around his snout on the glass as he pushed his nose against it.

"You funny dog!" Melissa laughed as she unlocked the door and was barged out of the way by the return of Jasper making sure he was not missing out on something trying to push pass Sydney for which he received more rumbling growls for his trouble. When she propped the door open with the 'hedge-frog' boot cleaner (a variation on the hedgehog ones that just made no sense at all) an imprint of Sydney's nostrils were still visible on the glass of the door. Melissa checked around for any obvious signs of spiders and then fairly happy that there were none about she pulled her dressing gown tightly around her and sat down on the concrete step. Sydney and Jasper happily wandered around the garden, Sydney stopping to raise his nose in the air and sniff at something from time to time but predominantly following Jasper around to wee over the top of every one of his wees which Jasper would then go back and wee on top of and then Syd would go back and wee on top of that again until both of them cocked their legs and nothing actually came out. Melissa could not help but smile at their antics as she pondered poor Tom's predicament and wondered what she could do to cheer him up. Hearing the kettle click off Melissa got up and brushed off the backside of her dressing gown and went off to make a mug of tea. On her way back through to the kitchen she spotted the Argos catalogue amongst the general debris, including a 'state of the arc' car stereo, a large plastic ride-on kids train in pieces and several piles of mail waiting to be opened all on one end of the large pine dining room table.

Followed by two dogs keen to see if Melissa had any food with her, all three made their way into the lounge. Melissa plonked herself down on the sage green leather sofa, wincing as the back of her bare legs made contact with the cold hide surface. She put the heavy and thick Argos catalogue down on the seat next to her and placed her favourite massive emerald green mug of tea down on the small wooden coffee table and in her haste slopped some of the steaming tea over the brim. Scowling at her clumsiness she picked up the mug and wiped the bottom of it on her dressing gown which left a large wet distorted ring shape where she had dragged it along the fluffy material. Then trying unsuccessfully to mop of the spill on the table with the TV guide magazine; which just sent tea squelching out of the end of the cover page to run into several small rivulets into the table's carved edge. Melissa eventually resorted to unfolding the rolled up cuff on the overly long dressing gown sleeve and having picked up the magazine and flicked the excess tea off it, unceremoniously mopped up the remainder with the turned down cuff. As Melissa replaced the mug on the table once more she glanced up and caught Sydney's one eyed glare.

"I know, but don't look at me like that." Melissa said at what she took as Sydney's disapproving look. "It could have been worse...I could have used the cushion!" Melissa said as she waved the cushion hanging over the arm of the adjacent chair at him to emphasise her point. Both dogs stayed sitting hopefully in front of her as she directed the TV remote at the TV and flicked through the channels. Looking away from the screen her attention was drawn to the long thick stream of drool hanging precariously from the side of Jasper's funny jaggedy edged pink and black lips, which all dogs fascinated her by having. (Why did they need serrations? She wondered often).

"Stop dribbling you horrible dog!" Melissa told Jasper as the drool stream grew longer and swung from side to side, every panty breath exaggerating the velocity of the swing.

"Here you are." Melissa delved into her pocket and fished about until she brought out several broken pieces of Rich Tea biscuit and passed some first to Sydney and then to Jasper. Jasper was just about to take the biscuit from Melissa's outstretched hand when there was a metallic rattle and dragging sound from the front of the house outside of the lounge window. The noise made Jasper move his head abruptly around in order to prepare to defend his home from would-be attackers and upon seeing the window cleaner appear at the window dragging his ladder along the gravel until it was upright and leaning against the wall, Jasper turned tail and rushed over and flung himself at the sofa and up and onto the windowsill where he began to bark – not however before the violent movement of his head caused the swinging drool to disconnect from his mouth and plummet to Melissa's utter disgust, right into the centre of her steaming tea where it sunk below the surface but not before the force of the impact caused a tidal wave and spilled more tea out over the edge of the mug.

"JAAAAASSSSSPPPPEEEEEERRRRR! YOU HORRIBLE DOG! LOOK WHAT YOU HAVE DONE – AND STOP BARK-ING AND GET OFF THE FURNITURE!" Melissa got up and took her mug off to the kitchen raising her free hand in acknowledge-ment to the window cleaner who was busy laughing at the dopey dog doing his best to appear ferocious but not quite pulling it off. Having an audience this time Melissa went and got a cloth to clean up the table with and then she went back out and poured her mug's contents down the sink, appalled as she watched the egg-white like drool slither out last and do one lap of the plug hole before finally undulating over the edge and into the dark depths of the awaiting drain beneath. Melissa squeezed an exces-sively large amount of lemon scented (or flavoured as she always referred to it) washing-up liquid all over the inside of the mug before barraging it with a deluge of steaming hot water from the mixer tap above it. Once the sink was a foaming mass of glistening bubbles, crackling as they burst, Melissa switched off the tap and re-boiled the kettle and made a second lot of tea in her second favourite mug which depicted a cartoon scene of afternoon tea with a mountain of cakes on a pale yellow background. By the time Melissa had returned to the lounge Jasper had vanished but she could hear him following the window cleaner from room to room about the house. Sydney had given up waiting for more food and Melissa could hear him snoring gently from behind his hidey-hole which he always went to for refuge in between the nearly touching arms of the two-seater sofa and the armchair at the opposite end of the lounge to where she finally sat back down to begin her perusal of the Argos catalogue for present inspiration for Tom. Melissa being Melissa, naturally began her search in the toy section because she made it a rule never to give anyone a dull and useful present, and it was not very long before she found exactly what she was looking for.

Melissa arrived at the hospital dead on two o'clock. Miraculously she managed to drive straight into a vacant parking space and even more miraculously was stopped by a woman in a car on her way to the parking meter who wound down her window and gave her her ticket which still had loads of time left on because the poor woman had not had the right change to buy a lesser value one. Melissa found the ward fairly easily, even though she had to climb four flights of stairs to get to it; no mean feat with the amount of things she was carrying. As Melissa was just asking at the nurses station where she might find Tom and Lucy it seemed that they had spotted her first.

"Oh my God! Whatever have you got there?" Lucy called over, chuckling at the sight of her friend. Beaming smiles at one another Melissa flushed red at all the attention from everyone checking out the newcomer into the eight bedded ward. Tom was lying flat on his back grinning broadly at her as she quickly went over to his bed.

"Thanks for coming Melly, it means a lot." Tom reached out a hand to touch Melissa to emphasise the point.

"Yeah thanks Mel, welcome to living hell."

"Yeah, I'm sure it must have been a terrible couple of days."

"No! I mean this ward! All they do is snore and fart. You'll see." Lucy rolled her eyes at Melissa.

"Shut up yer whinging you. I want my presents!"

"Tommmm!" Lucy chastised as Melissa laughed and tied the large silver 'get well soon' helium balloon to the foot of his bed.

"Right...well as Lucy said you are not allowed to move for six weeks I figured that you would need some kind of entertainment." Melissa said as she pulled the first package out of her bag. "Oh, and you'll need these too." She said delving into the bag again and producing a packet of batteries.

"Lucy what is it?" Tom asked as Lucy had snatched the box away and out of his sight. Lucy was laughing as she said "You're bloody mad you are! The nurses are going to kill us!"

"What? What is it?" Tom demanded. Lucy waved the picture side of the box at Tom who read out loud 'Dash The Dog?' Who the fuck's he when he's at home?"

"Tom! Language!" Lucy admonished.

"Oh sorry. Who 'on earth' is Dash The Dog?" Tom reiterated in his best BBC news announcer voice. Meanwhile Lucy had wasted no time getting the toy out of the box and installing the batteries.

"He's brilliant! Look Tom!" Lucy put Dash The Dog the little cream and brown plastic toy on the floor by the side of Tom's bed so that he did not have to move to see it and set it going.

"Oh wow Mel! That is great!" Tom exclaimed as Lucy sent the remote controlled dog with his rigid brown plastic flappy ears and springy wagging tail zooming around and around in the space between the beds.

"Let me have a go then, it's my present!" Tom whined reaching out his hand for the very simple remote control. After twenty minutes or so all the nurses on duty had come over and watched Dash being sent all over the ward and the whole ward seemed cheered up by their antics especially when one of the nurses up turned an empty cardboard-looking bed pan over Dash in an effort to stop Tom whizzing it around her feet and to all of their surprise the little toy was powerful enough to drive on unhindered.

"Hey Shaun! Do you need the loo?" Tom shouted over to the lad the same kind of age as himself who was covered in plaster casts in the bed diagonally opposite.

"Well now that you mention it...." Shaun laughed as Tom sent the bed pan covered dog zooming over to him.

"Bloody excellent prez Mel! I love it!" Tom laughed as he watched Lucy snatch the dog up as it passed near her feet and switched it off on the control on its belly.

"Ohhhhhhhhhhh!" Tom whined mimicking a child as he looked pitifully at Lucy who had put the toy on the cabinet out of his reach.

"Meany!" Melissa laughed at Lucy. "Not to worry Tom, this one is fun too!" Lucy unwrapped the next gift for Tom within view this time.

"Ohhh no! You'll get us barred!" Lucy laughed shutting her eyes for an overly long time whilst she absorbed the latest gift and slowly raising them heavenward in dread afterwards.

"What? What is it? Show me!" Tom begged swiping at Lucy who kept moving it away just out of his reach.

"It's called Butt Head, look I'll show you." Melissa told Tom as she reached into the wrapper and removed a fluorescent orange and yellow Velcro covered hat and pulled it tightly down over her wild curly hair and tied it under her chin. All of the people who could see her were most bemused at the weird thing she was now wearing, not least Lucy, Tom and Shaun whose tears were running down their faces with laughter, especially after Melissa took another hat the same over for Shaun to put on and he nearly knocked himself unconscious clouting himself on the head momentarily forgetting one of his plaster casts was there. Melissa, when she could stop herself laughing long enough, tied Shaun's hat on for him and he sat there propped up on his pillows grinning like the Cheshire cat with his ridiculous hat on.

Again the commotion had attracted the nurse's attention and they all stood and watched as Tom was given three Velcro covered balls to throw at Shaun and Melissa who alternated between trying to help them reach their targets on their heads and ducking out of the way. By now the whole ward were in hysterics and all the patients and visitors were cheering every time a ball made contact. Melissa was holding onto her stomach where it was aching so much from all the laughter but eventually the most sensible of all the nurses could see that the novelty of such entertainment was beginning to wear off for some of the patients and so she came over and told them to stop for today.

Tom wiped the tears from his eyes still unable to stop laughing at the ridiculous spectacle Melissa made in the hat and some more laughter erupted when she removed the hat and it had left red marks all down the side of her face and under her chin where the strings had been.

"Oh Mel, you have really made my day, thank you ever so much." Tom said seriously.

Melissa flushed red at the compliment and said "There is one other present." And she rummaged around in the bag some more.

"Wicked! That really has made my day!" Tom's eyes lit up even more, if it was possible as Melissa plonked on his bed the most enormous bag of pick and mix sweeties bursting out the top; over the edge trailed jewel coloured jelly snakes and long liquorish lengths. As he excitedly plunged his hand in and rooted about he sent an avalanche of cola bottles and pink and white chocolate mice overflowing onto the bed.

"So what's the food like then? Is it as terrible as everyone makes out?" Melissa asked Tom, smiling as he lined up a row of different sweets along his chest.

"Well it's OK, there's just not enough of it. No snacks or supper. No munchies for watching the telly with."

"Yeah, he's been here less than 48 hours and I've been sent out to MacDonald's twice and to fetch pizza!" Lucy said rolling her eyes upwards again to emphasise her hassles.

"You are allowed that stuff in here?" Melissa asked disbelievingly, "But it's all really smelly!"

"Yep, I Know but Tom sweet talked the nurses and they said that as long as they get offered the chance to put their orders in when I go – and every one else on the ward for that matter – then it's fine!"

Melissa shook her head in wonderment at what they were managing to get away with and as she was just checking her watch the distant rattling of approaching crockery signalled the arrival of their evening meal.

"Well, I had best leave you to it." Melissa picked up her handbag and rummaged around for her car keys.

"Ohhhh don't go Melly, we're having kebabs later." Tom beseeched her. Melissa laughed and bent down to kiss him good bye.

"Thanks for coming Mel."

"Yeah, thanks for offering me a sweetie – NOT!" Melissa laughed at him.

"Yes good point, how about you share them around a bit?" Lucy lunged for the bag.

"Piss off! They're mine! When you break your back and are suffering terribly then Mel might get you some!"

"Cheerio!" Melissa grinned at them squabbling and walked off waving goodbye to Shaun who had looked up from struggling to turn the pages of a car magazine she had spotted on his table earlier. He went to wave with his plaster covered arm and winced with pain the split second he tried to do so. Melissa smiled to herself and as she passed by the nurses station one of the older nurses came across to her.

"Well you have certainly livened this place up. We could do with a few more visitors like you." Melissa blushed furiously.

"Yeah, sorry about the noise."

"Nonsense! It was just what Tom needed. You take care now." And she smiled warmly at Melissa and walked over to the nearest patient.

Melissa made her way back to the car with a spring in her step and a smile that she could not remove from her face. They had all had a great afternoon and clearly she had not lost her touch at buying presents.

The next day when Melissa had just sat down with her lunch on a tray on her lap having just finished the lunchtime shift at the pub the telephone rang. As was habit, Melissa's Mum answered the 'phone and listening to her chatting happily away for ten minutes or so Melissa was most surprised to find out that the call was actually for her.

"Melissa! It's Lucy for you. Come on, she hasn't got all day!"

Melissa lost for words at the surreal scene her Mum had created where she was somehow responsible for keeping someone waiting that she never even knew was there on account of the fact that her Mum had been yakking away to her for so long that time had become an issue, took the 'phone from her Mum's outstretched hand and sat down on the bottom of the stairs.

"Hi Lucy! Sorry about that, I had no idea it was you!"

"Hey no worries mate, I love chatting to your Mum; she's so funny." Lucy chuckled.

"Everything OK there with Tom? You haven't been chucked out have you?"

"Naaaaah, nothing like that. We're all fine. Thanks so much for yesterday, it was just what he needed; he was so down until you showed up. Anyway you made a good impression. Shaun really likes you. Doesn't shut up asking about you and when you're coming back. He's single – well, just waiting for his divorce to come through. He has his own home. His own teeth. No car at the moment cuz he smashed his up, that's how come he's in here, but he seems like a top bloke. What do you reckon?"

Melissa was a bit lost for words. She hadn't given it a thought even. Lucy interrupted her thoughts, "Come in and see Tom again and we'll tell him to take you to the café to get us some chocolate or something and you can get to know each other a bit over a cup of tea."

"Lucy he's crippled! How on earth is he s'posed to go any-where? He nearly knocked himself unconscious yesterday with his own plaster cast."

"Don't be so negative. He is actually fairly mobile; he's been to the café a few times with his family so it's no problem. Go on. Say you'll give him a go. You know what they say…..if you take your earrings out for too long the holes grow over…so come on Mel before you forget what sex is and won't leave your smelly house full of cats!"

"I" Melissa answered through her smile "Will not be smelly old spinster cat lady….you know I prefer dogs!"

"Yeah, yeah, whatever. Say you'll come visit us again."

"Oh all right. But only to shut you up. I'm not happy about his though."

"YEEEEESSSSS! SHE SAID SHE'LL COME!"

"Who are you shouting to? Where are you?"

"We've got the mobile pay phone they bring round; I'm sat on Tom's bed."

"Shaun's there too isn't he?"

"Ummmm, well, yes. Well the pizza delivery guy has just been."

"You're having them delivered now? Unbelievable! I'll see you soon!"

"Bye Melly, don't be cross. Love you!"

"Love you Melly!" Tom shouted in the background.

"Yeah, bye friend!" Melissa said and replaced the handset in slow motion as she let the conversation she had just had sink in.

"Every thing all right Melly Belly?" Melissa's Father looked concerned.

"Ummmm yeah, I think so. I've got a date."

"Oh lovely. Excellent. Why?"

"Yes it is a wonder." Melissa said and sat back and fiddled with the remains of her lunch on the tray as she retold the conversation, excluding the references to sex, to her bemused Dad and her excited Mum who was whipping the tray away from her and ushering her to go up and get changed as soon as possible.

"Mum, I'm not so desperate that I need to rush off at the whim of any cripple who is enchanted by my sparkling wit and repartee!" Melissa said facetiously.

"You aren't getting any younger Melissa."

"Yes, thanks for that Mum."

"And anyway, what else are you going to do tonight instead? Exactly. Nothing. Go and see your cripple. You don't have to go again if you don't get on. It's just a cup of tea."

"What is this a conspiracy?" Melissa sighed and doing anything for a quiet life went upstairs to get showered and ready for her date.

Melissa drove around the various hospital car parks looking for the ever elusive parking space whilst the butterflies donned their boots and did a tap dance around in her stomach. Finally after fifteen minuets of infuriating laps around the hospital grounds Melissa spotted a doddery old couple headed along a path away from the building. Blocking the road she waited to see where they were headed and after several dirty looks from other frustrated would-be hospital visitors and a couple of loud blasts of car horns, the doddery old couple finally vacated their parking space in an old Austin Maestro with the compulsory crochet covered cushions resting on the rear parcel shelf. This time Melissa was not so lucky with a free parking ticket and indeed when she opened her purse did not have more than fifty pence in change including copper coins which the machine would not even take. By now her cheeks were glowing red with the stress of the pending date and the infuriating inability to park and now she had to decide whether to risk the wheel clamp by putting an insufficient value ticket on her windscreen. She knew that this was really not an option as hospital car parks were famed for their use of the dreaded yellow boot, so instead she rummaged through all the possible hiding places for change dotted about the car. As luck would have it the search turned up all manner of treasures including an old Murray Mint still in its wrapper which she discovered on further investigation was only a little bit sticky and so she shoved it in her mouth and screwed up the sticky wrapper and put it in the ashtray. It was a bit softer than normal but tasted fine. She counted up the coins and she had managed accrue seventy-three more pence. Opening the car door Melissa got out the car and checked all her pockets but to no avail. She then crouched down and ran her fingers tentatively along the carpet underneath the driver's seat and recoiled in horror as her fingers made contact with a green wine gum, until she knew that that was what she had put her hand on. Leaning over the side of the seat Melissa could see something shining up at her from the side of the seatbelt clasp. She reached her hand down and wriggled her fingers about in the confined space and eventually managed to flick the metallic object backwards under her seat to a more accessible position and to discover that her grazed skin was worth it for the twenty pence piece that she retrieved. Melissa had read on the board, on one of her many laps of the car park earlier, that she actually needed a minimum of £1.50. In one last attempt she looked inside the zipped up pocket inside her bag and finding nothing but a mascara and a tiny gold key, which she had no idea what it opened, she in desperation up-turned the whole bag so that it's entire contents spilled out overflowing the passenger seat and into the foot well. Shaking out the now empty bag so that all the bits of fluff and indeed a couple stray bits of popcorn and a hair-band fell out, Melissa then straightened out the lining and began to fill the bag back up. Lucy always referred to Melissa's bag as being the 'TARDIS' for no matter how small the bag whenever she emptied out the contents there always seemed to be a whole suitcase full of contents actually contained within it. Today was no exception and amongst the usual girlie clutter and purse was a tyre pressure gauge, a gold coloured metal screw-in hook that you might use to hang a mug from, and a full-size rubber handled screw-driver with interchangeable heads. Thrilled, Melissa finally glimpsed the answer to her prayers; a tiny taped up paper envelope only two inches wide and an inch high. It had lots of little particles of dark fluff, not dissimilar to that one might find in one's belly button, stuck to the edges and creases in the tape and when she turned the miniature package over in her hand it had her name scrawled across it in her own messy handwriting. Stripping one of the pieces of tape away from the end of the envelope three pound coins dropped out into her lap and the opening exposed the edge of some paper money. Unravelling the rest of the wrapping paper Melissa discovered three ten pound notes and one five. "Thank God for tips and for being untidy enough to lose and forget you had money!" Melissa said out loud as she folded the notes into her purse and then snatched up her bag and with a handful of change went over and bought a ticket. By the time she had displayed the ticket on the driver's door window, Melissa had developed quite a sweat and when she ran the back of her hand along her forehead had to wipe off the wetness accumulated on it in the back of the leg of her jeans. Locking up the car door and activating the alarm Melissa looked around her until she spotted a hospital plan showing where she was. When she found the 'YOU ARE HERE' arrow she was dismayed but not too surprised to discover that she was at just about the farthest point away from the ward that Tom and 'her date' were on. Without the slightest inkling of where she was going (not being able to make any sense of the map with so many lefts and rights between where she was and where she had to go) Melissa just headed for the nearest available door and with some trepidation entered the labyrinth that was the hospital. As soon as she was through the half window half panelled door with the safety glass wire criss crossing through the greeny-blue glass, that hideous hospital disinfectant smell hit her. The never ending corridor stretched out as far as she could see; all pale and dull and artificial strip lights leading off in an orderly uniform row. Melissa trudged through the echoing corridors listening to her footsteps reverberating around and after a couple minutes wished she had brought her roller skates. Eventually she came across the familiar sight of the entrance she had gone in the previous day which she could see out of one of the few windows, and so she decided to head for that instead of following the unhelpful signs which had sent her to everywhere other than where she actually wanted to go.

By now the butterflies' tap dance in her stomach was reaching it's crescendo and so when Melissa passed a door she afterwards registered was a toilet, did a u-turn and went in, barely getting her jeans and 'good luck' knickers emblazoned with 'NAUGHTY' in metallic, sparkly lettering across the front where Melissa had always thought 'FATTY' would have been more appropriate, down towards her knees when she had the most terrible case of the squits. Melissa's face flushed scarlet and she cringed as she panicked that someone might come in; clenching her buttocks and knees together in a vain attempt to reduce the out pour and especially the noise. The already airless, stifling cubicle was now hideously tainted with the warm stench of her stomach's fairly recent contents making Melissa want to retch as she pulled the neck of her t-shirt up over the end of her nose to try and muffle the smell. Even though she was hot and sweaty goose pimples prickled up all over her arms and legs and to her dismay the poo would just not stop coming. Whilst she sat there, head nearly touching her knees where she was doubled up with pain, Melissa heard the sound of the outside toilet door opening and the chattering of women's voices suddenly come to an abrupt halt and then retreat back out of the door, undoubtedly deterred by the vile odour. Flushing to the core with embarrassment Melissa decided enough was enough and bundling up an enormous amount of rough off-white paper from the large metal dispenser to her right she proceeded to wipe her bottom so that she could leave. To Melissa's disgust it seemed to have gotten everywhere and it took several more serious bundles of the coarse, harsh paper before she was finally brave enough to pull up her not so lucky 'lucky pants'. Seeing the toilet paper was almost up to the brim she swiftly pulled the flush and hoped to God that it was man enough for the job as she did up her jeans. Two more flushes later Melissa finally left the cubicle and thoroughly washed her hands. Her face reflected in the large mirror above the old fashioned sink was nothing short of gruesome. She had pale almost yellow-white rings around her eyes, nose and mouth and very flushed red cheeks.

"Yep….thanks for that then God. Excellent look for a first date!" Melissa raised her eyes heavenward to tell off the deity whom it only suited her to believe in when things were going badly. Melissa went back into the cubicle she had just vacated and pulled out a long length of the toilet roll which she then folded up into a big wadge and wetted it until it was sodden underneath the cold tap. Patting away the excess water she held it to her burning forehead and then dabbed it over her face. She re-moistened the tissue to cool it back down again and repeated the process until she glanced up and saw the trail of white blobs that she had managed to deposit all over her face where the tissue had disintegrated. "BLOODY MARVELLOUS! YOU MUST REALLY HATE ME!" Melissa accused the heavens once more as she dropped the soggy tissue into the bin which landed at the bottom with a loud splat as the weight of it made the bin liner make contact with the metal bin's base. Melissa ran her hands through her hair, from a habit of stress and not to style it, as she looked ghastly. There was nothing for it, she was just going to have to go and sit down some where for a bit until she cooled off. She was just heading out the door when she slowed up to turn and double check that she hadn't left her keys or anything behind when her stomach did another flip and Melissa rushed back into the toilet cubicle and had to go again. 'Oh, this is just bloody ridiculous' she thought to herself. 'It's just a cup of tea with the guy and he is completely crippled. There is no way I can get so nervous over something so trivial. I didn't even fancy him enough to register what he looked like. Not to mention if I don't get off here soon I'm going to end up with a big red loo shaped ring on my ass and I'm getting old, my skin is not as elastic and resilient as it once was – I might be scarred for life!'

One hour, two bottles of mineral water and two more foiled attempts to leave the toilet on other visits later, Melissa eventually climbed up the final flight of steps to the ward. The flowery green and yellow curtain was pulled securely around Tom's bed and as she smiled at the nurse at a nearby bed she could hear Lucy's dulcet tones from behind the curtains.

"You smelly pig! Why must you fart every single time you go for a wee?"

"It's a bloke thing, you don't understand. We get pressure build up; it has to come out!" Tom's voice could be heard mocking her.

"Pressure release my ass……"

"No, *my* ass actually!"

"Oh yes very funny. Ha bloody ha!"

The nurse appeared at Melissa's side and discretely popped her head through the curtains.

"Are you all finished there Tom?" The nurse asked as she vanished inside the curtained area and returned shortly afterwards with a funny shaped bottle thing with a cloth covering the top which left a strong smell of man's urine in her wake. Melissa screwed up her nose in distaste having had quite enough of toilet related smells for one day and watched as the curtains moving wildly about before Lucy appeared out of where they joined up and began to pull them back along their tracks to reveal Tom lying in the exact position that he had been in when she had left yesterday.

"Mel! Am I glad to see you!" He has been driving me mad!"

"I *am* here you know!"

"Yes, *AND INJURED!*" Lucy whined at him.

"Hi guys." Melissa laughed, "Me thinks you may have been playing the injured card a bit too much today then Tom?" Melissa smiled and waved at Shaun who was sitting on the edge of his bed.

"A bit!" Oh Lucy read me this, fetch me that, scratch me here, buy me that! And any slight hesitation or refusal on my part and all I get is '*but I'm injured!*'"

"Well I am! I…"

"Yeah I know….could have died."

"Lucy you are a hard woman." Melissa smiled at her.

"Don't you bloody start! You are supposed to be on my side!"

Just then an enormous ripple of farts echoed out from some-where across the ward. Tom laughed and Melissa with an incred-ulous expression on her face looked at Lucy.

"Yeah, I know. Men are filthy pigs! Last night it was like being in front of a surreal orchestra bombarded with farts of varying pitches and tones for hours on end. No 'excuse me's' no nothing"

"So are you coming for that cup of tea then Mel?" Shaun had managed to clunk, scrape and slide his way over to them and was grinning happily to see her. He was wearing a hideously bright green t-shirt but due to his well sun tanned face he, unlike most, carried off the colour quite well. He had spiky almost black hair which looked clean and shiny, although that was probably just the styling product, and he had startling green eyes which twin-kled nicely as he smiled. He had a large plaster cast covering from where his shorts stopped down to the end of his toes. Only the very end of his brown toes were visible from out the end of the hole in the cast. In his right hand Shaun leant on a hospital issue, metal crutch with a grey plastic handle and a rubber stop-per on the end. With her black suede cowboy boots on, which no matter the fashion Melissa could not be parted from, Shaun was about the same height as her which Melissa calculated with her approximately two inch heels must make him about five feet ten inches tall. All in all things were looking up Melissa thought to herself.

"Umm yes, great, I'll follow you." Lucy watched as Melissa slowly followed Shaun who was hobbling quite proficiently across the shiny grey tiled floor.

"Have fun you two, and if you can't be good be careful!" Tom bellowed out all down the ward at which Shaun picked up his crutch to wave at him and nearly fell with his efforts. Lucy and Tom exchanged smiles as Melissa and Shaun disappeared off through the lift doors. Melissa's face having taken on a slightly worried expression as the lift doors closed.

Remarkably, or so Melissa thought, they got on very well. Shaun was funny and all the ladies working in the cafeteria, along with several obvious patients in varying states of disrepair all chatted with him and commented on how much better he was getting about. Melissa carried the tray and they sat down by the nearest table to the open doors where Melissa was glad of the refreshing breeze blowing gently in and making the paper napkins flutter about. They both ate large sugary jam dough-nuts, Melissa decided that she may as well now that she was completely empty, and they both laughed as he managed to bite into one side of his doughnut and send jam jettisoning out of the opposite side and onto his plaster cast. Melissa had no such difficulties as anyone who has eaten as many doughnuts as her knows you always check around the outside first to find the hole where the jam was injected – not so much as to avoid mess but waste!

Shaun told Melissa about the horrific car crash he was in which squished his car into an unidentifiable shape and was surprised to hear him admit that he had been driving like a lunatic at the time, but nonetheless made a mental note never to get in a car with him if they went out in the future. Melissa found him easy to talk to, he did not come across as particularly gifted in the brains department from a few strange things that he said but Melissa dismissed this as nerves and although being the same age as herself, which was a good ten years younger than the men she was usually interested in, she decided that in the absence of any other offers, in particular now that 'her man' had buggered off to France, that when he asked if she would go out with him one night next week once he had been discharged from hospital, that she would accept.

When they got up to the ward there was a definite atmosphere between Lucy and Tom. Specifically Tom was refusing to speak to Lucy.

"Problem?" Melissa asked giving them both a lollipop each that she had bought in the café and looking from one to the other. Lucy started laughing sitting in the ugly blue plastic covered wingback chair next to the bed which creaked and squeaked as she moved about unwrapping her bright red lollipop.

"Do you want me to unwrap yours for you Tommy?" Lucy asked him in her conversing with a baby voice.

"Piss off!"

"Ooooooooooh that's not very nice." Lucy said having removed her lolly from her mouth to speak. Bemused Melissa and Shaun watched and waited for an indicator as to what had gone on when all of a sudden Melissa spotted Tom's feet. Barely controlling her laughter Melissa looked at Lucy who saw where Melissa had been looking. Lucy started shaking uncontrollably as she fought to contain her laughter with her lips firmly pursed around her lollipop stick.

"Niiiiicccceeee nails Tom. Possibly a bit dark for your skin tone don't you think?" Melissa said finally guffawing loudly joined by Lucy who by now had tears pouring down her face.

"What? What is it mate?" Shaun asked, completely clueless to the source of their mirth.

"That BITCH painted my toenails when I was asleep!" More guffaws burst forth from the two girls. Shaun struggled on his crutch and good leg to shuffle nearer to the foot of Tom's bed for a better look.

"Oh yes. Nice one Lucy!" He laughed as Tom obligingly wriggled his scarlet painted toes for him to see.

"It's not bloody funny! I'm telling my Mum on you!" Tom could keep a straight face himself no longer.

"You had better ask her to bring in some nail varnish remover when she comes visiting then." Lucy said as she looked into the mirror of a small black compact whilst dabbing at the mascara runs her laughter had caused down her cheeks with a tissue from her bag. In mock sulk Tom shoved his lollipop in his mouth and turned his head away from Lucy.

"Well again, it's been lovely but I really have to go. Play nice together you two and Shaun thanks for the tea and doughnut, Lucy will give you my number." Melissa leant over and kissed Shaun on the cheek, just like she might kiss her Gran she later thought, and then bent down to kiss Tom who turned his head around at the last second to plant a kiss firmly on Melissa's lips.

"Mmmmmm, that tasted of strawberry thanks. See you all soon. Byeee Lucy, enjoy tonight's orchestral rendition – I'll be thinking of you."

"Bye Melly – BITCH!" Lucy laughed at her and mocked sniffing and wringing out her sodden tissue from wiping her eyes at her sorrow from Melissa's departure.

CHAPTER THIRTY
BIRTHDAY

It was a Monday night. Melissa did not usually work on Mondays but Bruno had been invited out to dinner and so Melissa had agreed to swap shifts with him. Ironically it was 'her man's' birthday today; Melissa knew this because it was the same date as her Granddad's and because she was obsessed with him and hung off his every word. Bruno had left the pub in good spirits, in both senses of the words and had looked very smart in his undoubtedly hand tailored French-navy blue suit and marshmallow pink shirt with a dark subtly patterned blue silk tie which beautifully complimented both colours. He was looking particularly handsome having spent several days throughout the last fortnight on the beaches he loved to escape to at the slightest sign of sun, getting beautifully baked to the most perfect shade of caramel. Laughing and skipping about in his excitement and to make Melissa laugh at his antics he had eventually left at about 7.30pm.

"What have you forgotten?" Melissa called out laughing with her back to the door as she heard the door hinge creaking open.

"What this place looks like for a start!" An unexpected voice replied.

Melissa swung around and knocked over a nearly empty bottle of Green Chartreuse that she had been dusting around.

"Hello. How are you Mel?" Daniel remained just inside the doorway dressed from head to toe in black which had a very striking effect on him and made him appear darker and more mysterious than normal. All that was missing was the box of Milk Tray Melissa thought to herself swooning. Melissa clumsily groped about trying to right the knocked over bottle whose lime green contents were still sloshing about inside from the spill and simultaneously straighten her top which in her enthusiasm momentarily revealed the scalloped edging of her black lace bra.

"Hi. Long time no see. How are you? You look amazing!" Melissa gushed unable to stop herself in her excitement and nerves.

Daniel laughed at the flattery and flushed slightly and sat down on his usual stool.

"Nice to see you kept my stool for me."

Melissa laughed and waved an empty pint glass at him.

"Hell yes! Haven't you started pouring it yet?" Daniel teased. Melissa watched as the Murphys slowly filled the glass; black and white swirling around as one and then gradually separating out to leave one perfect and aesthetically pleasing looking pint of stout.

"If you only knew how much I have been looking forwards to this!" Daniel said momentarily holding it up to admire it then swallowing several large gulps. Pulling the glass away and wiping the frothy moustache away from his upper lip Melissa watched him completely mesmerised as he returned the glass down to the bar for his traditional top up. As Melissa expertly flicked the handle of the Murphys pump down to top up the glass Daniel drew out a handful of change from his pocket and began to extract the Euros from the 'real' money. Hearing the sound of his change chinking together Melissa looked up from studying the filling glass and said "And you can put that away, I'm buying you this one." Daniel's brow furrowed slightly with confusion. "Happy Birthday!" Melissa said putting the refilled glass down on the bar in front of him. Daniel beamed at her, his white teeth accentuated by his sun-bronzed skin. 'Was it only her that didn't have a suntan around here?' she wondered to herself.

"How on earth did you know it was my birthday?" Daniel asked clearly quite flabbergasted.

"You told me ages ago and as it is the same date as my Grand-dad's it was easy to remember." Melissa flushed at the look he was giving her.

"Well thank you. That's very good of you." He said and took another swig from his glass.

"Oh, I nearly forgot…" Melissa said as she hurried out of the bar and out of the front door of the pub towards her car. After deactivating her alarm Melissa quickly unlocked the passenger side door and reached into the glove compartment where she retrieved a very small box wrapped up in metallic blue and silver striped paper. Without bothering to reset the alarm in her haste Melissa hurried back into the pub lest Daniel might run away, and went back round to the safe protection of the bar. Daniel had watched her every movement with a very confused look upon his face.

"Another?" Melissa asked him as he replaced his empty glass down on the bar staring curiously at her.

"Do bears shit in the woods?" Daniel said at which Melissa laughed removing the glass with froth still clinging to the sides and putting it onto the draining board.

"It's nothing much but I saw this and thought of you. I've had it in the car for ages." Melissa glowed red with embarrassment at the intensity of his stare as she placed the tiny box down in front of him and at how embarrassed he seemed to be and reluctant to take it. She busied herself pouring his second pint and died a little inside at the realisation that he was not keen to have anything from her.

"I only got it because I knew how much you wanted one." Melissa tried desperately to win him over. 'Was he cross?' she wondered as she tried to read his severe face.

Daniel slowly reached for the box and carefully examined it from every angle turning it over and over in his tanned hands.

After what Melissa considered to be an excruciatingly long period of time Daniel eventually undid the tape from one end and slid out the plain white cardboard box from within the wrapper. The box was the exact size of an OXO cube box, a fact that Melissa knew because it was an OXO cube box that she had carefully covered in thick white paper so that it did not look quite so naff. Again Daniel examined the little box from all directions and eventually he opened up the flap at the end and emptied out the silver toy car it contained onto his palm.

"It's an Aston Martin…" Melissa gabbled "….I would have bought you a real one only I thought you might have been too proud to accept it."

Daniel held it nearer to his face for closer inspection and then smiling he placed it down on the bar and gently pushed it along.

"It's great. Thank you. And no…I don't think that I would have been too proud to accept a real one next time you feel the urge to make a purchase." Daniel smiled at her genuinely and then drank from his fresh pint.

Melissa laughed and exhaled a huge breath that she had not been aware that she had been holding and watched as he ran the toy backwards and forwards along a small section of bar in between them.

"So anyway, what brings you back? Have you had enough of France?" Melissa asked hopefully.

"Still loads to do out there I'm afraid, but the lads are working really hard considering the heat at the moment. I had to come back to sign some paperwork and check up on the other businesses. You know what they say about while the cat's away…."

"Absolutely, human nature to skive when the boss is not around, that is why I intend to have an easy night tonight; Bruno has gone out."

Whilst Daniel was taking another drink from his glass the door creaked open and a youngish man that Melissa had not seen before held it open whilst with much clattering and banging of crutch on flagstone and plaster cast knocking against the wooden cladding in the foyer, in hobbled Shaun grinning inanely at Melissa as he finally made it through the door and the stranger let it close behind him.

"All right then babe?" Shaun called out excitedly. Melissa's jaw dropped as she watched Daniel turn his dark gaze onto Shaun bedecked in a bright orange t-shirt and bad taste Hawaiian style patterned shorts making his way precariously over to the bar stool at the bar the opposite end to him. Melissa cringed; 'BABE' was like something out of a low budget American TV series.

"Pleased to see me then Babe? I thought I would surprise you seeing as how I got discharged early. Tom and Lucy told me where to find you; they said to say hello by the way. Oh and this is my best mate Mike…Mike this is Melissa."

"Hello Melissa." Mike stepped up to the bar and offered his hand over for her to shake. Mike appeared to be fairly normal and Melissa suspected that he probably spent a lot of time in the local library, collected stamps and was partial to wearing anoraks and frequenting train stations. Melissa had felt the colour drain from her face particularly as she saw an odd expression briefly cross Daniel's face as he concentrated on looking at the bottom of his pint while he swiftly finished off the contents. Melissa's face fell as she could see that he was, as indeed was she, unimpressed by the new company.

"Right I'll be off. Thanks for this." Daniel gestured with his hand clasped firmly around the present and put his lips together to form a sad looking smile which did not reach his eyes as Melissa knew it normally did. Melissa sadly watched him leave and her shoulders physically slumped in dismay as he did not do his customary backwards glance upon going through the door.

"So I bet I was the last person you though would turn up tonight." Shaun grinned at her as he spilt one of the lagers that Mike had ordered for them both over the leg of his hideously garish shorts.

"Yeah, you're not wrong there." Melissa answered wishing he would just piss off and die. Daniel's arrival and indeed departure had made Melissa look at Shaun through fresh eyes and considering him to be the cause of Daniel leaving and particularly on his birthday made Melissa only have feelings of contempt for him right now. However unrealistic her crush on Daniel, he had been in to see her and now she did not know when she might actually get to see him again.

Shaun continued chattering on and Melissa tuned him out so that he was merely background noise; a minor disturbance.

"Byeee then Melissa, nice to have met you." Mike said as he put his empty glass down in front of her and carefully mopped up a small spill with the corner of the beer mat and then meticulously replaced it and lined up its edge to be exactly parallel to the bar. Melissa came back to earth with a thump.

"Yes, right, byeeee!"

Mike turned and raised a hand at the door as he left.

"And then there were two." Shaun said chuckling quietly.

"He's coming back for you later is he?" Melissa asked slightly puzzled.

"Naaaa, I said you'd drop me off home. You don't mind do you?"

Melissa stared at him in disbelief. 'First you call me 'BABE' then you frighten 'my man' away and now you expect me to put up with you for the rest of the night then be some sort of glorified taxi!' Melissa thought to herself and wondered why it was that she could never voice these feelings of truth – be it all nasty – when she needed to.

"Nice of you to bother asking." Melissa said sullenly.

"Ha, yeah well I knew you wouldn't mind."

'Shows how much you know then!' Melissa thought sulkily and prepared herself for a tedious night.

What seemed like days later after the rigmarole of actually getting Shaun and his crutch and plaster casts ensconced safely in the car; well safely was not strictly accurate on account of Melissa's patience having run so thin that she ended up forcing him into the seat by closing the door against his leg. Naturally she apologised to him but muttered to herself all the way around the car to her seat about the fact that that was not all she'd like to shut in the car door. Twenty minutes later just grunting yes and uh huh from time to time in case he cared, which Melissa was beginning to doubt, suspecting that he was actually rather too fond of his own voice, they pulled in to 'Chaz Court'.

"Surely you know where 'Chaz Court' is?" he said as Melissa asked him to repeat the name three times because the way he said it, it came out as 'Chazcourt' and she assumed it was some sort of foreign name until he referred to it by it's actual title of 'Charlton Court' and then she realised that he was actually a bigger dick-head than she had given him credit for.

Melissa hurriedly got out of the car and waited for him to untangle his limbs and casts and get out, and waited and waited and waited. The nine pints he had consumed throughout the course of the very long evening, probably in some deluded attempt to impress her, had begun to take effect upon contact with the outside air. Where as before he was a stumbling, clumsy cripple, now he was a very pissed, stumbling clumsy, wreaking of lager and a definite hint of 'l'eau d'armpit' cripple.

"Give us a hand Mel – I'm stuck!" Shaun beseeched her.

Melissa who had been standing impatiently next to the open car door with her arms folded across her chest and her right foot tapping irritably at him, bent down slightly and peered in at him. He had some how managed to get his plaster cast covered arm stuck under his good leg which in turn was jammed against the bad leg, resting on top of the end of the metal crutch.

"Oh for God's sake!" Melissa muttered louder this time and reached in to begin to start untangling him.

"Ohhhh, don't be cross with me Melly." He whined as he watched her trying to make some order out of his position. Melissa did not answer him and roughly moved him about until she was able to heave him half out of the car resting some of his weight on his crutch.

"Right, after three I'm going to heave you out, but you have to help cuz you're much too heavy for me."

"OK Melly. I love you." Shaun said as his head flopped to one side and he closed his eyes.

"OYYYY BLOODY WAKE UP!"

"Uhhhh, what…..no need to shout." Shaun opened his eyes and pursed his lips together into an exaggerated pout.

"Right, after three…..one….two….three…" Melissa pulled at him from under his armpits, the last place she actually wanted to put her hands but due to his injuries the only suitable place left. Shaun's nearly dead weight lifted up about four inches and then the end of the crutch skidded out from underneath him and he slumped heavily back into his seat pulling a helpless Melissa sprawling down on top of him.

"Weeeeeelllll Melissa….you're very forward…..you only had to ask…" Shaun said grinning lasciviously as she hurriedly extracted herself from about his person.

Fiercely glaring, barely managing to contain the smoke and flames from billowing out of her nostrils, Melissa rubbed her moist hands off disgustedly on the sides of her trousers and Melissa stepped backwards away from the car and indignantly straightening her clothing whilst Shaun resting his head back against the head rest fought to keep his eyes open. Melissa looked at him and tears of frustration appeared in her eyes. 'I will not cry!' She told herself crossly as she watched him fighting consciousness slouched in front of her. 'And to think I nearly went out with you, you pissed tosser!' she thought to herself as a tiny bit of drool began to escape from his mouth.

"OYYY PISS HEAD!" She bellowed at him angrily. "GET OUT MY SODDING CAR!"

Shaun's eyes fluttered up and he grinned up stupidly at her causing her to grab at her hair in frustration. It was no use; she was going to have to try the same manoeuvre again. 'Where was a nosey neighbour when you needed one?' Melissa wondered looking around at the windows of the surrounding houses for any signs of life.

"We're going to have to try again." Melissa told him. "You ready?"

"OK Melly." He looked up at her adoringly. Melissa made a weird involuntary snorty sound through her nose of disdain and inserted her hands into his damp armpits again.

"After three…one…"

"Oooooonnnnneeee…" Shaun repeated slurring.

"Two…"

"Twwwwwoooooo…"

"Three!"

"Ttttthhhhhrrrreeeeeee! We have lift off!" Shaun enthused as this time Melissa's increased anger induced adrenalin gave her the strength to lift him clear from the seat to an unsteady resting position; half his weight on his crutch the rest swaying against the swinging car door. '*EVERY ACTION HAS AN EQUAL AND OPPOSITE REACTION*' or so we are taught (or words to that effect) and this Melissa figured was a prime example of this as the force of her efforts caused her staggering backwards, tripping over the edge of the tarmac drive and into the awaiting spiky arms of a massive flowering hydrangea bush. Melissa scrabbled about in panic to remove herself from the bush's clutches, as having three of her least favourite plants in the front garden back at home she was well aware of their popularity with her spider 'friends' and other such creepies. Struggling furiously she eventually righted herself and madly danced about shaking every limb and flapping her jacket about hoping to rid herself of any unwelcome guests. Finally she bent over and shook her hair wildly, only standing up fully after she had made herself giddy, to then proceed patting an exploratory hand over her hair to be doubly sure no creepy crawlies had hopped on for the ride. Shaun had watched all this in utter fascination and had stumbled backwards in his inebriated state against the body of the car and was beginning to slither downwards. Seeing the start of yet another hideous situation Melissa rushed to steady him and stop him sliding down any lower, because she knew that once he got down there she would have absolutely no chance of getting him back up. Catching her breath, having momentarily steadied Shaun, Melissa's eyes dotted frantically about looking for some way out of this nightmare. In her mind's eye Melissa watched Shaun slither down the car's side and slouched in an unconscious heap at which point she would rush back to the car and speed off down the road leaving him to get crawled over all night by escaping creepy crawlies from the hideous Hydrangea only to be woken up the following morning when the neighbours dog cocks a leg on him. Unfortunately, as nice a thought as this was Melissa knew that her conscience would never let her do this and so bending to carefully wrap his cast covered arms across her shoulders, not out of consideration towards him but in case he inadvertently clouted her with it, they stumbled hap-hazardly up the rest of his garden towards what she hoped to God was his front door.

"Where's your key?" Melissa demanded as she propped him against the wall at the side of the glass panelled front door.

"Under the flowerpot." Shaun grinned inanely at her. Melissa looked around her in all directions.

"There aren't any sodding flower pots! Are you sure this is your house?"

"Round the back." Shaun slurred as he attempted to wave his bad arm in the direction of the back garden.

Melissa clamped her eyes hard shut and kept them closed for an inordinately long length of time before she slowly opened them once more and told him in a quiet but menacing voice, spoken directly into his ear "Wait here. Do not move!" Giving him a harsh shove to push him back against the wall he was in danger of swaying away from. Melissa rushed around the side of the house opened and went through a tall arched wrought iron swirl covered black gate which separated the house from the garage and found herself on the patio area of a fairly small garden. To Melissa's dismay however, from what she could make out in the full moon's light, was what it lacked in size it made up for in plant pots; because they were everywhere, all shapes colours and sizes and judging by the hideous and fousty smell all full of geraniums. Instantly Melissa was whisked back in time to her biology lab at school which was over run with the nasty scented plant growing on every available surface; smell not with-standing however she'd give anything to be back there right now. Melissa lifted up the first few pots nearest to the back door but the key was not under any of them. Quickly Melissa went back round to the front of the house to where she was greatly relieved to see that Shaun was still standing – well to a fashion – and was preoccupied with pressing his mouth against the wobbly shaped glass in the door and blowing out his warm breath until he then poked his tongue out and licked a face in the steamed up area. Frowning in disgust (as for the second time in less than an hour he had reminded her, and not in a good way, of her dogs, at what he was running his tongue over) Melissa tried again to locate the key.

"OYYY DICK HEAD! Which pot is the key under?"

"IIIIIIIII'mmmmmmmmmmmmnnnnooooooooottttttt telllllllll-liiiiiinnnnnnnggggg." Shaun sung back at her laughing. Melissa pushed to her limits pushed his head forwards hard so that his tongue that was still stuck out and his nose were squeezed what she hoped was painfully against the glass.

"Ugggghhhhh Meeeeelllll, ttthhhhaaat thurts." Melissa managed to make out.

"Good. Which pot?" Melissa glared at the back of his head still firmly pushing the back of his neck. Shaun spluttered out an indecipherable answer and so Melissa released her hold on him to allow him to speak.

"Don't be nasty to me Mel." Shaun squeaked at her, "It's under the green one by the fence." He flopped back against the wall and stuck his tongue out against the glass once more. Melissa traipsed off back into the garden but although the light from the moon was bright it was not sufficient to illuminate the pots enough to be able to distinguish dark blue from dark green. In the end there was nothing for it but to check underneath all of the pots nearest the fence. Gingerly Melissa grabbed around the belly of the large pots very conscious of the fact that any manner of beasties could be lurking in, around or underneath each one. Her breath quickened partially with the exertion of moving some of the heavier planters but mainly due to her fear sending her pulse racing. Pot after pot she lifted up, one after the other and none of them revealing the hidden key underneath it.

Melissa could feel rivulets of sweat meandering their way down her back; at least she hoped that was what it was particularly as she was still feeling itchy from her tussle with the Hydrangea. Frantically she continued her search but to not avail. In desperation she went over to the back door and raising her hand up to her face mimicking the shape of a visor or peak of a hat, as though this would some how help, Melissa peered in through the large, clear glass panel. Peering through she could make out the neon blue digits on the cooker clock and could see a bowl of half eaten food and one of water which judging by the cat flap in the bottom panel of the door she was leaning against, meant that Shaun owned a cat. With her left hand Melissa was leaning on the silver coloured door handle and inadvertently as she moved her position in order to see if the key was sticking out of the other side of the door lock, the handle squeaked loudly as it moved under the additional weight and before she knew it she was stumbling threw the opening doorway. Preventing herself falling by reaching out for the wall to her right Melissa saw that she left a big muddy hand print. Slamming the door shut behind her Melissa stomped in through the kitchen and followed the dim orangey glow from the street lights toward the front of the house and the door she had left Shaun leaning against. As she approached she spotted a light switch on the wall near the doorway through to what she assumed to be his lounge and as she switched it on Shaun's now illuminated face could be seen still squeezed up unflatteringly against the wobbly glass.

"YOU DOPEY BASTARD! THE BACKDOOR WAS UNLOCKED THE WHOLE TIME!"

"Yeah, I know." Shaun said stumbling through the doorway and knocking over a potted Yucca and causing some of the overly dried out dirt to spill out onto the pale laminate floor. "I never lock it." Shaun giggled at her raising his hand up to his mouth as if to appear remorseful for being naughty.

"SO WHY DID YOU LET ME LOOK FOR THE KEY YOU ROTTEN SHIT!"

"Now, now Mel." Shaun slurred. "Nasty." He reprimanded her. "You asked me where the key was…" He hiccoughed. "….not if the door was locked." More giggling punctuated with more hiccoughs erupted from him.

Melissa could not bring herself to speak she was so cross and watched as half leaning, half stumbling he fell through the door into the lounge and onto the sofa opposite the door. Melissa found the light switch and put it on revealing a very modern room with more of the pale wooden laminate flooring and bright red furniture, cream curtains and a few cream cushions scattered about. Contrary to the big plasma screened TV she had anticipated there was an old fashioned portable television resting on the end of a long beech wood effect coffee table, the result of divorce she presumed. Once she was happy that the telephone on the small nest of tables next to him was working so that he could call for help should he require it, Melissa covered his now loudly snoring body with the cream coloured throw that was over the back of the sofa and went out of the front door closing it gently behind her. Once outside on the doorstep Melissa breathed an enormous sigh of relief and then after first closing the wide open passenger door on the car (slightly concerned about what may have crawled in during her absence) she got in, did up her seat belt and drove off with out a backwards glance. Melissa was paused at the junction to the estate to give way when she saw the road sign with 'Charlton Park' emblazoned on it.

"CHAZ PARK MY ASS – YOU TOSSER!" Melissa shouted out to no one in particular and drove rapidly home.

CHAPTER THIRTY-ONE
HAVE YOU SEEN THE WART
ON HER NOSE?

It was a busy Saturday night. It had been a beautiful sunny day and everyone coming into the pub seemed to be in good spirits. Melissa had to stifle many a laugh as one customer after another had glowing red cheeks and burnt noses and Melissa's favourite the 'panda eyes' where they had obviously been exposed to the sun for some considerable length of time wearing sunglasses so that now they were entering a dark old pub and had to remove them to see showed their large white patches around their eyes in contrast to the reddened skin everywhere else.

In days of old of course, Daniel and Nigel would be on their second or third pint by now, with Nigel still flushed red even though they had finished their game of squash more than an hour before. Melissa wondered what 'her man' was doing now out in France and was startled when Rick, the waiter, who had approached without her noticing started speaking to her only a couple of feet away.

"Earth to Melissa....Christ Mel, you were miles away!" He laughed repeating again the wine order for the newly arrived couple, the lady of which had a vest top sun burn shape revealed for all to see by the misguided choice of the strapless red dress she wore now. Melissa held her hand to her heart as if to prevent it from jumping out from her chest. Rick had really made her jump, she really must stop day-dreaming about Daniel and accept that he was a lost cause and move on.

At 9.30pm the lights of a large vehicle pulled into the car park and drove up near the front door. Melissa glanced at the clock and like clockwork Dennis entered the bar just a moment or so later. He was walking with a stick, which he did not use very often and Melissa secretly suspected that it was actually for extra support when he'd had a few too many later.

"Bloody hell Dennis, no jacket? It must have been hot today!" Melissa smiled at him as he rested the crook shaped handle over the end of the bar next to where he always sat, tucked away in the corner but able to see everything.

"Too hot today Melissa. How are you?" He asked having completely not taken in anything she had said.

"I'M FINE DENNIS THANK YOU, AND YOURSELF? Melissa shouted at him enunciating every word.

"No need to shout young lady I'm not deaf!" He quietly told her and she smiled as a man who had been patiently waiting behind Dennis and caught her eye laughed to himself. Having nodded in the direction of his favourite beer pump (for evenings at least) as his way of ordering, he rooted about in his pocket and slapped a large handful of change down onto the bar which he then deftly managed to stop, but only just, from rolling off the edge from the force. Melissa, as was customary on the occasions that he did this, helped herself to the correct money being careful to use up all the coppers first and then the fives and then the tens and so on up the value of the coins.

"GOT ENOUGH?" He shouted. At which Melissa nodded and smiled. Dennis's deafness could go either way. Some days she had really easy conversations with him where he hardly missed a word; other days he shouted back but was quick to remind you that he wasn't deaf if you shouted back at him or alternatively and tonight unfortunately appeared to be it; he varied between loud and quiet with his hearing aid whistling loudly at varying frequencies dependant on how much he moved his jaw and more distastefully; how much ear wax was clogging it up. (A fact he saw fit to explain to her on numerous occasions).

Dennis had made himself comfortable in his seat and already spilled the first beer of the evening down his cream shirt. Melissa had gone on and served the man who had been waiting and meanwhile handsome Rob and his latest girlfriend, well, one of many, were sitting chain smoking at the opposite end of the bar to Dennis having already exchanged pleasantries; including Dennis telling Rob that smoking would stunt his growth even though he was 6ft 5" at which they all laughed and Dennis loudly coughed and cleared his throat, this time spitting the contents into a screwed up clean white handkerchief he took from his trouser pocket. Melissa frowned and caught Rob's eye and so had to look away whilst she quietly heard Rob fill his girlfriend in on some of his wicked ways.

Melissa carefully kept watch over the bar; from her vantage point she could spy surreptitiously on most of the customers in order to direct the waiting staff to them in case they were not all completely on the ball due to being so busy. Additionally with her 'bat ears' as the regulars had christened them due to her apparently exceptional hearing; she could eaves drop on several different conversations simultaneously, generally her attention was caught by key words like sex, affairs and any other related words and of course whispering. Whispering could even cause her to come out of the bar to find out what was going on. Melissa could defend this act of nosiness on account of the fact that they might be whispering about a problem with their meal – which of course as the manager she needed to know. As Melissa subtly watched everyone she paid particular attention to Dennis who had actually pushed himself forwards leaning on the arms of his wooden chair in order to see just exactly who was in the pub and with whom. Again Melissa noted that the similarities between her and the old man were quite frightening – nosey old git!

"Hey!" Dennis summoned Melissa over to him in what he probably assumed was a stealthy unobtrusive gesture.

"Yes Dennis." Melissa leaned closer to him as he put his hand up to his mouth clearly about to whisper something to her.

"HAVE YOU SEEN THE WART ON HER NOSE?" He shouted nodding the back of his head over in the direction of the lady in question. Melissa, aware that the whole pub, including the poor lady would have been able to hear him attempted to shut him up.

"DENNNISSSS!" She hissed at him putting a finger up to her lips in case he did not hear her.

"IF THAT WAS MY NOSE…" Dennis carried on regardless, "AND I HAD A WART AS LARGE AS THAT ON THE END OF MY NOSE I WOULD HAVE THE DAMNED THING CUT OFF! IT'S BLOODY AWFUL THAT IS!" Dennis nodded at Rob to direct him towards the lady concerned as a deathly hush had fallen over the whole pub and Melissa's face flushed with embarrassment to have been caught up in such an awful and public conversation. Wendy, the lady in question, by now quite understandably red herself from all the undue attention was standing up.

"I have an appointment for it to be removed next week Dennis – if that's OK with you!" She bravely faced him.

"YES GOOD. ABOUT TIME SO I SHOULD THINK!" He responded without a hint of remorse. Wendy turned and had a good look at everyone gauping at her around the pub until they belatedly had the good grace to look away and get on with their individual conversations. Melissa thought to herself how brave Wendy had been and really felt for her as she was such a lovely and attractive lady who clearly made an enormous effort with her appearance and Melissa could not think of a worse place to grow a wart and was mortified on her behalf to have had so much attention brought to it.

"Dennis that was out of order. I think you should buy Wendy a drink!" Melissa sternly told him. "I cannot believe you just said that, don't you think she feels self conscious enough about it already without you publicly humiliating her?"

"WELL IT'S ENORMOUS!" He continued. "SHE COULD BE QUITE ATTRACTIVE IF IT WEREN'T FOR THAT BLOODY GREAT THING.....AND RIGHT ON THE END OF HER NOSE TOO – SHE LOOKS LIKE A WITCH!"

"DENNIS ENOUGH! YOU HEARTLESS OLD BASTARD! NOW OFFER HER A DRINK OR I'LL BAR YOU!" Melissa threatened appalled at his unfeeling behaviour.

"It's OK Melissa, don't worry." Wendy called over to her, obviously more worried about putting her at ease than worrying about Dennis and his cruel tongue.

"YOUNG WENDY.....I'M SORRY IF I HAVE OFFENDED YOU IN ANYWAY...SO CAN I BUY YOU A DRINK?"

"Yes Dennis you can and one for Bob too!" She added, knowing that he was so mean with his money that he would not think to offer her partner one too.

"NOT A PROBLEM.....BUT YOU MUST AGREE WENDY.... IT IS ENORMOUS!" Wendy giggled her infectious laugh absolutely flabbergasted that he could be so rude and tactless and gradually every one else who had been caught up with their banter once more returned to their pre-wart conversations.

CHAPTER THIRTY-TWO
SHOE WEARING BEASTIE

It was Saturday afternoon and Melissa's parents had been on holiday (again) for four days already. It was their 40th wedding anniversary and they had gone over to Alderney on a tiny twelve seater aeroplane held together with parcel tape, according to her Mother's version of their hair-raising journey on the 'phone to her once they had safely landed. Until now Melissa had coped really well with being on her own and the worst thing of all – the laundry, which she had decided grew over night as she slept because she seemed to be spending every waking moment loading or unloading the washing machine and hanging up or bringing in washing. Day four of her parent's absence and Melissa was still hoping for some magic ironing fairy to have miraculously visited and turned the quickly growing pile of screwed up laundry into a nice neat pile or three. Every day that she looked into the lounge where it was all mounting up on the two seater sofa her face dropped a little to see that nothing had changed and indeed she was beginning to not be able to see where washing ended and sofa began. Having watched her Saturday fix of the omnibus edition of Coronation Street and Emmerdale, wasting a good section of the day lying out on the other sofa that was not yet covered with clothes, drinking tea and munching on whatever she could find which took no preparation, Melissa decided that she ought to do something productive with her day (completely managing to ignore the ironing pile throughout all of the soaps and after they were over) and thought that it was long over-due that her bedroom should be mucked out. Taking up a huge mug of tea with her for sustenance for her arduous ordeal ahead she set her favourite pea green mug down beside her bed and looked around in despair now that she was actually there deciding just where to begin. Seeing as the floor was thickly disguised with a carpet of black items of clothing, of which the colour made up a good 90% of her things, Melissa decided that here was a good place to begin and very quickly the mound of clothing became yet another laundry basket full but her room looked half done already. Next Melissa took a big slurp of tea and wiped her already sweating brow with the overly long sleeve of her hooded sports top. Melissa then picked up a large up-turned 'Arkive' file box which she had specifically purchased a set of ten for the purpose of tidying some of her clutter into (a plan that had been fairly successful until she forgot which of the ten boxes had what in and could not find the mate to a shoe she decided she very much wanted to wear – the result was carnage; ten box innards all over the room – again!) As she effortlessly swooped up the empty box her long since forgotten goose pimple armour made an unwelcome re-appearance as sitting under the box in the darkness, presumably having gained entrance through the handle holes, was the most enormous spider that Melissa had ever seen outside of a zoo. As the realisation struck the spider that his hiding place had actually been discovered he seemed to unfold his eight legs in perfect synchronisation thus making him reach his full height of even more monstrous proportions. Then before Melissa had any time to react he scuttled off at break-neck speed through a clear patch of carpet and under the drawer section of the bed. Momentarily frozen to the spot Melissa grabbed at her hair in absolute despair. There was nothing for it – she was going to have to hunt him down otherwise she was not going to be able to ever set foot in the room again. Melissa looked around and spotted a long handled cob webbing brush out on

the landing and thrusting it viciously under the bed ran it violently backwards and forwards on either side of the small black
castors. Feel sick with fear the sweat poured off her as she half
expected the beastie to come scarpering out in her direction.
Some time passed and even though Melissa's eyes shot about as
if watching a tennis match desperate for some sighting she had
no luck. The futility of the situation set in and Melissa knew
that she just had to accept that there was only one thing for it –
the bed had to be looked under and behind even though she
knew that the whole room would have to be moved to make this
possible. Very gingerly Melissa pulled the heavy winter weight
duvet off the bed and then hanging on to the very edge only and
at arms length (in case the spider had already managed to get
onto it) she dragged it roughly out onto the large square landing and with huge effort due to its mass, shook the duvet out
across the landing carpet laying it flat in order to inspect every
bit for her excessively legged friend. Seeing no sign of him that
way up she grabbed at the corner and flipped it up, flinging it
away from her and jumping back to check where she was about
to hold onto was not where he was sitting; every avoiding action
she took making her more and more scared of when the inevitable find occurred. Happy that he was not where she wanted to
hold the duvet to flip it over but not trusting that he had not just
hidden further away, Melissa grabbed and twisted and flicked in
one impressive movement. Fear making her heart rage and the
sweat drip from her hairline and trickle like a spider crawling
down her face. Frantically swiping at the sweat with her sleeve
again just in case the spider has some how got on to her in some
fantastical gymnastic manoeuvre that she has not spotted, she
stepped away and examined the rest of the duvet as she tried to
calm herself down. As it was nearly bed changing day anyway
and more to double check an additional potential hiding place,
Melissa continued her frenzied finger tip flinging about of the
duvet until she had successfully separated 'innerds' from 'out-
terds' and bundled it up next to the overflowing laundry basket.
This whole procedure was then re-enacted for both pillows and

the bottom sheet. Melissa was equally desperate not to have to see the beastie again but also to find it sooner rather than later, worried about how well her blood pressure was coping with the stress levels she had frightened herself up to. 'Death by Spider' she imagined the headlines; A local Rubenesque barmaid died last Saturday after being frightened to death by an extraordinarily large British house spider. Her final words as she gasped her last breaths were "You must find it; it was wearing my best shoes!" She died shortly afterwards and the spider – and the shoes, one assumes, are still at large.

Under the valanced lilac sheet Melissa had removed, the covering on the bed and drawer section beneath was a subtle brown, beige and gold ivy leaf pattern. Spider brown. Until today Melissa had always thought it a shame to have to cover up such a pretty covering, but now she was appalled at what a perfect spider camouflage her parents had purchased for her. Carefully scrutinising every square inch for signs of life and indeed everywhere around the bed too Melissa carefully approached in order to try and look down the side of the bed nearest the wall. Only two steps in as she checked the carpet for movement and Melissa happened to glance inadvertently at her feet and realising that as always they were bare, grabbed a pair of boots from the bottom of the open wardrobe and retreated whilst she gave them a violent shake upside down in case the beastie had taken a fancy to them too, then leaning heavily against the closed wardrobe next to her, shoved them roughly on her feet. Not bothering to do up the zips. Now at least he could not easily crawl across her bare skin and if needs must she would be able to stomp on him. So, back to the task in hand she crept across and leant over unsuccessfully trying to see down the side of the bed. It was no good, she was just going to have to bite the bullet and get on the bed. Gingerly she knelt on to the edge of the bed, eyes peeled for the slightest movement as she leaned as far forwards as possible without having to actually put her hands in any possible spider vicinity. As she finally shuffled nearer and could see all her dirty filthy habits come back to haunt her at the worst possible time; for all that was visible down the side and edge of her bed were loads of paperback books and tons of sweet and chocolate wrappers and even an empty seashells shaped chocolates' box. Melissa was appalled; she had no idea at the waste that she had let accumulate there. All the top ten books in various shapes and sizes, flung down there on completion or knocked over by accident and with no reason for rescue just left there, spines bent in two, covers bent open and pages crushed in the wrong directions up against the wall or side of the bed. The multitude of brightly coloured wrappers, Melissa was almost tempted to add up the calorific contents of the whole disgraceful stash and see just what she had consumed late into the nights as she had read.

Melissa grabbed the cobweb brush back from under the bed and carefully checking that the spider had not cadged a free ride on it first, she began to poke it about in all the debris hoping for and dreading some movement. Melissa thrashed it back and forth thinking that the gentle touch could have been the wrong one when all of a sudden the head of the brush flew off adding to the detritus. "Bloody marvellous!" Melissa cursed out loud. There was nothing for it and loathed as she was to leave the room should he suddenly make a break for it, she was going to have to bring in reinforcements; she needed Henry.

Thundering down the stairs loudly enough to disturb the sleeping dogs Melissa patted them a reassuring hello as she flew by and with a load of noise of plastic hose and metal tubing banging and thwacking against the woodwork and leaving a trail of mismatched wellie boots spilling out from the cupboard behind her, Melissa dragged the ever smiling Henry out of his home in the hall and clumsily up the stairs. Once set up in the room Melissa set to removing the junk from behind the bed. Luckily Henry's suction was sufficient to move books along the debris in order to then remove them and pile them neatly on the floor behind her. A considerable time and seventeen books later Melissa had removed all the junk and inspected it for beastie and sucked up a vacuum cleaner full of wrappers. Frustratingly however still no sign of her eight legged friend. There was nothing else for it Melissa realised; she was going to have to move the bed properly. Melissa dropped to a crouching position; knees creaking under the effort, and dragged open the only accessible drawer under the bed. It juddered slowly open trying to resist but finally its contents were on view, if that is you could see what can only be described as a cloud. The drawer contained lots of old clothes which although hardly worn were grown out of but kept in case of happier days. Digging through the 'cloud' of thick fluffy dust (like that from your belly button again but pale grey) Melissa realised it must have been years since she had actually looked in the drawer, a fact that became increasingly evident when she saw one or two items that should have had her arrested by the fashion police several years ago and so Melissa was quite bewildered that she had gone to the trouble of hanging onto them. Smiling as each item of clothing had with it its own special memory Melissa sorted through the drawer creating a pile to be kept and a very large pile to go to jumble. The jumble pile featured three brand new pairs of ribbed cord ski-pants wrapped safely in an old dry cleaning wrapper. Each pair were a different size which made Melissa think that at the time of purchase she had actually thought that they would stand the test of fashion time – big mistake there then. With the drawer finally empty and with no way of moving the heavy old drawer unit blocking the bed in down one side including obstructing half of the front of the other drawer of the bed, Melissa decided that brute force and ignorance was the way to go. She pulled out the drawer she had emptied a couple of inches to give her a hand hold and then grabbing under the other drawer hoping to God that the spider had not hidden there, she threw the bed up onto its side. Only the power given by the adrenalin released through her fear made this manoeuvre possible; of thinking that the spider might crawl across her unseen at any moment. And then the tricky part: removing her left hand now that the drawer so hard to open before had closed shut on it as it had turned over and gravity had intervened. On the carpet where the bed had been visible even through all the dust it looked fluffed up and new. The rest of the carpet was covered by the obligatory wrappers, a couple of bank statements and an untouched, still wrapped orange flavoured lollipop. Melissa smiled as she saw that as it must have escaped from her Christmas 'pillow case' eight months before. Henry to the rescue again as Melissa poked and prodded the uncovered metal pipe of the vacuum along through the debris. Then with no sign of movement she picked up all the hair clips, hair bands, two and five pence pieces and Chewit wrappers. Before long the space was clean and fluff free but Melissa was still gutted; and relieved, not to have found her spider. With another slow drag of the now grubby sleeve across her wet brow, Melissa picked up the large green mug and took a large slurp.

"Ugggghhh!" She exclaimed no sooner than she'd done it at the shock of the vile taste of cold tea that she had just drunk. Looking around her at the newly cleared floor but the worse mess of the complete bomb site appearance of the room behind her Melissa glanced at her watch and realised how much time had passed in her near hysteric state and that she had not yet had her lunch, taken the dogs out and only had an hour and a half left to do it in and get showered and ready for work. There was no choice; she was going to have to leave the spider hunt until she came home from work and if he had not shown himself by then she would just have to sleep in her parents' room!

At 1.30am Melissa finally made her way wearily up the stairs to bed. She had chatted briefly with her exhausted looking brother who had come over for a few hours to 'dog sit' and had been thoughtful enough to wait until Melissa was home safely before leaving. She had done the final hedgehog hunt of the night in the garden with Jasper who was obsessed with them and rather uncharacteristically vicious towards them if he found one until he was told to leave it alone; which he did immediately but then whimpered pitifully desperately wanting to separate it from it's prickly coat and finally, if not kept an eye on, trying to wee on it. Jasper clumsily barged past Melissa half way up the stairs and got a warning growl off of Syd as he knocked into him as he slowly creaked and groaned his was painstakingly up the double dog-leg staircase stopping on each level for a breather before stumbling up to the next level. Stopping at the top of the stairs Melissa plonked her large mug of tea down, minus what had slopped out on impact with Jasper, on the last post of the stair banister. Conveniently it had a nice square flat top which perfectly accommodated a mug. Tentatively edging into her bedroom Melissa scanned all around her and stepped right into the room and abruptly turned around to check the vicinity of the light switch because she had had the misfortune of touching a spider inhabited one before and would not be caught out the same way twice. All clear, Melissa flicked on the switch and a dull glow of light emanated from the large low energy bulb in the centre of the room and then it 'tinked' and 'pinked' into full life and the room was brightly lit. Melissa's eyes shot about looking for any sign of a retreating foe but even after bravely leaning over her bed, her search was unfruitful and taking her pill from off of the shelf inside the wardrobe, ever watchful for the beastie, Melissa carefully grabbed the book from her bedside table and gave it a damn good shake, just in case, and then switched off the light and left the room. Melissa crossed the landing to her parents' room and switched on the light still watchful in case the beastie had gone on a walk, or indeed invited friends around. As the light slowly brightened she could see Syd snuggled up on the bed who sensing someone or perhaps the light, flicked open his one eye and winked an acknowledgement and Jasper lay near him scuffing up the duvet and trying to make a nest. Upon seeing Melissa he instantly stopped nesting and flew off the bed at her in welcome.

"Yeah, and you can stop that matey, it's bed time. Go and lie down, there's a good boy." She said rubbing his soft downy ears affectionately as he stood playfully on the bed in front of her. "How did you two know we were sleeping in here anyway?" Melissa looked expectantly between the two gorgeous faces and then checked the room again for uninvited guests and plonked her book down on the bedside table on her Mum's side of the bed and then went off for a wee. On her return she grabbed the forgotten mug from off of the banister and rubbed the wet ring off of the paintwork with the edge of her palm and then wiped the wetness off of that into the side of her trousers. "Classy chick – hey boys!" She told the oblivious dogs, then slipping off her clothes and putting on a clean t-shirt from a clean laundry pile beside the bed, she flicked back the duvet to spider-check; well, as far as she was able with Syd sprawled out all over it, and made herself comfy before finishing off her mug of tea and then reading her book. Lying there Melissa was instantly aware of the most intensely annoying ticking coming in stereo from clocks on both sides of the bed and from the gentle and occasional traffic noise from the passing of far off vehicles outside through the open window. Not only was Melissa's room at the back of the house as opposed to the front like her parents' but she also would never dream of having her window open for fear of late night visitors of the eight legged variety and from moths dive bombing her head drawn to her reading light; consequently the sounds in the room were all very alien to those she normally experienced with one exception: that of the loudly snoring old spaniel lying half way down his bed with his happily twitching paws.

Melissa woke up with a start about forty minutes later because her book had fallen out of her hands and thudded on her head. Realising the lateness of the hour and how bright the bedroom light now seemed she stumbled dopily from the bed and switched it off. Syd was still lying in the same position but Jasper lay on his back against the wall under the light switch with his feet straight up into the air scratching at the wood chip wallpaper as he ran energetically in his sleep. Melissa moving did not disturb him from his dreams and she knew that it was his favourite position to lie in having done it from the very first night that they had adopted him. Snuggling down under the covers she said "Good night boys" in a very low voice so as not to wake them in case they had not been disturbed by all her moving about, and then went off to sleep.

Not having the inclination to go spider hunting before or after the busy Sunday lunch shift Melissa only went into her room to very carefully retrieve clean clothes. Monday however, she had no choice but to sort out her problem visitor as her parents were back the following day and after that she would have no where sensible to sleep with none of her brother's old rooms having beds in them any more. Hours and hours she spent moving furniture and her nik naks from one place to another – even taking the trouble to clean and dust everywhere too. At 1.30pm Melissa's stomach growled its complaint at having been ignored all day and so Melissa took the opportunity to make her lunch and a well deserved gallon of tea whilst she watched Neighbours on the television.

As the whiney sounds of the Neighbours theme tune started up Melissa switched the television off before she got sucked into the next programme that came on. Melissa trudged up the stairs leaving her lunch plate and mug in the lounge for the magic fairy to hopefully clear up later, assuming she could see her way past all the laundry of course. As Melissa made it to the top of the stairs again her face dropped at the contents of her bedroom spewed out all over the landing; shoes mattress, ski-machine and numerous boxes of what anyone other than Melissa would call junk. Melissa made her way past her belongings and clambering over the abandoned Henry vacuum cleaner still smiling up at her from the middle of the cluttered floor. Despondently Melissa continued with her apparently never ending task. Before she knew if she looked at her watch and it was already six o'clock. Melissa was gob-smacked; a whole day wasted on her least favourite chore in the whole world and all but finished moving everything she owned but still without finding the spider from hell. Unbelievable!

That night, even though the room was all put back to normal Melissa could still not bring herself to sleep in it knowing that the spider was still at large, so she and 'the boys' spent their last night in her parents' room, checking one last time before she went to bed that the spider was not poking its tongue out at her from high up on one of her walls.

The next morning Melissa got up bright and early and stripped the duvet covers and sheets off her parents' bed and wrestled to replace them for a nice fresh set. Begrudgingly Melissa put her book back into her bedroom still warily looking about for any signs of her arch enemy who had made the last few days hell and not looking forward to having to sleep back in there again that evening. Melissa was just pottering about warily adjusting a few more items and wiping the dust off of others – into the clothes she was wearing, not a duster, when the sound of Jasper chomping and smacking his lips together caught her attention; worried about what it was he might have found to eat. Jasper's face was a picture as he moved his jaw up and down whilst simultaneously drooling and screwing up his snout, not really sure that he was enjoying what he was chewing.

"What have you got there then?" Melissa asked moving over to him as he flumped heavily down so that he way lying down still chomping as he moved his head peculiarly from side to side. Melissa laughed, her brow creased with confusion at what it was he could have found to eat when all of a sudden a large dark brown sodden dollop that resembled a chewed up length of dark brown wool fell from the side of his mouth and to Melissa's horror started to move on its own. As realisation dawned that what Jasper had actually been chomping on was in fact her spider she cringed as her goose pimples prickled up all over her body, Jasper whacked a clumsy paw at the escaping beastie and grabbed it back into his mouth once more.

"Jasper NO!" Melissa yelled moving closer towards him. Jasper seeing her approach and knowing that from days of old that it normally meant he was about to have whatever he was eating forcibly removed, tossed his head back and swallowed hard a couple of times until the spider was gone.

"Uggghhh! You are gross!" Melissa shuddered; not that she would have thought for a second about trying to rescue it. Jasper leapt up for her to smooth him but wary that the spider might still be in his mouth and not actually dead she moved away. Melissa dodged his mouth a few times and enjoying the new game he suddenly shot off downstairs running madly around all of the rooms and then back up to her, around the bedrooms and down the stairs again having a funny five minutes. Melissa laughed at his antics and patted an inquisitive Syd who had appeared to investigate before she went back into her room reasonably happy that she was safe – at least for the time being.

CHAPTER THIRTY-THREE
TOP BANANA

It never ceased to amaze Melissa the varying degrees of weirdness that the customers who came into the pub displayed. For the last few weeks an odd couple had been coming in at least twice a week. She was an early fifties lady with greying tired looking and fairly unkempt hair which she tucked behind her ears when it escaped periodically. She wore thick brown, amber speckled plastic framed glasses which she perched on top of her head when she was not wearing them and she had a very stern demeanour, a cool calculating stare and she dressed her trim figure in muted shades of brown; the styling of which would have better suited a lady ten years her senior. He, contrastingly, was early thirties and had clearly some Asian blood in him with glossy black hair cut smartly framing his olive coloured face – actually make that caramel - for I have only ever seen black or green olives and it was certainly neither of them – and very dark brown eyes. He was quite handsome and spoke with a public school accent at a much higher pitch than Melissa would have expected. He was a non-stop talker and was always dressed in garish golfing sweaters and forever attracting puzzled glances from people at his propensity to practise his golf swing; including a complete follow through and gazing after an imaginary ball. After a few weeks of eaves dropping on the odd couple who always drank two bottles of expensive wine and chose to sit on the oval table in front of the bar, Melissa had discovered that they were both accountants and that she was his boss. Watching their body language together it was clear that she was quite enchanted by him and the attention he paid her, and she could often be observed dreamily gazing into his eyes as he waffled on about what Melissa had only heard as dull and immature crap.

As the weeks had moved on Melissa had observed their confidence increase and when they ate their dinner they sat right next to each other on the very large oval table and Melissa was sure that there was romance afoot between the two by the way they leaned in towards each other and mirrored each other's movements.

After about a month, having paid little attention to Melissa before; barely bothering normally to acknowledge her upon entering the pub, he suddenly decided to talk to Melissa as it turned out he was interested in buying the table that they sat at as it would be 'absolutely perfect' in his new house. Melissa explained to him that it was actually an antique, as indeed were most of the pieces of furniture in the pub, and so she thought it unlikely that Bruno would be interested in actually parting with it but promised that she would ask on his behalf.

"Oh fantastic!" He enthused, "You know there is a name for good people like you?" Melissa raised her eyebrows curiously at him, "Yes, I call people like you a 'Top Banana'!" He explained seriously as if he had just bestowed upon her the greatest honour. Melissa was momentarily lost for words and hearing movement to her left she glance through the gothic archway of the bar and watched as Marlena mouthed the words 'TOP BANANA!' and pointed seriously at her and then held her stomach as she mimicked a Father Christmas belly laugh as Charlie watched on and giggled helplessly.

Everything about the weird couple's behaviour amused Melissa and the other staff; the way they always made and enormous display of perusing and debating every dish advertised on the menu and the specials board but invariably opted for ham egg and chips for her and rare fillet steak for him. The way that he always referred to her by her initials 'J D' and he was always called 'N B'. They discovered that her initials stood for Jane Douglas from Melissa reading her name printed in full from the silver raised letters on the credit card. His initials however, were all they knew about him due to the fact that he always let her pay, even when it was clear from her reaction when the bill arrived that she thought it was not necessarily appropriate. When the staff referred to the gruesome twosome they either called them by their table number '3C' or by 'The Top Banana People' or if it was Marlena speaking 'Jane Dull as hell and No Balls' They found themselves speaking about them quite a lot because as the weeks lead into months it became evident that they had been adopted by 'JD and NB' and a night did not pass by where some oddity arose.

Melissa's favourite evening had been one Sunday when instead of eating at the table in front of the bar 'The Top Banana People' had decided to go around the corner into another room which only contained one enormous table which could seat up to twelve people. Melissa watched with great interest as they giggled their way around into the room pushing childishly at one another to get to the bar that serviced that room first.

"Hello Melissa! We'd like a bottle of your finest wine please.... not the usual stuff you fob us off with!" Top Banana Man said arrogantly as he snatched up a menu from a stack on that side of the bar.

"You're in luck!" Melissa said smugly at him and went out into the kitchen which led through to her red wine store and came back with a dark bottle of red wine which appeared almost black in colour. "Look! Complete with dust!" Melissa laughed as she wiped a thick coating of dust away from the shoulders of the bottle with a beer cloth. "This is one from Bruno's private collection but when I mentioned that you had been working your way through the more discerning wine drinker's part of the wine list then he suggested that you would probably appreciate this." As is human nature, flattery of overly inflated egos gets you everywhere and instantly, having barely read the label he said that it would be perfect for them. Bucking their normal eating trend on this occasion they both chose 'Eggs Flamenca' one of Bruno's favourite specials board dishes; a hearty combination of peppers, tomatoes and spicy chorizo sausage topped with two sunny-side-up fried eggs and crusty freshly cooked baguette. All the way through their meal appreciative noises could be heard amongst NB's constant chatter and JD's coquettish giggles. Melissa left them and the otherwise empty pub to it and went out to order a mug of tea and hopefully steal a couple of chips that were normally plentiful in the tray at the side of the fryers whenever Charlie and Marlena worked together. When she came back out of the kitchen, the heavy cream coloured door covered in uniformly positioned black painted metal studs closed slowly on its automatic hinge behind her causing the small, square stained glass window depicting a colourful trout, a pheasant and a duck within its lead confines, to rattle in its frame. Melissa tripped clumsily down the dark grey step, the back of her black rubber soled, hideously ugly but comfortable, clog having caught between the door and its frame. Having heard the door hitting an obstacle Charlie had grabbed the door open to look and Melissa glanced around to see her and Marlena laughing as she walked on trying to pretend that nothing had happened. As she ducked slightly to go through the wobbly wooden framed gothic arch which was the bar's entrance, and indeed exit, she spotted NB standing at the bar with a large white dish in between his caramel coloured hands, which were either very small or the dish was enormous Melissa registered causing a little smile to cross her face.

"Sorry to keep you waiting, I was just ordering my tea." Melissa explained approaching him. NB did not smile and stared at her as she looked at his plate. "Do you have a problem?" Melissa asked, genuinely concerned momentarily.

"No. You do!" He snapped back menacingly. "I have just found this! IN MY DINNER!" he thundered at her. Melissa leant her head further forwards to get a better look and read out loud the words 'eggs flamenca' and could not help but giggle as he watched her reading the sauce stained sticky label approximately half a centimetre high and four centimetres long which was laid out on the edge of his plate.

"Well?" He glared at her.

"I'd say you had Eggs Flamenca for your dinner." Melissa said barely containing a hearty chuckle.

"It's not funny! I could have eaten that. I could have put it in my mouth – do you know what glue is made out of? Ground up cows hooves that's what! Do you think that it's funny that I nearly had ground up cows hooves in my mouth?" Melissa pursed her lips together, hoping that she was pulling off the serious expression much better than it felt. Composing herself ever so slightly she passed the plate to Marlena who had come to the bar door way to observe the commotion, and then Melissa asked NB what he would like her to do about the situation, after profusely apologising of course.

"It goes without saying that of course I will not charge you for your meal, but can I get you a sweet or a drink to make up for it?" NB's expression altered momentarily as clearly a cunning thought had crossed his mind.

"I want that bottle of wine for free." He looked at her smugly.

"I cannot possibly give you that – it is a £35.00 bottle of wine!" Melissa answered, quite gob smacked that he could have such a nerve.

"You asked me what I wanted and I have told you. Don't forget I did have ground cow's hoof in my meal!"

"We both know that you did not." Melissa said very quietly getting very cross by his arrogance.

"Well, either you give me that bottle of wine free of charge or we won't come in any more; surely the bottle of wine is a small price to pay considering we come in twice a week and have been doing so for ages?" Now would have been one of those moments in which she really wished that Bruno had been around because he had a reputation of telling people to 'piss off out of my pub then and don't come back!' Normally Melissa would have been happy to have done the same but as NB pointed out; they did actually put quite a lot of money over the bar and customers like this were very hard to come by – however annoying – particularly in the winter months, and so as much as it pained her to do it she was going to have to give in.

"Well although I agree that the label being in your food was absolutely inexcusable, I do think that you are taking advantage some what in your request and I am not happy about it but on this occasion I will let you have the bottle of wine."

"Oooohhh Melissa! You really are a Top Banana!" He gushed, reaching out for her hand and kissing it as she looked at him in barely concealed horror.

"We promise we'll come in more often than ever now!" He yelled out theatrically as they eventually left the pub.

As soon as they had heard the outside door close all three girls burst out laughing.

"You really are a 'Top Banana' Melissa!" Charlie mimicked what NB had just said. "You'll be in trouble with Bruno now though giving away a £35.00 bottle of wine – their whole meal wouldn't have come to that!"

"That my dear girl is where you are wrong. The wine that I told them was from Bruno's private collection was in fact a free-bie from a wine company that was just shoved to the back of the wine cupboard where it has been collecting cobwebs for a year." Melissa grinned smugly at them.

"What and you were going to charge them £35.00 for a bottle of free wine?" Marlena asked incredulously.

"Yes….I can't stand that tosser! So I guess I had the last laugh after all – hey girls?" Melissa looked between the girls as all three of them chuckled.

CHAPTER THIRTY-FOUR
OPEN YOUR MOUTH TO CHANGE FEET MEL!

Nathan Douglas was one of the Flagon's Irregular Regulars. He was a very slight man, approximately 5ft6" if he balanced on his toes and he sported a very curly hairdo which reminded Melissa of a recently clipped poodle, only in a non standard poodle shade of auburn. He had a friendly, lively looking face and a mischievous smile was always found appealingly crinkling the freckled skin around his eyes. He was always very smartly turned out, and if you bothered to look, all garments were carrying expensive designer logos; although Melissa always got the feeling that he had been dressed by his mother. He was a local graphic designer who brought various clients and or his staff in once or twice every other month or so and Melissa and he always had a happy bit of banter since the day he found out her interest in cars and so turned up the next day, not in his usual Volvo estate, but in what Melissa described as a 'custard yellow' convertible Ferrari that Melissa told him was a bit too eighties for her taste and needed a damned good hovering and dusting and that he ought to be ashamed of himself, as even she, who prided herself on being allergic to cleaning would bother to clean out a car of that calibre. A month or so later he appeared at the pub in a British racing green Aston Martin which he delighted in telling her that he had bought off of an eccentric elderly lady who's husband had died a couple years before and the beautiful car had been left under the protection of a ramshackle barn where the chickens had been free to crap on it at will. A similar tale she had heard the like of before on television but never about such a valuable car. Melissa was suitably appalled at such treatment of such a gorgeous car and she sat in it and revved the accelerator listening to the beautiful rumblings of the powerful engine and enjoyed breathing deeply inhaling the smell of the almost silky cream leather upholstery. Nathan did offer Melissa a ride in both vehicles but she made her excuses that if she wasn't driving it herself that there was no point – thank you, but only because she knew of Nathan's driving record which included several rather spectacular crashes in more modestly priced cars. Nathan was particularly smug to be able to tell Melissa that the Aston Martin was not a replacement for the Ferrari but an addition to his collection for when it wasn't convertible weather. Two days later a customer reported thinking he had spotted Nathan in a lay by some miles away with an Aston Martin with its bonnet up and smoke billowing out.

After quite a long period of not having seen Nathan in the pub, one Sunday evening with 'The Top Banana People' already ensconced on their usual table in front of the bar already on their second bottle of wine and a number of other diners dotted around the pub, he reappeared.

"Hi Mel! How the devil are you?"

"Not as well as you by the look of it! You could have had a wash before you visited me!" Melissa said cheerfully admiring his darkly tanned skin.

"Mel, this is Lenny, my driver." He introduced an attractive, very tall black man with sun glasses perched on the top of his head, dressed in khaki cargo pants and a camouflage pattern green t-shirt.

"Your driver?" Melissa asked incredulously smiling at him appreciatively as she took in his excellent physique and wondered where she could get one. "Hello." She said shyly as she tried to pull her tongue back in and wondered if she had been dribbling.

"Yeah, I know. I lost my license."

"Oh, I'm sorry to hear that, but the offer still stands if you need chauffeuring around in your Aston or Ferrari.

"Yeah I'll bear that in mind! Two lagers please." Nathan chuckled and looked around to see who was in the pub.

"Weeeelllll, hello, how are you?" Nathan turned to 'The Top Banana People's' table and put his hands on the edge of the end of the table opposite them and leant towards JD and NB rather strangely.

"Nathan." NB nodded politely at him.

"Nice holiday?" JD enquired looking curiously ill at ease.

Melissa watched the exchange as she took the money for the lagers from Lenny and he went and joined Nathan who had now sat at the table with JD and NB.

Several customers came and went for the next fifteen minutes or so and then remarkably, for the first time ever, NB appeared at the side of the square bar nearest the kitchen which was rarely used by customers due to being tucked away around the corner, and asked for the bill which he paid for in cash removed from a pristine leather wallet that had a finish on it rather like the brown lines on a hazelnut shell. Melissa smirked to herself, assuming that the reason for its excellent condition would be on account of its irregular use, and passed across a hand written receipt with a black and white hand drawn illustration of the beautiful old pub depicted along the top, along with his change. No sooner had she pushed the food order slips that pertained to their table onto the point of a large nail pushed into a wooden block kept as a record at the side of the till, Melissa looked up at the noise of the door to see 'The Top Banana People' hurrying out without so much as a backwards glance. Melissa frowned as she wondered what all that was about and then went across to the table they had vacated to remove the glasses and still half full wine bottle resting in its shiny stainless steel cooler which slid slightly in her grasp where it was moist from the condensation covering the inside.

"That was funny wasn't it?" Nathan asked Melissa grinning broadly looking between her and the very handsome Lenny.

"What's that, that the boss is shagging the much younger employee?" Melissa laughed as she blurted out her indiscretion. "That's nothing; you should have heard what a chauffeur that took them out on her birthday was saying about them!"

"Well yes, that and the fact that when I got back to our house this evening from Lenny having fetched me from the airport, on the table was a note saying 'gone out for dinner – don't wait up'.

"Right." Melissa said looking puzzled.

"Yeah, and the very first pub I walk into there those two are!" He laughed heartily.

"O-Kaaaayyyy?" Melissa's face was furrowed with bewilderment.

"The funniest thing about that lady shagging her employee Melissa is that in the words of some great saying... 'that's no lady....that's my wife!" Nathan said laughing more heartily the more he thought about it.

"Ohhh God!" Melissa exclaimed, the colour flushing her cheeks. "I'm sorry; I had absolutely no idea that she was your wife. You never came in here with her!"

"Mel, Mel, Mel. Don't worry yourself; we've been living separate lives for ages. It's just funny that I walked into the very pub that she's canoodling with her toy boy in!"

Melissa could not believe how badly she had put her foot in it this time and carried the glasses and cooler back around the safe side of the bar. 'Whoops!' She thought to herself.

Much later when Charlie and Marlena were sitting at the bar after they had finished for the evening Melissa relayed the whole story to them who could hardly contain their tears they were laughing so much.

"You won't be 'Top Banana' after tonight Mel!" Charlie giggled flicking the glowing end of her cigarette into the ashtray beside her.

"Of course you realise that now JD has seen that you know Nathan, A.K.A. her husband! That she will assume that you knew who she was all along and have been having a good laugh at their expense." Marlena suggested seriously to Melissa who was scowling and picking some muck out of her thumb nail with the end of one of the match sticks from their home in the red brick on the bar.

"Hey! If we're really lucky they will stop coming in here!" Melissa grinned as the thought came to her.

"Oh yes, lets cross our fingers and wish for that. 'Top Banana' my ass!" Charlie said and exhaled smoke out through her nostrils to accentuate the point whilst Melissa looked distastefully on and Marlena smiled before taking several large mouthfuls of lager from her pint glass.

CHAPTER THIRTY-FIVE
THE WEDDING

The day of Melissa's oldest brother Ben's wedding had finally arrived. The official invitations had arrived at the beginning of March and what seemed like forever later the big day August 31ˢᵗ was finally here. Melissa was brought her big steaming mug of tea at 9 am but stayed underneath the covers fighting off the over excited Jasper for another fifteen minutes until he got bored with her and flung himself off of the bed and barged through into her Dad who was propped up by a mass of pillows, lying in bed with his white vest on and his silver haired 'bed head' sticking out as he browsed through the rather cumbersome Daily Telegraph news paper with the radio burbling away in the background and the remnants of a hearty English breakfast on a tray next to him. Well, when I say remnants, I actually mean eight precisely chopped up pieces of bacon rind put on the rim of his plate.

"CALM DOWN YOU BLOODY SILLY ANIMAL!" Melissa's Dad yelled gruffly at Jasper as he thundered across the large landing towards him. Jasper, not unexpectedly, paid no attention so Melissa's Dad dropped the paper and grabbed the breakfast tray to stop it flying after Jasper's imminent crash landing occurred. Sure enough, Jasper lunged towards him and stomped over the newspaper to get to her Dad.

"GET DOWN!" Melissa's Dad hollered holding a tight grasp on the tray whilst trying to rescue the paper with the other hand which Jasper was crumpling up with excited feet. Jasper by this point was way too excited and his beautiful white teeth were exposed in a big mad smile as he executed a magnificent hand brake turn on the top of the splayed out newspaper before zooming off across the landing and hurling himself back onto Melissa's bed. Sydney popped his head up from his sleeping place on the floor at the side of the bed and growled deeply at Jasper for causing such a disturbance but before he had time to make himself comfortable once more Jasper went shooting off out through the door and across the landing.

"NO JASPER! STAY DOWN!" Melissa's Dad shouted having only just straightened up the ridiculously large newspaper and glaring at the dog over the top of his silver framed glasses. Jasper crashed onto the huge bed once more but was gone again before Melissa's exasperated father had time to swipe at him with the paper. This time Jasper raced away and with his feathery tail tucked up in his undercarriage rather like a racing greyhound, he tumbled his way down the staircase and Melissa could hear him thunder across the hall, into the dining room and out of the open back door. Through her open bedroom window (the hot nights had made her finally circum and risk the spider entry) which looked out across the back garden, she could hear Jasper racing around and her Mum shouting at him to calm down. A hollow clunk and a rattle then the rasping rolling sound Melissa could only assume was an empty bucket that hurricane Jasper had whipped up in his path and then again the thunder of feet up the staircase across the landing followed by a smart turn just short of her parents' bed and he rushed back across into Melissa's room, spun around on the bed causing Melissa to shout out in pain as his high velocity weight made contact with her body and then he shot off again leaving a growling spaniel in his wake as he flung himself down the stairs once more and out and across the garden. This time however, Melissa heard an almighty splash and a scream from her Mother. Melissa leapt out of bed and fought her way through the obstacles to the window where she was just in time to see her Mum pulling a very soggy dripping collie out from amongst the lily leaves and over the stone edge of their large garden pond. Jasper looked very sorry for himself as water poured everywhere off his thick coat causing a large wet area beneath his feet on the path which quickly spread and began to dry out on the already hot concrete. Melissa's Mum's hair clung to her head at the front and her light blue dressing gown appeared dark in a large wet patch down its entire length where Melissa assumed she had absorbed a large quantity of Jasper's tidal wave from where she had been quietly relaxing with her book and drinking a mug of tea enjoying a bit of peace before the hectic part of the day properly began.

"DAD! COME QUICK! YOU'VE GOT TO SEE THIS!" Melissa yelled across to her Dad as he adjusted the waist on his pyjama bottoms to prevent them slipping down whilst about to enter the bathroom. He came across the landing and stopped in the middle where there was an excellent vantage point of the garden below from the large window half way up the stairs. Once her Dad had taken in the scene they looked at each other and burst out laughing.

"Oh dear, what a naughty boy!" Her Dad said somewhat facetiously and then they both roared with laughter as the inevitable doggy shake ensued covering every thing within a ten feet area with a shower of water.

"UGGGGGGGHHHH! JASPER!" Melissa's Mum called out, her face a picture of disgust as she removed a length of curly pond weed from her face and flung it unceremoniously at the continuously moving water which was still lapping up the edges of the pond as a consequence of the disturbance. Jasper meanwhile was looking very sad at his predicament; his soggy ears were flat back against his head which was hung sadly down with his dark brown eyes showing his bewilderment at all that had gone on.

"JASPER!" Melissa shouted as she appeared at the back door way. "Have they been being nasty to you then?" Jasper's face perked up immediately and he raced over to welcome her.

"Don't you be nice to him – look what he's done to me. I had already had my shower!"

Melissa tried unsuccessfully not to laugh as she made her way over to her Mum. "Give it chance Mum – essence of pond water may catch on!" Melissa grinned as she pulled off another piece of weed from her Mum's shoulder.

"Very funny!" Melissa's Mum said as she headed inside. "And don't you think you are coming in here till you're dry!" She said to Jasper pulling the door closed behind her.

Jasper watched forlornly as he was shut out then gave a massive shake to expel the remaining water and then grabbed a tennis ball and flopped down into the grass with it, happily squashing it repeatedly between his teeth. Melissa sat on the back door step and enjoyed the sunshine and the wildlife that their left-to-nature (to lazy to properly maintain it) garden attracted. As she quietly watched the beautiful petrol blue dragon flies hovering low over the water Jasper plopped a dribbly tennis ball on the ground in front of Melissa's feet. As Melissa looked down to pick it up she suddenly had a proper look at her feet glowing up at her. To her absolute horror they were bright orange. "Oh my God! I look like I've been Tango-ed!" Melissa flung the ball away for the patiently waiting dog. Melissa licked her finger and gave the toes of her right foot a hard rub, but it was no good the fake tan was not budging. Melissa had used a quite expensive tanning product, not wanting to take any chances with a cheap dodgy one, but when she had first put it on two days ago it had hardly shown, even after waiting for the obligatory eight hours development time. The product information said that if you had not been happy with the strength of your colour that you should re-apply. However, Melissa four hours after the second application still did not think that she looked a very good shade and so re-applied another coat for good measure. This was not really the shade she had been aiming for particularly on closer inspection when her knees, heels, toes and hands all had an extra special orange glow to them too. Panic stricken Melissa rushed in just in time to let Sydney out into the garden to join Jasper and shut them both out. Her Mum had vanished, presumably to shower the pond life off, so Melissa stood at the kitchen sink and with a handful of washing-up liquid she lathered up her hands trying to rid herself of her weird coloured stain. The packaging had warned her to wear gloves which she did do – except for the last time, but she was sure she had thoroughly scrubbed off every trace. Wrong!

Melissa rubbed her hands under the running water when they were fully rinsed but as they were no different to look at she frantically looked about her for a helpful aid. Spotting the green pan scourer she gently rubbed this across her palms. Gentle did not work so she applied another big squeeze of washing-up liquid and scrubbed hard. After five minutes of this she gave it up as a lost cause and went upstairs to panic there instead.

Her Mum was just leaving the bathroom as Melissa clambered up the last of the stairs. Grabbing her fresh underwear and a large fluffy towel Melissa went into the bathroom and closed the door behind her where she immediately plonked herself down on the loo. The bathroom smelt of her Mum as it was still steamy from her Mum's shower and the smell of her conditioner and Tweed talcum powder (a smell that Melissa had always associated with her Mother as she had used it all through Melissa's childhood. Melissa was not sure if you could actually buy it any more but having three brothers and lots of birthdays, Christmases and Mothers days too it was a fairly safe bet that her Mother would never run out of it). Melissa looked down in despair at her knees whilst she sat there. Now she understood why the instructions said to pay special attention to moisturising them and her heels etc. Hindsight is a marvellous thing – well the power of having it before the event certainly would be!

As Melissa pulled the flush she happened to glance down and spotted the bottle of apple scented toilet duck cleaner at the side of the loo. Reaching down with her orange hand resting on the sink for support as she over extended, and opened the dusty louvered door beneath it Melissa quickly peered around checking there was no obvious sign of spider inhabitation and then removed a sponge backed bathroom scourer from the cello-phane wrapper. Pushing the door gently closed with her left foot until the catch clicked Melissa undid the lid on the toilet duck and squeezed a small amount of the thick green goo onto the scourer and rubbed it over her hands – gently at first and then harshly when it had no effect, but at least it had a nice 'fresh from the orchard' apply smell. After a few minutes of vigorous scrub-bing Melissa rinsed her hand to have a look. After mush scrutiny all she could see was that it was red, but surely that was progress so she proceeded to rub her other hand, knees and feet. When she was completely red in all these areas Melissa stripped off her pale lilac nightshirt, with a very sad looking Eeeor on the front, and went over to open the glass door of the shower cubicle. Just as she was about to get in she stopped in her tracks and walked back in front of the sink and the large mirror that hung above it. Managing to stare only at the body parts currently on her mind and not at all the belly rolls, Melissa turned her harms around so that her elbows faced the mirror in order that she could see that which she had spotted to grab her attention – namely her orange elbows. Repeating her toilet duck and scourer procedure she scrubbed hard at both elbows and then discarding the sponge-scourer in despair it bounced around the sink and Melissa shut herself in the shower. After applying her hair conditioner the previously hot water, of course, ran cold and so Melissa had to complete her task under the ice cold stream of water. Not all bad though Melissa thought, as it was having quite a good cool-ing effect on all her toilet ducked and scoured areas. Wrapped up in her large fluffy bath sheet Melissa put the lid down on the toilet and sat on top of it. Armed with a pumice stone (one of her life's constants that had always lived on the side of every bath her parents had owned, of which there were numerous) Melissa began rubbing at her heels with the little piece of volcanic rock in her hand and tried not to think of everyone else's rancid feet it had ground dead skin off of. After much scrubbing and much grunting and groaning at the effort of being bent over for such a long time, not to mention some very worrying creaks coming from the toilet which was being subjected to her wriggling mass, the pumice stone did seem to be doing the trick. Quite some time later, although not pleased with her still very orange hue, at least Melissa was pleased that all her wrinkly joint areas were toned down and not drawing quite so much attention to themselves. Wrapping her bath robe around her and loosely tying the belt she went out onto the landing and plugged in her hairdryer. Melissa always dried her hair upside down and without the aid of a mirror, as it was very curly and pretty well did what it wanted whenever it wanted, so Melissa had stopped trying to fight it a ling time ago. It was whilst she was bent over with her substantial behind facing anyone exiting her parents' bedroom that her Mum came out.

"What on earth have you done to your skin? You're orange!"

Melissa jumped at her voice, not having heard her approaching over the noise of the powerful hairdryer.

"Hey?" Melissa yelled as she stood up right and then switched off the power.

"Hay is what horses eat." Melissa raised her eyebrows and rolled her eyes. "I asked you what have you been doing to yourself?"

"You have already seen me this morning and you didn't notice then."

"Well I have now." Melissa's Mum wet a finger and before Melissa could stop her rubbed it up and down her arm.

"Muuuuummmm! That's gross! It won't come off I already tried."

"Just checking. Why on earth would you want to paint yourself that colour?"

"I didn't want to, it carried on working over night and well, I'm stuck with it now."

"You should have just worn tights like normal people."

"You know I hate them. They never fit properly and the only ones that do have a cotton gusset! No one under 70 should have a cotton gusset! Vile things! You spend all day pulling them up and the crotch spends all of its time mid-thigh so that you walk around like you've crapped yourself. Anyway, not only am I too clumsy and ladder them the second I look at them but also I am wearing open toes and I don't want ugly seams poking out the ends of my posh sandals."

"In my day you wouldn't have dreamt of leaving the house without your tights on!"

Melissa scowled at her Mother and bent over to unplug her hairdryer. "Muuuuummmm!" Melissa said swiping another wet finger away; this time from the back of her leg. "It won't come off!" Melissa's Mum frowned and made her way downstairs, holding her long hem line up off the floor as she carefully teetered down the stairs in her overly high heels.

Melissa put the hairdryer down on top of a box of Christmas decorations which some how had not quite made it back up into the loft with the others, even though it was now August, and kicked the sticking out lead in towards the linen bin to avoid tripping man or beast up with it some future point in time. Walking into the bathroom Melissa wiped the overly long sleeve of her dressing gown over a section of the still steamed up mirror in order to adjust her hair into place. Melissa never used a brush as it tended to make her curls rebel into a fuzzy wave which was far worse than the mad curls, so after running her hands through her hair a few times and tossing her head she covered it all over with maximum hold hairspray. Melissa having so much hair called for a lot of spray so it went on for quite some time, however when she finally let go of the trigger part of the can it did not, as was customary, actually stop. On and on the hairspray fired out and with every attempt to stop it leaving Melissa covered in more and more sticky liquid all over her hands, her face and the bathroom in general. Finally after a huge struggle Melissa managed to remove the lid of the can fully and finally the spraying abated. Melissa flung open the bathroom window and inhaled deeply for several moments coughing and pulling faces at the awful taste the air born vapours had left in her mouth. Melissa wafted the window backwards and forwards a few times in order to get the air moving better when her Dad hurried past the open door.

"Whatever you are spraying Melissa you have used more than enough! The whole house stinks!"

"I know!" Melissa said barely staying calm "The damn thing would not stop spraying – it jammed – I had to pull the lid off!" Melissa's Dad's only reply came in the form of a whole series of loud sneezes one after the other as he made his way down the stairs, one sneeze per step; the effort of the sneezes greatly hindering his journey. Finally after the sneezing came to an end Melissa closed the bathroom door to block out the profanities shouted up the stairs relating to his now well sneeze sprayed outfit, while she washed all the sticky hairspray from her skin and cleaned her teeth.

Remarkably the rest of the preparations went without a hitch and Melissa arrived downstairs exactly on time to say goodbye to the dogs and to put her and her Mum's hats, still in boxes, in the boot of the car.

Fortunately even though there was a rain shower on the journey for fifteen minutes or so, by the time Melissa and her parents arrived outside the pretty church the weather had cleared and the gentle breeze had sent the rain clouds on their way leaving behind a beautiful sky which had she had more time and less people to talk to Melissa would have searched for the cloud faces and objects that lurked within their fluffy confines.

"Hey Mel!" Have you been TANGOED?" Melissa was brought back to earth with a bump.

"Wow! Look at you! You finally found a barber!" Melissa yelled back across the graveyard upon seeing her brother, the groom, finally with short hair after years of having made it his mission in life to avoid the scissors. "I'm really shocked. You actually look quite handsome."

"Ummm. Yeah, well you look orange!" Ben shrugged off the compliment. "You do know that it is a wedding, not a funeral don't you?" Ben gestured at Melissa's completely black outfit "I thought that you wearing that dress you were making." Before Melissa could answer an elderly couple had tapped Ben on the shoulder and escorted him away. Melissa was momentarily taken

back to that whole dress incident that she was trying to wipe unsuccessfully from her mind. As her guest for the evening so that she would not be left chatting to age-ed relations who she only met at weddings and funerals, Melissa had invited Sally in the absence of a male person to escort her. Aware that the evening do was to be quite a posh affair Melissa had gone off with Sally to buy her outfit. Melissa was all sorted with hers as months before she had stumbled, literally tripped over the roll, across some beautiful purpley-pinky material which she had immediately fallen in love with that felt like a thicker version of silk but which had an almost matt finish. So chuffed was Melissa with the found treasure that she kept sneaking a look into the old fashioned brown paper bag that the shopkeeper had put it into all the way home; and even more amazingly she had managed to find the perfect evening dress pattern that would suit her down to the ground. Melissa wasted no time before she had cut out the pattern and lining pieces and she had even telephone Sally when she had come out of the shop with her purchase because she was so thrilled at her good finds. Melissa finished the dress the next day and tried it on. She was so pleased with it that she rushed downstairs complete with hat and heels to show her parents, who both agreed that by the time the wedding date arrived she would have lost sufficient weight to really do the out fit proud. So....
the day that Sally and Melissa went shopping together would go down in history with Melissa as a very bad day. The first place they went to was Debenhams. As they wandered through the maze of racks Melissa looked up and spotted a beautiful satin dress on an elegant black mannequin. "There, look Sally!" That is the exact same colour as my dress. Isn't it gorgeous?" Melissa gushed excitedly.

"Oh yes, that's beautiful. Really unusual. How much is it?" Sally asked making her way over to the rail.

"£89.00" Melissa said innocently. "They have one in black too."

"Hmmmm, yes, that's nice too." Sally said expertly flicking through the rail of purple ones looking for her size. Melissa watched on in bewilderment as Sally draped the one she had found that was the right size over her arm and then selected a black one the same.

"Where are the changing rooms?" Sally said as she scanned the room whilst picking up a third black dress to try on.

"But you can't get the purple one." Melissa said, her face distorted with confusion.

"Why not?" Sally challenged, barely turning her head around as she walked towards the changing room door.

"Because it is the exact same colour as I am wearing."

"ANNNNDDDD?" Sally yelled from the entrance to her cubicle.

"ANNNNDDDD! I spent a lot of money and time and effort on making and fitting into that dress and we both can't wear the same bloody colour!" Melissa raised her voice and caught her angry red faced reflection in a mirror.

"Why not? Lots of people will wear black."

"That is hardly the same." Melissa tugged exasperatedly at her hair and felt the prickle of tears threatening.

"Of course it is. Why should I have to wear the same colour as every one else?"

"You don't, but then you shouldn't wear the same colour as me when that colour is so unusual. We'll look like a right couple of Muppets!" Melissa tried to make light of the unbelievable situation, fervently hoping to herself that she would not like the purple dress once it was on. A long while later Sally emerged from the changing room and passed the two black dresses to the lady attending it.

"I'll keep this one." She told the woman as Melissa looked round in time to see her go up to the counter with the purple dress.

"You are actually going to buy it are you?" Melissa said as the threatened tears were gaining in numbers.

"Yes, I really like it."

"BUT YOU CANNNNT!" Melissa whined at this betrayal. Sally stiffened up at the counter but handed her card over to the embarrassed shop assistant who was not quite sure what was happening or where to look.

"We'll look ridiculous! OK, correction…*I'll* look ridiculous. We will look like two best friends at primary school copying each other. Only it isn't primary school and you'll look gorgeous and I'll look like a big fat moose! I cannot believe that you are actually doing this! You can buy anything and you'll look fabulous in it; I've actually made mine. I cannot take it back and I don't see why I have to – it's my brother's wedding!"

"I don't see what your problem is." Sally looked impatiently at her.

"That is because you are the gorgeous one!" Melissa said as Sally took her bag from the assistant and Melissa stomped off with angry tears running down her red cheeks.

"GREAT HAT MELISSA! And I mean *GREAT* – it's huge! I love it!" Melissa's Aunty brought her back from her sad memories and gave her a big hug which nearly set the tears off again.

"Hello little Aunty. Have you grown?" Ben had reappeared and had wrapped his long arms around their vertically challenged aunt and given her a hearty squeeze after she had released Melissa from her overly enthusiastic clutches. Melissa could not help but laugh as she barely reached up to his armpit, even with high heels and a hat on. Mid squeeze another stranger reached to shake her brother's hand and that of the other family members who had gathered around. Much pumping of arms occurred; Melissa grinned to herself as the stranger's hand shaking technique reminded her of how in the old films they used to pump up the water.

"And hello to you Mel!" The stranger said. "You look very striking. Unusual choice of colour but the black really looks smart."

"And slimming hey Mel!" Her Aunty piped up winking at her.

Melissa glanced around and saw her Gran appear being supported by her cousins as she slowly walked the length of the old church path. She was smiling all over her face at the excitement of the occasion and at the attention her Grandsons were giving her as they escorted her along.

"Hello Granner!" Melissa went over to kiss her Gran on the cheek.

"I'll give you Granner!" Melissa's Gran tutted but with an appreciative twinkle in her eye. When Melissa was very young printing words on t-shirts started to become 'the thing'; the lettering was black and sort of velvety to the touch. Ben bought a t-shirt with SLUG written across it for their brother Tony because it was the nasty nick name he called him at the time and Tony made their Gran a hideous big square shopping bag in his Home Economics class (in the first year of secondary school before he was old enough to pick his chosen subjects) and Tony got it printed with the legend 'GRANNER' as a Christmas present. She was not the least bit impressed with the new name but unfortunately for her they were impressionable young kids and thought it was great and so she got stuck with it.

"Looking good boys. Nice to see you." Melissa said to her handsome cousins. "See you in a while." And Melissa left them to go over and watch the bride arriving.

Barely had Melissa teetered to the end of the never ending path in her ridiculously high 'slut shoes' as she affectionately referred to them, when she heard her name being whispered harshly as if summoning a dog. Looking around to see the source of the noise her Mum was rather comically sticking her large hat covered head around the door frame of the church door and crouching down as if this would somehow make her less conspicuous. Upon gaining Melissa's attention she started beckoning her furiously to come to her with her dainty pearlescent cream handbag flailing around wildly on her arm as she desperately tried to stop the hat falling off with the hand of the other. Disappointed to be dragged away before getting a glimpse of her sister-in-law to be, Melissa sighed deeply and teetered as fast as she could to her ever more wildly gesticulating Mum.

"Where have you been? The Bride is arriving!"

"Yes Mum, that was the general idea."

"Hurry up and get in here." Her Mum led the way to their pew and Melissa's patiently waiting Dad near the front behind her brothers.

They all looked around when she appeared. "See, I told you she'd been Tangoed!" Ben, her Dad and her other two brothers all laughed heartily, gaining them the attention of the whole congregation.

"Well, it's actually worse than that." Melissa said holding the underside of her wrist up to her nose. "I keep getting really strong wafts of Bovril!" At this her youngest brother nearly cried with laughter and Melissa kept sniffing herself with a puzzled expression on her face.

Melissa's Mum took a swipe at each of her brothers to stop laughing but that just amused them even more. Even though they were all facing the front on the pretext of behaving, their shoulders were still rocking as they continued to laugh at Melissa's misfortune.

The ceremony went without a hitch and the Bride fulfilled the looking beautiful requirement as expected and Melissa participated in her favourite pastime of people-watched during the three-quarters of an hour of photographs. Melissa's Gran's step sister scowled at everybody and in particular her husband, who in utter contrast to herself was a really happy smiley person who no one would have blamed it he had done away with her and buried her under their patio. Melissa's Aunty, who was currently lumbered with escorting Granner around the graveyard obstacle course, was gritting her teeth into a smile whilst her eyes betrayed the overwhelming urge to lift up some turf and give her a push shouting 'INCOMING!' Her un-married brothers were flirting outrageously with the bridesmaids and her Grandad, on her Mum's side, was busy taking cuttings from various plants overflowing the church walls from the house next door and was unashamedly popping them into a polythene bag he always kept with him for this exact purpose. Eventually the wedding procession made its way to the local Golf Club where it took another hour to get various imaginative photographs; including Melissa's very big brothers all squeezing into a golf cart which was not so much artistic as Noddy and Big Ears. The Golf Club reminded Melissa of a crematorium from the outside but with lots of posh cars parked outside and thankfully no Hearse. Inside however, it was a beautifully designed building and lovely and cool after the hot still day in a completely black outfit. After everyone made their way down the wedding line Melissa found the table plan and along with her youngest brother Alex they made their way over to their allocated table; the rest of the family all being on the top table. When they approached the table the eight place settings were as yet unoccupied except for two; a youngish couple whom neither of them had met before.

"BABY WARNING! HIGH CHAIRS! WARNING!" Melissa mimicked a loud hailer as she spotted two high chairs amongst the place settings. She was just turning pulling a face at Alex about this hideous turn of events when the un-amused parents who could not have failed to miss Melissa's warning announcements both magically appeared as if off of the Star Trek Teleporter, but without the funny noise and distorted molecules.

"Oh, ummmm hello." Melissa greeted them whilst her cheeks flamed red with embarrassment.

"Hello. Don't mind my sister she doesn't get out much." Alex tried to make amends as they all introduced themselves. Having sat down and had a good poke about with everything on the table the man directly opposite spoke to her whilst she was mid-bubble blowing from the diddy champagne bottle replicas put at each place. Embarrassed again at her childish enthusiasm for the little bubble blowing set she tuned into Nick opposite.

"Yes, I reckon the last time I saw you was when we all stayed at yours the night before our ski-ing trip when your Dad took us to the airport. You must have been about twelve."

Melissa studied the man's features more carefully then realised that yes she did indeed know him.

"You probably know me better as Donk." He interrupted her thoughts as she tried to place him.

"Oh God, yes Donk. Yes I know that name. Well why ever didn't you say? Does anyone even call you Nick?"

"Yes. I do." The mother of his child answered abruptly and looked disapprovingly down her nose at her. Melissa flushed again and did a closed mouth smile as a small nod towards an apology.

"So why do they call you Donk?" Melissa asked trying to make conversation. With that her brother sprayed a mouthful of champagne out. Melissa looked around at him with surprise. "Oh, is it something really embarrassing?" She looked at Donk beginning to think that this was a bad line of questioning.

"It's short for Donkey?" Donk made it a question as if to say 'Do you get it now?'

"Ohhhhh." Melissa said looking puzzled still whilst Alex started giggling beside her having caught Donk's attention.

"So why Donkey?" Melissa asked, the penny still not having dropped and Alex spat at even more champagne.

"Melissa!" Alex laughed at her.

"What?" She still did not understand and looked at all the laughing faces staring at her.

"What are donkeys and horses renowned for being well endowed with Melissa?"

"Oh God! Right. OK. Ummmm very good. I get you now." Alex was still tittering helplessly the champagne adding to his merriment. Donk smiled at her all proud of himself and amused at her embarrassment and the mother of his child looked at her with disdain. Melissa tipped her head forward and hid behind the brim of her enormous hat.

The meal was lovely but the company was a bit of a strain with the exception of Donk and her brother the other people at the table were more interested in their children. Melissa was very glad when the speeches were over and of course the cake appeared and then they were all shooed away to the bar and the garden so that the evening do could be set up.

Sally arrived at 7pm and walked in looking stunning in her purple dress and sun-bed tan. Melissa tried not to think about her betrayal and of her own beautiful dress tucked away in her wardrobe at home. Melissa watched the people around giving her admiring glances and hated God for being so unfair. Melissa was technically an atheist other than when things were going wrong and against her in which case she was fond of cursing God for punishing her, especially when she had not done anything to deserve such treatment. Ted at the pub was always telling her that his Mum was always saying "Do good will come good" Melissa told him in no uncertain terms after about the fifth time that this was 'utter bollocks' and he would just heeee heee heeeee at her and say it again.

"Ladies and Gentlemen!" Came a loud booming voice over the speaker system cutting off the cheesy but good wedding music. "The Bride and Groom are just about to depart but before we all make our way outside to wave them off we need all you single ladies to gather around as the Bride is going to throw her bouquet. Come on now ladies, don't be shy!" Announced the pompous Master of Ceremonies who reminded Melissa of the Mayor of Toy Town in Larry the Lamb from her youth. The Master of Ceremonies was vertically challenged and very rotund. His black hair was slicked back and he strutted about the place like The Olde Flagon cockerel, chest out and with a John Wayne swagger. The cockerel however (Gregory Peck) had good reason for his arrogant stance because he was absolutely beautiful; the same could not be said for the MC.

Several younger women and girls made their way over to where the bride was waiting about to damage over one hundred pounds worth of beautiful flowers. All thirty-something women tried to hide out in the shadows not wishing to draw attention to their old spinster status until forcibly shoved forwards by the interfering do-gooders who had spotted them lurking in the dark recesses of the large room. Melissa and Sally were literally grabbed by the scruffs of their necks and deposited with the other women by Melissa's kind brother Alex. After having been more or less dragged unceremoniously to the front, as soon as her brother's back was departing Sally and Melissa encouraged the unashamed bouquet catching wannabees to go in front of them and stood at the back of the group. With Sally still mourning the loss of her drink which had been prised out of her hand by Alex, and looking around in a forlorn and tiddly state, just before the Bride threw the bouquet Ben whispered into her ear which made her look up and scan the crowd and make eye contact with Melissa. Guessing what was afoot the second Gemma turned her back to throw the bouquet Melissa side stepped several paces to the right and grinned smugly at her brother who was shouting across to his new wife that she needed to redirect her throw. It was too late; the beautiful bouquet of roses and lilies was hurled aloft. Melissa watched the trajectory of the flowers which almost appeared to go into slow motion as they arced high up into the ceiling and began their dramatic descent right towards an unsuspecting Sally. Sally by now more than a little worse for wear in celebratory drinks stood still with her arms hanging limply by her side as she finally became aware of the hurtling bouquet heading her way. Melissa watched on in utter astonishment as Sally did not move or react in any way as all of a sudden the flowers literally splatted into her chest and fell to the floor. A loud cheer went up from the wedding guests a long with a few groans from the bouquet catching wannabees. Sally was appalled. Her face was a picture of abject horror as she looked to the flowers at her feet and then at the big wet mark on the front of her beautiful purple dress all across her front where the wet stems had impacted. A young girl carefully picked up the slightly worse for their flight bouquet and passed it graciously to Sally who ungratefully nearly snatched them from her and took them back to their table and flopped them down next to her drink which she gratefully guzzled as she watched the closed bud of the snapped off head of a red rose rock gently backwards and forwards on the table. Melissa and her brothers Tony and Alex were in absolutely hysterics at the scene they had witnessed; tears were literally streaming down their faces and when they stopped laughing momentarily Tony re-enacted the point of impact again and they all burst out laughing once more and the more Sally stayed poe-faced completely unimpressed with the whole debacle the more it made them all laugh.

CHAPTER THIRTY-SIX
STANLEY

It was a Tuesday night and Daniel had not been in the pub since that God awful visit on his birthday when the dopey cripple had been off-loaded onto her for the evening. By Melissa's reckoning it had to be two months which had passed but to her it felt like at least six. Melissa's whole reason for getting out of bed of a morning had left the country, leaving Melissa with the dull long winter evenings stretching out relentlessly in front of her. Everyone noticed that Melissa had lost her sparkle and even though she did her best to hide it, she could not disguise her sadness; even causing the dogs to nudge her affectionately with their uncanny sense of knowing when things are not right.

Marlena and Charlie did their best to try and cheer her up by taking her out for fish and chips at their favourite local haunt in Slapperton where they were known by name due to the frequency of their visits, but when that stopped working as a cheering-up device they knew they were in trouble.

Melissa started frequenting the gym more often but instead of chanting her mantra of old she just stared into space and walked on autopilot until the machine beeped and slowed down and she moved on to the next piece of equipment. Week by week the pounds were beginning to come off but such was Melissa's lethargy she had even stopped bothering to weigh herself.

Charlie was blown through the door at 6.30pm and the door creaked noisily shut behind her whistling eerily as the wind howled against the front of the building and through the gaps around the door frame. Just as Charlie was taking off her thick black fleece and unwrapping her stripy scarf in several different shades of pink which were clashing with her red nose and cheeks, Marlena appeared from the kitchen carrying three mugs on a tray and a packet of digestive biscuits which were there for making cheesecake bases with.

"Oh well done Marlena. Excellent timing!" Charlie said grabbing her blue mug with a picture of a happy cartoon horse on the front with the slogan 'Dopey Mare' underneath.

"Thanks Marlena. But what on earth have you got Charlie?" Melissa asked staring at Charlie's mug which was piled high with whipped cream and chocolate sprinkles.

"Hot chocolate with whipped cream and sprinkles!" Do you know nothing?" Charlie laughed before taking a noisy slurp and pulling the mug away leaving a dollop of cream on the end of her nose which all three girls laughed at.

"And what have you got?" Melissa asked Marlena.

"Coffee of course." Marlena said smugly.

"And?" Charlie asked laughing.

"And what?"

"You never drink anything that doesn't have alcohol in it; you probably clean your teeth in vodka!" Charlie laughed and put her finger in the cream of her drink and licked it off as Melissa watched and smiled.

"Cooking Brandy today." Marlena laughed.

At seven o'clock car lights appeared in the car park and so Marlena and Charlie slowly made their way off to the kitchen, pausing out of sight just long enough to see who it was that arrived. As soon as the girls realised that it was TV Trevor that had been blown into the pub along with his scruffy dog Wellington, the girls relaxed once more and came back into the bar to say hello and make a fuss of the dog. Wellington was a lovely natured bearded collie-cross who always looked in need of a bath but was in no way neglected – kind of the dog equivalent of Bob Geldof. TV Trev as he was fondly referred to in the pub due to his job in a television studio, was a quiet watchful, mild mannered type who said little but gave the impression of having taken in every little detail of his surroundings. He was a very unassuming character but in the typical 'still waters run deep' theme he was always very well informed about everything going on both worldly news wise and matters of public gossip and scandal issues. Much to Melissa's disappointment however he always played his cards very close to his chest and she was only aware of his level of gossip knowledge after trying to share some with him, only to find that he had known about it for days already.

"Who else arrived then?" Charlie asked peering out through the window but only having the room reflected back at her in the diamond shapes making up the glass.

"No one that I saw." TV Trev replied helpfully shrugging his shoulders.

"Did you come in the car then?" Melissa asked.

"Yes, I'm afraid we did. Wellington said it was too windy for a walk and that it would mess up his hairdo." TV Trev said as Charlie ruffled up the already messy and long hair on the top of his head that Wellington was peering out of as it flopped over his gentle brown eyes.

"Got any gossip and scandal for us then?" Melissa asked hopefully as she took TV Trev's money he was proffering to pay for his glass of red wine.

"No gossip I'm afraid, but I do have a funny story if you like."

"We like!" Charlie enthused and sat down at the table in front of the bar to be able to better smooth Wellington as TV Trev entertained them.

"Well I was leaving the Headless Horseman last night, or rather at 1.45am this morning." TV Trev chuckled referring to the nearest pub to them at The Olde Flagon and approximately one mile from TV Trev's home. The Headless Horseman was a very popular drinking pub and even in the days before the revised licensing laws it was always possible to drink there until the early hours. As pubs The Olde Flagon and The Headless Horseman were worlds apart. Melissa never went there herself but took immense pleasure from shared appalled customers telling her that they served up cold baked beans in tomato sauce with their salads. "So as I got out to my car along with Wellington, Stanley…" (a stocky little Jack Russell who lived about a mile away from The Headless Horseman in completely the opposite direction to TV Trevor and Wellington, and who hated Wellington with a passion whenever they encountered him if they walked by his house) "…Was waiting by the driver's door. So knowing that Stanley was normally keen to see Wellington off I hurriedly opened up the back for him to get in and no sooner had I undone my door than Stanley had hopped in and went and sat on the passenger seat facing out the windscreen. So I could only assume that he wanted a lift and so I drove him home and when I pulled up at the gate outside his house and got out, he hopped across my seat and out of the car and ran up the drive, without so much as a thank you or backward glance!"

"That's amazing! How did he know that it was your car? Have you given him a lift before?" Melissa asked amazed.

"No, never! I have no idea. I can only assume that he must have been able to smell Wellington."

"Bloody clever idea though catching a lift home!" Charlie said as they all laughed.

"So were the dogs all right in the car together?" Melissa asked still intrigued.

"Amazingly yes. Not a peep out of either of them. Wellington looked a little furtive but Stanley looked arrogantly out of the window as if I was his own personal chauffeur!"

"He could have been waiting all night. He didn't know that you were going to drive home." Marlena pondered as Wellington sat next to her for her turn to adore him.

"Well you have to admire his style. There are not many dogs that walk to the pub and hitch a lift home. What a clever chap!" Melissa said smiling as she imagined TV Trev's reaction to finding Stanley there waiting.

This became the first tale of many which Melissa was to hear about Stanley; each one more entertaining than the last. Stanley lived about a mile away as the crow flies from The Olde Flagon and spent most of his days on sentry duty at the end of the drive way leading up to his house. He would stay there in all winds and weathers watching the world go by, what little of it there was along the narrow country lane and he would bark as people approached to let them know that he was on duty and guarding his home and owner – unless of course, as was common, he got a smell up his nose and scampered off on the trail of a bitch on heat or any wildlife that he like to chase. He also had something of a thing for joggers; chasing them up the road just for sport. Stanley was owned by Quentin the Accountant; a more contrasting coupling you would not find. Stanley was a rugged, thick set terrier with a very stocky body and an enquiring, attractive, but not obviously handsome face. The face description would have suited both owner and dog in actual fact but that is where the similarity ends. Quentin in his early fifties, very outgoing bordering on eccentric, was a very well dressed, 'terribly' well spoken, very intelligent and highly educated tax advisor. Melissa took to him immediately for his fast wit and enquiring mind. He was fascinating to watch; hardly pausing for breath with his persistent questioning of everyone he met. He was tall and slim and much to the amusement of all the slightly less eccentric regulars, he was always wearing a blazer or a smart jacket with a brightly coloured 'tank top' underneath in the bright shades that only the 'posh' seem to pull off, along with chequered shirts starched to within an inch of their lives and always fastened with gold cufflinks and in a different, generally multicoloured scheme again: a highly patterned tie. Although he denied it profusely, the regulars were always ribbing him about the fact that they thought he wore sock suspenders and a tiddly Regular of either sex could often be spotted running their hands suggestively up his calves in an attempt to prove their theory right. Quentin did not ask the usual run of the mill questions that strangers meeting for the first time always used; his were always strange or mind expanding or thought provoking ones, the most recent example to come to mind being that of his quest one evening upon chatting with Marlena was to remember the name of a famous Polish person of historical importance – the answer on this particular occasion having involved every poor person to set foot in the pub, being Copernicus. Melissa found his company such light relief from the dull, normal bar discussions which repeated themselves on a monthly or even weekly basis dependant on the levels of alcohol consumed at the time of their origin, and so she always looked forward to his visits.

TV Trev and Wellington left after the glass of wine was consumed, no doubt off to the next pub on their 'walk'. Begrudgingly the girls felt that they probably ought to do some work at least for a while and so Marlena and Charlie vanished off into the kitchen. Melissa was just doing a spot of dusting when the door creaked open again and in walked Quentin smoothing down his hair as the door closed behind him.

"Well speak of the devil!" Melissa laughed and said hello.

"How can you have been talking about me, you're all on your own!" Quentin said raising a black eyebrow at her and comically swaying from side to side in an effort to peer around the corners of the pub walls to double check.

"You've just missed TV Trevor." Melissa laughed again holding a little short glass against the Famous Grouse optic.

"A large Grouse and water please young Melissa!" Quentin said smiling at her as she loitered under the whisky optic for his go ahead.

"How on earth did you know?" He feigned surprise at her knowing his drink of choice.

Laughing again Melissa filled a large glass jug from the tap under the bar and quickly wiping off the excess dribbles down the outside with a tea towel, placed the jug and the short glass on the bar in front of him.

"Steady on there Melissa, I can't possibly drink all that!" He said peering over the edge of his dark framed glasses at the three-quarters full jug. "So why were you talking about me huh?"

He screwed his eyes up menacingly. Melissa relayed the story of Stanley catching a lift home last night and Quentin was most impressed.

"I shall have words with young Stanley about not thanking Trevor and Wellington for the lift home though; I didn't bring him up to be ill-mannered!"

"Hello Quentin!" Marlena said placing Melissa's refilled large mug of tea down on the bar in front of her.

"Thanks Marlena." Melissa said immediately warming her hands on it.

"The lovely Marlena!" Quentin said appreciatively admiring her legs for an overly long time reminding Melissa of a scene from one of the Doctor in the House or Carry On films. Marlena vanished as quickly as she appeared back into the kitchen.

"Lovely girl that Marlena. Remarkable eyes!" He said staring after her into space. "Well talking of Stanley, I ran into one of my neighbours today and it would appear that this is not the first time that Stanley has done this you know!"

"You're kidding!" Melissa laughed intrigued.

"No. She was telling me that she was visiting a friend over in Leafybridge and when she came out of the friend's house she saw a little chap running happily along the road that bore a striking resemblance to my Stanley. So not really thinking that it would be him she called out his name and he came running over and the second that she opened up her car door he apparently leapt straight in – and as you said with Trevor, he sat on the passenger seat just waiting for the lift home. My neighbour thought it was most funny and so obliged him by bringing him back but when they got here he would not get out of the car. She tried and tried to encourage him out but he wasn't having any of it and even lay down on the seat to prove his point."

"So what did she do? Would he bite?" Melissa asked fascinated by Stanley's cheek.

"No, not my Stanley! Bless her, she had to go to Slapperton and so she took him with her, so they spent the afternoon there. When she came back he was happy to get out, again without a word of thanks by all accounts." Quentin guffawed loudly as he clearly visualised the scene.

"That is excellent. How clever!"

"Of course! I can't believe you thought otherwise; he is *my* dog after all!"

The door creaked open again and this time Stephanie and Sebastian blew in laughing as they too tried to straighten down their wind blown hair.

"Hi Mel!" They chorused.

"Hello, the usuals?" Melissa laughed at them as they wrestled out of their coats and hung them over the back of the big heavy chairs around the table in front of the bar.

"Yes please Mel." Stephanie smiled and said hello to Quentin who was watching the attractive blonde with undisguised pleasure.

"Stephanie and Sebastian, this is Quentin. Quentin, this is Stephanie and Sebastian." Melissa very formally introduced them to each other gesturing unnecessarily at each person as she named them with her upturned hand. Politely they all said their hellos and then Melissa added an extra snippet of information; "Quentin is Stanley's owner."

"What 'THE' Stanley?"

"My bloody dog knows more people than I do!" Quentin laughed and Melissa filled Stephanie and Sebastian in on the two Stanley tales she had just learnt of and they all discussed it and laughed. In the middle of another round of raucous laughing the door opened again and a man in his late thirties to early forties came into the bar. Melissa had not seen him before and once he had ordered and paid for his pint of lager he moved to walk over to the table nearest the roaring fire until he was hollered at by Quentin.

"Its no use hiding over there, we will talk to you anyway!" They all laughed including the stranger.

"Well that suits me fine. I would be very happy to be included in your conversation; you look like you are having a good time." And he turned and took up the remaining available stool at the bar.

"Now who are you?" Quentin demanded peering over his glasses at the stranger as he wriggled to get comfortable on his slippery stool.

Laughing the stranger replied "I'm Andrew; it's a pleasure to meet you all."

"Ah, Andrew, don't speak to soon, you may regret it. This is Sebastian and the lovely Stephanie. Most importantly of all your fabulous bar lady for this evening is Melissa and I am Quentin. I have a pretty bloody amazing dog called Stanley as it turns out but he is undoubtedly out at another pub this evening and anyway you probably already know him – everyone else seems to!" The happy little crowd all shook hands and Quentin entertained them again with the tales of Stanley for Andrew's benefit and even though they had all heard it before except him they all laughed again anyway, amazed at the ingenious little dog.

"We'll have to get Stanley Cam." Melissa stated.

""Stanley what?" Quentin asked raising a confused eyebrow expertly at Melissa.

"You know, a camera that you fit on him and see the world as he sees it." Sebastian explained warming to the idea.

"That would be marvellous. I feel a TV documentary coming on, quick get Trevor up here!" Quentin shouted.

"So Andrew, what brings you to these parts on such a fine evening?" Quentin asked and as if on cue the wind whistled around the gaps in the door again and the outside door rattled.

"I have been doing some work in the area and was just finished so I thought I deserved a pint before I return to Bristol."

"What do you do for a living?" Stephanie asked after having tipped her head back to exhale a large cloud of smoke from her freshly lit cigarette.

"I'm a builder I suppose."

"You suppose? Don't you know?" Quentin asked bemused.

"Well I am a stone mason by trade but I am quite good at carpentry as well so I tend to do whatever needs doing."

"So what have you been working on around here?" Quentin asked waving his now empty glass at Melissa for a refill and gesticulating with his hand to put a round in for everyone else.

"Today I have been measuring up for a job in a hotel. They have a beautiful vaulted ceiling in a cellar running under the grounds of the whole hotel and it has some repair work needing doing where the road outside was dug up and damaged it."

"Sounds interesting." Sebastian said.

"Sounds expensive." Melissa said as she passed Quentin a fresh drink and offered the others one on his behalf.

"Now then, back to spanking!" Quentin blurted out as Stephanie nearly choked on her drink.

"I don't think we had actually broached the subject yet Quentin." Sebastian said laughing.

"No? Damn, must have just been me thinking it then!"

"I never did understand; is spanking with your hand or an object?" Stephanie asked giggling.

"Hmmmm, I had always envisioned a ping pong bat myself!" Quentin said grinning mischievously.

"I always assumed you used your hand, but now you come to mention it a ping pong bat would make perfect sense." Sebastian said thoughtfully.

"Aaah yes, but the smooth side or the dimply one?" Threw in Andrew for good measure.

"Well that would depend on which way up they were facing surely?" Melissa added and they all fell about laughing and the evening continued in a rowdy downwards spiral which kept them all entertained and drinking steadily.

When Quentin started to stagger on his way to the gents and Marlena asked if someone had left a door open as she wanted to know if he was being blown by the terrible winds or was just pissed; they all decided that they should probably be making a move to go to their respective homes. In happy spirits they said their goodbyes and thanked each other for a pleasant evening and then they all left in their different directions at which point Marlena and Charlie joined Melissa at the bar bringing the grey ashtray that they had already dirtied with them.

"Who was that man?" Marlena asked.

"I haven't seen him before." Charlie said fiddling with the cellophane wrapper on her cigarettes.

""That was Andrew. He's a builder but he lives in Bristol so I doubt that we'll see him again, it's a bit far away really."

"Quite tasty though wasn't he?" Charlie said grinning wickedly at Melissa and Marlena in turn.

"I wouldn't say no." Marlena said seriously.

"You never say no to anyone!" Melissa teased.

"Hey fuckoffski!" Marlena laughed. This was the new word in the kitchen that the waiting staff had made up because listening to Marlena gabbling on the only thing they could pick up was the fact that nearly everything seemed to have a 'ski' on the end of it and so now they all added it to everything.

"What did you think Mel?"

"Not bad at all. But as I said, he lives too far away and he's probably married with five kids."

"Yes, or gay!" Marlena added helpfully.

Friday evening of the same week, Melissa had barely pulled back the bolts of the top and bottom of the heavy front door of the pub when in came Andrew the builder.

"Hi, Melissa isn't it?" He said smiling brilliantly as he followed her through the internal door and into the pub.

"Yes, that's right. Crikey you're keen!" Melissa said looking up at the clock on the wall behind the bar. "What can I get you?" Melissa smiled warmly.

"Oh, no…nothing actually." He said as his cheeks coloured slightly.

"Wow that has to be a first." Melissa laughed as her brow wrinkled in confusion.

"No, I'm sorry I am in a bit of a hurry, but I was just wondering…"

"Yeeeees?"

"Well I have been thinking about you all week and what a nice night we all had here on Tuesday and well I was wondering if you might like to come out with me one night?" Andrew gabbled out, now very red and stepping nervously from one foot to the other.

"Oh wow! I wasn't expecting that." Melissa flushed scarlet.

"Yes she would wouldn't you Mel!" Marlena appeared at the bar behind them.

"Ummm, yes, that would be very nice." Melissa smiled at him.

"Oh great, thanks. Byeee then!" He turned and rushed out. Melissa stared after him as the door shut and Marlena laughing said "Go after him!"

"Andrew!" Melissa called as Andrew was walking away from the front door towards a small silver Escort van.

"Yes?" He turned and faced her still smiling and flushed.

"When were you thinking?"

"Oh, yes God! Sorry!" Andrew said and slapped the palm of his hand against his forehead in disbelief at his blunder.

"Saturday week any good to you? Dinner? I know a really nice place."

"Ummmm yes, that will be lovely. Thanks."

"I'll call in with the directions sometime in the week. Must dash. Byeeee for now. Thanks!" said Andrew as he stepped backwards and bumped into the side of his van.

Melissa stood stuck to the spot as she waved him goodbye as he sped off whilst what had just happened sunk in. As she made her way back into the pub and Marlena finally became visible behind her smoke cloud she was laughing at Melissa as she hurried back behind the safety of her bar.

"*Melissa's got a date! Melissa's got a date!*" Marlena chanted childishly at her.

"Shut up!" Melissa laughed and turned away so that she would not be able to see her embarrassed face.

"At least he's got a big dick." Marlena said matter-of –factly.

"What?" Melissa looked around appalled "Don't tell me you have slept with him too?"

"Naaah, but he has a very big nose." Marlena laughed.

"What has that got to do with the price of fish?"

Marlena looked confused but ignored the question. "Big nose big dick. Everyone knows that!"

"I have never heard it before. Here they always say big feet... big....."

"Shoes!" Bruno added helpfully appearing behind the bar to top up his wine glass.

"What naughtiness are you girlies talking about now?"

"Ah, the perfect man. Bruno, have you ever heard about the fact that the size of a man's nose is in direct proportion to his... bits?" Melissa asked refusing to use any of the male genitalia references; none of which she liked the sound of.

Bruno closed the fridge door with a flourish whooshing his hand up above his head as he spun flamboyantly to face them whilst simultaneously picking up his full glass. Thinking for a moment he then turned sideways on so that they might see his profile and then slowly brought his hand up to touch his large, slightly Roman looking nose.

"Living proof!" He laughed and practically skipped out to the kitchen.

CHAPTER THIRTY-SEVEN
THE OLD GITS

Tuesday lunch and an average sort of day (in The Olde Flagon sense of the word) at the pub; if not a bit quiet. The fire was blazing brightly with an occasional swirl of grey smoke being sucked up the chimney from the still damp chips of coal that Melissa had emptied out of the bottom of the ancient and ridiculously heavy, even when empty, brass bucket onto it a short while before. Dennis, Burt and Reg of 'The Old Gits' arrived for their weekly lunch of four halves each of 'the black stuff – in handles', a cheddar ploughman's for Burt (most of the cheese from which Dennis and Reg would eat) a soup for Reg, a bowl of chips to share between Dennis and Reg (which they would then spend most of their time squabbling over the fact that the other one had eaten more than his fair share) and whatever took Dennis's fancy dependant on how expensive it was and whether or not it was Reg's turn to pay. Reg always accused Dennis of only ordering expensive things when it was his turn and that he took more turns than Dennis did. This in fact was not the case but it gave them something else to squabble over and it entertained any other customers who could over hear them carrying on; and indeed Burt who was forever catching Melissa's eye and smirking at the pair of them. All three were in their late eighties; Burt had one year on Dennis but he was slightly more rickety and used his stick to

aid his walking all of the time. Burt was Melissa's favourite of
'The Old Gits'; he had a smile permanently on his face and a mischievous twinkle about him and he was a perfect gentleman and
did his best to keep Reg's language and evil comments in check.
Reg was remarkably fit and young looking; particularly baring
in mind that he had endured a triple by-pass operation only a
few months previous at which time Dennis told everyone he was
going to have a heart 'put in' owing to the fact that he was such a
mean and spiteful old bastard. He was outrageous and hideously
outspoken, making spiteful comments clearly intended to hurt
(although on his frequent tellings off from Melissa he always said
it was only meant to be funny) and always at an overweight and
or unfortunate looking person's expense. In The Olde Flagon
of course that left all of them as sitting ducks and it was a constant source of amazement each visit how he didn't end up with
ground glass, arsenic or laxatives buried in his food or drink or
both; it was nothing short of a modern day minor miracle that
kept him unharmed – some of the things he said were so cruel
they even embarrassed Dennis and that really took some doing.

About an hour and a half after their arrival Dennis and Reg
settled their respective bills (as whoever bought the food did not
buy the drink just to add to the confusion). Burt very sensibly
had shuffled off to the Gents whilst this fiasco took place, grinning at Melissa as he ducked around the corner as they began
yet another row. Finally with everything all sorted the three old
men turned to leave and in walked Patrick Hilton and Jonathan
Mills from the local quarry where Dennis had once worked, and
warmly greeted the three still bickering old men. Patrick had
replaced Dennis as quarry manager when he finally retired (and
ten years later than he should have). Dennis was well looked
after by the quarry people; particularly because he was a large
shareholder and unable to stay away, even going in every day to
take the mail to the post office and to feed the swan which had
inhabited the flooded part of the quarry.

Patrick winked affectionately at Melissa as he heartily
shook one of each of The Old Gits' hands in turn, followed by

Jonathan, his second in command who comically raised each of his thick eyebrows at Melissa and asked if they had been behaving themselves for her.

"I haven't been to the lake this morning Patrick cuz I couldn't get in. Someone had damaged the gate and it won't open."

"Really? What sort of damage?" Patrick asked concerned.

"Must have been hit with a car I should think."

"Anyone checked Dennis' car for dents recently?" Melissa asked in a low voice. Jonathan and Patrick both laughed and Dennis swung around to look at her suspiciously.

"What wickedness are you saying about me now?" He asked waving his arm around in a mock effort to swipe at her with it.

With The Old Gits gone and Jonathan and Patrick comfortably occupying their vacated table with their pints of beer, the front door creaked open again.

"Oh no…here's trouble!" Melissa said in a loud voice as she smiled at Ted Dando as he awkwardly made his way in through the door. His uncomfortable amble always reminded Melissa of how she felt when she wanted a poo but was too embarrassed to go because she would either stink the place out or fart loudly or both. Naturally not getting to the toilet before both of these things happened would be far more embarrassing but she always believed her body did not hate her enough to let her down that badly yet. Ted's strange and careful wander was more likely due to leg ulcers which he had been cultivating for months ignoring his Doctor's care instructions for them; his beer taking priority over his antibiotics.

"The usual then Ted?" Melissa asked; the pint glass already in her hand and poised for action under his favourite beer pump.

"Hello Mel." He grinned widely, lecherously eyeing her up. "Yes please."

"Hello you old reprobate, how goes it?" Jonathan asked affectionately thumping Ted's arm as he came to the bar with a menu in his hand to place an order.

"We'll get that for you Ted." Patrick said walking across to join them and shaking his hand.

"Well thank you, that's mighty kind of you. Thanks Mel." He said as she placed the dark brown pint down on the bar towel in front of him and he stared at her a lot longer than would normally be considered polite.

"Stop staring at me you lecherous old git!" Melissa harshly reprimanded him.

"Yes Mel. Sorry Mel. Hee hee hee hee hee hee. Oh Mel what would we do without you? You're so lovely."

"Piss off you pervie old sod!" They all laughed at this friendly banter and then the men all started discussing the fencing work that Ted had been doing for them. With few customers left in the pub Melissa had very little to occupy her, excluding cleaning, so she loitered at the bar and took part in their discussions. Ted resting awkwardly on one of the most uncomfortable bar stools that Bruno could have found to purchase, with his back resting against the bar next to Melissa. The door creaked open again causing the conversation to stop; reminiscent of when someone entered a saloon on a western film, and everyone all looked up to inspect the new arrival.

"Not you again! Haven't you got a home to go to?" Jonathan laughed heartily at Dennis who was back again.

"Bloody 'lectrics off and the house is too cold to sit around in so I thought I may as well come back and warm myself in front the fire and have another half."

"Put that on our bill please Mel." Patrick said, obviously amused by the scene.

"Thank you." Dennis said settling himself down in his regular seat, no where near the fire, once he had thrown the crook of his walking stick handle roughly over the edge of the bar. "Haven't you got any work to do? Sat there propping the bar up? You're getting fat!" Dennis accused Ted.

"Dennis!" Melissa chided, not necessarily disagreeing with him but not feeling the necessity to voice such an opinion either.

"Actually I have just finished a morning of hard work. I've been fencing since 5am. And I've got to go out seeding that new land around the edge of the quarry this afternoon for your lot."

"They've never employed you have they? Times must be hard!" Dennis jested with him before he disgustingly cleared his throat making Melissa relieved that no one within hearing distance was actually eating at that moment. Thank God there were no longer spittoons in bars, Melissa thought to herself, although frankly spitting it out may have been preferable to the prolonged thinking about the vile fact that he had just swallowed whatever disgusting stuff he had just dislodged. On second thoughts she decided that it was better that he swallow it rather than for her to have to empty the spittoon at the end of each shift. By the look of the expressions being exchanged everyone else in the pub was equally impressed by the throat clearing incident.

CHAPTER THIRTY-EIGHT
THE MEETING

Melissa tossed and turned and turned and tossed and eventually being able to bare the lack of sleep no more finally got out of bed and went downstairs to make herself a cup of tea at 7am. Sydney sleepily raised his head up and spied out at her from under his long eyelashes as she put her foot out on the floor next to him; but presumably deciding that nothing of any interest would come of it due to the hour, he closed his one eye back down and snuggled his nose back in between his paw and the edge of the valanced sheet along the side of the bed. Melissa smiled at him as he lay there and moved as quietly as she could from the room and down the stairs pulling on her dressing gown as she went. From the first landing down the double dog leg staircase Melissa could see Jasper on the small landing down below lying on his back with his black and white legs out straight, half leaning against the wall beside him with his head thrown back and the tip of his tongue poking out through his upside down smile. He looked like one big bundle of black and white fluff until he sensed activity near him and spun himself frantically into an upright position and stared in the direction of the noise; namely Melissa coming down the stairs. He looked at her for a while through vacant eyes with his lower lids still slightly sagging down showing the pink edging to his eyes, clearly not fully awake, then all of a sudden the penny dropped, it was his Melly and up he leapt attempting to get a cuddle from his precarious position on the stairs.

"Get down you bloody silly animal! Good boy. You're all right. Come on out the garden with me." Melissa whispered at Jasper as she ruffled up his big mane-like hairdo around his neck and he happily raced on ahead of her to the back door where he stood impatiently waiting for her to unlock it.

"Yeah, yeah, I'm coming!" Melissa fiddled with the key whilst Jasper looked up at her with imploring eyes to hurry up, and bouncing excitedly around leaving wet smears up the bottom section of the glass where he kept accidentally bumping into the door with his nose. Finally as the lock released the door flew open from the pressure of Jasper leaning against it and he tumbled out into the still dark garden and immediately went over to wee in Sydney's favourite spot; on the base of the washing line pole, taking advantage of the older dog's absence. Melissa quickly shut the door behind him to prevent any further cold air from penetrating the warm house and went off to switch on the kettle watching as Jasper's black and white face appeared at the glass panel in the door and then vanished again obviously having been sufficiently distracted by something elsewhere.

Whilst the kettle boiled Melissa went out to the downstairs toilet and had a wee, stopping and holding the flow mid stream as a conversation Kathy and her had about pelvic floor exercises came back to her every time she had a wee since hearing that if you lose your muscle tone there then you start to wet yourself every time you laugh or sneeze. The fact that this conversation had taken place in relation to Kathy's pending pregnancy was neither here nor there because Melissa figured the amount of time that she spent laughing she'd be wearing a nappy – forget an incontinence pad. Resuming flow again Melissa wee-ed and wee-ed and wee-ed and eventually through the ridiculously thin partition walling she heard the noisy kettle switch itself off after boiling. As she came back through to the dining room and kitchen Jasper's face was visible again pushed up against the glass and he barked as she approached.

"Sssssshhhhhhh!" Melissa hissed at him. It's silly o'clock, you'll wake Mum and Dad up!"

"Too late!" Melissa's Mum called through from the kitchen where she was pouring the boiling water into three mugs.

"Sorry Mum, did I wake you up? I did try to be quiet."

"I always get up around now anyway, but more to the point what on earth are you doing awake? Did you wet the bed?"

"I couldn't sleep you cheeky cow!"

"You mind who you are calling a cheeky cow young lady." Her Mum chided scowling at her as she plopped the teabags into the pedal bin with a loud doing as the metal lid closed down after she removed her big fluffy slipper covered foot from the pedal.

"Hello boy. Did nasty Melly wake you up then shut you out in that nasty cold, dark garden?" Melissa's Mum asked Jasper as he bounced around her feet and gratefully accepted a Rich Tea biscuit from her.

"Did I wake Dad up as well?" Melissa asked guiltily as she spotted his mug on the unit next to her's and her Mother's.

"Hell no! You know him; he'd sleep through a bomb blast. It's time he got up. We're going to see your Gran today so if I have to do that then he can take me shopping and out to lunch first. Fairs fair…cantankerous old battleaxe!" Melissa's Mum picked up their two mugs and with Jasper bouncing on behind her made her way up stairs. Melissa's Gran (Granner) was an absolute nightmare these days. She used to be such a dear little old lady, very prim and proper, but lately, rather shockingly, she was causing so much trouble in the home she was in that Melissa's Dad had been warned that if there was any more agro that she would be asked to leave. The latest incident was over her glasses. For some reason Winnie, the lady who slept in the chair next to Melissa's Gran in the day room where all the in-mates spent most of their time, had put her glasses down on the chair next to where Melissa's Gran had already put hers. Winnie put her glasses back on later only according to Melissa's Gran had put on *her* glasses and not Winnie's own pair. Melissa's Gran had asked for them back but Winnie had told her that she was mistaken and that she was wearing the correct pair and refused to hand them over. Eventually in a fit of rage (never before heard of) Melissa's Gran had ripped them off of her face and Winnie had slapped her hand away and so Melissa's Gran had slapped her back and it had ended up with Zimmer frames at dawn and a terrible to-do that the conscious in-mates found themselves caught up in; probably the most exciting thing that had happened to them outside of the television soaps in years! A few days before this Melissa's Gran had lost her bottom set of teeth. There were several trains of thought as to how this may have occurred; either Melissa's Gran had wrapped them up in a paper napkin and put them on her breakfast tray in her room which ended up being thrown away in the rubbish, or that as her Gran insisted the girl came around and collected them up in a big basket full of everyone's teeth to clean and never brought them back, or as her Gran now suspected after the glasses incident – Winnie had stolen them too and so every time they saw each other (they had been separated in the day room) Melissa's Gran spent all her time staring at Winnie trying to see if she was wearing her teeth. For Melissa's father unfortunately, senility had set in too far unfortunately to be able to get his Mother to understand the fact that people's mouth shapes varied enormously and so the chances of her teeth fitting Winnie were highly unlikely and indeed why on earth would she want her nasty old teeth in her mouth anyway. No, Melissa's Gran was adamant that Winnie had her teeth and would not be dissuaded. Sadly two weeks after the fighting began Winnie died in her sleep (foul play was ruled out much to Melissa's Dad's relief) not feeling the slightest bit of remorse Melissa's Gran had straight away asked her Dad on his visit the next day to make sure he went and got her glasses and teeth back before the body was buried. Needless to say he did not, for which he never got a moments peace.

Melissa switched off the kitchen and dining room lights and went back upstairs where Sydney was snoring loudly and this time did not wake up even as she stepped over him and flopped down into her duvet (after first safely depositing her big green bucket of tea on her bedside table of course).

Melissa propped herself up with her pillows and picked up the latest supermarket top ten novel she was unenthusiastically trawling through and found herself re-reading the same paragraph over and over due to her anxiousness about the evening to come and what it would entail. Not being very good at the whole girlieee vanity thing she reached into the drawer of her bedside unit and pulled out a tatty cornered note pad and a pen and began to write herself a list of all the things she had to remember to do that day.

1. Legs
2. Feet
3. Toenails
4. Disconnect eyebrows
5. Clothes
6. Shoes
7. Find Hotel

Happy that she had somewhere to begin now, she lay the pad and pen back down beside her on the bed and picked up her mug of tea as she went over her plan of action. None of which could take place until after her parents had left the house otherwise they would be bothering her about where she was going and with whom.

By 8.30am Melissa was enthusiastically waving her parents off from her favourite spot by the kettle in the kitchen which overlooked their front drive. Having made herself yet another mug of tea she went back upstairs and rummaged through a few of her drawers, turfing underwear and odds and ends all about the floor until she found what she was after. Finally she found it; her electric sander as her Dad referred to it; otherwise known as a Babyliss Smooth and Silky – it was one of the hair removing people's best kept secrets; basically a revolving piece of sandpaper that whizzed around so fast that it broke the hairs off whilst at the same time acting as a magnificent exfoliating device, the only downside of which were the clouds of dead skin dust that it left around wherever you chose to use it. It was painless, and Melissa actually meant this – not like those evil epilators which also claimed they were – and it left your skin silky smooth afterwards. Melissa sat on her bed and began 'sanding' her legs and watched as her carpet and sheet got covered in fine Melissa dust. She did not mind this because the end justified the means and she was such an untidy devil anyway that it mattered little to her that powdered Melissa was all over her floor. On completion of this she then set to work on her eyebrows – not with the sander though. Melissa had never had much in the way of eyebrows which was fairly remarkable considering that both of her parents had been very over endowed in that department, indeed, if she had not looked so much like her Dad in every other way Melissa's eyebrows would have made her believe she was adopted. Her Dad's eyebrow hairs got so long that people were forever telling him that he had a hair in his eye and on helpfully going to remove it for him discovered to their embarrassment, and his pain, that it was actually attached. Melissa's favourite retort about her Dad's complaints of finding her long hairs everywhere all round the house was to ask him to in fact prove that they were hers and not in fact his eyebrow hairs that he had shedded. Her Mum's eyebrows were also fairly thick, no where near her Dad's league of course, however in her Mum's case weirdly, her eyebrows had gone grey, bordering on white, but conversely the hair on her head was predominantly brown still with just a few grey highlights making anyone observing assume that she dyed her hair but forgot to do her eyebrows. Melissa had very thin quite long eyebrows and truth be known she was actually quite pleased with their form, with the exception of the fact that she did not really have eyebrows but rather an eyebrow; owing to the fact that there was no gap in the middle. Once in a blue moon when Melissa remembered, she took the tweezers to the middle section but generally she forgot just making her look very cross all the time with one dark frown line all above her eyes. As it was unlikely that Andrew may be close enough to see her mono brow she deftly yanked out several hairs at a time until there was a couple centimetres gap above her nose and her eyes were running with tears. The thought of Andrew sent her stomach churning and before she had chance to check for any missed stragglers Melissa flung down the tweezers on the shelf of her wardrobe and raced off to the bathroom just in time to empty the contents of her bowels out at high pressure, in record breaking time and with record breaking stench. Sitting poised over the pan as she wondered what had just hit her Melissa felt goose pimples crinkling up the outside of her arms and legs and then she flushed hot and cold until another mass of high pressure poo left her body. 'Oh well, better out than in.' She thought to herself burying her nose under the collar of her dressing gown in an effort to muffle the terrible smell. Jasper at that moment came thundering up the stairs and stuck his head around the still open bathroom door. No sooner had he spotted Melissa she could see his nose twitching before he turned tail and sneezed himself back downstairs. Feeling fairly empty by now, Melissa decided to risk getting up, and so flushing the loo she washed her hands thoroughly and then sprayed around dome hairspray in an attempt to cover the smell. The overall effect was worse and so she flung open the large bathroom window, the little one already being open and seeming to have little or no effect, and then she shut the bathroom door on it. Looking at the time she realised that the omnibus edition of Emmerdale would have started on television and so grabbling a towel from off the handle of the ski machine Melissa went downstairs to the lounge and found the correct channel. The advertisements were on and so she went out and made yet another mug of tea and grabbed a handful of Rich Tea biscuits and also picked up the carrier bag that she had left on the dining room table the previous day. Once she had settled into her programme and shared the biscuits between her and the dogs she rooted around in the carrier bag and withdrew a large plastic foot file from its packaging and turned it over in her hands examining the two different coarseness faces. Then she lay out the towel on the floor beneath her feet and began filling away at the dead skin on her feet with the roughest side of the file. Sydney, interested in the carrier bag noise had hung around until suitably disgusted by what she had started doing, he turned tail and went off to hide in his 'hole' between the arms of the sofa and the chair at the other end of the room. As with her legs earlier, clouds of dead skin were becoming air-born and wafting up around Melissa as she violently filed at her feet. If her Mum came back and caught her now she would be in so much trouble on her Mum's best carpet and sitting on her expensive leather sofa. 'Wipe clean' was what Melissa thought about the leather suite and so filed away to her hearts content feeling where she had filed from time to time to check for smoothness and rubbing the little dusting of skin that had collected around the edge of the towel into the carpet with the foot that was not currently being treated.

"Don't look at me like that; you're not one to judge me when you lick your bum on this carpet!" Melissa told the apparently scowling Sydney who was staring at her. Raising his eyebrows as if to admit that she had him there, he closed his one accusing eye and went back to sleep.

Melissa's feet were always dry and horrible from so many hours of standing with the weight of a hideously overweight body on them she assumed. A good half hour of filing later and she was finally satisfied that they were good enough to be seen when the Emmerdale music signalled another tea break. When she had returned to her seat she rooted about in the carrier bag once more and this time brought out a pale green and white stripy tube of menthol foot cream for tired feet. The cream was a pale minty colour and the smell instantly cleared your sinuses even before you started rubbing it into your feet. The sensation was rather lovely as Melissa applied at least twice the amount needed and slithered her creamy hands all over her feet until they could absorb no more. Out of the corner of her eye on the radiator at the far end of the room Melissa spied a pile of odd socks which her Mum had left there when she had been doing the ironing (ever hopeful of finding each sock a mate) and so gingerly standing up and resting her weight on her heels Melissa carefully shuffled over to the radiator not worrying about the menthol trail she was leaving behind her and grabbed two socks from the mismatched pile and sat down on the sofa at that end of the room to put them on. The cold leather on the backs of her legs made her wince but she had quickly donned her odd socks and walked normally back to original seat feeling the heat from the menthol cream warming up her now covered toes and her remarkably smooth hands.

Melissa spent hours on and off for the rest of the day preparing for her big date. She tried on every outfit she had, at least twice and at least fifteen different pairs of shoes and boots leaving all discarded items strewn around the floor of her room which she would periodically trip over and stand on the heels of the most painful upside down shoes. Every time Melissa checked the clock to see the hours being whittled away before her very eyes, she invariably ended up rushing off to the loo again. She was really quite amazed at where it could all be coming from and so happily grazed on anything she fancied throughout the day knowing it would be back out again shortly.

Melissa's parents arrived back at around 5.30pm having stayed for a cup of what her Dad described as gnats pee tea and a dry old piece of fruit cake which her Gran had tried to convince him was made with dead flies and not currants. Melissa's Mum was fuming as her Dad had convinced her to go not having pre-warned her that he had in fact promised to take the old girl out for lunch and so as well as the continuous sniping about Winnie and the constant need to repeat everything (due to her refusal to switch on her hearing aid as it made everything too loud) they also had to go to the crappy pub not far from the old people's home because it was the only place they knew of with disabled access that had a view. The food was awful but Melissa's Gran insisted on having a view of the river, even if it meant being right next to the noisy kiddies section (Which of course with her hearing aid off was not noisy at all and so what were they making all the fuss about?) Melissa's Dad looked exhausted as he ended up doing most of the talking on account of the fact that his wife and mother did not really like one another. His Mother's most popular habit was on any journey was asking if the approaching car or one they were following was like her old one. This became particularly amusing when her old car was one of the first of the minis and she would ask if big estate cars were like hers and would argue until distracted by the next car that took her fancy that she was right and they were wrong. She, after all had been there and they had not.

"You all right then?" Melissa asked her Dad as she appeared at the final landing on the stairs still towel drying her wet hair in time to see the dogs excitedly greet him.

"No we're bloody not! Bloody woman! She told me it was about time I started wearing a panty-girdle now that I have let myself go." Melissa's Mum shouted as she disappeared off into the kitchen. Melissa smirked at her Dad who was trying hard not to laugh burying his head into the furry neck of Jasper as he stood on his hind legs with his front feet on her Dad's chest. Having extricated himself from the dogs Melissa's Dad was just lowering himself down in his favourite chair in the lounge when Melissa's Mum stormed in looking for him.

"And you needn't make yourself comfy there either! You can go up and change your shirt; you are taking me out for a proper meal!" Melissa looked at her Dad's shirt where he had spilt something greasy down it.

Reluctantly Melissa's Dad eased himself up out of his chair and left the room winking at Melissa as he went and patting Jasper as he bounced happily beside him.

"And don't tell me you've been sitting around in your dressing gown all day!" Her Mum looked disapprovingly at Melissa who had perched herself down on the arm of the sofa as she patted her wet hair.

"Of course not." Melissa fibbed "I've just had a shower and heard you come back so I thought I would come down for two minutes and be sociable."

"Hmmmmm." Melissa's Mum answered still eyeing her suspiciously as Sydney appeared at her Mum's side leaning into her leg in an attempt at getting some attention. "Shall we get you some dinner then?" She asked him loudly as he raised his head up and looked at her adoringly. At the very mention of dinner he was gone. Already half way to the kitchen before the sentence was completed.

"I think you can safely take that as a yes then." Melissa laughed as her Mum followed on in the same direction.

"Yes, I'm coming!" Melissa could hear her Mum laughing at Sydney as he had doubled back to hurry her along.

Melissa glanced up at the clock on the mantelpiece and seeing that it was now 5.45pm got up with a start. She still had her hair to do and put some make-up on, but not before she went to the loo again she assessed as she rushed off in the direction of the downstairs loo. A short while later heading back up to continue her pre-date preparations, Melissa stepped to one side and held on tightly to the banister rail as Jasper passed her going in the opposite direction halfway up the stairs responding to the call for dinner which her Mum had bellowed out. Melissa smiled as she watched him go and could hear the sound of Sydney's metal name tag jangling against the side of his metal dish as he presumably tucked into his already. Then she continued on up where her Dad was waiting for her at the top rather than having to pass on the stairs which apparently was supposed to be terribly bad luck. Melissa did not believe in this however and neither she suspected did her Dad, more likely that it was the most sensible option rather than squeezing two overly large cuddly shaped bodies past each other in a restricted space.

On the landing Melissa bent down to retrieve her hairdryer and switch it on. She was sure that there were quieter jet engines than the row that it made when she turned it up to full power and blew her hair around haphazardly as she bent over so that her hair fell downwards towards the floor. Half way through the drying process she could hear something being shouted to her over the noise and so she switched it off for a moment and heard her

Mum yelling up to let her know that they were off out and that they would see her later – and of course the obligatory "Don't forget to lock up if you go out, leave a light on and the radio on for the dogs." Agreeing to all this and wishing them a nice time Melissa flicked her hair back upside down drying it once more until there was no damp left and then energetically she tossed her head back causing her long brown curly mane to shower down over her shoulders in quite pleasing ringlets she was pleased to discover as she peered into the toothpaste splattered mirror in the bathroom. Fortunately as she admired her hair and thanked the Gods which she did not believe in, the toothpaste splatters reminded her that now would be a good time to brush her teeth as she could just about guarantee dribbling toothpaste down her top if she waited until later. Having wiped her mouth in the hideous not to mention scratchy, orange nasty circular patterned towel which they had inherited from their Gran when she moved into the home (which was in fact older than Melissa) she tossed her head upside down again and sprayed half a can of maximum hold hairspray over her dark and shiny locks, stopping only when she ran out of air sufficiently to cause her to cough. Giving it a moment to dry a little she then flung her hair back so that she was now standing upright once more and felt slightly giddy from the rush of blood and then watched as the weight of her thick curls brought her big eighties hair under control to more in line with King Charles Spaniel ears, the dark spiralling ringlets catching the light from the unshaded bathroom light bulb causing Melissa to smile with relief that at least her hair looked all right even if every thing else was a disaster.

Melissa pulled her black top carefully over her hair and then, whilst she remembered, applied her deodorant, careful so as not to cover her brand new black bra that along with matching knickers she had eventually found after hours of only shopping and only being able to find thongs, because if there was one thing that Melissa knew: it was that fat arses and thongs did not mix, even though she was appalled to discover in 'Fat Bloater Evans' as she referred to the outsize women's clothing store she often frequented, did in fact stock very sexy see-thru thongs up to a size 32!) pleased with herself that she had remembered not to put it on when she first got out of the shower because she always managed to smear white streaks all over whatever it was that she most wanted to wear. Once she had put on the top, she was about to put her make-up on and then thought better of it, and so covered herself back up with her dressing gown once more. Picking up her mobile phone to check the time Melissa was appalled to see it was so late and in her haste to apply her make-up managed to jab the mascara wand right into her left eye which streamed black tears all down her cheeks on both sides and sent spiders legs imprints over her eyelids making her have to wipe the whole lot off and start again and leaving her with a rather red looking eye which she could not stop weeping sufficiently to dry the lashes enough to apply the mascara again without it going on much less think than the other eye which made her look like she was squinting. The more it went wrong the more Melissa panicked and the more she panicked the redder her face got and she could feel the moisture appearing in the small of her back and on her forehead. With her mouth wide open as she concentrated on applying the mascara to the most watery eye she dropped the mascara wand and the mascara brush bounced off her chest, rebounded off against the door length mirror she was standing in front of in her bedroom leaving a wiggly black smear and then it landed on the pale grey carpet. Cursing under her breath she bent over and picked it back up and pulled off the multicoloured array of hairs it had managed to attract from where both dogs had shed their fur and then as she stood upright she banged her head against the corner of the knickers drawer that was slightly protruding from the wardrobe that the mirror was attached to. "Oh SHIT!" Melissa shouted out loud dropping the mascara brush again as she reached up to hold her head at the point of impact. Carefully she picked up the brush *again*, now with one of her long hairs also attached to it (or may be her Dad's eyebrow ones) and arose slowly so as not to whack her head again. Giving up on her make-up for a moment Melissa put the rest of her outfit on, hoping that she would have more luck with her eyes in a couple of minutes time. Melissa was dressed from head to toe in black, which was not uncharacteristic as everyone knew it was the most slimming colour (God only knew how fat she would actually look she thought if this was the slim version) but for all her dodgy make-up she was actually quite pleased with the overall effect of her black trousers and new long-line fitted black jacket that was actually a designer label that she would never normally give a second look at but which was in a sale and so was only £90.00 which once she had tried it on knew she had to have it; if for no other reason its beautiful slippery silky silver lining. The boots she had chosen were suede stiletto heeled and very pointed, and Melissa loved how they made her feel and the extra height that they gave her; even though she did not really need it. She did not really know what to put on underneath them, normally she wore socks but should the night pan out unexpectedly she did not want to put him off with her sock clad feet, so even though it felt horrible, she slipped her bare but now silky smooth feet into the boots and wriggled her toes as they made contact with the unfamiliar feel of the leather insole.

Finally having one last swipe of the mascara across her eyes she accepted that she could do no more in the time and so tee-tered off downstairs and took her long black coat with a thick fake fur collar from off the back of the dining room door where she had left it and then after checking that the back door was locked she made her way back out into the hall way where the dogs were circling restlessly, watching her sensing that she too was about to go out and leave them. Melissa bent down and gave them both a big hug kissing them affectionately on the top of both of their heads and saying aloud as she did so "Don't kiss the dogs!" which is what her Mum was always shouting at her. Suddenly she realised that she did not have her car keys with her, or indeed her handbag for that matter and so rushed back into the dining room and picked up both from the end of the table, closely followed by Jasper who chased after her thinking perhaps that there had been a change of plan. As an after thought Melissa rushed across the kitchen as fast as possible on her tip toes so as to avoid punishing the lino with her colossal weight magnified by the tiny surface area of her heels and got a biscuit out of the barrel which at the sound of the lid opening they both instantly appeared behind her. Making them follow her back out into the hall way before she gave them the treat to ease her guilt at abandoning them; all three chomped at Rich Tea biscuit and Melissa switched on the hall and landing lights and then went out the front door waving to the dogs as they looked sadly after her. "Wish me luck!" She yelled "I haven't put the radio on for you 'cause I'm sure Radio Bristol drives you as mad as it does me!" and then switching on the outside light and barely missing shutting her hand in the door as she reached out to stop her long coat tails from being shut in it, she closed the door and leant against it to make sure it was locked and then hurried off excitedly down the drive to her car which as she turned around to face the house as she got into the drivers seat could see Jasper up on the windowsill spying out at her with his nose squashed up against the glass.

Melissa had figured that it would take her about thirty-five minutes to get to the hotel where they were having dinner, assuming that it was where she thought it was. It was in Bristol somewhere but frankly if it wasn't a chip shop, cake shop or cinema and it didn't sell shoes, then there was very little chance of her actually knowing where it was. Once Melissa had reached the dual carriageway, which in her estimations meant that she was only about two miles away, she managed to get all caught up in some traffic on a large roundabout with cross hatches and traffic lights on it that when she finally got off of it she ended up in the wrong lane entirely and ended up taking the slip road off onto the motorway. Now being the unadventurous country girl that she was this was actually very unnerving and unfamiliar territory; and worse still, it was taking her in completely the wrong direction away from the hotel and her date. Panicking as she merged with all the confident Saturday evening people venturing out, she glanced at the digital clock above her CD player and realised with dismay that she was already five minutes late. Late along with motorways were two things that Melissa just did not do. So keeping in the left hand lane she sped along for a good few miles until she found an exit road and then once she was off of the hair-raising stretch of road she drove slowly until she found some familiar names on sign posts and followed them until she was right back on the round about where it had all gone wrong some twenty minutes before. Panicking with nerves about being lost and late and the impending date, the sweat was pouring off her and she still did not really know where the hotel was even once she had managed to negotiate the roundabout successfully. Finally after stopping at a very rough looking pub and asking the bouncers for directions (and having to ask if she could have a desperately needed wee) Melissa eventually pulled in through the magnificent stone gateposts topped with some sort of large carved mythical dragon-like beasts with forked tails entwined around and over the top of the post lit up eerily by some cleverly directed lighting on the ground which cast brilliant shadows and highlighted their evil faces. On through the gates the ground covering changed to gravel which crackled pleasingly beneath her tyres as Melissa slowly followed the twists and turns of the long drive way edged by firs and regularly spaced old fashioned style lanterns until eventually at the end of a long straight section Melissa could finally see the beautiful building lit up ahead of her in all it's glory. It was spectacular and Melissa found herself braking to stop and have a proper look.

There was a massive stone staircase with a row of ornately carved ballastrading winding up to beautiful large double doors; both sides of which were open with an impressive set of internal glass doors visible just behind them where a welcoming glow could be seen from the bottom of a massive chandelier just visible from Melissa's vantage point. Melissa counted sixteen windows across the top floor of the building and was just admiring the columns that punctuated them when car lights appeared behind her forcing her to move on. In front of the grand external staircase was a large turning circle with a three tiered fountain topped with three entwined dragon-like creatures the same as the ones on the gateposts, gushing gallons of water out of their mouths and down over the carved stone gigantic clam shells which made up the tiers, catching the light and sparkling magnificently as it fell from one tier to the next. It was edged by beautifully cropped box hedges and more subtle lighting and off to the left of the turning circle Melissa saw an old fashioned white sign post complete with pointing finger directing her to the car park. Reluctant to drive away from the magnificent frontage Melissa drove into a spot under another of the old fashioned street lamps and switched off the ignition and watched as the spot-light motors whirled and swallowed the protruding headlights back into the bonnet of the car. Melissa was really panicking now and could feel her heart racing as she reached across to pick up her bag which had slid onto the floor when she had braked too harshly. Just as she was lifting it from out of the foot well a knocking at her window made her jump and drop the bag again. Looking around in panic she suddenly realised that it was Andrew peering in through the window. Visibly relaxing at the fact that it wasn't some one there to mug her he pulled opened the door of her car.

"Hello, you had me worried; I thought that you weren't coming."

"I am so sorry; I ended up on the motorway and had to do a big loop. I meant to call but couldn't seem to find anywhere suitable to stop and then I thought it would waste more time doing it so I left it and now I see that I am..." Melissa looked at the time on her dashboard, "Oh my God!...over an hour late! I am so sorry – I can't believe it!"

"Hey, you're here now. Come on in, I reserved the table for now so we can go straight in – perfect timing." Andrew offered out his hand to help her up from her low position and embarrassed she accepted it but made a point of not actually putting any weight on it; pushing herself up out of her suede covered seat instead with her left hand and hoping that he did not notice how much of a struggle it was to not look ungainly exiting such an impractical vehicle. Andrew realised she was not making full use of his proffered hand and in one swift movement slid his hand further over her hand and yanked her towards him so that she collided fully into his chest. Melissa quickly stepped back, turning to see where she was putting her feet as she did so, worried that she had winded him banging into him with such force and her colossal weight, in time to catch the kiss that he had intended for her lips to end up on her cheek very close to her ear. Embarrassed they both looked at each other and laughed, Melissa involuntarily raising her hand to her face to touch where he had kissed her and breathing in the musky smell of his aftershave.

"Hhhhmmmm, you smell nice." Melissa said inhaling deeply with undisguised pleasure.

"Do you like it?" Andrew said and offered his neck forwards for another sniff. Melissa suddenly feeling unbelievably self-conscious and aware of every tingling extremity leant obediently forwards into his neck beneath his ear and breathed the rich scent in deeply moving her nose underneath his well defined jaw line just millimetres away from touching him. As Melissa closed her eyes enjoying her proximity to Andrew he reached one arm around her and pulled her towards him grasping his other hand firmly around the back of her neck and angling her face up towards his; leaning his head down towards her as she looked up expectantly until he kissed her ever so gently on the lips lingering in the same position for an unimaginably long time until he sighed deeply and pulled away. Melissa opened her eyes which were sparkling and bright with the excitement of his touch, disappointed that he had stopped, but pleased to see in the light cast by the old fashioned lamp that glistened above them that her feelings certainly of lust at least were mirrored in his smiling face.

"Shall we go then?" Andrew asked not actually having let her go.

"Well actually I was rather enjoying myself out here." Melissa looked up wickedly at him.

"I would have to agree but plenty more where that came from." Andrew laughed finally releasing her from his grasp where upon Melissa stepped backwards towards the car to shut the door and felt her knees buckling. Reaching out to steady herself on the open car door she hoped he would think that she had just stumbled and not realise that he had in fact been the cause.

"Woooahhh, steady there!" Andrew laughed reaching out to stop her falling.

"Bloody heels, terrible invention!" Melissa smiled embarrassed as she recovered and locked the door and then Andrew reached out a gentlemanly arm to escort her inside with. Melissa laughed as he created a crook with his arm for her to latch onto and tentatively slid her hand through which he squeezed affectionately.

"Shall we?" He gestured in the direction of the magnificent building.

"Certainly Sir." Melissa laughed and hoped to God that she did not trip them both up on the gravel in her heels.

The two of them moved along towards the welcoming glow of the hotel with only the noise of the gravel crunching beneath their feet. As they reached the bottom of the grand stone staircase Melissa pulled her arm out from his saying "I'd better go it alone from here; steps and I don't get on at the best of times, let alone with my slut shoes on!"

"Your what?" Andrew raised his eyebrows at her.

Laughing Melissa explained "Oh God, sorry – it's what we call them at the pub." She scanned his face to gauge how appalled he was with her faux pas but he was smiling watching her as she hitched the bottom of her coat and holding it in her left hand she made her way steadily up the steps holding on tightly to the carved stone hand rail winding along the top of the balustrade.

Melissa glanced around her as she slowly climbed taking in the beautiful gardens illuminated below them and the beautiful carved stone pillars and sconces and some intricately carved gargoyles with the tip of an ancient verdigris stained copper spout poking out the end, cleverly highlighted by a green spotlight in the grounds below. Andrew watched Melissa's delighted expressions lighting up her face upon discovering each new distraction around them.

"It's a wonderful place. Have you been here before?" Melissa asked as she watched her expelled breath disperse and then looked up into the cold night sky sprinkled with stars.

"Yes, lots." Andrew said standing close to her at the top of the staircase following her gaze.

"Oh." Melissa said disappointed.

Andrew turned to look at her "I've never brought anyone here. My boss won the contract to do this place up. It was in a right state."

"Oh, how exciting." Melissa perked back up instantly. "Did you find any interesting things buried under floorboards or whatever?"

"Not really. Well, not that I was told about anyway." Andrew laughed putting his warm hand over Melissa's as she rested it on top of the remarkably smooth surface of the stone sphere which adorned the carved newel post at the end of the curvy balustrade.

Melissa looked up through her lowered lashes at Andrew and smiled shyly at him as he leant in again and kissed her tenderly once more and then pulled her gently by the hand across the top of the staircase and in through the impressively large doorway. Melissa found herself smiling uncontrollably as she concentrated on not stumbling on her quivering legs and her high heels. Inside the octagonal shaped foyer Melissa was transformed into another world of corsets and heaving bosoms as she had stepped into a by gone era with the massive chandelier glistening magnificently above their heads suspended from the ceiling several metres above them from the centre of a beautifully ornate dome adorned with plaster cherubs and surrounded by a large glass panelled area where the stars could be seen twinkling through the black sky. The staircase swept around the octagonal walls with a rich warm and highly polished mahogany banister rail topping intricately carved matching spindles interspersed with matt black wrought iron work of trailing metal ivy leaves meandering their way up the breathtaking staircase. The walls were a delicate duck egg greeny-blue with a mural of tropical birds and trees tastefully dotted about and circling up to the glass ceiling above them. In the middle of the ornately patterned parquet wooden floor sat an imposing dark green leather topped heavy legged wooden desk with a state of the art computer monitor and key board positioned at one end ill at ease with it's antiquated surroundings. Behind the desk a long and wide corridor could be seen leading off into the distance with numerous oversized wooden doors with brass handles and door plaques surrounded by more duck egg blue walls fabulously setting off the warm acorn coloured doors. To their left another large corridor led off along the front of the building with several big comfortable wing-backed well stuffed old fashioned plushly covered armchairs visible in front of the floor to ceiling shelves full of multicoloured leather bound books. To their right a mirror image corridor led off out of sight, symmetry clearly featuring very strongly throughout the building's layout. Through the large Greek colonnade style pillars standing century on either side of the large double doorway diners could be seen sitting at starched cloth covered tables adorned with sparkling cutlery, crystal glasses and pure white candlesticks in silver holders.

"This is absolutely fabulous. I don't think that I have ever seen anything so beautiful. Amazing!" Melissa said as she moved her head about as she struggled to take everything in.

A black suited rotund little man appeared and took Melissa's coat and showed them into the library off to the left where he took their drink order and presented them each with a large leather bound peacock blue menu which was lined with a beautiful silk replica of the mural around the staircase. Melissa sunk much further than she anticipated into the plush two seat sofa which they were directed to and tried to right herself without making a further spectacle. Andrew laughed easily and offered her a hand again which she gratefully accepted and wriggled herself to the front and more firmly stuffed edge of the seat where she perched quite uncomfortably until Andrew sat down next to her and was swallowed up into the squashy cushion in much the same way that she had causing them both to laugh and forcing the waiter to force back a smile. The waiter placed their drinks safely out of harms way on a low rectangular coffee table inlaid with a beautiful marquetry hunting scene in several different coloured timbers preserved from harm under a big glass panel. Relaxing back into the squashy cushions next to Andrew, Melissa turned her head slowly around admiring the wonderful plaster cornice way up above them with grapes and vine leaves running along it's length and repeated again on the large circle above the amazing chandelier with a waterfall of large teardrop shaped crystals dangling on golden wires. With the exception of the spaces around the tall windows draped with exquisite peacock blue curtains which were painted the same duck egg blue as the foyer, the walls were floor to ceiling covered with books on shiny dark wood varnished shelves complete with an old fashioned brass railed wooden stepped ladder which could move around the length of the room on two long highly polished brass tracks. The room was arranged with several groupings of varying colour coordinated sofas and seats around other low tables. There was an ancient looking couple sat in high wing-backed chairs in front of the large blazing fire. The lady was knitting something with a ball of multicoloured wool which she raised the needles to shoulder height from time to time causing the ball to bounce about at her feet as it extended the length of yarn free for her to work with. The man wearing an obviously hand made pullover was puffing on a big old pipe which he did so lost in thought as he gazed into the flickering hearth surrounding them both in a haze of sweet smelling tobacco smoke.

"Hey, Earth to Melissa!" Andrew laughed gently enjoying her wondrous expression as her eyes darted everywhere.

"Oh sorry...miles away."

"You haven't even looked at the menu yet. The Maitre d' will be after us in a moment." Andrew laughed drawing Melissa's attention to a very serious looking man who was surreptitiously spying on them from behind the bar near the library ladder. Melissa followed his gaze as the man realising he had been spotted stepped backwards behind a pillar and they both giggled. Melissa turned the thick cream pages attached to the menu on a thick gold cord which ended in a fancy tied tassel which hung out of the bottom of the covers. Birds from the mural were flying discretely in fainter colours across the pages and Melissa ran her hand over the embossed pages appreciatively and then fiddled with the tassel as she read the exquisite descriptions underneath each of the dishes. The rotund black-suited waiter appeared and took their order followed straight behind by the Maitre d' with a contemporary rectangular glass plate containing a selection of tiny bite size delicacies.

"Oh, aren't they wonderful. Much too pretty to eat." Melissa said admiring the dish on the table in front of them.

"You speak for yourself!" Andrew laughed and picked up a mini quiche and popped it whole; grinning mischievously at her before chewing it up. Melissa laughed and examined each of the tiny offerings before choosing the same little quiche as Andrew had shoved in whole; but taking a little bite off of the end to reveal a small piece of cooked salmon amongst the fluffy egg centre.

"Still warm!" Melissa exclaimed surprised as she happily popped the rest of the little quiche in her mouth. "Mmmmm, lovely!"

Andrew reached for a fat, or 'Rubenesque' as Melissa always referred to fat as being, mushroom shape which was covered in golden breadcrumbs. Biting into it revealed it was indeed a mushroom with gooey cheese and chive mixture covering the dark gills. Liking the look of that one as well Melissa chose a similar nibble from the platter and bit into it. Unfortunately the cheesy sauce plummeted in a big globule and splatted onto the leg of her black trousers.

"Oh shit!" Melissa exclaimed, causing the knitting lady to raise a disapproving eyebrow in her direction.

"Sorry." Melissa called over to her sensing her glare. The Maitre d' appeared as if by magic, still clearly spying on them, with a white damask cotton napkin. Andrew took it gratefully from him and the Maitre d' quietly suggested that should Madam wish to attend to it that the ladies cloakroom was just out of the door and to the left past reception. Melissa was flushing beet-root red with all the attention and as much as she would just as soon pick it off and spit on her finger to rub the stain away like she did when it was only her and the dogs watching, she decided her current audience would be even more appalled than Sydney normally was and so reluctantly she struggled out of her seat and armed with her starched to within an inch of it's life napkin and her handbag she headed off shame faced in the direction the Maitre d' was pointing towards.

"Bloody marvellous!" Melissa shouted out loud as she saw her flame red cheeks and dishevelled hair from where she had got herself so hot and bothered on the journey there. Wetting the napkin under the sparkling bright taps Melissa admired the room around her in it's reflection in the mirror. Subtle peach tones covered the walls and curtains and there were piles of fluffy mint green towels on the wide low windowsill and at either end of the set of three sinks in chocolate-brown wicker baskets. In between the sinks suspended from the wall were similar wicker baskets filled with cotton wool balls in pretty pastel shades and miniature emery boards, tampons and sanitary towels in citrus coloured wrappings, sachets containing wet-wipes and a tiny gold canister of hairspray and a little bundle of cotton wool buds on baby-pink stalks. Behind the taps in cut glass pump dispens-ers were peach coloured liquid soaps and similar ones contain-ing a white moisturiser for hands. Directly behind her was a dark brown wicker chaise longues with plump vibrant orange, pink and mint and emerald green cushions propped up along its back. Two colonnade style pillars were topped with Verde gris coloured urns overflowing with trailing flowers which Melissa fingered a leaf of trying to ascertain as to whether or not they were real. Undecided she looked about her and then ripped a leaf in half, instantly feeling bad to discover that it was in fact real and now that she had vandalised it as she guiltily tucked the broken part into the foliage poking out the top of the urn. Melissa fluffed up her hair for a bit but gave it up as a bad job and made her way back out of the toilet holding the door open for a stunningly attractive blonde lady who smiled a thank you with perfect white teeth. Just as Melissa was putting her bag over her shoulder she looked up and saw the back of a large and trim looking man wearing a well cut black suit with the collar of a perfectly starched and brilliant white shirt protruding out filled with a strong and firm looking tanned neck. Melissa having something of a fetish for men in suits lingered slightly longer whilst she ogled at the fine specimen before her until sensing her presence he turned around. Melissa coloured slightly from having been caught out letching, as she suspected that she was turning into old Dennis sooner rather than later, and then on closer inspection the colour completely drained from her face along with the strength from her knees.

"Melissa! What on earth are you doing here?" Daniel asked smiling brilliantly at her.

"I could ask you the same thing. You are supposed to be in France!" Melissa answered rather harshly feeling hurt that he was in the country again and had not bothered to come in and see her. Before any more could be said the stunning blonde re-emerged from the toilet and looking slightly confused at the interloper talking to Daniel sidled up to him and grabbed his arm staking her claim whilst looking Melissa up and down.

"Arabella, this is Melissa. She runs my favourite pub." Daniel said smiling warmly still at Melissa his eyes sparkling. Clearly unimpressed Arabella pulled an imaginary piece of fluff off of Daniel's jacket so that she was completely up against him and then with her back to Melissa said "That's nice but we really ought to be going in, we're running awfully late darling. Nice to meet you Melanie." Arabella had skilfully turned Daniel around and was manoeuvring her prize possessively away from Melissa.

"Oh, yes right. Catch you later Mel. I'll be in the pub in the next few days." Daniel called over his shoulder as there was a loud cracking sound somewhere deep within Melissa's body as a very vital organ was wrenched in half.

Standing there rooted to the spot with tears in her eyes, angry with herself for how stupid she had been to think for a moment that Daniel as handsome as he was would have ever looked at her twice was brought back from her thoughts and directed back to the library by the Maitre d' who had appeared like magic (just like the shopkeeper on Mr Ben from her youth she thought) and relieved her of her soggy napkin. Melissa watched Andrew struggle out of the sofa in order to stand up as he saw her approaching and giggled at his efforts.

"Shall we make our way through now so that you can make some serious mess of your clothes?" Andrew smiled back at her straightening the bottom of his navy blue jacket as he finally got to his feet.

"Now now. You should not mock; it's not just me I can spill things on." Melissa valiantly put on a brave face although all she really wanted to do was go and batter the blonde bitch from hell with a very heavy object and then cry herself to sleep. The crying at least would have to wait. Sod Daniel bloody Palmer, Andrew was a nice man and she was going to have a nice night even if it killed her!

Andrew offered up his arm and Melissa laughing at his old fashioned but charming gestures latched on and they both followed behind the officious Maitre d' who led them through the foyer and out into the restaurant beyond. As they went passed the large wooden panelled doors Melissa could not resist studying everything around her and she saw the look of disapproval on the face of the Maitre d' as he turned around expecting them to be right behind him and they were in fact several paces behind as Melissa had gone so slowly in order to be able to properly admire everything and so as not to trip over her own feet and to delay for as long as possible another meeting with Daniel and the Bitch.

Exactly as she knew would happen Melissa and Andrew were led to the table right next to Daniel's. Fortunately at least the Bitch had her back to Melissa so that she did not have to put up looking at her all night, but unfortunately it did mean that she had the best view of Daniel who smiled warmly at her as she sat clumsily down knocking over one of the sparkling wine glasses with the heavy bump her (feeling lardier than ever) thigh gave the table. With a lot more skill than an English football goalie the waiter nearest them dived for the glass and managed to catch it before the rim made contact with the cutlery it was aiming for and Melissa reddened and apologised as the waiter righted the glass and continued with his other duties Melissa had waylaid him from. Arabella the Bitch turned sharply at the clinking of the disturbed cutlery and to see who Daniel was smiling at and then frowning at Melissa said something to Daniel which made him laugh and Melissa looked down at the table wanting the ground to swallow her up.

Quite a while into the main course Andrew looked over to where Melissa's eyes kept wandering and waved at Daniel. Attention grabbed Melissa concentrated on Andrew and realised how rude she was being.

"Sorry, do you know Daniel too then?"

"Yes, just a bit." Andrew chuckled as he watched Melissa grab a tiny prawn from off of her lap and put it on the side of the plate. "He's my boss."

"Oh my God! What a small world!"

"Yeah, I would never have come here if I'd known he would be here. I thought he was over in France. I'll have to phone round a few of the lads later and warn them that he is back." Melissa did not like this minor act of disloyalty to 'her man' but hey, the blonde bitch had just reminded her in no uncertain terms that he was never going to be that.

"Your's nice?" She enquired as Andrew put his cutlery neatly together on his plate.

"Lovely, really nice. Your's?"

"Really good yes. Little blighters keep trying to escape though!" Melissa flushed again as she retrieved yet another prawn from her lap.

Andrew was very chatty throughout the whole of the meal and so Melissa could listen and keep half an eye trained on Daniel who she noticed did seem to be keeping just as much attention fixed onto them; but thought to herself that that was probably just wishful thinking. As the courses came and went the more loud and slurred that Andrew became and by the time that the cheeseboard arrived and she sadly watched Daniel escort Bitch lady out of the restaurant waving goodbye to Melissa as he paused and turned at the door with a slightly sad look on his face, Melissa realised that Andrew was in fact as pissed as a fart. Marvellous!

Melissa because she was driving had stuck predominantly to water and so now, just like in the pub, was in her normal position of having to listen to the drunken ramblings of the heavily inebriated who think that everything that they say is the funniest thing ever; normally however she got paid for putting up with it, tonight it was really quite the last thing that she needed.

After the cheeseboard was removed an enormous silver pot of tea was delivered to their table which even in her miserable state Melissa was quite touched at and thanked Andrew for his thoughtfulness.

"Oh, how lovely. Fancy you remembering that I drink gallons of tea. This is brilliant!" Melissa enthused as she thanked the waiter but sent him away and told him she could manage the operations from here. Andrew looked confused and smiled a glassy eyed smile at Melissa as he watched her stirring the contents of the rather large teapot as he continued to drink vintage port that he kept signalling to the waiter to keep on topping up. Finally they left the restaurant at around midnight. All the while Melissa obsessing over what Daniel and the skinny Bitch were up to. As Andrew followed Melissa out she heard a clatter and turned round to see he had staggered into a table and in true pinball machine fashion had then rebounded off into the opposite one. A waiter came scampering out from the direction of the kitchen scowling as he surveyed the carnage that were his carefully laid out tables ready for breakfast presumably the following day. So apologising profusely Melissa grabbed Andrew's arm and put it awkwardly around her shoulders in order that she could steer him out of harms way.

"You are so lovely Melissa. Come up to my room with me." Andrew slurred.

"You have a room here?" Melissa asked rather appalled at his presumption.

"Only so I could have a drink and not worry about driving home."

"You live in Bristol; a taxi would have been cheaper." Scowled Melissa as she leant him against the doorway whilst she readjusted her hold on him.

"Naaah, the owner did me a good rate, like she will have for Daniel cuz of all the work we did here. Although by the way she was all over him earlier I suspect he may just get his room for free!" Andrew giggled mischievously.

"What do you mean? That woman with Daniel is the owner of this hotel?"

"Yes. She's beautiful but a complete bitch! Now about that room, you coming to tuck me in?"

"No I am not! Anyway Daniel is married!" Melissa glared at him. "It's late, I have a long way to go, so thanks for a lovely evening but I'll be on my way now."

"Yes, married…very funny!" Andrew laughed loudly.

"Oh, I see you mean it doesn't stop him from playing away?" Melissa asked sadly assuming by his laughter that Daniel must be a serial womaniser.

"He's not the problem…she is!" Andrew said exploding into more guffaws.

"What she is unfaithful to him?" Melissa asked appalled, finding it inconceivable that anyone would ever want to give up on 'her man'. Andrew couldn't reply for laughing and the tears were pouring down his face.

"You mean you don't know?"

"Don't know what?" Melissa asked angry that she seemed to be the source of his amusement.

"His wife prefers the ladies."

"What…she's a lesbian?"

"Hell yes! Now are you coming up to tuck me in or what?"

"But they still live together!"

"Well yes, but so does Dominique."

"Who is Dominique?"

"She is his wife's bit of stuff and Daniel's P.A.!"

"And they all live together?" Melissa asked dumbfounded at this revelation.

"Hell yes, and why not?" Good P.A.'s are really hard to come by. Come to bed with me Mel!"

"No! I'm going home!" Melissa needed time to process all this new information. How could she have known him for all these years and not known about his wife. They lived in the gossip centre of the universe, how was it possible that no one knew or hadn't mentioned it if they had known Melissa thought to herself amazed.

"Oh all right then – if you are sure I can't tempt you. I'll just walk you to your car." He said breaking himself loose from her hold having stood him back up and straightening his jacket before holding out his arm to escort her away. Just as he was about to take his first step however he staggered clumsily towards Melissa and knocked her staggering across the foyer.

"I think I'll be better off without you as an escort thank you."

"Ummmm Melissa, could you do me a favour before you go!" Andrew asked as he started slithering down the wall he was now leaning against.

"What's that?" Melissa asked impatiently needing to be on her own.

"I seem to have lost the use of my legs. They have gone all bendy. It must be something I ate." Andrew said pulling at his right knee in an effort to get it to move as he started slithering towards the floor. Melissa grabbed him roughly and walked him awkwardly over towards the bottom of the staircase. Where were the magical bloody staff when you needed them? Melissa thought to herself.

"What room are you in?"

"Oh great Mel, I knew you'd come." You won't be disappointed." Andrew smiled wickedly at her as he swayed with the effort of retrieving his room key from his pocket.

"52. Just at the top of the stairs and along the landing." Andrew pointed up at the top of the large staircase ahead of them and nearly fell with the effort.

"OK, where's the lift?" Melissa asked as she swung her head sharply about making Andrew screw up his eyes as he was concentrating on her movement which was making him dizzy.

"There isn't one."

"Why am I not surprised to hear that? Come on. Don't let go of the banister or else you'll have us both over!" Painfully slowly they staggered their way up and around the great sweeping staircase. What had impressed her with its size and magnificence had soon lost its appeal by the time they got half way up, particularly as they went up several of the steps twice owing to Andrew staggering backwards and forwards several times on the way and laughing uncontrollably as he slithered down the banister rail. Finally at the top of the landing they turned right and staggered five or six doors along and as Andrew tried and failed several times to get his key in the lock concentrating so hard that the tip of his tongue was poking out between his lips. Melissa propping him up on one side looked about her and her jaw dropped as though she was catching flies at the scene she was unfortunate to be witnessing at the other end of the long corridor. Daniel was standing outside of the door at the very end and in the open doorway Arabella blonde Bitch was smiling seductively and before her very eyes she watched her lean in towards Daniel and putting her hand up around the back of his neck (as they do in all the films with red painted talons for nails) and one hand on his bum, she kissed him. Melissa went all hot and cold and thought that she might be about to faint, simultaneously

Andrew finally managed to unlock the door as he fell through the door dragging Melissa who was still meant to be holding him up with him he yelled out "Come on then Melly, take me to bed!" and the door on its self closing hinge firmly closed behind them. Not before however the disturbance had caused Daniel to turn around away from his embrace and see Melissa apparently 'rushing' into Andrew's bedroom.

Melissa was feeling ill. Nothing or nobody had ever made her feel so awful before. The walls of the room felt as though they were closing in on her and having disentangled herself from Andrew and pushing him backwards so that he was sitting on the floor with his back up against the side of the bed as he smiled like an idiot at her and started nodding off.

"Night Andrew. Thanks again." Melissa said quietly before she let herself back out into the now empty corridor and slowly made her way down the grand old staircase. Once she was at the bottom the Night Porter who was sitting at reception now that she did not actually need him, stood up and asked if he could do anything for her. She was just about to say no when she suddenly remembered her coat and so asked him if he could please find it for her. The Night Porter went off in the direction of the library and Melissa heard him tell someone that he would be back in a moment to get Sir another brandy. Not giving it another thought Melissa gratefully accepted the coat which the Night Porter held out for her and helped her into and she smiled sadly at him and went out of the large front doors into the frosty night air and as soon as she had got back into the safe confines of her car burst into tears.

Meanwhile back inside the hotel the Night Porter returned to the library and poured Daniel another very large brandy who was sitting on his own sadly staring into the flickering fire as Melissa's car whizzed by the windows behind him.

CHAPTER THIRTY-NINE
DOG PORN

Melissa drove through the night like a thing possessed. Due to the lateness of the hour the roads were fairly clear which was lucky because Melissa was completely oblivious to anything anyway and even though she repeatedly switched on her windscreen wipers it did nothing to clear her blurred tear filled vision. She looked a picture; her thick black eyelashes were now black dribbles running the length of her face and the backs of her hands were smeared with black too from wiping away the tears when she realised that the windscreen wipers were no use. She had been driving and crying for more than twenty minutes and her eyelids had puffed up unattractively and trails of snot kept appearing from her nostrils which were irritatingly ticklish and so from having swiped them away with the back of her hand left her with black smudges there too.

Melissa could not understand why she was getting so worked up. He had never been hers. He had never expressed so much as an interest in her other than in jest. But then hey, many a true word spoken in jest Melissa told herself and then banged her steering wheel hard with her fist in frustration. That bitch Arabella was stunningly beautiful and undoubtedly his wife was every bit as gorgeous and skinny too. Although she was a lesbian? Melissa thought to herself running the conversation she'd had with Andrew over and over in her mind. Not possible. It was just a malicious rumour started off by jealous or bitter employees. Melissa was bound to have heard something about her surprising sexual preference by now; particularly if she was having it away with Daniel's own P.A.

Before she knew it, Melissa was only a mile or so away from the village where she lived. Glancing down at the digital clock above the CD player she noted the time and as it was not yet 2am decided she would see if Marlena was still in the land of the living. Ten minutes later as she pulled into the dully lit car park with only a few of the night time exterior lights on, she looked up and sure enough Marlena's window was still brightly illuminated and Melissa could see the multicoloured flashes of the ever changing television screen playing on the ceiling in the gap in the curtains. Bruno's car was not there making Melissa smile to herself happy in the knowledge that at this late hour not to be home could only mean that he had 'pulled'. Abandoning the car across the marked out car parking spaces Melissa got out and closed the door and calling out to Bessie that it was only her as she was barking at her from her bed without bothering to get up (which she could tell by the funny echo of the room she lived in) Melissa let herself in the still unlocked back door and into the kitchen.

"Slapper! Are you awake?" Melissa yelled up the stairs as she went over and lifting up the kettle to check it had sufficient water in by its weight; placed it back onto its base and switched it on. There was a movement on the stairs and Marlena followed by an inquisitive Buddy appeared shortly after in the doorway at the bottom.

"God! Are you OK? You look terrible!" Melissa said swinging round to see Marlena in a blue track suit with her long black hair tied back in a lose pony tail and without a trace of make-up on – a sight never before seen.

"Says she! What on earth has happened? Has he hurt you?" Marlena went nearer Melissa for a better look.

"No, it was Daniel!"

"Oh Christ, bloody Daniel! Forget about him he has moved to France! It's over! Andrew seemed nice, what's up?" Marlena looked bewildered. Normally Melissa was the bubbly confident one. "Bring that into the bar, I need a pint!" Marlena said as Melissa flicked the soggy used teabag into the bin.

"Start at the beginning." Marlena said making herself comfortable on her regular bar stool which involved putting her legs across two other stools next to each other and then wriggling until she remove a squat looking cigarette packet from her pocket and a green plastic lighter, that had been left behind in the pub by some one the day before. Melissa slumped down in one of the chairs around the oval table in front of the bar and put her feet up onto the next chair along slopping her tea down her front and cursing as she did so. Buddy came over and gave her a friendly nudge before she vanished out through the pub and they could hear her footsteps pitter-patter up the staircase above their heads. Marlena listened intently as Melissa told her all that had gone on. Other than being fascinated at the lesbian news and at the many coincidences of the evening especially of Daniel being Andrew's boss and of course that of all the places they could have gone to for their first date it had to be the same place as Daniel and that he wasn't even supposed to be in the country, Marlena was fairly unsympathetic as really nothing of any relevance had ever happened between them; it was all just fantasy in Melissa's head.

This was exactly why Melissa had come to see her, well that and no one else she knew would be up and of course she could not possibly go home looking like Alice Cooper crossed with a puffer fish.

"So what about Andrew?" Marlena asked enthusiastically.

"What about him? Melissa answered miserably.

"Melissa!"

"He was lovely and funny but I only had ten minutes with him before I saw Shit Head and Bitch Face and so that ruined that. Oh, and he got pissed out of his mind!"

"That was probably just nerves. Are you going to see him again?"

"What's the point?"

"Because Daniel isn't interested. You have to move on."

"I'll think about it." Melissa said miserably, scowling as she tried fishing a tiny fly out of her tea several times unsuccessfully with her finger.

"What are you doing?"

"There is a bloody fly trying to drink my tea! Ah…got it!" Melissa said wiping her finger onto the edge of the table.

"Andrew deserves another crack! The best way of getting over one bloke is to shag another!" Marlena said matter-of-factly as she tapped a new cigarette's tip down onto the bar before twirling it around and lighting it. Melissa looked up at her and smirked.

"That's just you, and you never 'get into' the bloke in the first place to need to get over them."

"Hmmmm, yes. Fair comment." Marlena exhaled a large smoke cloud and flicked at a small clump of ash which had dropped onto her leg.

"Anyway, you could do with the practise. You ought to go out with him for a while and if you don't want him I wouldn't mind having a go."

"You are awful!"

"He's a nice looking bloke and if you did not have your Daniel blinkers on you would see that."

"He got pissed out of his mind on our first date!"

"You probably made him nervous! Anyway…and what a first date. How many men go to the trouble of taking women out to big fancy stately homes? It must have cost a packet! See him again and then decide. If you haven't put him off by mooning over Daniel all night!"

"I s'pose you are right. Perhaps I'll let fate decide. If he 'phones me before Monday I'll give him another chance."

"If he got as pissed as you say he probably won't wake up until Monday!"

"Exactly. Fate decides."

"And you accept the fact that there is no chance with Daniel because if his wife is a lesbian he could have asked you out ages ago."

"Yes. I am a sad deluded cow! Daniel means nothing to me."

"Correct. Now as much as I am finding it most entertaining you looking like some sort of explosion in a paint factory I think that you probably ought to go and wash some of that mascara off of your face."

Melissa smiled and slowly got up and wandered over to the entrance to the ladies loo.

"Well rather laugh at me the least you can do is make me another cup of tea!"

"Laughing is much funnier, but OK." Marlena said and watched the door close behind her sad friend.

Sunday afternoon Melissa was just falling to sleep reading through a print out of her book which she had not added to now for so long that she needed reminding about what she had written, when her mobile 'phone shrilled out waking her with a start.

"Hi Melissa? It's Andrew. Are you OK? I am sorry about last night. I hope I didn't show myself up too badly."

"No, you were quite funny. Do you feel all right? I thought you would be as sick as a dog."

"Actually I have just come to now." Andrew said rather sheepishly.

"But it's half past five!"

"I know. Apparently the cleaners let themselves in at mid-day thinking that I had vacated but once they had ascertained that I was not actually dead they left me to it – lucky the room is not booked for tonight!"

"So do you feel ill?" Melissa was eager to think that he was getting some come back for her shoddy date.

"My tongue feels like it could do with a shave but other than that I'm actually remarkably all right. Anyway...I was wondering if you fancy trying again...another date I mean. I promise I won't get pissed?"

"When?" Melissa asked non-committally.

"Next Saturday night?"

"No sorry. I better not take another one off so soon. Week-ends are the busiest time."

"OK, what about the Monday after that?"

"Ummmm…yes…OK thanks. When and where?"

"I don't know, I'll have a think and let you know. I'll call you in the week to confirm details OK?"

"Yep…fine. I'll wait and hear from you. Thanks for calling Andrew, oh and by the way, thanks again for the lovely meal."

"You're welcome. I'm off to get a drink. Bye bye."

* * *

"So he rang!" Marlena was already sitting at the bar with a third of a pint of lager left in the bottom of her pint glass in front of her, the pub telephone up turned next to it and next to that an ashtray brimming with squashed up dog-ends and ash.

"Wow! How long have you been sitting here?" Melissa said picking up the telephone and returning it to it's charger behind the bar. "Uggggh, it's all warm!" She exclaimed wiping off her hand in distaste at the warm telephone.

"About an hour and a half. I have been talking to my Mummy."

"An hour and a half! What on earth have you been talking about?"

"The usual. What I have been doing, what she has been doing…"

"Don't you mean 'who' you have been doing?" Melissa smiled.

"Well yes, that too!" Mummy has three boyfriends on the go at the moment!"

"Do they all know about each other?"

"No, and neither do their wives!"

"Isn't she worried that she will meet someone like her and get the acid treatment?"

"No, not really. I think she sees men as the enemy now and just takes them for whatever she can."

"That's quite sad." Wouldn't she rather have someone to love, just her and him; a couple?"

"She will never trust a man again. She has quite a happy life really. As a mistress you get treated remarkably well and don't get lumbered washing their dirty socks and pants!"

"Yes, I suppose there is a lot of truth in that."

"Anyway...Andrew?"

"He rang up about an hour ago; he had only just woken up and doesn't feel half as ill as he should!"

"AND?"

"AND...I'm seeing him next Monday."

"What tomorrow?"

"No next Monday."

"Tomorrow is next Monday."

"Well I mean next, next Monday then." Melissa said as Marlena's brow furrowed with confusion.

"You English are very odd."

"Yes, says the weird Polish person!"

"Offski!" Marlena laughed lighting up yet another cigarette. Anyway, was Stanley hanging around outside when you arrived?"

"No. Has he been here then?"

"Yes. Bruno's been going mad where he has been trying to get in with Bessie all afternoon."

"Rotweiler and Jack Russell puppies, that would be interesting to see."

"Yes...what a thought....Rotweiller sized head on a Jack Russell sized body!" The two girls suggested more and more silly combinations until it was time to open the pub and Marlena vanished off into the kitchen and Melissa emptied the nearly full ashtray into the bin.

At about 11.30pm Marlena was just letting Melissa out of the pub and saying goodnight when by the driver's side of Melissa's MR2 Stanley was sitting patiently staring at them as they came through the door. Upon seeing the two girls he immediately got to his feet, like the true gentleman he was, and Melissa and

Marlena both looked at each other and laughed after both saying their hello's to him.

"Have you been up here courting then?" Melissa asked Stanley seriously as she looked beyond the car and through to the garden gate where Bessie was sitting as close up to the gate as she could get and whining miserably.

"Oh Bess! Is he playing hard to get?" Melissa asked laughing as Bessie shuffled excitedly around on her bottom, rather like when she was waiting to get a biscuit.

"I think your chauffeur has just arrived hey Stanley!" Marlena said laughing as Melissa put her keys in the door lock and watched as Stanley stepped back a little but faced the door ready to get in.

"You cheeky bugger!" I hope you've got clean feet!" Melissa laughed as Stanley hopped straight in and made himself comfortable on the passenger seat not paying the slightest bit of attention to Melissa and Marlena who were both in hysterics.

"Right, ummm I'm off to Stanley's then! I'll see you tomorrow." Melissa said not quite sure how she had got volunteered into having the scruffy little dog on her suede and leather seat.

"Right, I'm off to 'phone my Mummy again – she's never going to believe this!" Marlena laughed and waved them off as they drove out of the car park, Stanley keeping his eyes trained on the road ahead. Melissa chatted to Stanley for the short journey back to his house but as they drew up close to the large converted barn that Stanley and his owner Quentin lived in, it suddenly occurred to Melissa that anyone seeing her might think that she had dog-knapped him.

"You had better speak up for me at my trial when I get arrested!" Melissa told him sternly as she stopped and got out at the bottom of his drive. Melissa stood with the door open expecting him to hop straight out but Stanley looked at her and then faced forwards once more.

"You cheeky bloody animal! My side not good enough for you – or is it that you expect the full chauffeur service?" Melissa asked as she stomped around the front of the car being momentarily blinded by the headlights which she had left on main beam along the pitch black lane devoid of any street lamps or white lines even. As Melissa opened the door and flamboyantly bowed and gestured for Stanley to get out he immediately obliged and without a backward glance or a thank you, went bounding off up the long drive and around the side of the house. There were still several lights on throughout the building and so after hurrying back into the safety of her car Melissa waited to make sure that Stanley did not reappear and then turned around, reversing into Quentin and Stanley's driveway and after checking one more time for signs of him she drove back up the road the way she had come laughing at Stanley's initiative.

Over the next week Stanley was a regular visitor to the pub and so was Melissa to Stanley's house, returning him home at the end of his courting session concerned that he might get run over on the road if left to his own devices. Each time even when Melissa turned up in her jeep instead of the MR2 he was waiting for her at the end of her shift. At the end of the week Quentin finally turned up at the pub.

"Your dog is a floozy!"

"Good evening to you too Melissa!" Quentin said taking a step backwards as he did to mimic the blow he had received from her verbal battery.

"Your dog is not only up here corrupting poor innocent Bessie but he also has the nerve to expect a lift home afterwards. I feel like some sort of a pimp!"

"What!" Quentin laughed astonished as Melissa put down his usual double whisky and a jug of water in front of him. "That's my Stanley you are talking about, what on earth has been going on?" He groped about in his pocket for some change for the drink which Melissa rung into the till as she explained her new found job chauffeuring Stanley.

"But that's brilliant!" Clever old Stanley! But are you sure he is interested in Bessie? She's that bloody great Rotweiller out there isn't she?"

"There is nothing wrong with our Bessie, and she is just a bit 'Rubenesque'!"

"What?" Quentin asked in his clipped news reader's voice.

"We larger girls prefer 'Rubenesque'…if you don't mind!" Melissa said gesturing to her own body and Quentin smiling as the penny dropped.

"He will never reach; we will have to find him a box to stand on poor brave lad!" Quentin heartily guffawed.

"You may well laugh but it's not funny! And he certainly does not need a box to stand on; today when I arrived I was witness to nothing short of dog porn!"

"What?" Quentin was coughing as his drink went down the wrong way.

"You heard me. DOG PORN!"

"What on earth are you talking about woman? Did he get in with her then?" Quentin asked enthralled like a proud father.

"No he didn't have to! When I arrived Bessie had her bum pushed right up against the gate and Stanley was licking her bits!" Quentin screwed up his face somewhat appalled at the graphic picture Melissa had painted for him.

"But how on earth did he reach? Bessie is twice his height at least?"

"She bent her knees!"

"Ah ha! So it is not Bessie who is being corrupted it is my poor Stanley!" Quentin accused heartily laughing. "Bent her knees indeed!"

"She did! And what's more she was loving it! I had to look away. It was dog porn!" Charlie and Marlena who were in the bar when he arrived were not far off of wetting themselves as she relayed the story.

"Tell him what happened today!" Charlie managed to burst out in between laughs.

"What there is more?" Quentin asked flabbergasted. "You had better get me another Melissa!"

"Well I was coming up your road having been to Slapperton at lunch time and I saw Stanley just as I turned up towards The

Olde Flagon. He looked around as I turned the corner and was then sat down in the verge. I stopped to see if he was all right and as I went around the front of the car he must have gone around the back because when I got to where he had been sitting he had vanished. So as I was looking around wondering where he had shot off to I spotted him sitting in his seat ready to go."

"That's my boy!" Quentin laughed proudly.

"So I turned the car around and drove him home to yours but as I drove him up the drive I noticed that your car wasn't there but I wasn't too worried because I know he can get in, so I got out to let him out. Normally he happily hops out provided that I open his door in the correct chauffeur manner." Which Melissa demonstrated for them "But he was having none of it. In the end I got cross with him and shouted at him to get out and was very firm but he just lay down and turned his head away from me. I stood there for a couple minutes wondering what to do and after a couple minutes I went back around my side and got back in. Just as soon as I did up my seat belt Stanley sat up and looked out the window all happy again. So anyway I thought he might be like my Gran and just like a ride out from time to time, so I took him for a drive for about quarter of an hour or so..."

"You did what? You took a dog for a drive?"

"Yes and laugh all you will but when I brought him back to yours afterwards he got out happy as you like and trotted off around the back of the house."

"I don't know who is more mad; you or the bloody dog!"

CHAPTER FORTY
ANYTHING BUT HORROR

The Monday of the date arrived. It was Melissa's day off but even though she had all the time in the world available to her to do her girlie preparations this time she had no inclination to want to bother and went so far as to almost cancelling the date twice were it not for Sally confiscating her telephone and trying to distract her with the lure of chips and cake out shopping for the day. Melissa was not really in the mood for shopping either. Even though for the wedding she had managed to shed three stones in weight; when no one seemed to notice the difference after her starting at a 'Rubenesque' sixteen stones in weight, she felt rather discouraged from bothering and with the added incentive of 'her man' gone now too – and this time she had to face the fact that it was forever, there seemed little point in doing anything at this moment in time; remarkably even shoes did not bring a smile to her face.

"Hey, buck up Melissa! Give this Andrew bloke a go. He might have a big willy!" She giggled wickedly getting a disapproving look from a shrivelled looking old lady with a knitted burgundy red floppy up-turned flower pot shaped hat on.

"You're as bad as Marlena. That is exactly what she said when she saw that he had a big nose!"

"What about his feet?"

"I can't say I noticed but that is what the nose thing is all about in Poland."

"Really? Does that work does it?" Sally smiled.

"I don't suppose it is any more scientific than the feet thing." Melissa laughed. "What are you doing?" Melissa asked Sally.

"Trying to remember all my ex's nose sizes and comparing them with their…"

"Feet!" Melissa interrupted before they faced the wrath of flower pot hat lady who was still in close proximity.

"Yes, good old Marlena is right. Well who'd have thought it?" Sally carried on chuckling and looked closely at a nearby man's feet and then straight up at his nose.

"SALLY!"

"What? He won't know what I'm looking at." She laughed and wandered off around the shoe department in the men's section.

Melissa met Andrew in Bristol outside of the large multiplex cinema. He was late. Melissa scuffed about from one foot to the other watching her breath condense and the minutes tick by. Eventually when the huge car park was looking very full up she spotted Andrew's work van, a smaller version of Daniel's, head towards her and then turn off into one of the very few parking spaces left. Melissa wondered to herself as he heart had momentarily ceased to beat, if the longing for Daniel would go away ever, then telling herself off for allowing her pathetic fantasy to depress her real world she smiled warmly as Andrew having parked up wove in and out of the cars towards her.

"Sorry I'm late. You been here long?"

"Come on in it's chilly out here." Melissa held the door open for him to go in to distract herself for having a go at him for keeping her waiting for twenty minutes; conveniently forgetting her worse fiasco with time keeping from their first date.

"What are we going to watch then?" Melissa asked looking up at the big digital display to see what films were on and when.

"Oh, it's OK; I already booked the tickets on the 'phone earlier." Andrew said inserting his credit card into the machine to collect them.

"You did? What are we watching?" Melissa said quite dismayed at not having been consulted.

Andrew whipped the tickets out of the dispensing part of the machine and pocketed his card turning away from her as he answered. They were walking by one of the speakers blasting film trailer's sound tracks out for the large screens dotted around the huge foyer as he spoke and so Melissa heard only a garbled sound but decided to hope for the best and pray it was not horror which she could not stand.

They quickly grabbed some popcorn and a drink and due to his tardiness and the incompetence of the bored kiosk workers at serving them they sat down just as the film was beginning, much to the annoyance of the disgruntled people Andrew forced to move to let them by, insisting that they sit right in the middle half way up the rows of seats.

Nearly two hideous hours later they emerged from the cinema. Andrew happily relaying the goriest moments particularly enjoying the scenes where numerous people were hideously massacred.

"I'm just off to the loo." Melissa said as they approached the illuminated sign for the ladies toilet.

"Right oh. See you back out here in a mo." Andrew smiled vanishing off to the gents.

Melissa walked through the toilet door and caught her unsmiling face in the wall of mirrors. Making her way to the cubicle furthest away, because it was the one most likely to still actually have toilet paper in (she and Marlena had discovered from their frequent visits) she shut herself in and sat down. As Melissa sat there and wee-ed she flung her head back and looked up towards the square ceiling tiles and muttered to them that they must really hate her. She probably meant God truth be known but the ceiling tiles were nearest and someone needed to take the blame for the most enjoyable part of the evening being finally able to relieve ones self.

When she had washed and dried her hands and returned to the corridor Andrew was waiting happily browsing through a stand of freebie advertising postcards of which he grabbed a couple. Upon seeing Melissa his face lit up with a bright smile and he offered her his arm in a jokey gentlemanly fashion and escorted her out of the building. Outside the weather had grown colder and there was a fine drizzle being lit up by the bright illumination all around them of the cinema and the next door bowling alley.

"So what now? Shall we go for a drink somewhere?"

Melissa looked at her telephone to check the time. "If you don't mind can I take a rain check on that one? I've had a bit of a day of it. Sorry."

"Horror films not your bag then?" Andrew looked at her tired face.

"Not something I would have chosen but it made a nice change." Melissa said trying not to be rude.

"Hey, no problem. Your choice next time! And when is that?"

"Oh, I don't know….when are you free? Not weekends though." Melissa said surprised that he was still interested.

"I tell you what…rather than us stand around in the cold why don't we go on in and get a drink?" Andrew smiled beseechingly

"You are terrible!" Melissa laughed "And I'm going home – you probably have to be up at the crack of dawn anyway so get off home!"

"Can't blame a guy for trying. How about you think about where we go next time and I'll ring you tomorrow. Not the cinema though hey – I have barely said ten words to you all night and most of them have been sorry." Andrew escorted Melissa over to her car and kissed her goodbye on the lips with the car door in between them and Melissa ducking in quickly to get in out of the rain. Melissa drove home thinking that although he was bit thoughtless regarding the choice of film that he was actually a nice bloke and that she really would make an effort next time. If there was a next time.

The next day Melissa got up early as she had to go to the bank to pay some bills and forgot to take them with her when she was out with Sally. She showered and changed and headed off to Slapperton in order that she could pay her bills and then go on to work from there. Melissa could not find anywhere to park near the bank and so she ended up doing a lap of the town's one way system and parking in the furthest car park away. The irony of this was not lost on her. Slapperton was a bustling market town and there were quite a few people queuing in the bank all armed with paying-in books and the like as they waited glaring at the mother of the screaming toddler who was doing nothing to try and stop the hideous and disproportionately large noise coming out such a tiny body. The mother, presumably, just stared angrily into space from out of her badly applied make-up covered face, exuding hostility from every pore and piercing hole, of which there were many, daring anyone to say anything. Melissa looked at her and wondered if she had looked as frightening as that after her Saturday night crying fest. Finally the owner of the scream-ing child was served and after much swearing at the cashier's inability to give her money, Melissa assumed, she left. Melissa got served a short while after that and was greatly relieved to get out of the stuffy bank and took in a couple of large breaths of fresh air and was just fastening the zip on her bag when she looked up in time to spot Daniel on the other side of the bank door to her just before she realised that he was with yet another beautiful woman and yet again she was kissing him. Melissa's heart stopped and she felt hot but simultaneously the blood left her face. She looked away but it was no good, she had to see and so feeling sick to her stomach she watched as they hugged affec-tionately and then pulled away from each other smiling broadly and still holding onto each other's extended hands. They chat-ted for a moment and then they hugged again. This was just too much for Melissa to bear and so keeping her head down, just in case he noticed her watching, she hurried away stumbling as she did on a slightly uneven curb stone. Tears appeared in Melissa's eyes but she held them back. Angry with herself again for over-reacting so badly. Melissa was just stepping out into the road when a silver Mercedes SLK sports car beeped it's horn at her and flushing with embarrassment and hoping that she still had not been spotted she hurried away. Had Melissa waited just a minute longer she would have watched the beautiful woman who had just been kissing 'her man' get into the same Mercedes that had just beeped at her, and kiss the woman in the driver's seat a whole lot more passionately than she had Daniel. Unaware she scurried off at a fast rate of knots. Many more run-ins like this and she would end up having an accident. Fast cars and broken hearts are not a good combination. Melissa thought as she stamped on the brakes screeching the car to a halt at the same time as the woman with her Satan child from the bank crossed the road in front of her shouting more expletives at her to which Melissa gave her a very heart felt V sign and sped off once more.

CHAPTER FORTY-ONE
GONE WITH THE WIND

When Andrew rang later that day it was arranged that they would meet up again on Thursday morning as coincidentally they both had the day off. Melissa drove into Bristol 'again' thinking it seemed to be she that was making all the effort here and eventually after taking several wrong turns she arrived outside Andrew's house that he shared with his brother. It was a tiny end of terrace little house unbelievably containing three bedrooms, which considering the width of the frontage would fit into Melissa's four bedroom house about three times, she found very hard to believe because theirs was not of impressive proportions. As she pulled into the small cul de sac Melissa saw a large silver works van with the bold italics of Daniel's building firm emblazoned in black on all sides and again there was the momentary flip of her stomach, particularly as it was the same size as the one Daniel himself normally drove around. Melissa turned the car around in a big arc and parked further up the road away from the van at the side of a block of garages with white painted doors. By now her face was so flushed and she had become so hot and bothered from getting lost that she could feel a trickle of sweat running down her back. Quickly she checked her reflection in the rear view mirror and then wiping away the imprint of her eyelashes in mascara from off of her eyelid with a classily licked finger tip she decided against messing with her hair as she suspected she would only make it worse and so grabbing her bag from the passenger seat she exited the car. Once she had locked the car and activated the alarm she pulled the bottom of her jacket down to make sure that it wasn't caught up and revealing her bum and then she tugged at each sleeve trying in vain to make the sleeves appear as though they covered up much more of her long arms than they actually did. Fully adjusted she set her sights on the house behind Andrew's van and walked purposefully towards it. Any onlooker would have been well deceived into believing her confident gait. As she drew closer Andrew appeared at the front door and as he pulled the white PVC door further open towards him Melissa lost her poise and tripped over her own feet stumbling embarrassingly but not completely falling over. Andrew watched on trying to contain a laugh but only managed to stop at a very wide smile and Melissa turned instantly beetroot coloured which she knew did nothing to enhance her large face and big cheeks.

Finally she stepped over the threshold and passed a line of paired up shoes with their toes all up against the white skirting board and Andrew shut the door behind her and where upon she leant forward for her anticipated kiss and he simultaneously turned away to lead them through to the kitchen and turned back to speak to her just in time to realise what she had and indeed he hadn't done. Melissa watched as he instantly coloured up to a tone not unlike her own and they both laughed awkwardly at each other. Once in the kitchen he filled up the dark green jug kettle and switched it on and pulled two matching green mugs from off of their branches on the bleached pine mug tree.

"Tea I assume?" Andrew asked hovering a tea bag over each mug.

"Oh yes. Great. Thanks." Melissa managed to get out in an almost staccato fashion.

"So ummm how have you been?" She continued, managing to pull her self together.

"Yes, fine thanks. You?"

Melissa burst out laughing and he looked around at her puzzled. "Well hark at us, we'll be discussing the weather next!"

"Well yes, but it has been particularly warm lately don't you think?" He laughed and as he did she looked up at him as he did so he suddenly stopped and took a few steps towards her staring intently into her eyes the whole while and then placing his large hands gently onto her waist, or at least the place formerly known as her waist, he gave her a strong tug and forced her to step towards him at which point still with a serious expression on his face he bent his head down and kissed her firmly on the lips. Melissa felt an almost electric charge course up from deep within her and felt her face glow hotter, this time from the adrenalin rush and not from embarrassment. She became very aware of her breasts which were firmly squeezed up against his firm chest and of her embarrassment of a belly which she was sure had touched him before her boobs did as he had moved his arms so that he now embracing her in a very tight and very passionate way. Melissa opened her eyes to look at him, which had involuntarily closed; next thing she thought her right foot would be lifting off of the ground behind her like in the old films (may be Marlena was right about the best way of getting over someone). The thought made her smile and feeling her mouth change shape under his lips Andrew's eyes flashed open and he looked at her in concern.

"What's the matter?" He asked holding her away from him as he stared into her eyes.

"I'm sorry; I just had a laugh coming. I can't help it. If I feel embarrassed or nervous I tend to laugh. Don't take it personally." She tried to reassure him "It's a family trait; my Mum always has to stop whoever she is helping in the middle of moving furniture to have a laugh. Sorry." Melissa looked away and then back at him through partially closed lashes. Then without saying another word he drew her back towards him and kissed her again until she pushed him away and guffawed with laughter. Andrew looked like he had been slapped which made Melissa laugh even more.

"Oh God, I'm so sorry!" She spluttered through her laughter as she tried desperately to stop the laughter. "You just make me nervous I suppose. Please pay not attention. Come back and kiss me…please." Andrew's face softened a little and he obliged her but he was less relaxed and kept glancing up at her through his long dark lashes to check that she was not about to laugh. Finally much to Melissa's relief the giggles subsided as it was clear he was beginning to take offence, may be he was not as confident and self assured as she had first thought.

Finally when they had both relaxed into the task at hand the kettle started bubbling furiously and the lid clumped loudly against it's surround where it had not been shut properly and the water spat out from the spout and up over the sides where Andrew had overfilled it until it clicked loudly off and the red light on it's handle went out. Distracted at the noise Andrew pulled away and went to clean up the spilt water with a tea towel which he grabbed from a plastic hook stuck to the door underneath the sink. Melissa watched on in amusement as he mopped up the mess and then filled up both mugs with water which sent more water gushing out over the edge of the spout where it was still too full. Andrew turned at the sound of her giggling again and flinging the sodden tea towel down onto the counter her walked towards Melissa and said "That's quite enough out of you!" and grabbing her by the arm he frog marched her out of the kitchen, through the small and very tidy lounge and up the staircase which led out of it with Melissa nervously laughing all the way and the teabags left stewing in the hot water. Andrew's expression remained stern the whole time and it crossed Melissa's mind for a split second that she should be worried but seeing a wicked glint in his eye she let herself be shoved somewhat forcibly across the landing and into the first doorway on the right. Even though they were alone Andrew deftly pushed the door closed with his left foot whilst still having a firm hold on Melissa's arms and then without so much as a by your leave he gave her a shove backwards onto the waiting bed, the shock of which momentarily left her speechless and before she had time to think or worry about holding her stomach in he had straddled over the top of her and forced her back into the squishy duvet cover and firmly kissed her. Melissa was shocked by the reaction of her body to his manhandling of her and felt an instant heat in her groin and her breath became quicker, and not just because he was squashing the air from her lungs with the weight of his body either. Before she knew it he had stripped her naked and was just standing over her admiring his prize having removed his own shirt and in the process of undoing his black leather belt when the door bell shrilled out. Instinctively Melissa reached out and covered herself up as best she could with a pillow and pulling it away Andrew laughed at her and said "It's OK no one knows we're here, it's probably just an Avon lady or something." Having undone the belt already he was beginning to unbutton the fly of his faded blue jeans when the door bell rang out again.

"Didn't you ought to go and see who it is?" Melissa asked grabbing another pillow to cover herself up with.

"It won't be for me and I think we have much bigger matters to attend to don't you?" He said looking down pointedly towards the front of his jeans which were beginning to strain at the fly some what. Melissa glanced down to what he was looking at and grinned shyly and looked away. Smiling wickedly at her he moved over to the window and shifted one of the louvers in the dark wooden blinds and bent down slightly to peer out.

"It's the Police!" He stood up abruptly and winced as he tried to pull closed his jeans. Melissa looked panic stricken, the affect that the Police always had on her even though she never broke the law, excluding speeding of course, and Andrew rushed out of the door pulling his still mostly buttoned up shirt roughly over his head. Melissa heard him take the stairs several at a time and the bell ring out again just as he got to the bottom and opened the door.

"Martin Brooks?" Hello, I'm PC Fisher." A trim but pale Policeman stood on the door step.

"Ummm, no. I'm Andrew his brother, can I help you?"

"Well sir I need to speak with Martin I'm afraid. Can you tell me when he will be back?"

"Not for another two weeks, he went on holiday yesterday."

"Aaah. Right. Well may be you can help me then." PC Fisher said referring back to his black note book which he had produced. "Mr Brooks' car has been discovered burnt out in Bristol…"

"There must be some mistake officer, that is Martin's car there." Andrew said pointing to the red Escort parked in the driveway the other side of the white picket style fence they were standing next to.

"Oh right. We have him as the registered keeper of an H registration brown Austin Metro." PC Fisher peered sternly at Andrew.

"Oh that old thing. He got rid of that a couple of years ago." Andrew chuckled at the memory of the tatty battered old heap with missing hub caps and a red bonnet where it had been involved in an incident with a low flying pheasant the first week after he had bought it.

"This is a very serious matter Sir. From my information it is clear that he failed to inform the relevant authorities about the change of ownership. Please tell him to make sure he writes a letter to the DVLA and explains when he sold the vehicle and to whom upon his return." PC Fisher folded away his notepad and touched the brim of his hat and simultaneously nodded in an old fashioned way bidding his leave and said goodbye and then turned and walked down the path and over to his car reminding Andrew of the closing scene from The Bill. Quickly closing the door behind him Andrew thumped loudly up the stairs and had removed his shirt by the time he got back through the bedroom door. Melissa was sitting on the end of the bed looking anxious as he burst back through the door with his stereotypical builder's checked shirt in his hand.

"You've got your clothes back on." He looked at her disappointedly. "Have you changed your mind?" He looked concerned.

"It's not that, I just didn't want to get caught here with all my kit off in case he came in."

"Oh, well that's all right then. I'll just have to undress you all over again. What a hardship. We men really do have to suffer for our art." Andrew said bending over and kissing her as he pushed her back on the bed once more.

Before long they were back to where they were when they had first been rudely interrupted with Melissa lying somewhat self consciously on the bed doing her best to hold her stomach in and bending her legs at the knees in order to raise her thighs off the bed so that they might also appear slimmer, not entering her head of course that raising her legs gave him an altogether different view of her that would leave him fairly unaware of her thighs. Again Andrew stood before her and slowly ran his eyes over every square inch of her, and by golly there were a lot of them, taking it all in as he dropped his jeans to the floor which chinked as they landed from the belt buckle making contact with the loose change in his pocket. Melissa nervously watched as he pulled his jockey pants carefully over his enlarged 'Will' (as he had affectionately referred to it when he had been drunk in the hotel that awful night, a fact that had amused Melissa no end and much preferred to the vile names everyone else used both medically and in slang) and dropped them down on top of his jeans. Just as Andrew was leaning forward and put his right knee on the bed dangling 'Will' dangerously close to her thigh a loud alarm started going outside and the reflection of a bright revolving orange light was intermittently lighting up the bright magnolia walls. Melissa did not know where to look; at the flashing light or the mesmerising appendage and so her eyes darted between the two. Catching them both unawares they both jumped at the alarm and Andrew stood back up and peered out through the louvers of the blinds once more, Melissa stared at his still jiggling about and fascinating bits.

"It's OK; it's only the dustbin lorry. Give me a heart attack, blumin' noise!" With that the lorry noise doubled as the hydraulic rams could be heard whining into action as a wheelie bin was picked up and emptied into the jaws of the large sky blue lorry followed by more noise as it chewed up its latest offering. "And again….where were we?" He said swinging around causing 'Will and the boys' much fascinating turbulence. Andrew caught her looking and smiled at which she flushed furiously and looked away.

"Don't be embarrassed. You're not disappointed are you?"

"Hardly!" Melissa answered before she could stop herself, distracted once again by the unfamiliar shapes and movements. Men and their ego's she thought to herself as she was shocked to see that Andrew was better endowed than the stripper that they had been to see on Kathy's hen night and he remained the talk of all get togethers to date and not just because of his dancing and gyrating either. Melissa inexperienced in these matters had just gone along with the whole being impressed at the size of the guy not wishing to betray how truly lacking in sex she had been, he could have been tiny for all she knew and painted orange! It was a funny old night, as he was always plagued by girls after the strip show he had come and sat himself down with Melissa and her friend Anna as they waited outside for their lift home. They had gotten into a fascinating discussion about the fact that he was actually a quantity surveyor by day but just wanted to earn a bit of extra cash and be screamed at by adoring women. More fascinating was the fact that when Melissa asked how it was that he managed not to get aroused, particularly when he had women eating ring doughnuts from about his person (which he was keen to explain that he had to make the hole in the middle of it bigger) and he told them that he has a rubber ring he puts on like an elastic band that keeps him semi erect all the time, consequently appearing huge at all times. Snapped back to reality Melissa knew that Andrew had asked her something but all she was doing was watching 'Will' still swinging about like an erratic clock pendulum.

"Sorry what?" She looked up at his laughing face.

"A bit less sorry for himself than he would have been on Saturday night hey!" Andrew repeated clearly proud at his latest achievement as he looked at it admiringly. Melissa looked back to 'Will' she was reminded of traffic accidents where you really did not ought to look for fear of what you might see but slowed down your car none the less for a damn good stare. To her surprise it had grown some more even whilst she was looking at it. For now it had taken on something of a bend, similar to that of a banana, but so very much bigger and it had become darker and more menacing. Unfortunately as he walked forwards towards her his movement caused additional undulations and immediately all Melissa wanted to do was draw some eyes and tusks on to turn the image into the true elephant it had become.

"What now?" Andrew asked as he watched the smile forming on her face. With that Melissa looked away from the elephant and caught the look in his eyes, but the movement he made in raising his hand up to his head to emphasise his confusion caused the trunk to sway from side to side and Melissa burst into uncontrollable giggles once more. She tried to contain them. She knew how inappropriate they were, particularly at this precise moment in time but all she managed to achieve was to stifle them which made her shake uncontrollably and caused tears to pour down her face. Her giggling was confusing to Andrew but sufficiently contagious that he could not help but join in until she managed to blurt out never to let her loose near a marker pen and managed eventually to explain why. Not unexpectedly Andrew did not find this anywhere near as funny as Melissa did. What is it with men, she wondered, had they not looked in the mirror?

How could you do anything but laugh and want to make cartoon characters from them. More evidence she mused that if there was in fact a God, which she doubted, then she would have to be female and with a sense of humour not too dissimilar from her own. Whilst she was still giggling Andrew eased himself gently down covering her with his body and she felt the end of 'Will' bump into the end of her girlie bits (also hating the words vagina and fanny and not to mention the 'c' word which made her cringe with the harshness of the word in whatever form it was used) and slid snugly down and rather pleasingly she was surprised to find between her thighs. The whole sensation amongst her giggles was rather erotic especially as he kissed her gently all over her mouth, neck and shoulders. As yet nothing particularly sexual had occurred but now Melissa had a very enlightened view to the thrill of the chase being all it was cracked up to be as she involuntarily shuddered. Ridiculously exited just by the weight of his naked body on top of her.

The sharp repeated blasting of a loud horn was enough to concentrate her thoughts rather rudely away from the sensuous things that Andrew was doing to her. He carried on regardless and from the movement that Melissa was aware of between her legs 'Will' seemed spurred on by it like players at a football match. After a couple minutes the blasting noise was still as persistent as ever and trying unsuccessfully to tune the noise out it was interrupted by the bloody doorbell again, closely followed by loud banging on the door.

"They'll go away!" Andrew whispered as Melissa tensed up after the door noise. Right on cue the bell rang again. "For God's sake! What's a bloke s'posed to do to get a bit of peace around here?" He shouted frustrated and pulled his jeans on over his naked body and ran off, clearly having trouble tucking his elephants trunk back in. Andrew thumped heavily down the stairs and moments later she heard the door close but no sound of movement inside. Quite frustrated at the source of her tingling having been so abruptly taken away Melissa slid to the end of the bed and holding the pillow that Andrew had discarded onto the floor from earlier, in front of her to cover her modesty, she peered out through the gaps in between the louvers of the blind into the cul de sac below. She saw Andrew barefooted and chested running along the black and by the look of how he was picking his feet up like a gecko, hot, tarmac back from his newly positioned van now over on the opposite side of the road to Melissa's own vehicle half covering the pavement in order that vehicles could still get by.

Melissa heard the front door close and then the pounding of Andrew's feet up the stairs and then looking flushed from his exertions he appeared in the doorway.

"Bloody dustbin lorry got stuck between that car that's up on blocks and my van, so they've been going door to door to find me. Ought to learn how to bloody drive and they wouldn't have got it stuck in the first place! Some of us had urgent business we were attending to!" He smiled wickedly at Melissa still hiding behind her pillow at the window. "And on that note, now I need a pee!" And rushed out of the room. Melissa laughed and then smiled to herself at their misfortune today.

"What are you smiling about now?" Andrew said returning into the room and pushing himself up against her back as she was still spying out of the window.

"How did you know that I was smiling when you couldn't see my face?" Melissa gasped slightly as she felt him slide his hand around and underneath the pillow she was still holding and pull her backwards further into his groin whilst simultaneously keeping his hand firmly wandering into interesting locations that were feeling remarkably warm and damp. Melissa felt her knees begin to buckle from his attentions and shocked herself as she had to hang on to the windowsill to actually not stumble from their failing. She had always thought that going weak at the knees was a figure of speech no from the result of some skilful manhandling. Things after that got more and more heated and Melissa could feel 'Will' getting harder and hotter as Andrew moved against her, eventually he whispered urgently for her to bend over and rest her hands on the bed and then continued trailing urgent kisses all around under her ear and around her neck.

"You aren't planning on shoving that up my bum are you?" Melissa suddenly panicked feeling self conscious and embarrassed as she assumed the position and watched with fascination and a strained neck as he expertly unwrapped a condom from it's packet with his teeth and put it on.

"God no! Not unless I slip!" Andrew laughed. Melissa relaxed slightly and then winced to herself as she felt hopefully full sized 'Will' slide inside her.

Melissa could feel a laugh coming on as Andrew thrust excitedly into her, all she could see in her mind's eye was the sight of her bent over the end of the bed with her head nearly touching the duvet, looking between her splayed apart legs seeing a dismembered pair of skinnier and thankfully hairier legs than her own swaying about, as well as wincing with each thrust and wondering what vital organs he was reshuffling. All of a sudden Melissa could feel a weird sort of pressure building up within her and it was getting stronger with each powerful surge. Simultaneously Andrew groaned, shuddered and presumably came and somebody trumpeted a fanfare in appreciation. Melissa suddenly realised as the fanfare continued that there was not as she had hoped and prayed a brass playing musician in the room and that it was in fact coming from her. Coming and coming and coming. Was it never going to end? Melissa could not believe that this was happening to her and leant forwards to bury her head properly in the duvet which in doing so let rip another few bars of the tune that she could not quite place. After several moments had passed Melissa peered out from under the cover and caught Andrew's bemused face.

"I am *SO* sorry. I have never been so embarrassed before in my whole life!" Melissa said and hid her burning cheeks away again.

"Don't worry, it couldn't be helped. I must have pumped some air into you. Sorry I got a bit carried away."

"SOME AIR? It's amazing that there is enough left in the room for us to breathe!" Melissa carefully wriggled forward on her elbows and just as she was delicately lowering herself down a fan fare blew out again. With that the laughter started and Melissa laughed and laughed and laughed until the tears were streaming down her face, punctuated from time to time with a single parp which set her off laughing even more.

Upon returning home later that afternoon, the date, to Melissa's relief having been cut short on account of Andrew's sister ringing him and requiring some help putting together some flat-packed furniture, Melissa went straight around to Sally's garage where she worked as a receptionist, her face burning and cringing with shame every time she thought about it, and told her everything.

"So I don't suppose I'll be seeing him again!" Melissa groaned holding her head in her hands as Sally laughed at her vivid re-enactment of the day's events.

"Well if nothing else…he'll never forget you!" Sally laughed and made them another cup of tea. "Anyway now that you are back here you can give me Samantha's number please I need to ring her about getting Mother-in-law's seat back that she borrowed."

"Yep, no problem." Melissa said rummaging through her pockets and then her bag. "That's odd; I must have dropped it in the car, back in a minute." Melissa headed back out to her car and after a fruitless search came back inside. "I can't find it, will you ring my number a minute whilst I look again." Melissa went back outside to her car again and came back in a short while later. "I must have left it at Andrews."

"Call him and ask him to bring it with him next time he comes to work."

"I would but I only have his number on the telephone. Anyway, I can't be without my 'phone for that amount of time, I won't be able to text anyone."

"Oh no! How will you cope?" Sally asked facetiously.

"I am just going to have to and fetch it. You coming? We could go for dinner and see a film or something."

"As it happens you have timed it perfectly as Mark has promised to take the kids go-karting tonight so just let me check that Mum is still all right to pick them up from school and then I'll finish off this letter and I will be all yours."

"OK. I'll be back in at 3.30pm, I just have to get some fuel and check my tyres whilst I am here."

The traffic was heavy heading into the city, worsened no doubt by all the children being collected from school. Melissa and Sally finally arrived outside Andrew's house, without getting lost once, at 4.30pm.

"I'll only be a second." Melissa told Sally and hurried across the cul de sac and rang on Andrew's front door. As she waited Melissa was making silly faces at Sally and doing a spot of impromptu tap dancing on the doorstep. The van was there and so she knew he was back and rang the door bell again. Eventually Melissa could see Andrew's outline through the wobbly glass panel in the double glazed door and as he flung it open she was surprised to see that he was bare chested and sock-less wearing only his jeans. Not as surprised as he was to see her standing there however and his face blanched significantly.

"Mel!" He said stepping forwards and pulling the door closed behind him.

"I'm sorry; I left my telephone here earlier."

"Oh right, I'll just get it for you." Andrew scarpered off into the house and a moment later a petite little red-head with startling blue eyes and pretty freckles wearing nothing but a pale blue towel to cover her modesty, appeared on the stairs calling out Andrew's name and asking what the hold up was.

Melissa's jaw dropped open and Andrew appeared holding Melissa's telephone in his hand, his head moving from Melissa to the semi-naked red-head and back again like a spectator at a tennis match.

"Melissa, I can explain!" Andrew said as Melissa lunged forward and snatched the 'phone from his hand causing Andrew to flinch thinking that he was about to have pain inflicted upon him.

"You and your sister always put furniture together naked do you?" Melissa said storming down the path hearing the red head shout out "Sister?" as she got into the car and Andrew stood pathetically in the doorway watching as Melissa drove off.

"What was that all about?" Asked Sally straining her neck to look out of the rear windscreen.

"That was me being shown up for the complete idiot that I am!"

"Why, what happened?"

"He had another girl there!"

"That doesn't mean anything." Sally laughed thinking Melissa funny to have over-reacted so badly.

"It does if he answers the door with only his jeans on and she comes down the stairs wearing a smile!"

"What she was naked?"

"Well may as well have been, she was wearing a towel!"

"My, he's a fast worker, you haven't been gone more than a couple of hours; the bed was probably still warm! You got your 'phone though I take it?"

"I knew I shouldn't have slept with him!" Melissa ignored her question. "The first tarty thing I ever do and it is an unmitigated disaster!" Melissa wiped the tears that were beginning to appear away with the back of her hand.

"At least it made you forget about Daniel for a while." Sally said not knowing what else to say.

"DANIEL! IF IT WEREN'T FOR BLOODY DANIEL I WOULD NEVER HAVE GOT INTO THIS MESS IN THE FIRST PLACE!"

"You can't blame him because the first man you play hide the sausage with since meeting him is a two-timing bastard Mel!"

"YES I CAN AND I DO! I am very good at being unreasonable. Annnnnndddd...that using shit bag made me watch a crappy horror film!"

Melissa said tears abated replaced by anger. "God I feel like such and idiot! Come on, I need calories!" Melissa ordered and leapt out of the car in front of Pizza Hut and slammed the door behind her.

CHAPTER FORTY-TWO
POST MORTEM

The night after spending all of Thursday evening eating every-thing in sight Melissa arrived at the pub very down hearted. Even Bessie's bouncy welcome did little to cheer her and so Melissa wandered about setting the quiet bar up ready com-pletely on autopilot until she was disturbed from her thoughts by Charlie and Marlena both bursting in through the door bear-ing Melissa's large mug of tea that she had put the kettle on for.

"So....tell us all!" Charlie and Marlena simultaneously sat on a bar stool each and Charlie rested her head in her hands with her elbows on the bar as if to be in full listening and attentive mode. Charlie soon gave this up as a bad job and rubbed her elbows quickly before her and Marlena both lit up their first of the evening's many cigarettes. Melissa regaled them with all the glory details which the girls lapped up; laughing hilariously at the whole trumping situation until the tears poured from their eyes. Both girls were shocked and appalled that he should have managed to get another girl into his bed so quickly and prob-ably on the same sheets Marlena was quick to point out. Char-lie helpfully added that someone may have been there before Melissa too; not to mention the night shift. All the girls were contemplating this when the door creaked open and all of them in true Western saloon bar fashion turned to face the door to see who had arrived, when to their absolute shock, the last possible person they all thought would turn up was Andrew walking in through the door.

"Wow! You've got a nerve!" Charlie said harshly glaring at him, stopping him dead in his tracks.

"I'd have said he has got no brain coming in here after what he's done!" Marlena said glaring harshly also.

"What do you want?" Melissa said looking at him through very narrowed eyes.

"To apologise and to get a drink."

"No to both!" Melissa said folding her arms across her chest.

"Melissa, you must let me explain!"

"There is nothing that you could say that I will want to hear!"

"Melissa, I am so sorry. I never meant for you to see that. I did not know that you were coming. It is not my fault. It's that damn Fosseway Magazine, since I advertised in there I haven't got a moments peace. I have got more women than I know what to do with!" Andrew misguidedly looked for understanding.

"You advertised in The Fosseway Magazine?" Melissa and Charlie said in unison.

"Yes, just before Christmas."

"That doesn't mean that you have to go out with all the women who answered your advert. And especially not all at once!" Melissa yelled.

"I know…things just got a little bit out of hand and once I had been out with them I did not have the heart to say no to another date. I have met some really great people."

All three girls looked at him and each other saying nothing until the silence was broken by the creaking noise of the front door creaking open.

Standing in the doorway and blocking out a fair bit of the light was an enormous woman wearing a bright large flower-print dress and large very masculine looking shoes. She had pink framed National Health very thick lensed glasses and even from the door signs of a dark moustache were very apparent. Melissa smiled warmly at her as she barged past Andrew towards the bar and ordered a juice. As Melissa was pouring the drink over some ice in a glass the lady nervously gabbled on about the fact that she was meeting a blind date here. As Melissa looked up to gauge Charlie and Marlena's reaction to this latest piece of news she saw the colour drain from Andrew's face.

"Was the advertisement in The Fosseway Magazine?" Melissa asked smiling brightly.

"Yes that's right. How on earth did you know that?" The lady said downing the drink in a couple of large swallows and crunching up the ice.

"Because I suspect this is your date." Melissa said and pointed to Andrew.

"Are you Andrew?" The lady eyed Andrew appreciatively. "Excellent! I can see that we are going to have a lot of fun together! Shall we go?" She asked as she more or less manhandled him out of the door and pinched his bum as they went much to all of their surprise and amusement.

"Cheeky bastard! Fancy arranging to meet someone else here!" Marlena said shocked at his nerve.

"He's not all there is he?" Charlie said flabbergasted.

"He won't be by the time she finishes with him!" Melissa nodded in the direction of the door.

"I think he sees himself as doing some kind of service in dating all these sad lonely women." Charlie said as she got off of the stool and pushed it back against the bar its feet scraping loudly along the shiny black covered floor that edged the carpet in front of the bar to avoid spills staining the flooring.

"That would make me a sympathy fuck – thanks a bundle for raising my self esteem!" Melissa scowled at them emptying the ashtray they had shared.

"No, you have to turn this around!" Marlena said sharply "You shagged him to get over Daniel and move on! He means nothing to you. 'It' meant nothing to you! Now you are free to get on with the next man!"

"Yes, because there are so many of them around!" Melissa said grumpily.

"We could always ring up The Fosse way ads again." Charlie giggled wickedly.

"That's why Andrew came to the pub in the first place and look how badly that turned out!" Melissa scowled.

"I think it is a good idea. They can't all be sad losers!" Marlena said as she too scraped her stool along into its proper place.

"Yes…you're right, they might be worse!" Melissa straightened up the beer cloth in front of her.

"Yes, knowing Mel's luck she could get the male equivalent of what Andrew has just gone out with!" Charlie said giggling at the thought.

"PISS OFF BACK TO THE KITCHEN YOU EVIL BITCHES! I shall stay here and feel sorry for myself – alone!" Marlena and Charlie headed off towards the kitchen laughing happily as they went.

CHAPTER FORTY-THREE
THE OUTSTANDING BALANCE

The weeks went by, one following into the other and things resumed to a more even keel in the pub. Marlena continued to regale them all with her wicked antics having continued to see Jack most weeks for a clandestine rendezvous generally somewhere wholly inappropriate and with a high risk of being discovered; such as in busy car parks with shoppers coming and going all around them and even in the cellar of his own club and when his wife was in the building. Melissa returned to the gym again but her heart wasn't really in it as she pounded the treadmill like an automaton, each step reminding her of her old mantra she used to chant to motivate her flagging steps.

One Tuesday morning Marlena arrived for work having found a note from Bruno asking her to do a few things as he had gone out for the day and left early. As she made her way down the list she noticed that the last but one thing was go to the bank followed by 'pay Daniel's bill – invoice attached – money in till'. Bloody marvellous! Cheeky git! Why couldn't he have taken it yesterday? Melissa thought crossly to herself. The absolute last place that she wanted to go was to his house. Charlie brought out her big mug of steaming tea and put it on the bar next to Melissa.

"Have you seen this?"

"What is it?"

"Bruno's list of jobs for me!"

"He always leaves one, what's up?"

"That one!" Melissa slid the note around and pointed to the bottom chore.

"Oh, is that for fixing the fire door? That was ages ago! Well he won't be there anyway. He would have come in for a drink if he was back."

"Yes I suppose you are right."

Melissa left the pub after the lunch time shift had ended, having put the paying-in book and cheques for the bank into her handbag she had then picked up Daniel's invoice and took the money which was folded up into a clear plastic change bag from the till. Daniel's house which was also where his company was based was only a couple miles from the pub and on the way to the bank from the pub so she had no excuse not to go. Seeing the large sign attached to the old stone gate post Melissa pulled in and drove up the long drive pulling in after a hundred yards to let a large flat-bed truck go past on its way out followed by two of Daniel's work vans in differing sizes all emblazoned with his initials on the silver background. Beyond her the beautiful old house nestled comfortably at the end of a stripy green lawn and the old mullioned windows sparkled in what little sunlight there was as the same diagonal shaped panes that made up The Olde Flagon windows were repeated here. Grey smoke circled up and away from two tall red brick chimney stacks at opposite ends of the building. In the summer beautiful purple wisteria twisted over the edges appearing from a distance like grapes on a vine, but now only the creeper's pale stem meandered its way over the front of the building giving it a slightly eerie feel of decay on such a dull and miserable day. Melissa followed the road around to the left at a fork which led away from the house and around the side to some large workshops and storage sheds. Here two smaller vans also with Daniel's logo were parked up outside of a small cottagey looking building which in a different setting was exactly what she would have chosen to live in with ornate gabled ends and small mullioned windows dotted about.

Melissa got out of the car and headed for the front presumably office door, looking around her as she went for any signs of life. Finding none she knocked on the door and hearing nothing and it being an office after all, turned the old brass door handle and walked on in. Inside was as endearing as the outside with low wooden beams across the ceiling and whitewashed interior walls. Two large modern desks were all that was in the room adorned with numerous computer screens, a fax and all the usual office paraphernalia with a wall of shelves containing masses of files arranged in blocks by colour.

"Hello!" Melissa called out when no one came. Melissa cocked her head to listen out for signs of movement but there was nothing. Again she called out and at the same time she heard a telephone ringing somewhere further away into the building. After only two rings it was answered and a short time after that the old oak door with an old fashioned black painted latch which rattled as it lifted, opened opposite her and with a telephone held up to his ear looking more handsome than ever in walked Daniel. Melissa felt her knees buckling and clumsily shuffled forward to lean against the desk for support and she could feel her cheeks burn with embarrassment.

"Melissa!" Daniel smiled, surprised that anyone was there. "John, something has come up, I'll call you back in a while.... yes....no problem....bye." Daniel said and removed the telephone from his ear and switched it off.

"How are you? You look really well!" Daniel looked at her smiling widely.

Melissa self consciously put her hand up to her hair and then thinking better of it as a lost cause brought it back down again.

"Yes, I'm fine thanks. Bruno sent me down with this – your bill for the fire door."

"Right, yes. Fine. Thanks." Daniel said taking the outstretched invoice and money from her hand. "Come on through." Daniel indicated and held open the door he had come through and gestured towards it.

"After you." Melissa said happier to follow him.

The door led into a corridor with a section of low ceiling which after they went through another already open doorway became much higher and lighter with a stretch of windows running along its length which looked out over a large courtyard area which the workshops backed onto. They finally went through a large oak framed doorway, the heavy oak door to which had an arch shaped top and was propped open with a small dark metal anvil. This led into a large hall way with a beautiful old wooden staircase and several more arch shaped doors leading off in all directions.

"You have a beautiful home and it smells wonderful." Melissa breathed in deeply through her nose appreciating the smell of presumably beeswax polish with a background hint of the burning log fire.

"Thank you." Daniel laughed as he watched her sniffing and held open one of the arched doors. Melissa went through into a very grand office, filled floor to ceiling in old leather bound books on old wooden shelves with a large leather topped desk in the window and a burgundy leather armchair behind it that was worn pleasingly on the arms and hinted at its great age. The window was vast and looked out across the courtyard with storage sheds on the left and an uninterrupted view of rolling hills and trees beyond. Daniel smiled as he watched her taking it all in as he moved behind the desk and sat down.

"Take a seat while I write you out a receipt for Bruno." Daniel gestured to a smaller version of his own chair on the other side of the desk. Melissa sat down as Daniel tapped a few keys on his computer until a printer started chuntering and whining behind him somewhere out of sight.

"I should check that's right. Bruno is famous for his blonde moments."

Melissa told Daniel as he opened a drawer in his desk and put the money she had given him in it.

"Well if it makes you happier…" Daniel got it back out and undid the fold of money in the clear plastic money bag.

"Big firm like yours…shouldn't you have some staff to deal with all this sort of thing?" Melissa asked surprised at the lack of people around.

"Well my admin lady Julie has left early because she has a dentist appointment today and my P.A. Dominique has run off over to France with my wife." Daniel told her looking straight at her for a reaction.

"Oh….ummmm, I'm sorry to hear that." Melissa said looking concerned for him.

"Yes, bloody inconvenient, she was a really good P.A.….you don't know anyone do you?" Melissa looked at him to see if he was kidding but was unable to tell.

"No chance that she might come back?"

"No, she is French too so now they are living with my Mother-in-law in a bloody great castle, not much reason to come back as far as I can see." Daniel said quietly.

"Ummm actually I meant your wife, not your P.A." Melissa chuckled.

"Oh hell no, when we all went out after Christmas that was so she could stay out there when the chateau was restored and live there with her Mum. You look confused. My wife and I have been more like brother and sister for years, she and Dominique are the couple, I live in one half of the house them in the other, it has been very amicable and I got to keep the best P.A. I ever had a while longer."

"Right, ummmm I best get going… I have to get to the bank before it closes." Melissa stood up.

"Right yes…here you are." Daniel said passing Melissa the printed receipt for Bruno. Melissa thanked him and turned and walked out of the door stopping in the hallway whilst Daniel caught up. "I should go through that door." Daniel said pointing at the largest of all the doors which was just visible through a fancy stone archway on top of two ornate stone pillars.

"Oh, right." Melissa said and headed in the direction Daniel had pointed. As she neared the pillars a terrible smell filled her nostrils and she wrinkled her nose.

"Quite hideous isn't it." Daniel laughed as she had put the back of her hand up to her nose.

"Yes, I take it back, your house smells vile. What on earth is it?" Melissa said as they carried on walking and the smell intensified as they were halted by the large door in front of them.

"Ummm..I think it must be those." Daniel said pointing backwards to a high spot just behind Melissa. Melissa's eyes followed the direction he was pointing toward and screwed up her face as she tried to figure out what it was she was looking at.

"I looked everywhere, and I just couldn't get hold of any fresh ones at short notice so I bought frozen." Daniel told her searching her face for a reaction.

"Sprouts?" Melissa said looking up at the sad drooping, stinking and dripping bunch of sprouts above her head.

"I know it's a bit early for Christmas but I enjoyed my last sprouts so much that I thought that it was high time we tried out some more – assuming that you are up for testing out defrosted, smelly sprouts versus the fresh ones that you provided." Daniel was smiling at her hopefully, his eyes sparkling as the penny finally dropped.

"You hung up frozen sprouts for me?" Melissa said smiling with tears forming in the corners of her eyes. "How did you know I'd come?" Melissa said staring up at him and looking confused as a million thoughts rushed around in her head.

"I asked Bruno to send you. I could not think how else to get you here. It was my money you brought me, Bruno paid that bill ages ago."

"You set me up! But you've got a woman – women!"

"No I haven't!"

"But I saw you. At the hotel and at the bank." Melissa said looking sad again.

"The woman at the hotel is the wife of the owner and they had invited me to dinner to celebrate the completion of the work we did for them in the hotel only he got called away leaving me to entertain his wife for the evening."

"But I saw you kissing. Upstairs when I was helping that drunken pillock to bed."

"You saw that? 'She' actually kissed me and as soon as you had gone into matey boy's room I went downstairs for a drink; that woman is like a bitch on heat!"

"I didn't stay with him you know." Melissa said getting flustered.

"No, I know. I heard wheels spinning on gravel when I was in the library and looked around to see who the hooligan was only to see your number plate whizzing off into the distance."

"What about the other woman?"

"What other woman?"

"I saw you hugging a beautiful woman outside of the bank in Slapperton, then someone picked her up in a silver SLK and nearly ran me over!"

"Ohhh, that was my wife and the SLK driver was Dominique driving my wife's car. That was the day they went back to France and I lost my P.A."

Melissa was lost for words as Daniel slowly stepped towards her.

"So about these sprouts…"

"You bought these just for me?" Melissa looked up at him now that he was just inches away.

"Yes you daft cow, now will you please hurry up and kiss me so that I can get rid of them, they stink!"

Melissa laughed as Daniel covered the final distance towards her and putting his hands gently on either side of the becoming more well defined curve of her waist; he pulled her towards him and gently kissed her laughter away. After a short while he pulled away to see her eyes sparkling back at him as he wrapped his arms further around her and squashed himself up against the full length of her body. Melissa's knees weakened and his previously closed eyes flashed open concerned at her sudden movement. Laughing Melissa whispered "It's just my knees.... you make them go weak."

"I thought that was just in the movies!"

"Yes, so did I. Now where as I have to say that I am very impressed with your sprouts and they are without doubt better than mine....yours also win on smell. Can we open the door and let some fresh air in?" Melissa laughed as Daniel flung open the big arched door and they both rushed to gasp in sprout free air bumping into each other in their haste to get out. Laughing as Melissa pushed Daniel out of the way and got out first Daniel snatched at her fleeting hand and pulled her roughly back to him where he kissed her all over again cheered on by a load of Daniel's builders who were just returning for the day and amongst their group as Melissa looked up at them and waved she spotted Charlie, Marlena and Bruno all lurking smiling like lunatics, particularly Bruno who was surrounded by burly workmen; his favourite type!

If you have enjoyed this book look out for:

Red Shoes and No Knickers

Also by Jill Madge coming soon!

Printed in Poland
by Amazon Fulfillment
Poland Sp. z o.o., Wrocław